THIRD EDITION

Physical Education for Lifelong Fitness

The Physical Best Teacher's Guide

THIRD EDITION

Physical Education for Lifelong Fitness

The Physical Best Teacher's Guide

National Association for
Sport and Physical Education

*an association of the American Alliance for Health,
Physical Education, Recreation and Dance*

Human Kinetics

Library of Congress Cataloging-in-Publication Data

Physical Best (Program)
  Physical education for lifelong fitness : the physical best teacher's guide. -- 3rd ed.
      p. cm.
  Includes bibliographical references and index.
  ISBN-13: 978-0-7360-8116-0 (soft cover)
  ISBN-10: 0-7360-8116-X (soft cover)
  1. Physical education and training--Study and teaching--United States. 2. Physical fitness--
Study and teaching--United States. I. National Association for Sport and Physical Education.
  GV365.P4992 2010
  613.7--dc22

                              2010022973

ISBN-10: 0-7360-8116-X (print)
ISBN-13: 978-0-7360-8116-0 (print)

The Web addresses cited in this text were current as of August 2010, unless otherwise noted.

Acquisitions Editors: Sarajane Quinn and Scott Wikgren; **Developmental Editor:** Ragen E. Sanner; **Assistant Editor:** Anne Rumery; **Copyeditor:** Bob Replinger; **Indexer:** Andrea Hepner; **Permission Manager:** Dalene Reeder; **Graphic Designer:** Joe Buck; **Graphic Artist:** Dawn Sills; **Cover Designer:** Keith Blomberg; **Photographer (cover):** © Human Kinetics; **Photographer (interior):** © Human Kinetics, unless otherwise noted; **Art Manager:** Kelly Hendren; **Associate Art Manager:** Alan L. Wilborn; **Illustrator:** © Human Kinetics, unless otherwise noted; **Printer:** McNaughton & Gunn

Printed in the United States of America   10 9 8 7 6 5

The paper in this book is certified under a sustainable forestry program.

Human Kinetics
Web site: www.HumanKinetics.com

United States: Human Kinetics
P.O. Box 5076
Champaign, IL 61825-5076
800-747-4457
e-mail: humank@hkusa.com

Canada: Human Kinetics
475 Devonshire Road Unit 100
Windsor, ON N8Y 2L5
800-465-7301 (in Canada only)
e-mail: info@hkcanada.com

Europe: Human Kinetics
107 Bradford Road
Stanningley
Leeds LS28 6AT, United Kingdom
+44 (0) 113 255 5665
e-mail: hk@hkeurope.com

Australia: Human Kinetics
57A Price Avenue
Lower Mitcham, South Australia 5062
08 8372 0999
e-mail: info@hkaustralia.com

New Zealand: Human Kinetics
P.O. Box 80
Torrens Park, South Australia 5062
0800 222 062
e-mail: info@hknewzealand.com

E4736

CONTENTS

PART III Curriculum and Teaching Methods 145

PREFACE

In the face of a growing obesity pandemic, physical educators confront a long-standing responsibility that has taken on even greater importance—the health and wellness of a diverse, increasingly sedentary population of children and adolescents. With this responsibility comes an opportunity to have a powerful and positive effect on hundreds of young people each year. By teaching them the skills and knowledge that they need to live physically active lives and by giving them the appreciation and confidence to do so, you are preparing them to avoid many major diseases and to live healthier, less stressful, and more productive lives.

The role that physical education plays in preparing students for lifelong health is clear; the link between participation in regular physical activity and good health and improved cognitive performance is increasingly well documented. Physical education in the schools affords the best opportunity to reach most of the population. But a physical education program that successfully prepares students for healthy lives must be far more than the roll-out-the-ball programs that are stereotyped in the media, that some adults remember from their experiences with physical education, and that, sadly, are still seen in some schools today.

PHYSICAL BEST CONTENT

This book was developed to provide a comprehensive guide to incorporating health-related fitness and lifetime physical activity into quality physical education programs. It provides a conceptual framework based on current research and includes a wealth of examples from experienced physical educators. It provides specific advice on integrating all aspects of a quality health-related fitness education program. Examples from the third edition include how to teach fitness concepts through enjoyable physical activity and how to use fitness assessment as an educational and motivational tool.

For veteran teachers, this book outlines strategies for emphasizing health-related fitness while still maintaining all the components of an existing program. For new teachers, this book details aspects of creating an effective fitness education program by illustrating details with specific examples from master teachers.

Part I introduces health-related fitness by providing an in-depth look at physical activity behavior and motivation. Basic training principles for fitness are also examined. Because nutrition is an essential component of body composition, part I concludes with an overview of nutrition that includes the foundations of a healthy diet, relating body composition to other health-related fitness components, and updated dietary tools.

An overview of health-related physical fitness concepts is provided in part II. Specifically, the third edition addresses aerobic fitness, muscular strength and endurance, flexibility, and body composition as they relate to the teaching of kindergarten through 12th-grade students. Because knowledge of fitness has been rapidly evolving and some disagreement still exists (even among exercise physiologists) about appropriate exercise protocols, discussions of controversial topics along with recommendations for addressing these issues in your program are provided. Suggestions are provided at the end of chapters 5, 6, and 7 for ways to address motor skills by using activities that deal with aerobic fitness, muscular strength and endurance, and flexibility.

In part III strategies are outlined for developing a health-related fitness education curriculum that will serve varying program needs. Effective teaching methods that encourage the inclusion of all students—in the gymnasium, on the field, or in the classroom—are examined in chapter 10.

Assessment is an important component of effective teaching, and part IV provides a detailed look at assessing health-related fitness. The discussion includes appropriate uses of fitness assessment results and ways in which to assess fitness concept knowledge, participation in physical activity, and evidence of growth in the affective domain.

The book concludes with a glossary, appendixes that provide ready-to-use worksheets and masters, and a reference list that can be used as a reading resource guide. The third edition also introduces online resources that instructors can use to help teach the material given in the book, including a presentation package and test package. The presentation package presents 196 slides of key concepts covering all 14 chapters in PowerPoint format. The test package consists of 160 ready-made test questions that feature multiple-choice and true-false questions covering the content from all chapters.

HOW THIS EDITION WAS DEVELOPED

Good teaching is both an art and a science. The first edition was developed by combining extensive research on the science of physical activity for children and young adults with the vast knowledge and experience of master physical education teachers from across the country. The second edition was a revision of then-current research and was spearheaded by Gayle Claman, then the Physical Best Coordinator at NASPE. The third edition builds on the information developed in the first two editions by focusing on updated research and current guidelines for youth physical activity and fitness. This edition provides enhanced practical tools and information throughout. Page ix provides a list of physical educators who were involved in the editing of this third edition. The *Physical Best Activity Guides*, described further in chapter 1, have also been updated with many new activities at both levels. Each activity book has a CD that includes many new resources.

YOUR PHYSICAL BEST

As a physical educator, you have an important job, one that can literally shape the future health of the nation. We hope that you will find this book both informative and inspirational in being the best physical educator you can be.

Suzan F. Ayers, PhD
Coeditor, Associate Professor
Health, Physical Education and Recreation
Western Michigan University

Mary Jo Sariscsany, EdD
Coeditor, Associate Professor
Department of Kinesiology
California State University, Northridge

ACKNOWLEDGMENTS

Many physical education professionals contributed their time and expertise to this project. This process started with reviews of the second edition by the Physical Best Steering Committee and staff from Human Kinetics. Without the work of these individuals, we would not have been able to identify the content that required updates and additions. In addition to the Physical Best Steering Committee, many researchers and educators generously shared their ideas and experiences, which are referenced throughout the book. We thank both the new contributors listed on each chapter and those who provided content for the second edition, which served as a springboard for the cutting-edge content provided in this edition. Susan Schoenberg, professional services senior manager for NASPE, played a significant role in coordinating the revision, as did Joe McGavin and Mary Ellen Aull from NASPE. The following people served as content experts for the second edition:

Debra Ballinger
Towson University
Chapters 2, 12, 13, 14

Jennie Gilbert
Illinois
Chapters 3, 5, 6, 7

Melody Kyzer
North Carolina
Chapters 4, 8

Joan Morrison and Ginny Popiolek
Maryland
Chapter 11

Diane Tunnell
Washington
Chapters 1, 9, 10

The contributors for the third edition of the *Physical Best Teacher's Guide* worked selflessly for over a year to provide updated content in rapidly changing areas. This revised edition would not have been possible without their help. The contributors for this third edition are the following:

Chapter 1   Suzan Ayers, *Western Michigan University*

Mary Jo Sariscsany, *California State University, Northridge*

Chapter 2   Debra Ballinger, *East Stroudsburg University*

Chapter 3   Sean Bulger, *West Virginia University*

Chapter 4   Linda Nickson, *Stow-Munroe Falls High School*

Chapter 5   Jan Bishop, *Central Connecticut State University*

Chapter 6   Joe Deutsch, *South Dakota State University*

Chapter 7   Brian Mosier, *University of West Georgia*

Chapter 8   Scott Going, *University of Arizona*

Chapter 9   Bane McCracken

Chapter 10   Mary Jo Sariscsany, *California State University, Northridge*

Chapter 11   Joan Morrison, *Lisbon Elementary School*

Ginny Popiolek, *Harford County Public Schools*

Chapter 12   Celia Regimbal, *University of Toledo*

Chapter 13   Mary Jo Sariscsany, *California State University, Northridge*

Chapter 14   Christina Sinclair, *University of Northern Colorado*

Sandra Nelson, *Coastal Carolina University*

Finally, we would like to thank those who contributed to the second edition of the *Physical Best Teacher's Guide* because their contributions laid the groundwork for this edition and set the tone for the continued growth of the Physical Best program over the past five years.

OVERVIEW OF THE PRESIDENTIAL YOUTH FITNESS PROGRAM

The Presidential Youth Fitness Program (PYFP) is a voluntary program that includes a health-related assessment, as well as educational and motivational tools, to support educators and empower students to adopt an active lifestyle.

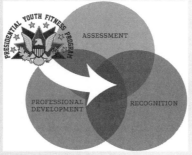

Launched in September 2012, PYFP offers a comprehensive school-based program that promotes physical activity and fitness for improving the health of America's young people.

PYFP is built around three pillars:

1. Professional development and education
2. Assessment
3. Recognition and awards

Although seemingly separate in nature, these pillars are linked by the expertise and contributions of the program's partners and their collective interest in equipping physical educators with the materials and information they need to deliver a high-quality, beneficial health-related fitness education experience to their students.

PYFP is built from a partnership of five organizations: American Alliance for Health, Physical Education, Recreation and Dance; Amateur Athletic Union; Centers for Disease Control and Prevention; The Cooper Institute; and President's Council on Fitness, Sports and Nutrition. These organizations came together with a goal to provide one national youth fitness test that focuses on health and equips educators with the resources and knowledge necessary for helping their students lead active lives.

The Three Pillars

Here is a closer look at the program's three pillars.

1. Professional development. PYFP will equip educators with the knowledge and tools required for implementing a high-quality fitness education experience for students and for promoting and engaging them in physical activity regardless of a school's physical education budget. That includes integrating elements of the Physical Best program, with access to resources to support the successful teaching of health-related fitness. Online and in-person training opportunities are available at www.presidentialyouthfitnessprogram.org.

2. Assessment. FITNESSGRAM® is the adopted assessment of PYFP. Developed in the early 1980s by The Cooper Institute, Fitnessgram includes a variety of health-related physical fitness assessments of aerobic capacity, muscle strength, muscle endurance and flexibility, and body composition. Scores from these assessments are compared to Healthy Fitness Zone® standards to determine students' overall physical fitness and to suggest areas for improvement when appropriate. Using Fitnessgram keeps the focus of fitness assessment on promoting and improving personal health rather than performance and athletic ability.

3. Recognition and awards. Providing an opportunity to recognize students for reaching personal fitness goals and physical activity behaviors is the final pillar of the Presidential Youth Fitness Program. Students who reach the Healthy Fitness Zone on at least five test items are eligible for the Presidential Youth Fitness Award. Understanding how to use recognition in a responsible manner that includes all students is a key part of the professional-development package. In addition, schools have the opportunity to be recognized for creating an environment that supports PYFP and physical activity, in general, as described through the development of comprehensive school physical activity plans (visit www.aahperd.org/cspap).

The three areas around which the program is built come together to provide a robust experience for teachers and their students.

Physical Best and the PYFP

Physical Best, including the teacher's guide and activity guides, complements PYFP's mission by providing the how and why of teaching health-related physical activity and fitness-enhancing skills and behaviors. The program's partners seek to provide a fun and beneficial experience for *all* youths, regardless of ability or health status.

This book provides additional guidance and information on using the Presidential Youth Fitness Program.

The Physical Best activity guides include a variety of activities that can count toward a student's daily physical activity and, therefore, set him or her on a path to earning a Presidential Active Lifestyle Award (PALA+), one of the awards that make up the PYFP recognition pillar.

For the latest resources and information on the Presidential Youth Fitness Program, visit www.presidentialyouthfitnessprogram.org.

PART 1

Foundations of Health-Related Fitness and Physical Activity

Part I introduces the Physical Best program. Chapter 1 examines the Physical Best philosophy and program components. Information is provided to explain the comprehensive nature and unique qualities of Physical Best. Chapter 2 focuses on how and why children and adolescents choose to be physically active. Suggestions for physical educators are provided to help motivate students to become more physically active. Age-appropriate information provides connections between motivation and the Physical Best program. Chapter 3 presents applications of the philosophical and behavioral concepts of the Physical Best program, including an overview of the basic training principles for aerobic fitness, muscular strength and endurance, and flexibility components of health-related fitness and chapter 4 discusses food, diet, and nutrition.

Introduction to Physical Best

Suzan F. Ayers and Mary Jo Sariscsany

Regular participation in physical activity has a significant positive effect on people's health and well-being. In turn, improved health and well-being positively influence quality of life and society as a whole. Organizations such as the American Academy of Pediatrics, the American Medical Association, the American Heart Association, the Centers for Disease Control and Prevention, the U.S. Department of Health and Human Services, as well as the allied health community emphasize the importance of lifelong physical activity to good health. This is true for all people, including those with physical and mental challenges, the sedentary population, and even elite athletes.

Chapter Contents

BENEFITS OF LIFELONG PARTICIPATION IN PHYSICAL ACTIVITY

According to the Division of Adolescent and School Health (DASH), the National Center for Chronic Disease Prevention and Health Promotion (NCCDPHP), and the Centers for Disease Control and Prevention (CDC) (2008), the prevalence of obesity among children aged 6 to 11 years has more than doubled in the past 20 years, and among adolescents aged 12 to 19 obesity has more than tripled (Ogden, Flegal, Carroll, & Johnson, 2002). Overweight children and adolescents are more likely to become overweight or obese adults, and children who became obese by age 8 were more severely obese as adults (Ferraro, Thorpe, & Wilkinson, 2003). Although students must know the risks of a sedentary lifestyle, they should also know the many benefits of getting enough physical activity and remaining active for life. Emphasizing the benefits that they will see today is especially important. Regular physical activity in childhood and adolescence can (USDHHS, 2008)

- increase strength and endurance,
- build healthy bones and muscles,
- control weight,
- reduce anxiety and stress,
- increase self-esteem, and
- improve blood pressure and cholesterol levels.

Positive experiences with physical activity at a young age can help lay a foundation for being active regularly through life (USDHHS, 2008). The U.S. Department of Health and Human Services recommends that young people (ages 6–17) participate in at least 60 minutes of physical activity daily (USDHHS, 2008). In 2007 only 35% of high school students had participated in at least 60 minutes per day of physical activity on five or more of the last seven days, and only 30% attended physical activity class daily. Participation in physical activity declines as children age (CDC, 2007).

Physical activity has a positive effect not only on an individual's health but also on society as a whole because a physically active population is able to be more productive. Physically active people have healthier attitudes, which allows them to handle the larger problems associated with work or home in a more positive, reflective manner.

In recent years, society has shown an unprecedented interest in health. Newspaper articles discussing health issues appear on a daily basis, and more and more "healthy living" classes are being offered through community resources. Newspapers include daily advertisements focusing on personal health. Television stations devote time to promoting health issues, and fitness classes are aired in weekly television lineups. Technology has allowed quick access to the latest health reports. Internet sites provide easy access to questions and answers about health-related issues. Government documents such as *Promoting Better Health for Young People Through Physical Activity and Sports: A Report to the President* (Secretary of Health and Human Services and Secretary of Education, 2000) are published and disseminated on a regular basis. Professional organizations such as the American Alliance for Health, Physical Education, Recreation and Dance (AAHPERD); the National Association for Sport and Physical Education (NASPE); and the Centers for Disease Control and Prevention (CDC) research and pub-

lish data on the importance of physical activity.

In addition, First Lady Michelle Obama is spearheading a national public awareness effort to address the childhood obesity epidemic within one generation. This effort, Let's Move! (www. letsmove.gov/), is supported by the interagency federal Task Force on Childhood Obesity developed by President Obama. The overarching goals of this group (www.whitehouse.gov/the-press-office/presidential-memorandum-establishing-a-task-force-childhood-obesity) include

- ensuring access to healthy, affordable food;
- increasing physical activity in schools and communities;
- providing healthier food in schools; and
- empowering parents with information and tools to make good choices for themselves and their families.

School-based physical education is strongly recommended because of its effectiveness in increasing physical activity and improving physical fitness among adolescents and children (Task Force on Community Preventive Services, 2002). Physical education can add significantly to the health and well-being of children and adolescents through physical activity. Although this concept is not new, significant research supports the role of physical education in health improvement. Physical education programs can help prepare children and adolescents to live physically active and healthy lives. Physical educators can help the community understand the relationship between physical activity and a healthy life. Community support can increase when people understand the positive influence of an effective physical education program on children and adolescents. Physical educators can develop strong relationships with allied community health practitioners, physicians, and local government. When people think of schools as contributing to both the cognitive and physical well-being of children and adolescents, greater support can be developed. Physical education not only teaches children about a wide range of healthy habits but also provides them opportunities to participate in health-enhancing physical activity.

WHAT IS PHYSICAL BEST?

In the early 1980s AAHPERD and NASPE recognized the need for a program that would help youth understand the importance of lifetime physical activity through regular physical activity. This program would focus on educating all students from a health-related viewpoint, regardless of their abilities. Thus, in 1987 Physical Best was developed.

Physical Best is a comprehensive health-related fitness education program. It provides a series of activities and conceptual information to be included in a quality physical education program. Physical Best is standards-based and assists both teachers and students in meeting the NASPE national physical education standards for physical education pertaining to health-related fitness. Physical Best is designed to assist students in achieving their individual physical best.

It is important to clarify that the Physical Best program was not designed to be used as a stand-alone curriculum. The materials that make up the Physical Best program can be used in conjunction with existing curricula and should be considered instructional materials, not a curriculum framework.

To aid in understanding the mission of the Physical Best program, clarity among a few commonly used terms must be established. *Fitness, physical activity,* and *exercise* are frequently presented in the popular media as synonymous terms.

▶ **Health-related fitness** is a measure of a person's ability to perform physical activities that require endurance, strength, or flexibility. This kind of fitness is achieved through a combination of regular exercise and inherent ability. The components of health-related physical fitness are aerobic fitness, muscular strength, muscular endurance, flexibility, and body composition as they relate specifically to health enhancement.

▶ **Skill-related fitness** is often confused with health-related fitness components. Skill-related components often go hand in hand with certain physical activities and are necessary for a person to accomplish or enhance a skill or task. Skill-related components include agility, coordination, reaction time, balance, speed, and power. An individual can still achieve and maintain a healthy lifestyle and lifelong participation in physical activity without possessing a high degree of skill-related components. Health-related and skill-related components are not mutually exclusive, but the Physical Best program primarily focuses on the health-related components of fitness (see figure 1.1 on page 6).

Further, the USDHHS (2008) offers technical definitions of these terms:

▶ **Physical activity** is strictly defined as any bodily movement produced by skeletal muscles that results in an expenditure of energy. It includes a broad range of occupational, leisure time, and routine daily activities from manual labor to gardening, walking, and household chores. These activities can require light, moderate, or vigorous effort and can lead to improved health when performed regularly.

▶ **Exercise** is physical activity of a repetitive nature that is planned or structured to improve or maintain one or more of the health-related fitness components.

Figure 1.1 *(a)* Health-related fitness includes components of aerobic fitness, muscular strength, muscular endurance, flexibility, and body composition, and *(b)* skill-related fitness includes components of agility, coordination, reaction time, balance, speed, and power.

PHYSICAL BEST'S MISSION

© NASPE

The mission of the Physical Best program is to foster healthier youth by providing quality resources and professional development for educators. The mission incorporates partnerships with like-minded programs and organizations. The program emphasizes teaching health-related fitness concepts and attitudes through activity in a manner that includes all children, is enjoyable, and promotes a physically active lifestyle.

Physical Best focuses on the positive benefits of physical activity (not just exercising), offers a variety of enjoyable activities, and develops knowledge and skills needed to be confident and successful through a variety of movement activities across the lifespan.

Physical education in the nation's schools is being shortchanged at a time when an increasing number of American adults view physical activity as important to their health. It should come as no surprise, then, that the availability of physical education and the rate of physical activity among young people are declining.

This information is reflected by data provided by the 2007 Youth Risk Behavior Survey (YRBS), which found that 34.7% of high school students met the recommended physical activity level of 60 minutes per day for five of the seven days before completing the survey. Conversely, these same YRBS data revealed that 53.6% of high school students attended physical education class at least one day per week and 30.3% attended daily physical education.

Shape of the Nation 2010 (NASPE) noted the following:

- ▶ Between 57% (elementary) and 90% (high school) of all states require certified physical education teachers to provide planned instructional programs of physical education. This has remained consistent since the 2006 edition of this text. Half of all states grant temporary, emergency certificates to teach physical education with the minimum requirement being a bachelor's degree in any area or in teaching.
- ▶ In 59% of all states, students can substitute other activities (i.e., ROTC, interscholastic sports, marching band) for required physical education credit.
- ▶ Among children (ages 6-11 years), 33% are overweight and 17% are obese. Among teens (ages 12-19 years), 34% are overweight and another 18% are obese.

According to the fifth annual *F as in Fat: How Obesity Policies Are Failing in America, 2008* report (Levi, Vinter, St. Laurent, & Segal), adult obesity rates have increased in 37 states over the past year while no state saw a decrease. Although this report focused on adult obesity rates, one of the recommendations for combating obesity included increasing the amount and quality of physical education and activity in schools and childcare programs. The key issue is, How should we be preparing children and adolescents for daily physical activity? Implementing a planned program of instruction provided by certified physical educators and eliminating the option of exemptions, waivers, or substitutions is a reasonable starting point.

WHAT MAKES PHYSICAL BEST UNIQUE?

The comprehensiveness of the Physical Best program is what makes it truly unique—combining the latest scientific research with practical experience and activities of physical educators from around the country. The following list highlights the many features of the program that make it a valuable tool for physical educators and students alike.

▶ *Comprehensive conceptual framework*—Physical Best provides a framework for educators to teach conceptual information about physical fitness and nutrition within the activity setting. It provides students with information to help them understand and value the concepts of physical fitness and its relationship to a healthy lifestyle. It also provides information on assessment, goal setting, and motivational strategies. In addition, the Physical Best program offers ideas and suggestions for integrated curricula (across subject areas, in the three learning domains—cognitive, affective, and psychomotor) as well as parental and community involvement.

▶ *Active participation*—The activities are designed so that all students are involved and remain active most of the time. Teams are limited in size (two to four students per team) so that each student has numerous practice opportunities. Multiple stations are set up so that students do not have to wait long for a turn.

▶ *Individualized activities*—Activities are designed so that students can work at their own fitness or activity level. The program also provides avenues for students to excel by moving beyond the minimum. The activities may provide various levels to achieve, different practice times, variety in the number of trials, choices of task difficulty, and so forth. Individuals have the opportunity and freedom to choose activities that are interesting to them. They can also modify an activity to suit their needs, goals, and abilities without losing the health-related benefits of the activity. In short, Physical Best emphasizes enjoyment in participation and encourages students to strive for personal success in a positive learning atmosphere.

▶ *Tools for lifelong activity*—Students will gain the knowledge, skills, and self-motivation to engage regularly in one or more physical activities as an ongoing lifestyle choice.

▶ *Health-related physical activity* (fitness and skill development)—Students are provided with safe and sequential activities that will help maintain or improve the components of health-related physical fitness (aerobic

Monkey Business/fotolia.com

Students must be taught the skills, knowledge, and attitudes that set the groundwork for daily physical activity.

fitness, muscular strength and endurance, flexibility, and body composition). Activities focus on personal improvement rather than attaining unrealistic standards. The program incorporates the latest fitness testing (Fitnessgram) and combines assessment and activities into a plan for individual improvement.

▶ *Adherence to standards*—Physical Best was developed to help teachers meet national standards for physical education, health education, and dance education (see chapter 9). It also supports the *Healthy People 2020* objectives as well as the 1999 *Surgeon General's Report on Physical Activity and Health*.

In the past, some physical educators have said, "I teach football, basketball, volleyball, and softball." Physical Best teachers say, "I teach children and young adults the *how* and *why* of a physically active, healthy lifestyle." The how and why components are combined into a comprehensive K through 12 health-related fitness education program with resources and professional development training to make the Physical Best program truly unique—and truly valuable for student and teacher success.

PHYSICAL BEST COMPANION RESOURCES

With the foundation of knowledge in health-related fitness that this book provides, you will be ready to move on and motivate students with the *Physical Best Activity Guide: Elementary Level* or the *Physical Best Activity Guide: Middle and High School Levels*.

Physical Best Activity Guide: Elementary Level

This guide contains the information needed to help kindergarten through fifth-grade students gain the knowledge, skills, appreciation, and confidence to lead physically active, healthy lives. The easy-to-use instructional activities have been developed and used successfully by physical educators across the United States. This guide includes competitive and noncompetitive activities, demanding and less demanding activities,

and activities that allow for maximum time on task. Above all, the activities are designed to be educational and fun. Packaged with the book is a CD containing reproducible charts, posters, and handouts that accompany the activities. New features for the third edition include many new activities in each chapter as well as the addition of a new chapter, titled "Combined-Component Training," containing activities that combine teaching of the areas of fitness. In addition, some of the student worksheets are provided in two formats—PDF for teachers who just want to print the provided example and a plain editable version that teachers can manipulate to meet their students' needs before printing.

Physical Best Activity Guide: Middle and High School Levels

This guide is similar in scope to the elementary guide but is geared toward 6th- through 12th-grade students. The information allows a deeper and richer understanding of the importance of daily physical activity. The middle school and high school level guide contains an additional section focused on personal health and fitness planning. This section provides students with an introduction to the skills needed to be physically active for life after they graduate from high school. Other features for the third edition include a CD-ROM containing printable materials that supplement the activities, editable versions of some student worksheets, and many new activities in each chapter.

RELATED RESOURCES

During a typical school year, many educators use more than one program and a variety of teaching resources, overlapping various approaches on a day-to-day basis. With this in mind, it may be reassuring to know that although Physical Best is designed to be used independently for teaching health-related fitness, the following resources can also be used in conjunction with the Physical Best program.

Fitnessgram

Fitnessgram (developed by the Cooper Institute) is a comprehensive health-related fitness and activity assessment as well as a computerized reporting system. All elements within Fitnessgram are designed to assist teachers in accomplishing the primary objective of youth fitness programs, which is to help students establish physical activity as a part of their daily lives.

Fitnessgram is based on a belief that extremely high levels of physical fitness, while admirable, are not necessary to accomplish objectives associated with good health and improved function. All children should have adequate levels of activity and fitness. Fitnessgram is used to help all children and youth achieve a level of activity and fitness associated with good health, growth, and function.

Fitnessgram resources are published and available through Human Kinetics, as are the materials for the Brockport Physical Fitness Test, which is a health-related fitness assessment for students with disabilities. For complete information about Fitnessgram, visit www.fitnessgram.net.

Fitness for Life

Fitness for Life is a comprehensive K through 12 program designed to help students take responsibility for their own activity, fitness, and health and to prepare them to be physically active and healthy throughout their adult lives. This standards-based program has been carefully articulated following a pedagogically sound scope and sequence to enhance student learning and progress. It is compatible with the Physical Best program in philosophy and with the goal of lifelong physical activity habits. Research has shown that *Fitness for Life* is a program that is effective in promoting physically active behavior after students finish school.

Fitness for Life and Physical Best complement one another effectively, because the *Physical Best Activity Guides* can be used both before and after a *Fitness for Life* course, as well as during the course to provide supplemental activities. Both programs are based on the HELP philosophy, which promotes Health for Everyone with a focus on Lifetime activity of a Personal nature. In fact, the two programs are so compatible that the Physical Best program offers teacher training for *Fitness for Life* course instructors.

HELP PHILOSOPHY

The HELP philosophy is shared by NASPE, Fitnessgram, Activitygram, and Corbin and Lindsey's *Fitness for Life*.

H stands for **HEALTH** and health-related fitness. The primary goal of the program is to promote regular physical activity among all youth. Of particular importance is promoting activity patterns that lead to reduced health risk and improved health-related physical fitness.

E stands for **EVERYONE**. The Fitnessgram program is designed for all people regardless of physical ability. Used together, Fitnessgram and Activitygram assessments are designed to help all youth find some form of activity in which they can participate for a lifetime. Too often activity programs are perceived to be only for those who are "good" rather than for all people. Physical activity and fitness are for everyone regardless of age, gender, or ability.

L stands for **LIFETIME**. Fitnessgram and Activitygram have as a goal helping young people to be active now, but a long-term goal is to help them learn to do activities that they will continue to perform throughout their lives.

P stands for **PERSONAL**. No two people are exactly the same. No two people enjoy the exact same activities. Fitnessgram and Activitygram are designed to personalize physical activity to meet personal or individual needs.

Reprinted, by permission, from C.B. Corbin and R. Lindsey, 2005, *Fitness for life,* 5th ed. (Champaign, IL: Human Kinetics), 5.

NASPE Resources

NASPE publishes many useful resources that are available through the online AAHPERD store at www.aahperd.org/naspe/publications.

These resources include the following:

▸ *Moving Into the Future: Standards for Physical Education, 2nd edition*

▸ *Beyond Activities: Learning Experiences to Support the National Physical Education Standards*

▸ *Appropriate Practices Documents (Elementary, Middle School, and High School)*

▸ *Physical Activity for Children: A Statement of Guidelines for Children Ages 5–12*

▸ Assessment series (titles relating to fitness and heart rate)

▸ Advocacy publications and brochures

▸ K through 12 publications relating to conceptual learning and school-based wellness centers

PHYSICAL BEST CERTIFICATION

Physical Best provides accurate, up-to-date information and training to help today's physical educators create a conceptual and integrated format for health-related fitness education within their programs. NASPE-AAHPERD offers a certification program that allows physical education teachers to become Physical Best Health-Fitness Specialists. The Physical Best certification has been created specifically for updating physical educators on the most effective strategies for helping their students gain the knowledge, skills, appreciation, and confidence needed to lead physically active, healthy lives. It focuses on application—how to teach fitness concepts through developmentally- and age-appropriate activities and the Fitnessgram assessments.

To earn certification through NASPE-AAHPERD as a Physical Best Health-Fitness Specialist, the following steps are necessary:

▸ Attend a one-day Physical Best Health-Fitness Specialist Workshop or complete a college or university semester-long course including Physical Best content.

▸ Read this book, *Physical Education for Lifelong Fitness: The Physical Best Teacher's Guide 3E,* the latest versions of the *Fitnessgram/Activitygram*

Test Administration Manual, and the *Physical Best Activity Guides.*

▸ Using the required resources just mentioned, complete an online, open-book examination. Successful completion of the examination will result in certification.

For more information on certification as a health-fitness specialist, or to learn about becoming a Physical Best Health-Fitness Instructor (to train other teachers), call Physical Best at 800-213-7193.

The Physical Best certification seal.
© NASPE

SUMMARY

Physical Best complements and supports existing physical education programs by teaching and applying health-related physical fitness concepts to promote lifelong physical activity. Physical Best excels at providing this component of a well-rounded physical education curriculum by

▸ basing its philosophy and materials on current research and expert, field-tested input,

▸ teaching the benefits of lifelong physical activity,

▸ offering national certification as a Physical Best Health-Fitness Specialist,

▸ focusing on the positive (such as student strengths and enjoyable activities), and

▸ individualizing instruction so that all students may benefit and succeed.

The Physical Best approach enhances the likelihood that students will pursue healthy, physically active lifestyles after they leave quality physical education programs and move into adulthood.

Physical Activity Behavior and Motivation

Debra Ballinger

Chapter Contents

Adults have various reasons for being physically active or inactive, and children do too. This chapter looks at motivational factors affecting physical activity levels. Recent research has established that participation in physical activity as a child or adolescent is positively related to adult participation (Biddle et al., 2005; Daley, 2002; Beunen et al., 2004; Telama, Yang, Hirvensalo, & Raitakari, 2006). Some activity motivation factors are common to both children and adults, but others are not. Using the acronym MOTIVATIONAL PE, strategies are offered to help students learn how to set goals. This important tool can help teachers influence children and adolescents to increase and maintain a health-enhancing level of physical activity.

Although children may appear to be the most active age group in our society, research conducted on daily physical activity levels reported that activity declines as children get older (Biddle et al., 2005; Corbin, Pangrazi, & LeMasurier, 2004; Norman et al., 2006). Even more drops were found in children between 9 and 15 years of age (Nader, 2008; Youth Risk Behavior Survey [YRBS], 2007). Why are some children more physically active than others? Why do some children stay more physically active than their peers during adolescence? Is activity level always a choice, or do factors outside the child's control have more influence on activity levels? The answers to these questions lie within the habitual patterns of behavior of children and adolescents. Individuals' behaviors are influenced by internally and externally controlled factors. If teachers are to become effective facilitators of behavioral change, they must first understand the factors that are influential in the formation of physical activity habits.

According to Hellison (2003, p. 32), "even though most kids are oriented to the present, learning to choose and stay with activities that meet both long- and short-term interests and needs in some balance is one of the hallmarks of mature self-direction."

A study of children ages 9 through 15 (Nader et al., 2008) revealed some behavior patterns that lead to a better understanding of the decline in physical activity as children get older. Children at 9 years of age met or exceeded 60 minutes of moderate to vigorous daily physical activity (MVPA) on both weekends and weekdays. By the age of 15, however, only 31% of youth met the suggested MVPA guidelines during weekdays, and only 17% met the guidelines on weekends. Age and sex were also found to be related to activity levels; boys were generally more active than girls. The declines in activity increased throughout late adolescence and into adulthood.

Although teachers cannot control or change gender, age, geographical location, or family income, they can help students understand the relationship between lifestyle and well-being. Educators can teach about the relationship between sedentary behaviors and health concerns. They can emphasize that as children get older,

they will face increasing barriers to finding time to be active and competing tugs on their time. They can emphasize the importance of making regular physical activity in school and at home a priority for staying healthy. After students learn the importance of physical activity, teachers can help them understand internal and external influences that affect physical activity motivation and behavior.

Research findings indicate that children's physical activity levels can be influenced by both **internal**, or personal (i.e., biological and psychological), factors and **external**, or environmental (i.e., social and physical), **factors**. Understanding these personal and environmental influences on student behaviors can help teachers encourage students to develop more physically active lifestyles. Teachers must understand how these differences affect student activity behaviors, and students must be taught about how individual differences affect their efforts toward becoming their physical best.

INTERNAL FACTORS INFLUENCING PHYSICAL ACTIVITY BEHAVIOR

Internal factors, sometimes called personal factors, can be grouped into biological and psychological categories.

Biological Factors

Gender, age, and race have been studied as possible biological influences on physical activity behavior. Studies investigating gender and age factors have shown clear trends: Boys are generally more active than girls (YRBS, 2009; Biddle et al., 2005; Blankenship, 2008), and a substantial decline in physical activity levels occurs between the ages of 6 and 18. Table 2.1 shows that fewer than one-quarter of high school girls and less than half of high school boys met daily activity guidelines to be healthy. The guidelines suggest that to be healthy, children and adolescents should accumulate, at a minimum, 60 minutes of moderate to vigorous physical activity daily.

Table 2.1 Percentage of High School Students Who Met Recommended Levels of Physical Activity* and Who Did Not Participate in 60 or More Minutes of Physical Activity on Any Day, by Sex, Race or Ethnicity, and Grade

| | Met recommended levels of physical activity | | | | | | Did not participate in 60 or more minutes of physical activity on any day | | | | | |
| | Female | | Male | | Total | | Female | | Male | | Total | |
Category	%	CI**	%	CI	%	CI	%	CI	%	CI	%	CI
Race or ethnicity												
White, non-Hispanic	27.9	23.7–32.6	46.1	42.6–49.6	**37.0**	**33.9–40.3**	28.2	24.4–32.3	16.7	14.6–19.0	**22.4**	**20.1–24.9**
Black, non-Hispanic	21.0	18.1–24.2	41.3	38.9–43.7	**31.1**	**29.3–32.9**	42.1	38.5–45.8	21.8	19.0–24.9	**32.0**	**29.3–34.8**
Hispanic	21.9	18.7–25.4	38.6	35.5–41.9	**30.2**	**27.6–33.0**	35.2	31.6–39.0	18.8	16.1–21.8	**27.1**	**24.3–30.0**
Grade												
9	31.5	27.6–35.8	44.4	41.2–47.7	**38.1**	**35.3–41.0**	26.1	22.8–29.7	17.1	14.6–20.0	**21.5**	**19.4–23.8**
10	24.4	20.4–28.9	45.1	41.8–48.3	**34.8**	**32.2–37.6**	31.7	27.6–36.2	16.3	13.9–19.1	**24.0**	**21.6–26.6**
11	24.6	21.2–28.3	45.2	41.0–49.4	**34.8**	**31.9–37.7**	34.3	30.4–38.3	18.0	15.6–20.6	**26.2**	**24.0–28.5**
12	20.6	17.2–24.4	38.7	34.7–42.8	**29.5**	**26.4–32.9**	36.2	32.5–40.0	21.5	18.6–24.7	**28.9**	**26.2–31.8**
Total	**25.6**	**22.8–28.6**	**43.7**	**41.1–46.4**	**34.7**	**32.5–37.0**	**31.8**	**29.2–34.5**	**18.0**	**16.4–19.8**	**24.9**	**23.2–26.6**

*Were physically active doing any kind of physical activity that increased their heart rate and made them breathe hard some of the time for a total of at least 60 minutes per day on five or more days during the seven days before the survey.

**95% confidence interval.

Adapted from Eaton et al. 2007.

As previously stated, children's physical activity levels decline between ages 9 and 15 as measured by accelerometers. Survey results report a steady decline throughout the high school years as measured by questionnaire responses (YRBS, 2009; Grunbaum et al., 2002). A biological explanation would point out that this change parallels the onset of puberty and therefore may be caused by changes in biological factors (hormonal, growth) as well as social and lifestyle factors.

Recent descriptive studies (YRBS, 2007) report that black students are more likely to be obese (18.3%) than white students (10%) between the ages of 12 and 19. On average, 62.7% of black students also reported spending three or more hours watching television daily on school days, compared with 43% of Hispanics and 27.2% of

white students reporting the same behaviors (see table 2.2 on page 16). The accumulation of time spent watching television, using cell phones, texting, and playing video games is certainly competing with time that could be spent being more physically active. These behaviors seem to indicate that biological determinants may contribute to differences in obesity but are likely not the exclusive causes for the decreases in physical activity in this age group. Rather, environmental, social, and behavioral factors are more likely codeterminants of the rise in sedentary behaviors.

Differences in activity levels have also been based on gender and race. The CDC (2001a) reported that black females between ages 12 and 19 were more likely to be overweight (16.3%) than white females (9%). Furthermore, Hispanic

Table 2.2 Percentage of High School Students Who Played Video or Computer Games or Used a Computer* for Three or More Hours per Day** and Who Watched Three or More Hours per Day of Television,** by Sex, Race or Ethnicity, and Grade

| | Used computers three or more hours per day | | | | | | Watched television three or more hours per day | | | | | |
| | Female | | Male | | Total | | Female | | Male | | Total | |
Category	%	CI***	%	CI	%	CI	%	CI	%	CI	%	CI
Race or ethnicity												
White, Non-Hispanic	18.2	16.2–20.5	26.9	24.0–30.1	**22.6**	**20.4–25.0**	24.0	21.8–26.3	30.4	28.1–32.8	**27.2**	**25.1–29.3**
Black, Non-Hispanic	26.7	24.2–29.4	34.0	30.3–37.9	**30.5**	**28.4–32.6**	60.6	55.9–65.1	64.6	61.9–67.3	**62.7**	**59.6–65.6**
Hispanic	21.8	18.2–26.0	30.7	26.9–34.7	**26.3**	**23.3–29.5**	43.6	39.6–47.8	42.4	37.8–47.1	**43.0**	**39.5–46.6**
Grade												
9	24.9	21.5–28.6	30.5	27.3–33.9	**27.8**	**25.3–30.5**	37.2	32.5–42.1	42.0	38.5–45.5	**39.7**	**36.4–43.0**
10	22.6	19.5–26.0	30.0	25.7–34.6	**26.3**	**23.4–29.4**	35.9	32.6–39.3	38.1	34.9–41.4	**37.0**	**34.3–39.8**
11	17.9	15.0–21.3	29.5	26.7–32.5	**23.7**	**21.2–26.5**	29.6	26.2–33.4	35.4	31.1–40.0	**32.5**	**29.4–35.7**
12	14.8	12.2–17.9	25.6	22.2–29.4	**20.1**	**17.7–22.9**	28.9	25.9–32.0	32.8	29.2–36.6	**30.8**	**28.3–33.5**
Total	**20.6**	**18.6–22.7**	**29.1**	**26.6–31.8**	**24.9**	**22.9–27.0**	**33.2**	**30.7–35.9**	**37.5**	**35.0–40.0**	**35.4**	**33.1–37.7**

*For something that was not schoolwork.

**On an average school day.

***95% confidence interval.

Adapted from Eaton et al. 2007.

high school girls were more likely than either white or black girls to describe themselves as overweight (YRBS, 2007). This trend reverses in adolescent males; white males 12 to 19 years old are more likely to be overweight (12%) than black males (10.4%). Mexican American boys also were significantly more likely to be overweight than non-Hispanic black and non-Hispanic white boys (USDHHS, 2010). Although such evidence shows a relationship between race, age, obesity, and physical activity levels in adolescents and teens, insufficient longitudinal or experimental research has been conducted to understand whether obese youth were always prone to inactivity or whether they became inactive only after

they became obese. What is known is that obese children engage in less physical activity and tend to spend more nonschool time watching television (YRBS, 2007) than their nonobese peers do.

Psychological Factors

Psychological factors also affect physical activity behaviors. Researchers have studied the relationship of cognitive and psychological variables to levels of physical activity among children and adolescents. For adults, knowledge about the benefits of physical activity has been recognized as a powerful influence on exercise behaviors and a stimulus for change (Marcus & Forsyth, 2003).

YOUTH AND PHYSICAL ACTIVITY STATISTICS

Although youth are a more active population, two particular factors make it less likely for adolescents to continue an active lifestyle into adulthood. First, physical activity levels in both males and females decline steadily during high school. Second, American high school students do not engage in regular physical activities that maintain or improve their aerobic fitness, strength, and flexibility (USDHHS, 2001; YRBS, 2009).

These trends are shown in the results of the 2007 national school-based Youth Risk Behavior Surveillance (YRBS) system:

Physical Inactivity

- 34.7% met recommended levels of physical activity.
- 53.6% attended physical education classes on one or more days per week.
- 70% did not attend physical education classes daily.
- 35% watched television three or more hours per day on an average school day.
- 25% played video or computer games or used a computer for something that was not school-work for three or more hours per day on an average school day.

Research has also shown differences in strengthening exercise behavior among high school students (Grunbaum et al. 2002; YRBS, 2001):

- 53.4% of students had done strengthening exercises (e.g., push-ups, curl-ups, and weight-lifting) on more than three of the seven days preceding the survey.
- Male students (62.8%) were significantly more likely than female students (44.5%) to have participated in strengthening activities. This gender difference was identified for all racial or ethnic and grade subpopulations.
- White students (54.8%) were significantly more likely than black students (47.9%) to have participated in strengthening activities.
- Students in grade 9 (58.7%) were more likely than students in grades 10, 11, and 12 (53.9%, 51.1%, and 48%, respectively) to have participated in strengthening activities.

From www.cdc.gov/healthyyouth/yrbs/pdf/yrbs07-us-overview.pdf; reprinted from Grunbaum et al. 2002.

But knowing that it is healthy to be physically active does not always influence the physical activity levels of adults, and for children this knowledge is even less of an influence. Children place more importance on the value of an activity and on whether or not they feel competent and satisfied during the activity (Ward, Saunders, & Pate, 2007). Table 2.3 on page 18 summarizes some of the research in this area.

For students to persist in physical activities as they grow, the research clearly demonstrates that children and adolescents must feel generally competent in physical activities. They also need to feel confident in their ability to achieve a specific goal

(self-efficacy). Self-efficacy suggests that children and adolescents believe that they have a chance to succeed. Control over the outcomes based on effort is included in self-efficacy (Harter, 1999). To influence changes in children, teachers need to know how to motivate students to participate actively in class. Another component teachers must know is how to help students achieve satisfaction or feel successful following their effort. Students are taught that participation and effort can be quantified during activity by monitoring breathing or heart rate. Quantifying activity in this manner is important in focusing on the process of activity rather than the outcome or

Table 2.3 Psychological Factors and Children's Physical Activity

Variable	Relationship to motivation for physical activity
Self-efficacy	Belief that they can succeed will lead to attempts to participate in specific activities.
Self-control or self-determination (internal control)	Belief that they have control over the outcome leads to persistence in activity.
Intrinsic motivation	Individuals differ on levels of curiosity and preference for challenge or mastery of goals.
Value of activity	Students who perceive an activity to be important are more motivated to pursue it.
Global self-esteem and global self-worth	Related to motivation, but only in trying new activities—persistence depends on success or achievement and value of activity.
Satisfaction	Satisfaction is an outcome of success experienced in valued activities.

performance results. Recent research on children in sport and exercise psychology provides the physical education teacher with a much better understanding of how children and adolescents are motivated. This understanding can help teachers develop classroom strategies that may help reverse the trend of physical inactivity in adolescents.

To feel competent, younger children must be guided through skill acquisition and provided with many opportunities to practice at their own level, without emphasis on competition. Young children have a tendency to believe that merely trying hard controls outcome. Teachers can quantify the concept of effort by rewarding the number of practice attempts or minutes spent working toward a goal in younger children. As children learn and develop, they understand that effort does not always lead to success, and the reward system must be changed to award the achievement of goals. This developmental change is the reason that older children need to be given more choices of activities so that they can find activities in which they can succeed. To develop physical activity self-efficacy, children must be provided a variety of activities from which they can choose. This approach will enhance their chances of finding activities matched to personal factors such as strength, height, endurance, or other biological factors. Self-control is also enhanced when teachers provide students with choices of activities, including individual or team activities, and various levels of competitive or noncompetitive activities. Teachers can find a variety of developmentally appropriate activities in the *Physical Best Activity Guides*. Using a variety of

activities matched to the age and developmental level of students will increase student interest and student success, thereby increasing student self-efficacy. This approach will lead to greater student motivation in class. Teachers who use developmentally appropriate activities are taking the first steps to creating a psychologically safe classroom—one where children and adolescents can be successful, receive regular helpful feedback to improve their performance of physical skills, and have choices of activities used to accomplish fitness goals. Students who feel safe and who experience success will persist in activities both in the physical education classroom and during after-school hours.

EXTERNAL FACTORS INFLUENCING PHYSICAL ACTIVITY BEHAVIOR

Naturally, the world a child lives in influences his or her physical activity level and choices. Social and physical surroundings (environmental factors) must therefore also be taken into consideration.

Social Factors

Parents and siblings greatly influence a younger (elementary level) child's choices in life (Jackson et al., 2004), whereas an adolescent is more likely to seek peer approval and support. Researchers (Epstein et al., 2000; Nader et al., 2008) have recognized that parents must be included when trying to change students' physical activity behav-

Social interaction can be motivating to students. You should help students learn that fitness can be social as well as good for their physical health.

iors. Television and screen time in the home can and must be replaced with family activity time, such as taking walks or just playing outside. Substituting less active screen time (watching TV, playing sedentary computer games) with interactive screen play such as Nintendo Wii or Dance Dance Revolution can also be encouraged. Other adults, including teachers, coaches, and physicians, also influence a child's choices and can affect physical activity behavior.

The various people in a child's life can influence physical activity behavior in many ways:

▶ Peers—If a child's friends are out biking or in-line skating, the child is more likely to be doing the same. If a child's friends are more interested in television or video games, these will probably be the child's interests too. The older the child is, the more likely it is that peers will significantly influence physical activity behavior.

▶ Parents and siblings—As with peers, if a child's family is out hiking or playing basketball regularly, the child is more likely to feel competent in these areas. The child is more likely to be physically active if the family is active and the child is exposed early to activity. Conversely, if the child's family is sedentary and avoids physical activity, the child is less likely to be motivated to be physically active. Parents also influence a child's physical activity level by their ability to finance community-based physical activities. As any parent knows, chauffeuring for these activities alone can require a tremendous commitment of time and energy.

▶ Teachers—Most people can think of at least one teacher who greatly influenced life choices they have made in one area or another. In relation to physical activity behavior, teacher enthusiasm is contagious! Teacher enthusiasm shows that they value the content they teach and that physical education is important in life (Lavay, French, & Henderson, 2006).

▶ Physicians—According to the American Academy of Pediatrics (AAP) (2000), a physical activity prescription is a powerful strategy that can take advantage of the "white coat effect," emphasizing to patients that physical activity is as important to their health as any medication. Physicians are encouraged to include children and their parents in the physical activity goal-setting process. For many children, parents play an important role in any behavioral change; therefore, physicians are encouraged to target both the child and the parent (AAP, 2000).

Environmental Factors

Many environmental factors can promote or discourage physical activity. This area is especially important to consider because most physical activity must take place outside of physical education class and school itself. Recent research suggests that children do not engage in sufficient after-school physical activity at home or in the community (Dale, Corbin, & Dale, 2000; McKenzie & Kahan, 2008). The neighborhood that a child lives in can greatly influence physical activity behavior. For example, in many environments, parents are reluctant or unwilling to allow their children to play outdoors because of safety concerns. Indoor activities, such as watching television, reading, or playing computer games keep children entertained and occupied but are sedentary in nature, rather than active. Walking or biking to school programs were initiated by many communities in response to the national goals included in *Healthy People 2020*. In other areas, facilities and friends may be several miles away, so transportation can be a barrier to participating in physical activities that require more than one person. In contrast, a child living in another neighborhood may have greater freedom as well as more attractive and conveniently located physical activity facilities, such as parks, gymnasiums, and swimming pools. Temperatures that are too hot in summer or too cold in winter can also influence activity levels in various parts of the country. Teachers who recognize the limitations associated with such environmental factors often alter their curricular offerings to provide knowledge and experience in a variety of activities that correspond with their students' resources.

OVERCOMING BARRIERS TO PHYSICAL ACTIVITY FOR CHILDREN WITH DISABILITIES

"Easier said than done" could be the motto for many families who try to provide expanded opportunities to participate in physical activity to their children with disabilities. Although the Individuals with Disabilities Act (see chapter 11) mandates accessibility to public buildings and accessible transportation for all, families still need a lot of resolve to get these children into the arena of physical activity. Here are some examples:

- James, a teenager with cerebral palsy, wanted to prepare for a swim meet. To do so, he had to travel alone by bus to the pool. His mother felt comfortable with this because James is able to communicate clearly, but the bus driver refused to help James position his heavy wheelchair to use the lift. James' mother had to fight to get the bus company to change its "policy," forcing the bus driver to give James the assistance he needed.

- Sara's father wanted her to play soccer, but the city league was not receptive to including a child with a disability. Sara's father organized his own special team, which thrived for many years because of this parent's dedication.

Contributed by Aleita Hass-Holcombe, Corvallis (Oregon) School District.

WHY PHYSICAL ACTIVITY DECREASES WITH AGE

Developmental changes occur over a life span. The decrease in physical activity seen from childhood to adolescence is likely influenced by a combination of factors that may include cognitive, social, and psychological changes in interests and motivational factors. Physical development leads to changes in functional abilities such as strength, speed, and flexibility. Social factors include a desire to spend time with peers. If a high school student's friends are more interested in sedentary activities or if the only way to interact is by texting or talking on the phone, the person will find less time available for activity. Psychological needs for approval and competence also influence activity choices. Demands to work and raise money also contribute to decreases in time available for sports and active lifestyles. The prestige of driving a car affects the desire to walk or bike to and from school—and adds additional sitting time to an already sedentary school day. Environmental factors are interspersed within each of these areas.

Changing the downward trend in activity levels with increasing age involves examining all factors influencing activity levels and then tailoring the curriculum and environment to meet these changing needs. Although this task may seem impossible, expert teachers and researchers have responded to the challenge and have identified strategies incorporated into Physical Best and Fitnessgram that can be useful in reversing trends.

As students enter high school, they face increasing demands on their time. A survey of parents (USDHHS, 2005) reported that children aged 10 to 11 averaged 4.4 days of 20 minutes or more of physical activity. By the ages of 15 to 17, this average fell to 3.5 days per week. In the same report, 61.5% of children aged 10 to 11 and 61.6 % of those aged 12 to 14 participated in sports; by ages 15 to 17, the rate had dropped to 53.4%. Many students have jobs after school. More than a third of young people in grades 9 through 12 do not regularly engage in vigorous physical activity (YRBS, 2007). According to *Shape of the Nation* (NASPE, 2006) 65% of states require physical education for middle or junior high school students and 83% of states mandate it for high school students. Teachers must clearly communicate and help high school students understand that physical activity must be a regular daily behavior occurring outside of school.

With changing family demographics that include more single-parent homes and more homes with both parents working outside the home, many older students must hurry home to care for younger siblings. Because of either transportation issues or time demands, many students cannot rely on participation in organized sports to meet the daily activity requirements. They simply do not have time to play. Secondary-level teachers need to teach how alternative physical activity choices such as walking, biking, hiking, aerobics, yoga, strength training, or leisure pursuits can meet physical activity requirements. Activities that can be done alone, without teammates or partners, must become part of the curriculum. Teachers need to realize that skill competency does not necessarily equate to being competent in team sports. The challenge for today's secondary teachers becomes finding a greater variety of activities that high school students can fit into their busy lives.

This objective can be met by individualizing instruction (see chapter 11) and by offering more choices in before-, during-, or after-school programs. Adolescent students tend to gravitate toward peer partners of their own skill and interest levels. Providing activities that do not require

Involvement in community events can be a powerful motivator for getting young people to be active.

teams but rather can be accomplished with one or more friends is a trend that should be explored in physical education programming. Successful programs have created environments similar to fitness centers, where students can use ergometers, treadmills, and weight machines to address personal fitness plans.

In such programs, students are taught to set personal fitness and activity goals, and are encouraged to become personally responsible for monitoring their progress toward these goals. The teacher serves as a facilitator of student goals and teaches the skills and concepts that students need to assume self-management over their physical activity goals. In general, then, physical education programs for older students must focus on teaching students to apply what they learn in class to community settings and activities available to adults, while helping those students develop the basic skills that they need for their activities of choice.

MOTIVATING STUDENTS TO BE ACTIVE FOR LIFE

Secondary-level teachers need to be skillful at teaching goal setting, and they should understand strategies for teaching students how to change behaviors that are contrary to healthy lifestyles. Teachers need to refocus their thinking about teaching skills and movement competencies. Just as fitness is necessary to play sports, sports can be used as a venue to achieve increases in fitness and physical activity. Furthermore, teachers can help students identify and overcome barriers that prevent active behaviors. All teachers should understand multiple ways to motivate their learners.

For more than 30 years, psychologists have examined extrinsic and intrinsic motivation as critical determinants influencing behavioral change. Extrinsic motivation, requiring the use of rewards, tokens, or social reinforcers, is effective, especially for younger students and students with disabilities (Blankenship, 2008). Reliance on extrinsic motivation, however, leads to dependence on others for behaviors to become habitual. Intrinsic motivation comes from within—from the student's own desire to succeed, to grow, and

to be independent. Teachers have spent countless hours debating which type of motivation is most effective to foster learning and behavioral change. The question is best answered by recognizing that the job of today's teachers is to foster independence and to empower their students—intrinsic motivation will increase as self-confidence and self-esteem grow and as students assume responsibility for their own behaviors (Hellison, 2003).

Extrinsic Motivation

Extrinsic motivation occurs when a desired object or socially enhancing consequence (reinforcer) is presented to increase the likelihood that a behavior will be repeated. Extrinsic motivational tools in physical education often include the use of material reinforcers, social reinforcers, activity reinforcers, or special outings (Blankenship, 2008). Material reinforcers include such rewards or tokens as trophies, certificates, T-shirts, money, points, stickers, or stamps. Extrinsic reinforcers work well with younger children and initially can enhance the value of an activity to adolescents. Stickers (at the elementary level) and T-shirts (at the middle and high school levels) are often effective in rewarding effort or conveying the sense of belonging to the group. High fives, public acknowledgement, verbal praise, smiles, or signals such as thumbs up are examples of social reinforcers. Posting student accomplishments on bulletin boards or sharing them over public address systems also serve as social reinforcers. These activities provide extrinsic motivation by enhancing students' self-esteem through peer and teacher recognition. Activity reinforcers can also be used to motivate students. For example, offering a choice of games to play or allowing students to choose activities to pursue during free time enhances enjoyment. Teachers are in control of this type of extrinsic motivation. The teacher controls the time spent, but students have opportunities to become part of the decision-making process. Special outings can also be used as extrinsic rewards. Students who achieve target goals might be rewarded with a field trip to the bowling alley, a ski area, or another physical activity event.

Although extrinsic rewards may motivate children to achieve activity goals, they tend to lose their effectiveness over time. Cognitive evaluation theory (Blankenship, 2008; Ryan & Deci, 2000) has been used to explain why the use of extrinsic motivation may not be sustainable. According to the theory, rewards are effective only when they are perceived as valuable. When students begin to see the reward as more controlling or as a bribe to comply with teacher directions and less indicative of having accomplished something special or unique, the reward loses its value as a motivational tool. More specifically, when extrinsic rewards are used too often, children may come to view the rewards as the reason to participate. They may have made the choice to participate in these activities without the rewards. Extrinsic rewards must be selected carefully. Rewards should be valued by the recipient and directly related to the activity. To remain effective motivators, extrinsic rewards can be used to reward achievement of student goals and should be chosen by the student rather than the teacher.

The Fitnessgram program introduces new tools, such as the Activitygram Activity Log, for children to monitor their activities, including steps and activity time. A motivational tool for teachers to use in physical education class includes classwide or schoolwide challenges. By creating group competitions, motivation is enhanced for children and youth in the competitive stages of life (beyond about third grade). By using the Activity Log tools, teachers can create challenges and help students set goals for daily, weekly, or even yearly activity levels. Seeing progress toward group goals can transfer to increases in intrinsic motivation as well. The latest version of Fitnessgram also can be used to link at-home activities with those introduced at school. When children can log into the programs from their own computers, they can take ownership of their personal activity programs. The networking capabilities of the newer programs also help make the connections between school and home more explicit. Chapter 13 covers the Fitnessgram and Activitygram assessment reports in more detail.

Intrinsic Motivation

Intrinsic motivation comes from an internal desire to be competent and self-determined (Blankenship, 2008). A person who is intrinsically motivated participates in an activity simply because it is enjoyable or presents a challenge. Unlike extrinsic motivation, intrinsic motivation leads to a persistence in behavior and a long-term

DEBATING ABOUT REWARDS AND AWARDS

Whether or not to offer extrinsic rewards for physical activity participation or fitness assessment scores is a controversial topic. On the one hand, it is important to encourage students to do their best on assessments and be more active overall. On the other hand, intrinsic motivation may be longer lasting. The following are some guidelines for using rewards and awards judiciously:

- Reward the performance, not the outcome.
- Reward the students more for their effort than for their actual success.
- Reward little things on the way toward reaching larger goals.
- Reward the learning and performance of emotional and social skills as well as health-related fitness endeavors.
- Reward frequently when youngsters are first learning to apply new concepts.
- After physical activity and health-related fitness habits are well formed, you only need to reinforce them occasionally. In other words, you can use extrinsic rewards to change students' physical activity habits and then slowly wean them onto intrinsic appreciation of physical activity.
- Use rewards that have meaning to the recipients; ask students what they might find reinforcing. Be age appropriate in your choices.
- Rewards can be words of praise or chances to choose from a wider variety of activities, as well as more tangible items, such as stickers and T-shirts.

Reprinted, by permission, from R. Martens, 2004, *Successful coaching*, 3rd ed. (Champaign, IL: Human Kinetics), 158.

commitment to behavior change. Intrinsically motivated students view physical activity as enjoyable, and participation leads to feelings of personal satisfaction and competence. To promote intrinsic motivation, teachers initially can reward physical activity behavior extrinsically (e.g., with stickers, ribbons, gift certificates) and gradually substitute social reinforcers until the students understand the importance of physical activity. Teachers must incorporate knowledge and concepts during activity to facilitate this understanding of the importance of activity to long-term health. Without this knowledge, the children will focus on the fun but not be able to internalize the importance of lifelong activity. When the activity ceases to be fun or challenging, without the knowledge components, children will stop participating. As children mature, learning about the personal rewards of becoming physically fit and active can help them become more intrinsically motivated. This transition is best accomplished when goals and awards are focused on the process, such as being active, rather than the product, such as achieving a fast time in the mile run (see also chapter 13). Choice plus physical skill or movement competence is what creates an intrinsically motivated and physically active person.

Experts on motivation argue that an understanding of human drive is much more complex than a two-dimensional (extrinsic versus intrinsic) model. For example, Vallerand's (2001) model includes a third construct to explain human motives, that of amotivation, and he argues that motivation is multidimensional and hierarchical in nature. His work points out that to understand exercise (or activity) motivation, you need to know about the motives of people in other life contexts, such as education, leisure, and interpersonal relationships, as well as their perceptions of competence, autonomy, and relatedness (Vallerand, 2001).

It has been established that regular physical activity is associated with a healthier, longer life by lowering the risks of heart disease, high blood pressure, diabetes, obesity, and some types of cancer. Unfortunately, merely acknowledging the benefits of physical activity hasn't been sufficient motivation for behavioral change. Thus, one must ask what strategies work best in motivating people to become more physically active.

Prochaska, Norcross, and DiClemete (1994) and others (Cardinal, 2000; Carron, Hausenblas, & Estabrooks, 2003) have examined motivation to change as it relates to stages of readiness and awareness (see sidebar) and have demonstrated

Having fun is the primary intrinsic reason that students give for choosing to be physically active on their own.

Photodisc

that understanding the **stages of change** (SOC) (aka transtheoretical model) can help in changing behaviors, such as achieving exercise goals (see sidebar). In the SOC model, people are believed to pass through five stages when adopting a physically active lifestyle or any other life change. In the precontemplation stage, the person has no intention to change and is not motivated to do so. The second stage, contemplation, reflects thinking about change but still not being motivated to take action. The preparation stage involves some activity, but not of a regular frequency. To move from any of these stages to the action stage (regular activity behavior, for example) the person must have knowledge, support, and the tools to be successful at changing. For inactive students, teachers and physical education programs must find a way to provide these tools so that students can adopt lifelong physical activity behaviors (maintenance stage).

The SOC, or transtheoretical, model may be useful for middle and high school teachers working with more mature students, but more research is needed on adolescents to determine whether the adult model applies to exercise behavior modification in teens.

Teachers must understand that **motivational factors** for children differ from those for adults. Harter (1999) and Harter, Waters, and Whitesell (1998) found that children's self-worth varied and was influenced greatly by their perceptions of the people near them (parents, teachers, peers) and by their desire to please those people or be accepted by them. Therefore, because the context or environment is always changing, the motivational climate will also change, depending on the time, place, or people around the student. As an example, someone might be motivated to participate in physical education class if she has a desire to please the teacher, but she may just as easily be unmotivated if her friends do not value physical activity.

Self-determination theory (Deci & Ryan, 1991) also informs us that children and adults

CHARACTERISTICS RELATED TO EACH STAGE OF CHANGE (SOC)

1. Precontemplation
- Resists change
- Believes that change is not needed
- Not really thinking about or intending to change behaviors

2. Contemplation
- Thinks about changing within six months; may be indecisive about change
- May gather information about pros and cons of change (benefits, barriers)

3. Preparation
- Has achieved the desire to change but doesn't know how
- Believes that benefits of change outweigh barriers
- Lacks efficacy or confidence to maintain desired behaviors

4. Action
- Has a plan of action; has specific goals
- Is committed to acquiring the new behavior
- Is at risk for relapse—easily discouraged
- Finds confidence slowly increasing

5. Maintenance
- Has maintained behavior for six months or longer
- Is enjoying benefits of change—less likely to relapse
- Has increased confidence in new behavior
- Finds temptations to relapse less enticing

Adapted from Prochaska, Norcross, and DiClemente 1994.

HELPING STUDENTS MOVE THROUGH THE STAGES OF CHANGE

From precontemplation to contemplation
- Teach about benefits of healthy lifestyle
- Challenge unhealthy behaviors—show how they affect self and others
- Encourage students to self-assess behaviors and fitness (awareness enhances contemplation)
- Provide assessments

From contemplation to action
- Help students set goals
- Reward students for reaching goals

- Praise and recognize achievement of goals or change
- Encourage students when they are at risk for relapse
- Provide continued assessments

From action to maintenance
- Recognize sustained change
- Help to reassess; provide opportunities for assessment
- Provide options or choices of activities to enhance enjoyment

Adapted from Prochaska, Norcross, and DiClemente 1994.

have three basic needs: They need competence, autonomy, and relatedness. When children feel competent (able to achieve tasks), have a sense of self-control or input into activities, and see that activities are relevant to their lives, they will be motivated to become active. Simply put, teachers must know the needs of their students to be able to influence their behaviors. Teachers must have a repertoire of motivational strategies to use with their students.

CREATING PHYSICAL EDUCATION PROGRAMS THAT MOTIVATE

One major intrinsic motivator is fun. In fact, enjoyment is the primary intrinsic reason that students give for participating in physical activity (Blankenship, 2008). Enjoyable, intrinsically motivating activities have four characteristics: They create a challenge, provoke curiosity, provide control (chances for self-responsibility), and promote creativity (Raffini, 1993). The activities used should embody these characteristics. Another intrinsic motivator is the natural urge to learn. When children learn from a class activity, they are more likely to be motivated to continue being physically active. Finally, when teaching physical skills teachers should ensure that students attain reasonable form. When students lack basic skills,

WHAT IS *FUN*?

Throughout this book, emphasis is placed on making physical activity fun. Fun is not a widely accepted goal or objective of a quality physical education program; rather, fun has typically been perceived as a means to achieving the ultimate goal of having students adopt physical activity that results in healthy lifestyles. In fact, fun sometimes is considered a replacement for quality instruction, a substitution that is not necessary or realistic in quality physical education programs.

People are more likely to participate in activities that they enjoy. Fun for one person may not be fun for others. Some people like competition (e.g., playing team sports), some like cooperative social activities (e.g., participating in an aerobics class), and others prefer individual activities (e.g., cross-country skiing at a state park). Fun is accomplishing a new task, achieving personal goals, and learning new skills! The key is making physical education purposeful and enjoyable to achieve the goal of graduating students who will be physically active, healthy, and productive adults.

participation may not be an enjoyable experience. Students' self-efficacy and self-esteem may decline because of lack of success.

THE FOUR Cs = CHARACTERISTICS OF INTRINSICALLY MOTIVATING ACTIVITIES

- Challenge—When students are challenged and subsequently succeed, they feel competent. Feelings of competency enhance self-worth and lead to intrinsic motivation.
- Curiosity—Curiosity is innate. Curious students seek knowledge and strive to learn about themselves and the world. Curiosity leads to problem solving and feelings of efficacy—that they can successfully tackle the barriers that they face in life.
- Control—Self-control leads to feelings of autonomy, self-direction, and accomplishment. External control diminishes autonomy and motivation for self-direction.
- Creativity—Creativity is enjoyable because it allows students to be individuals and presents opportunities for self-expression. Creative environments are noncompetitive and allow everyone to feel special.

Regardless of the approach students must perceive physical education as relevant. Physical Best is designed to enhance the intrinsic pleasures of physical activity.

Too often students are turned off to physical activity when teachers attempt to get children active and physically fit. Boring laps, the antiquated no pain, no gain philosophy, and comparisons to others have too often been deterrents to physical activity. The *Physical Best Activity Guides* help teachers explore enjoyable and interesting activities that promote a conceptual knowledge of fitness in a positive, fun, and developmentally appropriate manner.

Goal Setting and Motivation

Goal setting is a mechanism that helps students understand their potential and feel satisfied with their accomplishments. Establishing goals is a good way to encourage changes in behavior that lead to improved health and fitness. Using goals created from personal assessments establishes ownership and fosters pride in the process. Written action plans help to establish a pathway to the destination that has been set. The types of behaviors (goals) that students require for improving health-related fitness can be determined from a preassessment. (See the Fitness Goals Contract and Activity Goals Contract in appendix A.) The goal-setting process is invaluable to physical education, as well as to other areas of life.

The positive relationship between motivation and self-determination, or autonomy, has been supported (Deci & Ryan, 1985) in sport and physical activity settings. Underlying assumptions of the theory are that people who have input or choices regarding their activities and goals are more vested in the time and energy (effort) spent working to accomplish these goals. Conversely, when goals are externally controlled, people lack commitment and are more likely to withdraw or to expend less effort in the activities. Goal setting can be divided into two distinct areas: (1) establishing an outcome and (2) working to achieve the outcome. For students' goals to be motivational and for students to incorporate goals into their physical activity behaviors, teachers must encourage students to use them regularly. Teachers should encourage students to set goals for learning new tasks, practicing drills and skills, and participating in physical activity and fitness assessments.

Goal setting does not have to take a lot of time or even extra planning. It is a cognitive strategy that promotes self-monitoring and motivation, and should be incorporated into good teaching. Young children can set simple goals, such as playing games for 30 minutes after school or riding bikes two days after school. After the first attempt, students are asked to state or think to themselves what they did and how participating in either of these activities affected their personal fitness. Students are then asked to establish a new revised goal based on the first attempts. Teachers may ask students to write them down in the beginning stages. After each activity attempt, however, the teacher reinforces the goal-setting process by merely asking the students whether they met their goals. If students were unable to meet their goals, they are asked to think about strategies that might help them achieve their goals. Asking students whether they thought that their goals were too difficult can help them refine and set attainable goals. This introduction to the goal-setting process teaches children the importance of decision making and self-assessment.

Older students should write down their goals, identify barriers to accomplishing their goals, and hold themselves accountable for meeting their goals. Reflection and critical thinking enhance learning, and are both important steps in goal setting.

Goals pursued because of autonomous (personal choice) motives lead to sustained effort while striving to achieve them. Goals pursued because of external regulation lead to decreases in effort and motivation over time. Furthermore, more challenging goals that are imposed on individuals (students) by external agents (teachers) have been associated with decreased effort over time.

Goal setting should be viewed as the process of writing or listing specific outcomes that are measurable, specific, and task oriented.

GOAL SETTING

When?
- From the beginning
- Throughout the year
- Daily
- In school and out of school

How?
- Involve students by asking them to choose their own goals.
- Start small.
- Use regularly, not just for long-term outcomes.
- Make goals specific and measurable.
- Encourage students to set challenging and realistic goals.
- Write down goals to enhance accountability.
- Provide strategies when students are stuck but encourage them to solve problems and identify their barriers.
- Give feedback on progress or have students self-assess progress.
- Create goal stations or integrate goals into all daily activities.
- Conduct periodic evaluation; without evaluation, students learn that teachers do not value the process.

What?
- Use Physical Best resources.
  - Tie activities to standards; explain that standards are the goals that teachers have to meet.

- The healthy fitness zones (HFZ) are the standards or goals that we need to achieve to live healthy lives (see chapter 13).
- Preassess—Ask students to compare their results to the charts and identify their personal strengths and areas needing work. Preassessment should occur when students have a clear understanding of what they are to assess. Meaning occurs when students have prior knowledge of what and why.
- Use Fitnessgram resources
  - The entire program is designed for individualized goal setting and self-assessment.
  - Use student printouts; the feedback in the student Fitnessgram and Activitygrams should be used to set individual fitness, nutritional, and activity goals.
  - The Activity Log and Challenges can be used to create group or class goals.
  - Goal striving = effort demonstrated toward goal attainment.

Student autonomy can be undermined if the focus of the goals becomes solely to achieve scores in the healthy fitness zone (HFZ), which are zones that reflect fitness levels required for good health (see chapter 13 for more information). Although the healthy fitness zone is a desirable target score that represents health-enhancing levels of strength, endurance, body composition, and flexibility, it should not become the focus of fitness assessment and teaching. Teachers must be careful not to overemphasize the achievement of the HFZ as their desired goal for all students. Rather, they should teach about health-related fitness—that the scores in the zones are related to health and well-being, that they differ by age and gender, and therefore that a variety of factors affect their personal health. When students choose the HFZ as their goal it is more autonomous. Some students may wish to set goals above the zone. Others may wish to set goals that progressively move them toward the zone. Although the outcome of student choice and the teacher's desired outcomes may be the same for many students, the *process* is the focus of goal-setting exercises. Applying an individualized approach helps students select their own goals. Student discussions can establish connections between an HFZ and its relationship to psychological and physical well-being, providing students with meaningful reasons to use an HFZ as the goal.

Goal setting takes experience and practice for both students and teachers. But when incorporated throughout the physical education curriculum, students of all ages can use the process to enhance motivation and effort. Many factors should be considered when using goal setting, including gender differences, current fitness level, information about fitness improvement, and growth and maturation. Achieving personal goals can encourage students to do well.

Goal-Setting Steps

1. Determine a baseline. The baseline is an accounting of the current fitness level or the behaviors needing change. Thus, in setting goals to enhance personal fitness, the first step is to assess the current level of fitness.

2. Clearly define the desired outcome. If in the initial assessment it is determined that improvement in flexibility in the right shoulder is needed, the student can use the Fitnessgram healthy fitness zone charts as a guide in setting the desired outcome. The desired outcome would be that the student would be able to touch fingertips when reaching with the right hand over the shoulder.

3. List the activities to be performed or strategies needed to achieve the desired outcome. Using the FITT guidelines helps the student ensure specificity in the setting of the activities: frequency (e.g., how many times per day or week a stretch will be performed), intensity (e.g., whether the stretch is to be performed by the person alone or with partner assistance), time (e.g., how long to hold the stretch), and type (e.g., the types of stretching that will enhance shoulder flexibility).

4. Identify a time line for reassessment and the accomplishment of the goal. Often, this is written at the beginning of the goal, as in the following: "At the end of six weeks, I will be able to touch fingertips when performing the right shoulder flexibility assessment."

5. Commit to the achievement of the goal. The best way to accomplish this is by using goal partners (the teacher can also be the goal partner for younger students). The goal partner and the goal setter both sign the paper, and the paper is then posted in a place that reminds the person to work toward the goal, perhaps on the inside of the student's locker door, on the refrigerator at home (e.g., for a nutritional goal), or in a daily journal. Students should be told to check daily with their goal partner and to provide encouragement. They can do this in person or by phone, e-mail, or texting.

6. Reassess and reinforce. Reassessment should occur not only at the end of the period but also at least weekly. Reinforcement occurs daily from both the goal setter and the goal partner after each reassessment period. For students who need extrinsic motivation, the reinforcement might come in the form of tokens (e.g., stickers) that can be exchanged at the end of the goal period for something of value—free time, choice of activities, points toward a grade, or even a day off.

Provide individualized motivation and support but do so in a way that is perceived as helpful rather than stigmatizing.

MOTIVATIONAL PE

For goal setting to be effective, teachers must demonstrate that goals are important so that students learn how to set appropriate goals. Time must be provided in class for evaluation and reestablishment of new goals. Teachers can help students identify fitness areas that they need to develop. Teachers can help guide students to make appropriate decisions throughout the goal-setting process. The acronym MOTIVATIONAL PE may be helpful in teaching goal setting. The Goal-Setting Worksheet is an example of applying these concepts with students (see figure 2.1).

▶ **M = Measure and monitor**. Goal setting begins with measurement. Taking stock of student needs is the basis for effective goal setting and motivation. After goals are set, they must be constantly monitored to determine whether progress is being made toward their achievement. Goals must be written in measurable terms. Teachers must have time to monitor the progress of all students to ensure that they are having fun and are making progress toward goals. Too often teachers and students set goals but then do not revisit them, or set new ones, after the goals are met.

▶ **O = Outcomes defined that are optimally challenging**. Teachers should use the Fitness-gram healthy fitness zone charts to identify achievable goals. They should provide knowledge about why fitness is important and how it is achieved. Teachers must help students define the desired outcome. Teachers are accustomed to writing objectives that specify conditions and outcomes that are measurable, and this format is the basis for a good goal. To have fun and not be bored, students must be challenged with tasks or goals that are difficult but achievable (i.e., they must be optimally challenged). Goals that are too difficult will be discarded; those that are too easy will not have value.

▶ **T = Time**. If a goal can't be reached within a specified time limit, then it is too difficult. Setting a time line for assessment is critical for appropriate monitoring of progress toward goal achievement. To remain motivated, students should have both short-term and long-range goals. The short-term goals should be achievable within one or two class periods, such as increasing the number of laps in the PACER assessment or increasing curl-ups by one per class session. Short-term goals are often process goals related to skill acquisition or form. Long-term goals should also have a time limit and should be achievable within a couple of weeks or a month. For students, focusing on a longer period may result in a loss of interest and enjoyment in the activity and the value of its outcome. The goals should specify the length of time needed to achieve the outcome, as well as a time line for reassessment.

▶ **I = Individualized**. Students own the goal, and it must be tailored to meet their individual needs. Goals should not be competitive and should vary in level of difficulty, time, type of activity, and in the number of goals set. Individualization helps students with diverse needs. Well-prepared classes include a variety of activities from which students can choose. Allowing students to choose a variety of activities to meet their individual goals prevents boredom and provides opportunities for increased success. Younger

students may need more teacher guidance, but as students develop, they should have autonomy in setting fitness goals and the activities that they will use to accomplish the goals.

▶ **V = Valuable**. For a goal to have value, students set their own goals and determine the reward to be earned. For younger students, activities that are fun are valued. Providing rewards such as tokens that can be exchanged for choice activity time often increases the value of goal achievement. For adolescents, value is often enhanced when goals are linked with those of other students. Sharing goals and having goal partners validate success are effective ways to enhance the social value of goal achievement.

▶ **A = Active**. Activity is a component of the goal-setting process. Active refers to the process of goal setting as well as to the achievement of its outcome. Students should select the aspect of fitness on which they wish to focus their efforts, record their own progress toward the goal, and have a say in the rewards received as a result of goal accomplishment.

▶ **T = Type**. Providing choices (types) of activities that may be used to achieve the desired outcomes will enhance motivation to achieve the goal. Allowing choices can also help overcome barriers to success. Consider a goal leading toward enhanced aerobic fitness. A student might write that he will walk 1 mile (1.6 km) each day, but then winter weather may prevent walking. Teaching students about various activities that are available to achieve a fitness goal enables appropriate substitution of a different activity. Alternatives such as walking 15 minutes on a treadmill or performing step-ups will lead to the desired outcome. Providing choices will facilitate greater success than prescribing specific activities. Task stations are used to provide students with variety and choice of activities.

▶ **I = Incremental**. Incremental refers to developmentally appropriate and safe progressions in levels of difficulty. When setting several goals, the easiest goal to accomplish should be the first goal. This approach will provide an initial successful experience. For optimal success, goals should be written so that the difficulty increases incrementally.

GOAL-SETTING WORKSHEET

Name_____Date_____

M = Measure and monitor

In class, my Fitnessgram scores were as follows: _____.
My scores falling below the healthy fitness zone were (list) _____.

O = Outcomes defined that are optimally challenging

Based on my Fitnessgram scores, I wish to improve fitness in the following areas:
(Example: abdominal strength and endurance)

T = Time

I will accomplish my goal in_____weeks.

I = Individualized

I will not compare my scores to my classmates' scores.
To reach the HFZ, I need to increase my score by_____(the exercise).
(Example: 10 curl-ups)

V = Valuable

I have chosen an important goal of _____.
(Example: increasing abdominal strength)
This is important to me because . . .

A = Active

By completing this sheet, I am taking active responsibility for increasing my health and fitness._____(initial)

T = Type

The following types of activities will help me to reach my goal: (list several activities)
(Example: curl-ups, pelvic thrusts, oblique curls)

I = Incremental

I will add_____(a number of exercises) to my score or add _____ minutes of _____ (activity) each week to achieve my goals.
(Example: two curl-ups each week or five minutes of jogging each week)

(continued)

From NASPE, 2011, *Physical education for lifelong fitness: The Physical Best teacher's guide*, 3rd edition (Champaign, IL: Human Kinetics). Debra Ballinger, PhD, Associate Professor, East Stroudsburg University.

Figure 2.1 Students can use the Goal-Setting Worksheet to identify and track physical activity goals using the MOTIVATIONAL PE concepts. See appendix A for a reproducible version of this form.

Created by Debra Ballinger.

▶ **O = Overload**. Within each goal, steps should be included that outline the process to achieve the student's physical best. The principle of overload should be clearly stated in the wording of the conditions of the goal. The overload principle states that to adapt and improve physiological function and fitness, a body system (cardiorespiratory, muscular, or skeletal) must perform at a level beyond normal. A sample goal is that the student will achieve a health-enhancing level of aerobic fitness by adding one lap in the PACER per day (overload in time and distance).

▶ **N = Necessary**. Adding to the concept of value is the point that the goal must be necessary, or important, to the student. By allowing students to determine their own goals, the chances that the goals will be important to them are enhanced. But the teacher must also provide incentives through instruction about the importance of health-related fitness so that the student has the capacity to understand which goals are important and necessary. Students should be challenged to respond to the question, "How will my life be different or better after I achieve my goal?" If the answer isn't obvious, then the necessity of the goal should be called into question.

▶ **A = Authentic assessment**. Assessment should be directly related to the goal and the outcome desired by the student as well as provide a connection to the needs and interests of the student. Weight-loss programs typically focus on reduction in girth rather than weight because this outcome is more authentically tied to what an individual client wants to achieve. Authentic assessment is also closely tied to the necessity component of goal setting.

▶ **L = Lifestyle**. Student goals must be tied to achieving a healthy lifestyle. Students learn why certain behaviors lead to healthy lifestyles and why others lead to self-destructive behaviors. Using a journal to track behaviors and the feelings related to them should be a joint activity with goal setting. If goals don't include connections to behavioral change, they become less valuable. This link is especially important when working with high school students. Teachers should help students see the connection between the goal and real changes that affect their futures. For younger students, linking goals with family activities and interests contributes to connections between school and home—and helps them better understand nutrition, exercise, and fitness from a global perspective.

▶ **P = Posted but private**. Commitment to the goal is critical. Commitment is best achieved by writing the goals and having them signed by the individual and a goal partner. The partner is a motivator in the process and a support system when progress isn't so obvious. Allow students to choose their goal partner, as well as the place for posting their goals. If lockers are truly private, posting the goals inside the locker door may work. Goal partners should be encouraged to check on progress daily (e-mail, instant messaging, or texting can be an enjoyable tool for today's youth to communicate about goals). Goals should only be shared with the permission of the student, and privacy must be maintained throughout the process. Recognition in public is acceptable for some students when goals are accomplished, but for others, public recognition can be embarrassing and counterproductive.

▶ **E = Enjoyable**. Enjoyment comes not only from participating in chosen activities that are fun but also from feelings of satisfaction in the accomplishment of challenging goals. Help students select activities that will ensure success as well as those that the students think are fun. Pairing students with friends as goal partners adds to enjoyment. Students don't even have to be in the same class to be paired. Enjoyment can also be enhanced for younger children by involving family members, parents, or other teachers in the process.

Promoting Physical Activity and Fitness Through Physical Best

Children and adolescents are not miniature adults. Teachers should look for age-appropriate ways to tailor the general strategies described in this section to the realms of home, school, and community. Table 2.4 offers several specific suggestions that the Physical Best program endorses. Emphasize enjoyment! If a child remembers only one thing from physical education, it should be that being physically active is enjoyable and interesting. Teachers can find new and fun activities in the revised *Physical Best Activity Guides*. Enjoyment is an important key to a lifetime of fitness.

Perhaps if Americans felt more comfortable with their ability to fit physical activity into their lives, they'd be more likely to spread the word and really get the ball rolling for a fitness revolution. After all, studies show that people who have confidence in their ability to be physically active and who receive support from family members and friends are more likely to begin and continue exercise programs (Dishman & Sallis, 1994).

BUILDING A FITNESS PROGRAM USING STUDENT GOALS

The Physical Best program supports student goal setting for improving their physical fitness levels, as well as affecting how they feel (affective) and think (cognitive) about physical activity. Students learn how to set achievable goals, and teachers provide opportunities for students to

Table 2.4 Strategies for Promoting Physical Activity in Children

Setting	Objectives	Strategies
Home	Families will be active together at least 60 minutes per day. Families will help students reduce screen time.	• E-mails to home • Set family activity goals • Homework: exercise with family • Journals to reflect on activity levels at home
	Parents will facilitate child's activity.	• Arrange transportation and car pools • Set family activity time daily • Set limits on TV and computer time per day • Encourage interactive video games such as Wii Fit, DDR, and so on • Teacher provides suggested weekly activities • School allows pedometer or heart rate monitor checkout for a 24-hour period
School	Students will maintain a health-enhancing level of physical activity each day on school days.	• Use Activitygram or activity log • Use pedometers in school • Use heart rate monitors in school • Set class activity goals—activity log • Interclass competition for walking • Increase physical activity during physical education by decreasing transitions, management time, and off-task behavior • Emphasize physical activity over physical fitness • Teach self-monitoring and self-reinforcement • Use goal setting to promote goal striving
Community	Access to safe and fun venues for all children.	• Open school venues during nonschool days • Open schools before and after hours • Provide community programs • Link activity times for children with public transportation • Regularly inspect playground safety • Have police regularly patrol venues • Secure grants to fund inclusive programs for children with special needs
	Establish corporate partnerships.	• Contact businesses to establish partnerships • Contact professional sport franchises to set up partnerships or special attendance nights

Adapted, by permission, from R.R. Pate, 1995, Promoting activity and fitness. In *Child health, nutrition, and physical activity*, edited by L.W.Y. Cheung and J.B. Richmond (Champaign, IL: Human Kinetics), 139-145.

use personal assessments to set, revise, and evaluate goals. The Physical Best program recognizes the achievement of goals set by students as an important reinforcement for student motivation. Goal-setting techniques and strategies can help students have positive experiences through movement activities, which can result in their feeling good about themselves as movers. Physical educators can support students' use of goal setting to enhance their lives and fitness abilities.

Just as individually adapted health behavior change programs teach adults behavioral skills to help them incorporate physical activity into their daily routines, Physical Best activities are created to provide teachers extensions and ideas for individualizing activities to meet a variety of student interests, preferences, and abilities. Activities are designed to help teachers teach skills such as goal setting, self-monitoring of progress toward those goals, problem solving, and critical thinking skills.

Table 2.5 provides some examples for setting fitness goals. In the table, the level of fitness is based on the healthy fitness zone (HFZ):

- ▶ Low—initial level is far from reaching the HFZ
- ▶ Moderate—initial level is close to the low end of the HFZ
- ▶ High—initial level is within or above the HFZ

Teachers can help students focus on appropriate fitness goals by ensuring that the healthy fitness zone wall charts included with the Fitnessgram assessment kits are posted where students can readily compare their scores to the HFZ for their age and gender.

The Fitnessgram software printouts offer specific feedback and guidance for students based on their age and their performance on the battery of assessments. (For example, students who are active only one or two days per week will find statements in their Fitnessgram that encourage them to increase the frequency of their activity to five or more days per week.) Teachers can use the Fitnessgram report to guide student goal setting. The Activitygram is useful for assessing school and nonschool daily activity levels and for providing information about blocks of time

Table 2.5 Guidelines for Setting Reasonable Goals and Expectations

Fitness component	Pretest below the Fitnessgram healthy fitness zone	Pretest close to or in lower end of the Fitnessgram healthy fitness zone	Pretest in or above the Fitnessgram healthy fitness zone
Aerobic fitness	Increase daily activity	Increase daily activity	Maintain activity levels
PACER	Increase laps by two to four per week	Increase laps by two to four per week	Continue behaviors
Flexibility	Stretch two or three times per day	Stretch two times per day	Maintain activity level
Back-saver sit-and-reach	Hold 8 to 10 seconds	Hold 8 to 10 seconds	Stretch all areas daily
Shoulder stretch	Learn two yoga positions	Stretch with partner two times per day	• Stretch daily • Continue daily activity
Muscular strength and endurance	• Perform strength activity on alternate days for low areas • Increase reps by two to five per set every other day	Increase weight 1 lb (.45 kg) per day and increase reps by two to five per set each day	• Maintain activities • Add two new exercises per week • Encourage a classmate
Body composition	Increase activity time by 2 minutes per day until maintaining 30 minutes per day	• Increase activity by 5 minutes per week • Add strength and flexibility or maintain if in HFZ	• Maintain activity level • Vary lifetime activities • Learn one new activity

SAMPLE GOALS FOR AEROBIC FITNESS

- I will increase my PACER laps by _____ number of laps (outcome or product goal) by performing aerobic activity _____ times per week for at least _____ minutes each session (process component of goal).

- I will do push-ups four times a week, and each week I will increase the number of push-ups that I do by at least one repetition until I reach my healthy fitness zone (process goal).

- I will exercise aerobically _____ times a week, running the 1-mile (1.6 km) distance at least _____ times a week, and timing and logging the results (process goal).

- I will perform aerobic activity _____ times a week, recording the amount of time, type of activity, and intensity of the activity (process).

- I will walk briskly _____ times a week for a total of _____ blocks (process and product). Each week I will increase the distance by _____ blocks (product).

- I will replace sedentary (inactive) habits with active habits at least three times per day (process).

- As I exercise, I will monitor my heart rate level to remain in my target zone (process).

- As I exercise, I will wear my pedometer and monitor my daily steps.

that the students might be able to use for fitness development and maintenance. Both reports can form the basis for individual goal setting to help students achieve and maintain healthy lifestyles.

It's OK to Excel

Emphasis has been placed on lifelong physical activity for all students. In the classroom, however, students will be at all levels of fitness. Students at low fitness levels shouldn't be ignored, and those at high fitness levels shouldn't be allowed to go on their own. Highly motivated students who want to achieve a high level of fitness for a variety of reasons should have opportunities to excel. Just as schools provide opportunities to students interested in science or math, they should provide opportunities to students who are interested in achieving excellence in fitness. Teachers can create an individualized fitness plan for a student who wants to compete at an elite level in a particular sport or activity (e.g., tennis, rock climbing, hiking). Another example is having a student serve as a mentor to other students; this opportunity could help the student decide whether he or she would enjoy a career as a physical educator or personal trainer. The first key is that this arrangement should be voluntary for both students. Individualized programs for these students will help them safely achieve their goals.

For example, two moderately fit students might establish goals for upper-body strength that fall at the opposite extremes of the range. One student might have class only two times a week, not receive much encouragement at home, and be somewhat overweight. The other student might have an hour-long class five times a week. Teachers and students will improve in the ability to set goals through practice setting and observing outcomes.

SUMMARY

The Physical Best program offers the following suggestions for motivating students to be physically active:

▶ Award the process of participation rather than the product of fitness.

▶ Teach students to set goals that are challenging yet attainable, enjoyable, and valuable to them individually.

▶ Develop students' basic skills by using developmentally appropriate progressions so that students become competent and feel confident when participating in physical activities that develop fitness for a healthy lifestyle.

► Recognize students for making progress toward lifestyle changes and goals rather than for achieving specific competitive outcomes.

► Emphasize self-monitoring and self-management programs that teach children to assess and evaluate their own fitness levels.

► Provide multiple opportunities for success and monitoring of personal goals.

► Redefine effort as goal striving and reinforce effort directed toward personal goals.

► Provide choices of activities to promote enjoyment and self-determination.

Basic Training Principles

Sean Bulger

Chapter Contents

Over the past several decades, researchers have acquired a more complete understanding of the health-related benefits associated with a physically active lifestyle. Habitual physical activity is one behavior known to provide a protective effect against a variety of chronic diseases in adults, including cardiovascular disease, hypertension, obesity, type 2 diabetes mellitus, and osteoporosis (Rowland, 2007). Although the link between physical activity and health has already been well established in adults, Rowland states that limited scientific evidence demonstrates that this relationship exists in youth. Despite this lack of direct evidence, experts contend that many of the chronic diseases affecting older adults are the product of lifelong processes that originate in childhood and adolescence. As a result, the promotion of youth physical activity has gained considerable support as a recommended strategy for reducing disease risk and improving public health. If children and adolescents participate in regular physical activity, they may gain immediate cardiopulmonary, musculoskeletal, and psychological benefits (Bar-Or & Rowland, 2004), but the more important goal is to establish a pattern of behavior that persists into adulthood. A number of leading professional and government organizations have indicated that school physical education programs are well positioned to make a significant contribution to the promotion of lifelong physical activity (e.g., AHA, 2006; CDC, 1997; NASPE, 2004b, 2008; USDHHS, 2000b).

Whether or not a physical education program is successful in facilitating a child's commitment to lifelong activity depends on a number of variables including the development of physical skills and self-monitoring capabilities, exposure to a wide range of movement forms, individualization of activities, provision of safe and supportive environments, and so forth (NASPE, 2004b). Another critical strategy for developing physically active adults is to teach youth basic training principles and FITT guidelines (frequency, intensity, time, and type). These concepts provide the conceptual foundation for safe and effective physical activity program design. Basic training principles are the scientific concepts that underlie program design decisions, and the FITT guidelines represent the key decisions that need to be made to address an individual's physical activity and health-related fitness needs. Although many instructors are likely to be familiar with this information, this chapter provides a quick reference to make the job of teaching this information easier.

UNDERSTANDING THE BASIC TRAINING PRINCIPLES

The basic training principles (overload, progression, specificity, regularity, and individuality) describe how the body responds to the physiological stress of physical activity across all five components of health-related fitness (aerobic fitness, muscular strength, muscular endurance, flexibility, and body composition). These principles are applied to bring about desired physiological changes through manipulation of the frequency, intensity, time, and type of the physical activity performed. The physiological changes that occur in response to regular physical activity or exercise are called **training adaptations**. Although the basic training principles represent the foundation for all physical activity programs, including school physical education, the magnitude of the training adaptations that will occur in children is limited because they do not respond to training as adults do. Another key concept when applying these principles to classroom activities is that they allow the instructor to individualize the lesson to meet the needs of the student–athlete, the sedentary stu-

dent, the disabled student, or the poorly motivated student. Expecting all students to maintain the same personal goals, physical activity interests, and physical fitness levels is unrealistic. Each student will respond to the activities in a physical education lesson differently, and adherence to the basic principles of training provides a basis for a more personalized approach. Rather than requiring all children to run around the track during fitness stations, for example, the teacher could afford students the choice of walking, walking and jogging, or jogging. If used across multiple lessons, this station accounts for all the basic training principles and allows the students to participate at a level that is consistent with their individual interests and needs.

The **overload principle** states that a body system (cardiorespiratory, muscular, or skeletal) must be stressed beyond what it is accustomed to in order to bring about a desired training adaptation. Overload is considered a positive stressor that can be applied through the careful manipulation of frequency, intensity, or time (Brooks, Fahey, & White, 1996). The overload principle should not be confused with the term *overtraining*. **Overtraining** is the condition caused by training too much or too intensely and not providing sufficient recovery time. Symptoms include lack of energy, fatigue, depression, aching muscles, loss of appetite and susceptibility to injury.

The **progression principle** indicates that an overload must be increased over time in a gradual manner to remain effective and safe (see figure 3.1, *a* and *b*). If too much overload is applied too soon, the risk for an overtraining or overuse injury increases, either of which may discourage or prevent a person from participating in continued physical activity. Conversely, the failure to progress frequency, intensity, or time may result in diminished training adaptations over an extended period. Teachers should emphasize that becoming more physically active and improving fitness is a gradual and ongoing process.

The **specificity principle** states that physical activities that produce training adaptations by stressing a particular body part or system do little to affect other body parts or systems (Brooks, Fahey, & White, 1996). For example, a person must perform resistance-training exercises that stress the quadriceps muscle group, like leg press or

Figure 3.1   Students demonstrate progression by increasing the intensity by moving from (*a*) a modified push-up to (*b*) a regular push-up.

knee extension, to develop muscular strength or muscular endurance of the quadriceps. Similarly, a student interested in increasing hamstring flexibility would need to include several stretches targeting that muscle group such as the back-saver sit-and-reach stretch. When training for aerobic fitness, a distance runner would employ a training program involving runs of longer duration and lesser intensity when compared with the program of a sprinter. In other words, the physical activity program should always reflect the desired training outcome or adaptation.

The **regularity principle**, based on the old adage "Use it, or lose it," states that physical activity must be performed on a regular basis to be effective. Any fitness gains achieved through physical activity will be lost if the person does not continue to be active. This basic training principle helps to reinforce the importance of physical activity across the life span because any improvements in fitness performance gained during an active childhood or adolescence are transient and will be lost following years of adult inactivity.

The **individuality principle** takes into account that people enter into physical activity programs with different biological potentials for change, personal goals and interests, current activity patterns, fitness levels, psychosocial characteristics, and environmental determinants. Giving children plenty of opportunities to make choices in physical education regarding the FITT guidelines is an important way to help them develop physical activity patterns that may carry across the life span. In the most complex form, student choice could involve an elective physical education program at a high school where students select from a number of lifetime leisure pursuits like rock climbing, tennis, golf, and weight training. In its simplest form, the choice could occur during a fitness tag game at the elementary level where the students select from a list of simple to complex alternatives to perform when tagged (e.g., line jumps, cone jumps, rope jumps).

APPLYING THE BASIC TRAINING PRINCIPLES

The American College of Sports Medicine (ACSM, 2006) Web site (www.acsm.org/AM/Template.cfm?Section=Home) defines **exercise prescription** as the process of designing an individualized physical activity program to enhance fitness, reduce risk factors for chronic degenerative disease, and ensure participant safety. When developing an exercise prescription, the practitioner must make key decisions regarding the FITT guidelines (frequency, intensity, time, and type) and an appropriate rate of progression. These decisions need to take into account a variety of issues including the participant's health status, current activity levels, past experience, personal preference, fitness goals, and so forth.

FITT Guidelines

The **FITT guidelines** represent how the basic training principles are applied during physical activity program design. Whether the program is designed for a college student–athlete, a high school student enrolled in a personal wellness course, or an elementary student joining an after-school fitness education club, the physical educator needs to facilitate responsible decision making regarding the application of the FITT guidelines. The precise manner in which those decisions are implemented will vary based on a number of factors including the program goals and outcomes, the physical activity setting or context, the developmental readiness of participants, and the instructor's qualifications. More specific FITT guidelines for each area of health-related fitness are discussed in chapters 5 through 8 of this book.

Frequency

Frequency describes *how often* a person performs the targeted physical activity. For each component of health-related fitness, the beneficial and safe frequency is generally three to five days per week, and aerobic fitness activities can be performed all or most days of the week. The exceptions are activities intended for increasing muscular strength and endurance. Most experts believe that these activities should be limited to three nonconsecutive days per week, unless different muscle groups are exercised on alternating days.

Intensity

Intensity describes *how hard* a person exercises and represents one of the most critical decisions in program design. The selection of appropriate exercise intensity depends on a number of factors including the participant's developmental readiness, personal goals, and current physical activity and fitness levels. For example, participants who have a goal of improving sport performance would need to exercise at a higher intensity when compared with those trying to achieve general health benefits. Furthermore, a student who is already physically active on a regular basis would be better prepared to tolerate higher exercise intensities than someone who was previously sedentary. When working with students with low initial physical activity or fitness levels, teachers should use activities of lower intensity to provide a more enjoyable experience and minimize any potential discomfort or soreness.

Time

Time, or **duration**, describes *how long* the activity should be performed. As with other aspects of the FITT guidelines, time varies depending on the targeted health-related fitness component, and it is inversely related to intensity. Primary-grade children will have more difficulty understanding this concept than will older children and will be less able than older children and adolescents to complete intense physical activities in a single bout.

Type

Type refers to mode or *what kind* of activity a person chooses to perform for each component of health-related fitness (see figure 3.2). For example, a person may improve aerobic fitness by walking, riding a bike, in-line skating, stair climbing, or engaging in any number of other physical activities

that elevate the heart rate for an extended period. Muscular fitness may be developed by contracting a muscle or muscle group against an external resistance provided by free weights, variable resistance machines, elastic tubing, body weight, medicine balls, or a partner. Flexibility may be enhanced by repeatedly stretching a muscle beyond its normal resting length using several training modes including static and dynamic stretches. Most important, physical educators should encourage students to select activities that they enjoy and that target their personal health, fitness, or sport performance goals. Instructors of elementary and middle school students should provide a variety of activities that will facilitate responsible decision-making at the high school level and in the future.

Valeriy Pistry/fotolia.com

Figure 3.2 All of these different types of activities improve students' health-related fitness. Best of all, they're having fun doing them!

FITT Age Differences

Many physical educators know how these basic training principles and FITT guidelines apply to adults, but they fail to keep in mind that children respond differently from adults and that the traditional idea of an exercise prescription should not be rigorously applied to young children. Physical educators should use instructional approaches that reinforce the process of engaging in enjoyable activity rather than the product of becoming physically fit through more structured forms of exercise training (NASPE, 2004b). Most studies indicate that habitual physical activity is not a strong predictor of fitness in children and that they

do not respond to structured exercise in the same manner as adults do (Rowland, 2007). As a result, the lifetime activity model, which emphasizes the accumulation of moderate physical activity in a less structured manner, represents a more appropriate application of the FITT guidelines for most children (NASPE, 2004b). When adhering to the lifetime activity model, a child would be encouraged to accumulate at least one hour, and up to several hours, of play each day through participation in a range of lifestyle activities, active aerobics, active sports, flexibility exercises, and muscular exercises while minimizing long periods of sedentary living. The physical activity pyramid (Lambdin et al., 2010; Corbin & Lindsey, 2007)

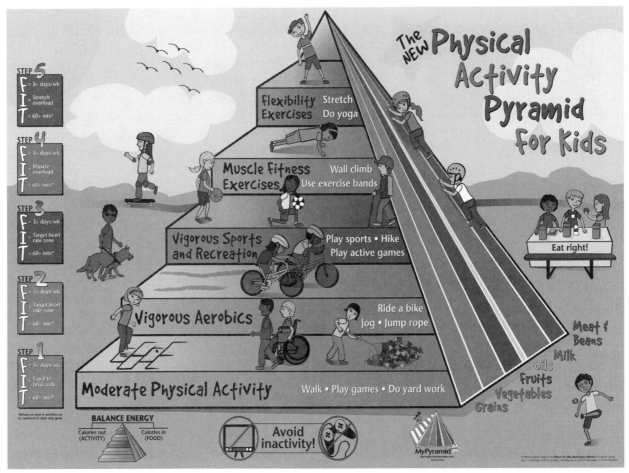

a

Figure 3.3 The physical activity pyramid, (a) for children and (b) for teenagers, is a tool that will help your students understand how to address each component of health-related fitness. The children's version is available for full-size printing on the *Physical Best Activity Guide: Elementary Level CD-ROM*. The teen's version is available for full-size printing on the *Physical Best Activity Guide: Middle and High School Levels CD-ROM*.

Figure 3.3a; Reprinted, by permission, from D. Lambdin et al., 2010, *Fitness for life: Elementary school classroom guide kindergarten classroom guide* (Champaign, IL: Human Kinetics), 11.

is an effective tool for teaching students how to weigh each component of health-related fitness while incorporating sufficient variation in their personal physical activity programs (see figure 3.3).

Aerobic fitness activities form a large segment of the physical activity pyramid (see figure 3.3) which parallels activity recommendations by the International Consensus Conference on Physical Activity Guidelines for Adolescents (Sallis & Patrick, 1994), and NASPE guidelines for elementary school aged children (NASPE, 2004b). The following is recommended for children and adolescents (6–17 years of age) (PCPF, 2008):

1. Children and adolescents should do 60 minutes (1 hour) or more of physical activity daily.

2. Most of the 60 or more minutes each day should be either moderate- or vigorous-intensity aerobic physical activity, and vigorous-intensity physical activity should occur on at least three days per week.

NASPE (2004b) guidelines for elementary school aged children state the following:

1. Children should accumulate at least 60 minutes, and up to several hours, of age-appropriate physical activity on all or most days of the week. This daily accumulation should include moderate and vigorous physical activity with the majority being intermittent in nature.

2. Children should participate in several bouts of physical activity lasting 15 minutes or more each day.

3. Children should participate each day in a variety of age-appropriate physical activities designed to achieve optimal health, wellness, fitness, and performance benefits.

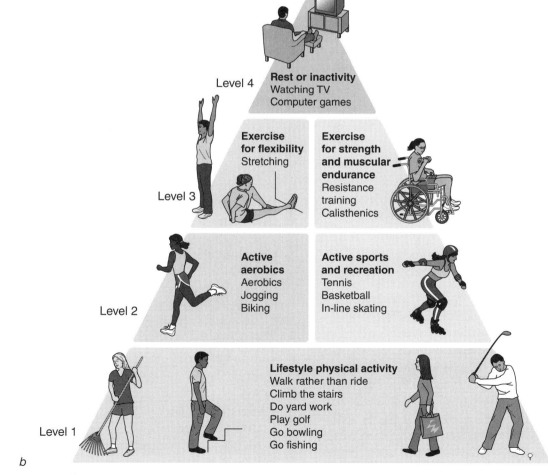

b

Figure 3.3 *(continued)*

Figure 3.3*b*; Reprinted, by permission, from C.B. Corbin and R. Lindsey, 2007, *Fitness for life: Middle school* (Champaign, IL: Human Kinetics), 4.

4. Extended periods (periods of two hours or more) of inactivity are discouraged for children, especially during daytime hours (pp. 9-10).

NASPE (2004b) suggests 11 guidelines for promoting physical activity in schools and physical education. As a physical educator, you can use these guidelines to enhance your lessons and to promote active lifestyles outside of the physical education setting.

- Provide time for activity throughout the school day—include recess and short activity breaks that supplement the allotted time for physical education.
- Encourage self-monitoring of physical activity.
- Individualize activity.
- Expose children to a variety of physical activities.
- Offer feedback that reinforces regular participation and encourages children to give their best effort; avoid giving feedback on how fast the performance was or how many repetitions were completed.
- Do not sacrifice class time for fitness-only activities—include fundamental skill development.
- Be an active role model.
- Care about the attitudes of your students. Help them set goals and then provide achievable challenges to meet those goals.
- Enhance exercise self-efficacy by teaching the value of various activities and ways to develop personalized exercise or activity programs that can be achieved.
- Promote activity outside the school environment.
- Consider lifetime activities that will carry into adulthood such as walking, jogging, hiking, or cycling. Physical Best provides an opportunity for students to learn why activities are important and what the benefits of the activity are for today and in the future.

To assist teachers in determining what activities are considered moderate, vigorous, or age appropriate, the following definitions are provided by NASPE (2004b). **Developmentally appropriate physical activity** "refers to activity of a frequency, intensity, duration and type that leads to optimal child growth and development and contributes to the development of future physically active lifestyles" (p. 8). **Moderate physical activity** is defined as "activity of an intensity equal to brisk walking . . . and can be performed for relatively long periods of time without fatigue" (NASPE, 2004b, 7). The authors suggest brisk walking, bike riding, some chores or housework, low-intensity games such as hopscotch or four-square, and playing low-activity positions such as goalie or outfield. **Vigorous physical activity** is defined as "movement that expends more energy or is performed at a higher intensity than brisk walking. Some forms of vigorous activity, such as running, can be done for relatively long periods of time while others may be so vigorous (e.g., sprinting) that frequent rests are necessary" (NASPE, 2004b, 8). For examples of moderate and vigorous aerobic fitness and muscle- and bone-strengthening activities, see table 3.1.

Although the FITT guidelines are still applicable when using the lifetime activity model for program design, they are being used in a less structured manner, which is thought to be suitable for younger children and inactive adults. At the elementary level, teachers should remove the stringent three-day-per-week training requirement, place less emphasis on minimum intensity levels, remove time limits frequently suggested as minimums for the development of fitness, and emphasize increased daily physical activity. Certainly, the adult model FITT guidelines can be presented, but the emphasis should be on increasing physical activity. To prevent students from losing interest, or to keep them from losing the desire to become more physically fit, help each student explore a variety of recreational activities and different ways to vary their physical activity choices. Encourage students to become involved in school athletic programs and before- or after-school fitness or activity programs. Demonstrate active behavior and be a role model for your students. Take the stairs, park away from the building, or take your classes outside and walk the longest distance to the activity area. Explain

Table 3.1 Examples of Moderate- and Vigorous-Intensity Aerobic Physical Activities and Muscle- and Bone-Strengthening Activities for Children and Adolescents

Type of physical activity	Age group	
	Children	**Adolescents**
Moderate-intensity aerobic	• Active recreation, such as hiking, skateboarding, in-line skating • Bicycle riding • Brisk walking	• Active recreation, such as canoeing, hiking, skateboarding, in-line skating • Brisk walking • Bicycle riding (stationary or road bike) • Housework and yard work, such as sweeping or pushing a lawnmower • Games that require catching and throwing, such as baseball and softball
Vigorous-intensity aerobic	• Active games involving running and chasing, such as tag • Bicycle riding • Jumping rope • Martial arts, such as karate • Running • Sports such as soccer, ice or field hockey, basketball, swimming, tennis • Cross-country skiing	• Active games involving running and chasing, such as flag football • Bicycle riding • Jumping rope • Martial arts, such as karate • Running • Sports such as soccer, ice or field hockey, basketball, swimming, tennis • Vigorous dancing • Cross-country skiing
Muscle strengthening	• Games such as tug-of-war • Modified push-ups (with knees on the floor) • Resistance exercises using body weight or resistance bands • Rope or tree climbing • Curl-ups or crunches • Swinging on playground equipment or bars	• Games such as tug-of-war • Push-ups and pull-ups • Resistance exercises with exercise bands, weight machines, hand-held weights • Climbing wall • Curl-ups or crunches
Bone strengthening	• Games such as hopscotch • Hopping, skipping, jumping • Jumping rope • Running • Sports such as gymnastics, basketball, volleyball, tennis	• Hopping, skipping, jumping • Jumping rope • Running • Sports such as gymnastics, basketball, volleyball, tennis

Note: Some activities, such as bicycling, can be moderate or vigorous intensity, depending on level of effort.

From US Department of Health and Human Services 2008.

to your students the importance of adding these activities to their lifestyles and the way in which it directly relates to them. For example, explain how improved aerobic fitness will enable them to play longer without getting tired. Discuss how improved muscular strength will help them perform their daily chores, such as taking out the trash, or how extra strength can help them play on the playground bars and equipment. In addition, act as a liaison between the student and the community by pointing out the various recreational programs available in your community away from the school setting (such as sport leagues, health clubs, and park district activities).

If a child, parent, and physical educator agree that a more structured, adultlike exercise prescription is needed to enhance a child's fitness or sport performance, then the program must adhere to the basic training principles and the FITT guidelines must be applied based on the individual's stage of maturation rather than chronological age (Bompa, 2000). As a rule, however, teachers and coaches of younger children should focus on age-appropriate activities that give all participants an equal opportunity to play, make friends, improve social skills, and at the same time enhance their fitness. At the middle and high school levels, students are closer to adulthood and respond to training and conditioning more like adults. At this point teachers can begin to transition to adultlike physical activity programs by helping students apply the FITT guidelines in a more prescriptive manner.

COMPONENTS OF A PHYSICAL ACTIVITY SESSION

Every physical activity session should follow a systematic approach that includes a warm-up, main physical activity, and cool-down. This approach helps to ensure participant safety by preparing the body for the demands of physical activity and by providing a mechanism for a gradual reduction in workload at the end of the session. Properly warming up before and cooling down after physical activity may also prevent injuries and aid in postexercise recovery, respectively. The main physical activity must also be conducted appropriately for students to feel and understand, through participation, the importance of being physically active.

Warm-Up

A **warm-up** is a low-intensity activity done before a full effort and should be organized to meet the goals of the main physical activity. The primary purpose of the warm-up is to prepare the participant for the moderate to vigorous physical activity that will occur during the session. For example, a person intending to engage in a vigorous physical activity, like a game of full-court basketball, would need to complete a more thorough warm-up than someone simply going out for a brisk walk. This type of structured basketball warm-up would incorporate a general warm-up followed by a specific warm-up incorporating sport-related stretches and movement patterns performed at progressively increasing intensities.

A general warm-up—including activities such as walking, jogging, swimming, or cycling—may be used to prepare the cardiorespiratory and musculoskeletal systems for the sport-specific segment of the warm-up and the main physical activity that follows. The specific warm-up may include a combination of static and dynamic stretches like walking lunges and high knees. The specific warm-up is also more effective if the activities target the primary muscles that will be used to perform the main physical activity. This type of structured warm-up routine offers the following benefits:

- Increases active muscle blood flow
- Increases blood flow to the heart
- Raises body temperature and may reduce the risk of muscular injury and soreness
- Facilitates temperature regulation by causing earlier sweating

Physical education classes, however, do not lend themselves to structured warm-up routines in many instances. In a 40-minute elementary physical education class, the allocation of 10 to 15 minutes for an extended warm-up may not represent the best use of instructional time. Furthermore, in this context committing large chunks of lesson time to less active types of exercise such as static stretching is not advisable. As an alternative approach, the Physical Best activities can be used throughout the year as warm-up activities during other units besides fitness education. For example, if throwing is the main activity, a general warm-up such as Power Ball Hunt in *Physical Best Activity Guide: Elementary Level, Third Edition*) could be used to explain to students, in age-appropriate ways, that warming up properly prepares the body for the main activity by gradually increasing heart rate and blood flow to the muscles and tissues of the body. A more specific warm-up could incorporate dynamic movements that target the prime movers acting on the shoulder joint including jumping jacks, arm swings in multiple planes of movement, and pull-up and push-up variations to prepare the arms for throwing activities.

Although gentle stretching and walking or slow jogging for about five minutes are common and safe warm-up activities, you must vary the warm-up to prevent boredom and carelessness in the routine. For younger children (and to prevent discipline problems), plan and lead warm-ups that provide instant activity as the students arrive at the lesson site (Graham, 2008). This might include challenge activities such as how many times students can jump back and forth across a line, how many successive turns of a jump rope the students can complete, a short circuit training course, or a dribbling activity. These instant activities may also work for older students by providing an opportunity for students to socialize while warming up. Also, for older students, post the warm-up in the locker rooms or at the lesson site and make the students responsible for carrying it out independently.

Main Physical Activity

The main physical activity represents the core of the lesson or physical activity session and is intended to improve or maintain one or more of the health-related fitness components. The frequency, intensity, time, and type of physical activity depend on the goals of the lesson, the length of the class period, and the current fitness level of individual students. Whether teaching kindergarteners or high school seniors, you should explain the purpose of the lesson and how the day's activity will help students reach class or personalized goals.

Children, like adults, will express and act on preferences among the many physical activities available. We strongly encourage you to provide a wide variety of activities and to allow a wide range of personal choice in your program, but you must ensure that your students understand the need to address each component of health-related fitness. In short, emphasize the importance of total fitness and the need to engage in an activity for each component of health-related fitness. The student who elects to swim laps instead of going cross-country skiing is addressing aerobic fitness appropriately, but both of these students still need to work on flexibility, muscular strength and endurance (for muscle groups not addressed by the activities), and body composition at some point.

Cool-Down

A proper **cool-down** includes a period of light activity following exercise that allows the body to slow down and return to near resting levels. Students must understand that the body needs this gradual recovery following exercise to reduce muscle stiffness and soreness, remove lactic acid, and prevent light-headedness, dizziness, or even fainting. Teach them to resist the urge to sit or lie down after physical activity; instead, they should gradually slow down their activity by walking or jogging for three to five minutes, or until the heart rate returns to near resting level. Continued light activity facilitates recovery by "milking" blood in the veins back toward the heart. An abrupt cessation of exercise facilitates pooling of blood in the extremities and decreases the return flow of blood to the heart, and subsequently to the brain, leaving the person susceptible to fainting. Stretching exercises should also be performed during the cool-down because muscles are warmest and most pliable then, providing maximum benefit toward improving flexibility. Refer to chapter 7 in this book and to the *Physical Best Activity Guides* for examples of stretching exercises and activities. The cool-down is also an opportunity for the teacher to bring closure to the lesson by reviewing key concepts learned and facilitating student self-evaluation of personalized goals for the workout.

SOCIAL SUPPORT AND SAFETY GUIDELINES

Besides using the basic training principles, FITT guidelines, and components of a physical activity session in a developmentally appropriate manner, physical educators must be careful to provide their students with a teaching and learning environment that is both socially supportive and safe. In the absence of these key features, physical education programs are not likely to influence physical activity and other health-related behaviors in a positive direction.

Providing Social Support

Adhering to the basic principles of training involves more than the physical aspects of training and conditioning or simply increasing physical activity level; psychosocial components must also be considered. Generally, children do not choose to exercise or remain physically active for the associated health benefits, but they are more likely to be physically active if they perceive their physical abilities as high (NASPE, 2004b). As a result, children must experience some measure of success when being introduced to new physical activities. Activities that are initially of excessive intensity or difficulty may prove discouraging.

The role of the physical education teacher as a primary source of social support is paramount. Physical Best emphasizes development of lifetime physical activity and education by calling attention to fitness as a lifelong process rather than a product of isolated training and conditioning. The literature demonstrates that physical education and sport in the schools can make meaningful contributions to the development of lifestyle physical activity and health-related fitness, fundamental movement skills, social responsibility, self-esteem and proschool attitudes, and perhaps cognitive development and academic achievement under the appropriate circumstances (Bailey, 2006). These positive outcomes are not the direct result of participation in regular physical activity, however, and we must be careful to acknowledge that "the effects are likely to be mediated by the nature of the interactions between students and their teachers, parents, and coaches who work with them" (Bailey, 2006, p. 397). In short, Bailey asserts that these important learning outcomes are most likely to be realized if the physical education environment is positive and characterized by high levels of student engagement, enjoyment, diversity, and social support from knowledgeable practitioners and well-informed parents.

Furthermore, self-perceptions of competence decline as children get older. Jacobs and Eccles (2000) and Jacobs et al. (2002) indicate that as children become aware of other children's levels of competence, they begin to realize where they stand in relation to other students. Also, as the child gets older, fewer opportunities are available for success in sport and activity because the level of competition increases. The child becomes selective, participating in the few activities that he or she believes offer opportunities to be successful. Physical Best activities provide many opportunities for positive encouragement of individuals and provide success for each child, which fosters improved self-esteem and perceived competence.

For more information on physical activity behavior and motivation, refer to chapter 2.

Establishing a Safe Environment

Because a number of dangers are inherent to physical activity participation, teachers must be careful to establish a teaching and learning environment that minimizes risk of injury. This responsibility includes regular inspection and maintenance of all facilities and equipment. Preventive maintenance is of particular importance in those high-risk areas where the potential for catastrophic injury exists (e.g., swimming pools, weight rooms, climbing walls, playground equipment). Furthermore, meaningful preinstructional planning, effective teaching methods, and qualified supervision should be considered mandatory in any physical education program. Physical educators should have a written emergency response plan posted, and they should practice it on a routine basis. The maintenance of current first aid and CPR certification is recommended for all physical education professionals.

Physical educators should also teach their students to become accountable for their own safety. Students seeking any level of health-related fitness must be encouraged to listen to their bodies and slow down if they feel overtired or suffer from soreness that is intense or lasts more than a day or so.

Doing too much too fast, weakness, lack of flexibility, biomechanical problems, and improper footwear are common causes of injury. Teach students to use proper pacing—beginning gradually and at low intensity and then slowly progressing to activities that are more intense and longer in duration. These concepts are difficult to communicate, especially with younger children who still gauge success by winners and losers of competition. Beginners frequently ignore early warning signs of overtraining and fail to recognize that they are overdoing it until it is too late to prevent injury or avoid undue fatigue. In regard to flexibility and muscular strength and endurance, students must understand that concentrating on only a few muscle groups and neglecting others can make an individual more susceptible to injury. For example, working only on pushing movements like bench press and shoulder press during resistance training can lead to muscle imbalances that increase risk of injury. Encourage students to take a whole-body approach to physical activity and health-related fitness.

SUMMARY

Remember, the discussion is about health-related physical activity—not Olympic training. Students, regardless of age, should be presented with reasonable choices of how intense they will work during a given physical activity session, based on their personal goals. Keep in mind that fitness is a journey, not a destination. All teachers want to see students develop lifelong health-related physical activity habits. Moreover, students must understand the principles of training and the FITT guidelines so that, ultimately, they can choose to increase their performance and fitness levels as they desire—and know how to do so safely. The goal is to progress toward self-assessment and self-delivery of health-related fitness activities.

Nutrition

Linda Nickson

The science of nutrition examines food, the level of nutrients and other chemicals in foods, and the way in which these are used in the body. The substances in food affect growth as well as health. All people have the same general needs (DRIs, or dietary reference intake), but the amounts of specific nutrients needed may increase or decrease because of gender, age, growth, disease, or activity level. One of the factors that make applying good nutrition principles more challenging is that food serves many purposes in our society other than nourishment. Americans eat to celebrate, to mourn, for entertainment, out of boredom, and for a myriad of other reasons. The key to good nutrition is for people to strive to meet their individual nutrient needs while still remembering that they should enjoy food.

Chapter Contents

FOUNDATIONS OF A HEALTHY DIET

Diet is the total intake of food and beverages consumed. No single food item or meal defines the diet. Good nutrition is vital to good health and is essential for the healthy growth and development of children and adolescents (*Dietary Guidelines for Americans*, 2005). Food habits are learned early and change throughout life. But parents and family tend to shape food habits early in life, and these habits may prove long lasting. Peers and marketing also affect these patterns as children mature into adolescence. Eating habits and preferences established by adolescence tend to carry into adulthood.

Many factors can affect food choices:

- Habit
- Emotional factors such as happiness or stress
- Convenience
- Nutrition knowledge
- Time limitations
- Religious beliefs
- Socioeconomic factors such as cost of food and availability of food
- Advertising
- Ethnicity
- Learned behaviors
- Genetics
- Health factors
- Ability to shop and cook
- Taste

Most foods have nutrient value and may fit into a healthful diet. In making sure that a person takes in good nutrition, the primary goals are to

- provide a variety of nutrient-dense foods and beverages,
- supply all the nutrients in adequate amounts by adopting a balanced eating pattern, and
- supply a recommended caloric intake within energy needs to maintain an ideal body weight.

The childhood years offer the best chance for parents and teachers to influence not only current but also future food choices, and thus to develop

Nutrient requirements may vary by age and activity level, but good nutrition is essential to optimal health throughout life.

good eating behaviors. Food habits developed in childhood and adolescence often continue into adulthood. Parents are the gatekeepers; they control and influence the availability and choices of food in their children's environment. Physical educators must help educate parents about nutrition and the concept of energy balance. Parents and teachers should do what they can to help establish good eating and activity habits at the elementary school level and make students aware of the relationship among nutrition, activity, and health, both now and for the future. The concept of balance and moderation in eating combined with an active lifestyle is crucial to maintaining an appropriate body weight as well as maintaining optimal health.

A person's total nutrient needs are greater during adolescence than at any other time of life, except perhaps during pregnancy and lactation. Caloric ranges are based on both age and, more important, activity level. Students need to determine their activity level (sedentary, moderately active, or active) to determine their estimated caloric needs. Nutrient needs rise throughout adolescence and then level off, or possibly even diminish slightly, as an adolescent becomes an adult (Institute of Medicine of the National Academies, 2001).

Of course, adolescents make many more choices for themselves than young children do, about both how active they are and what they eat. Social or peer pressures may push them to make both good and bad choices. Children and adolescents acquire information, and sometimes misinformation, on nutrition from personal, immediate experiences. They are concerned with how food choices can improve their lives and looks now, so they may engage in crash dieting or the latest fad in weight gain or loss. Conversely, increased calorie consumption is also commonly seen, especially of fat and carbohydrate, among adolescents.

A **kilocalorie** is a measure of heat energy. Technically, a kilocalorie is the amount of energy required to raise the temperature of one kilogram of water one degree Celsius. Popular sources often shorten the term *kilocalories* to simply *calories*. Different types of food have different energy values for equal weights.

Nutrient density refers to the amount of a given nutrient per calorie. Nutrient-dense foods are those that provide substantial amounts of vitamins and minerals and relatively few calories. A variety of foods with high nutrient densities should make up most of a diet. A sample listing of foods and nutritional information for each is included in table 4.1. As you can see, the reduced-fat Monterey Jack cheese is more nutrient dense than the American cheese.

CATEGORIES OF NUTRIENTS

Many people consume more calories than they need without meeting recommended nutritional intake. Meeting nutrient recommendations should go hand in hand with keeping total calories under

Table 4.1 Common Food Values

Food	Kilocalories	Protein*	Fat*	Vitamin C**	Calcium**	Fiber*
American cheese (2 oz, or 60 g)	213	13	18	0	349	0
Reduced-fat Monterey Jack cheese (1 1/2 oz, or 45 g)	120	12	8	0	360	0
Turkey pot pie (one)	410	16	24	0	80	0
Roasted turkey, white meat (3 oz, or 90 g)	134	25	3	0	16	0
White corn (1/2 cup)	66	2	1	5	2	5
Corn chips (13 chips)	160	2	11	0	72	1

*Indicates grams

**Indicates milligrams

Note the difference in nutrient density between the foods.

control. Doing so provides many important benefits including normal growth and development of children, health promotion for people of all ages, and reduction of risk for a number of chronic diseases that are major public health problems. The six categories of nutrients are carbohydrate, protein, fat, vitamins, minerals, and water. **Macronutrients** provide the greatest amount of energy and include carbohydrate, protein, and fat. **Micronutrients** include vitamins and minerals that are required in the human diet in very small amounts. **Phytonutrients** are components found in plants that are thought to promote health. Fruits, vegetables, grains, legumes, nuts, and teas are rich sources of phytonutrients. Phytonutrients can be divided into several major classes. We currently have the most information about carotenoids found in red, yellow, and orange pigments of fruits and vegetables. These fruits and vegetables high in carotenoids appear to protect humans against certain cancers, heart disease, and age-related macular degeneration (USDA Agricultural Research Services, 2005). More research is needed in this area to establish support of the nutritional value of the various phytochemicals. Phytonutrients are thought to serve as antioxidants, enhance the immune system, convert vitamin A, and repair damage caused by smoking and other toxic exposures—all of which reduce the risk of cancer and heart disease. All these nutrients are essential for good health.

Carbohydrate

Carbohydrate constitutes the majority of energy for people across the world. Carbohydrate also represents the preferred source of energy for the body, particularly the brain, and is categorized as being either simple or complex. **Simple carbohydrate** is food that is high in sugar. In general, simple carbohydrate is high in calories and low in nutrients. Simple carbohydrate also tends to provide a short, rapid burst of energy. Simple carbohydrate includes foods such as cakes, candies, sodas, table sugar, and juices (figure 4.1a). The USDA recommends choosing and preparing foods and beverages with little added sugar or caloric sweeteners.

Complex carbohydrate includes foods such as pasta, cereals, breads, and grains (figure 4.1b). In general, complex carbohydrate provides a longer, sustained supply of energy, which is optimal for physical activity. Whole grains are the preferred type of complex carbohydrate. Whole grains are higher in nutrients as well as fiber. Fiber may help to reduce the risk of colon diseases and possibly help to lower blood cholesterol levels. All carbohydrate contains four kilocalories per gram.

a

b

Figure 4.1 Foods containing (a) simple carbohydrate and (b) complex carbohydrate.

Current recommendations are that 45 to 65% of the diet should consist of carbohydrate, primarily complex carbohydrate. People should be encouraged to choose fiber-rich fruits, vegetables, and whole grains.

Protein

Protein is a constituent of vital body parts. Every cell contains proteins—muscles, blood-clotting factors, immune cells, and so on. Protein is the basic building block for the body but constitutes a relatively small amount of the daily calorie intake. The body's preferred use for protein is growth and cell replacement. The body can use protein for energy if no carbohydrate is available. Protein sources can be either animal or plant based. Examples of animal sources of protein include meats, cheeses, milk, and eggs (figure 4.2a). Examples of plant sources of protein include beans, nuts, and soy products (figure 4.2b). In the United States, most protein, approximately 65%, comes from animal sources. In contrast, the rest of the world obtains only 35% of its protein from animal sources. Unfortunately, animal sources of protein are usually higher in saturated fat than other sources (Wardlaw, 2002). Current recommendations are that 10 to 15% of the diet should consist of protein. Protein, like carbohydrate, provides four kilocalories per gram.

Fat

The human body needs **fat**, but not as much as most people eat. Fat provides energy, supports cell growth, absorbs some nutrients, and produces important hormones. Its key role is to help protect organs and keep the body warm.

Fat in the body provides a concentrated supply of calories, or energy, in a limited volume. Unlike

a   b

Figure 4.2 Protein from (a) animal and (b) plant sources.

protein or carbohydrate, fat provides nine kilocalories per gram. Because of the calorie content, consuming high levels of fat, regardless of the type, can result in excessive intake of calories, leading to weight gain, being overweight, or being overfat. Fat also gives food some pleasant sensory qualities. Fat makes food tender and adds a lovely smell when cooking. Think of the savory smell of bacon wafting across the kitchen. Fat can be more or less healthful depending on its level of saturation. **Saturated fat**, the main contributor of high cholesterol, tends to be hard at room temperature and comes predominantly from animal sources. Examples of saturated fat include lard, butter, and marbling in steaks and meats. Palm oil, palm kernel, and coconut oils represent the only major plant sources of saturated fat (figure 4.3a). Unsaturated fat is liquid at room temperature and comes from plant sources. Examples of **unsaturated fat** include olive, soybean, peanut, and canola oils (figure 4.3b). Unsaturated fat is divided into polyunsaturated and monounsaturated fat. Both forms of unsaturated fat can help to lower cholesterol levels and are beneficial when consumed in moderation. **Trans fatty acid**, or trans fat, is unsaturated fatty acid created during food processing in which liquid oils are converted into solid fat, a process called **hydrogenation**. This process creates oils that keep food fresh longer. The dilemma is that these hydrogenated (or partially hydrogenated) oils contain trans fat, which can increase low-density lipoprotein (LDL cholesterol) and decrease high-density lipoprotein (HDL cholesterol), both indicated risk factors for heart disease. The source of trans fatty acid includes hydrogenated and partially hydrogenated vegetable oil used in making shortening and commercially prepared baked goods, snack foods, fried foods, and margarine.

Excess intake of saturated fat has been found to contribute to chronic diseases such as heart disease, cancer, stroke, and obesity.

According to the American Heart Association, knowing which fats raise LDL cholesterol and which ones don't is the first step in lowering the risk of heart disease. Besides the LDL produced naturally by the body, saturated fat, trans fatty acid, and dietary cholesterol can also raise blood cholesterol. Monounsaturated fat and polyunsaturated fat appear not to raise LDL cholesterol; some studies suggest that they might even help lower LDL cholesterol slightly when eaten as part of a diet low in saturated fat.

a   b

Figure 4.3 Sources of (a) saturated fat and (b) unsaturated fat.

The American Heart Association's Nutrition Committee strongly advises these fat guidelines for healthy Americans over age two:

▶ Limit total fat intake to less than 25 to 35% of total calories each day.

▶ Limit saturated fat intake to less than 7% of total daily calories.

▶ Limit trans fat intake to less than 1% of total daily calories.

▶ The remaining fat should come from sources of monounsaturated and polyunsaturated fats such as nuts, seeds, fish, and vegetable oil.

▶ Most people should limit cholesterol intake to less than 300 milligrams per day. Those who have coronary heart disease or an LDL cholesterol level of 100 mg/dL or greater should limit cholesterol intake to less than 200 milligrams a day.

From American Heart Association 2010.

The CDC's *Dietary Guidelines for Americans 2005* recommends that Americans maintain total fat intake within the following limits:

▶ Children ages 2 to 3—30 to 35% of total calories

▶ Children and adolescents ages 4 to 18—25 to 35% of total calories

▶ Adults ages 19 and older—20 to 35% of total calories

Cultures with diets high in animal products, such as the United States, tend to have higher levels of saturated fat intake. Items high in saturated fat also usually contain cholesterol. Both contribute to high levels of blood cholesterol.

Vitamins

Vitamins and minerals allow people's bodies to work properly. They boost the immune system, support normal growth and development, and help cells and organs do their jobs. Although vitamins and minerals are provided by the foods eaten every day, some foods have more vitamins and minerals than others do. Vitamins and minerals are organic substances that contribute to the normal functioning of the body and are essential for normal growth and maintenance. Although vitamins contain no calories, they facilitate chemical reactions within the body that often yield energy (Wardlaw, 2002). Vitamins can be either **fat soluble** or **water soluble**.

The fat-soluble vitamins are vitamins A, D, E, and K. They dissolve in fat and can be stored in the body. Not surprisingly, the fat-soluble vitamins are found in high-fat foods such as fatty fish, oils, and nuts. The water-soluble vitamins are the numerous B-complex vitamins (such as B_6, B_{12}, niacin, riboflavin, and folate) and vitamin C. These vitamins need to dissolve in water before the body can absorb them. Because of this, the body does not store these vitamins and any vitamin not used by the body passes through the system. The water-soluble vitamins are found in enriched and whole grains, fruits, and vegetables. A fresh supply of these vitamins is needed every day. Eating a variety of foods and food colors is the best way to get all the vitamins and minerals needed each day. Vitamin supplements are widely available. Multivitamins are a good source of dietary insurance but should never be used as a substitute for a good diet.

Minerals

Minerals are nonorganic substances that are necessary for normal functioning of the body. Minerals are needed for growth and maintenance. Minerals are classified as either major minerals (the body needs larger amounts of these) or trace minerals (the body needs only very small amounts of them each day). Major minerals are classified as such if their daily requirement is over 100 milligrams or 1/50 teaspoon (Wardlaw, 2002). The risk of mineral toxicity is fairly high when using high doses of supplements, so knowing the recommended dietary intake (RDI) is important. Exceeding the RDI when choosing mineral supplements is not advised unless under the supervision of a health care provider.

Major minerals

▶ Sodium

▶ Potassium

▶ Chloride

▶ Calcium

▶ Phosphorus

▶ Magnesium

▶ Sulfur

Trace minerals

▸ Iron

▸ Zinc

▸ Selenium

▸ Iodide

▸ Copper

▸ Fluoride

▸ Chromium

▸ Manganese

▸ Molybdenum

Minerals, like vitamins, contain zero calories. Less than 2,400 mg (approximately 1 teaspoon of salt) of sodium should be consumed per day (based on a 2,000-calorie intake), and foods should be chosen and prepared with little salt. At the same time, consuming potassium-rich foods such as fruits and vegetables is important.

One of the most important minerals to athletes, particularly females, is calcium. Throughout life, the body continuously builds and breaks down bone. Humans turn over their skeleton every 7 to 10 years. The bone is built from minerals, primarily calcium. In fact, 99% of the calcium in the body is found in the skeleton (Zeigler & Filer, 2000). Nutritional factors affecting bone density include calcium, vitamin D, and fluoride, which build the mineral matrix that forms the hard interior of the bone. Weight-bearing exercises and certain hormones stimulate the synthesis of bone. In females with low body fat, the response to female hormones is limited, leading to brittle bones and osteoporosis. Maintaining a healthy body weight, including not becoming excessively thin, and performing weight-bearing activity stimulates bone production and helps prevent osteoporosis and brittle bones (see figure 4.4, *a* and *b*). Dairy foods are the primary source of calcium for children and adolescents.

The importance of calcium in the body brings up an important example of how nutrients like minerals and vitamins work together. The body needs vitamin D to aid in absorption of calcium. Without enough vitamin D in the body, insufficient calcium is absorbed from the diet. Under these circumstances, the body must take calcium from its stores in the skeleton, which weakens existing bone and prevents the formation of strong new bone. Recent research also suggests that vitamin D may provide protection from hypertension and some forms of cancer, boost immune function, reduce inflammation, and promote healthy neuromuscular function. Many foods in our diet are fortified with vitamin D. One of the best ways to get vitamin D is to spend 10 to 15 minutes a day outside in the sun without sunscreen. In instances of low intake, supplementation is indicated. A health care provider should be consulted for recommendations regarding any needed supplementation. Eating a variety of foods, of a variety of colors, is the best way to get all the vitamins and minerals needed each day.

Water

Many people are surprised to learn that water is an essential nutrient. It makes up 50 to 70% of

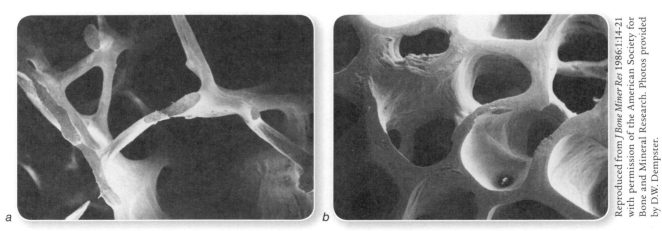

Reproduced from *J Bone Miner Res* 1986:1:14-21 with permission of the American Society for Bone and Mineral Research. Photos provided by D.W. Dempster.

Figure 4.4 View of (*a*) osteoporotic bone and (*b*) healthy bone.

the weight of the human body and serves multiple functions in the body:

- ▶ Water contributes to temperature regulation (each liter of sweat represents 600 kilocalories of energy lost).
- ▶ Water forms lubricants for the joints.
- ▶ Water is the basis for saliva and bile.
- ▶ Water helps to eliminate wastes through urine. Most people produce one to two quarts (liters) of urine per day (Wardlaw, 2002).

Water can be obtained from various food and beverage sources, but the best source is just simple water, tap or bottled. Items such as coffee, tea, and soda should not be considered good sources of water. These may contain caffeine, which is a diuretic. A diuretic causes increased fluid loss and increased urine volume. This process becomes especially important during exercise when fluid loss is already high because of perspiration. Although consuming beverages that contain caffeine can contribute to total water intake, thus helping to meet dietary recommendations, fluids with reduced caffeine or reduced sugar are preferred. The latest Institute of Medicine (IOM) report addresses the use of alcoholic and caffeinated beverages: "While consumption of beverages containing caffeine and alcohol have been shown in some studies to have diuretic effects, available information indicates that this may be transient in nature, and that such beverages can contribute to total water intake and thus can be used in meeting recommendations for dietary intake of total water" (Institute of Medicine, 2004, p. S-5).

In general, people need approximately 1 milliliter of water for every kilocalorie ingested. So a person who eats 2,000 kilocalories a day needs to consume a minimum of 8 cups (1,920 milliliters) of water per day (1 cup = 240 milliliters). By the time a person loses as little as 1% of his or her body weight in fluids, the person is becoming thirsty. Even mild dehydration interferes with both mental and physical performance. The early symptoms of dehydration include headache, thirst, fatigue, dry eyes and mouth, loss of appetite, and dark-colored urine. If a person continues to ignore thirst, the body will release antidiuretic hormone (ADH), which causes the kidneys to conserve water and concentrate the urine. This process also triggers the body to release the hormone aldosterone, which causes water and sodium retention. With continued dehydration, the cardiovascular, respiratory, renal, and temperature regulation systems are compromised. With a continued loss of up to 20% of body weight in fluids, coma or death is imminent (Kleiner, 1999).

Bottled water is not just H_2O anymore; store shelves and vending machines are filled with vitamin or fitness waters, which are fortified with various vitamins and other additives. Most are low in calories and pose little threat. Most manufactures identify the waters by flavor or ingredients, by benefit (Immunity), or by the target audience (Athletic Performance). People who eat a balanced diet will not likely benefit from drinking vitamin water (Mayo Clinic, 2009). The real question is whether fitness waters are any better than plain water. The simple answer is that they are better only if they help people meet their needs for fluid. Otherwise, plain water is fine.

Many high-powered energy drinks are being marketed to young adults today. Manufacturers promote beverages containing ingredients that have pseudoscientific names, but most of the energy from these drinks comes from the sugar and caffeine, not from the unnecessary extras that are unfamiliar to most people. Most of the high-energy drinks contain ingredients whose safety and effectiveness have not been tested. Some contain herbal supplements that are not regulated by the Food and Drug Administration (FDA), have little or no value, and can be potentially harmful in large amounts. Although one cup (240 ml) of coffee has about 125 to 150 milligrams of caffeine and a 12-ounce (360 ml) can of ordinary cola has 35 to 38 milligrams, an 8-ounce (240 ml) energy drink contains about 280 milligrams of caffeine. Energy drinks lack nutritional value and can contain hundreds of calories. Caffeine can cause side effects like jitters, upset stomach, headaches, and sleep problems, all of which can decrease energy, not help a person power up.

DIETARY TOOLS

Tools are available to help people make optimal food choices. These include the food guide pyramid, dietary guidelines, and food-labeling regulations. The U.S. government created these tools, and information on each is readily available. Nutrition software programs as well as online sites like www.mypyramid.gov are available to help people monitor their nutritional needs and behaviors.

Food Guide Pyramid and MyPlate

The U.S. Department of Agriculture (USDA) updated the food guide pyramid to depict graphically that people need to engage in physical activity and eat right to stay healthy. The new pyramid shows a person climbing up stairs to illustrate that physical activity and proper nutrition provide the best healthy balance. Recently the USDA created a new graphic, MyPlate, to provide a better illustration of food portions. Both graphics have educational value and can be used with Physical Best activities and as part of a fitness education curriculum. Figure 4.5 shows both MyPyramid and MyPlate. Complete information on MyPlate can be found at www.ChooseMyPlate.gov.

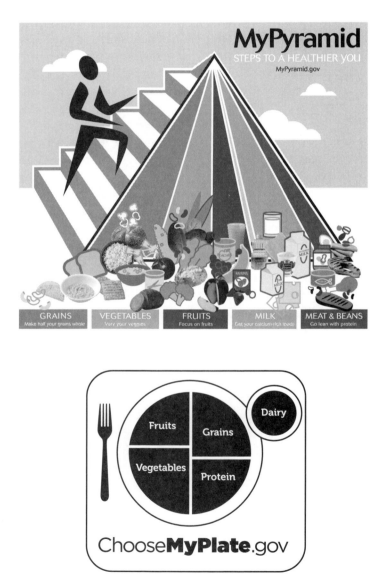

Figure 4.5 The USDA's MyPyramid represents healthy lifestyle choices, symbolizes a personalized approach to physical activity, and promotes healthy eating. The USDA's new MyPlate provides a new way to visualize food portions.

From USDA.

The food guide pyramid or MyPlate should be used as a general guide for healthful eating. In addition, the diet should allow for maintenance of an appropriate weight. Obesity is now at epidemic proportions in the United States. According to the Centers for Disease Control and Prevention, more than 66.5% of adults are overweight or obese, and the percentage of young people who are overweight has more than tripled in the last three decades. For Americans ages 2 through 5 and ages 12 through 19, obesity has more than doubled, and it has more than tripled among children ages 6 through 11. The current statistics show that of children ages 2 through 5, 12.4% are overweight. In children ages 6 through 11, that number increases to 17%, and among adolescents ages 12 through 16, about 18% are considered overweight (USDA Agricultural Research Services, 2005). For more details, refer to the "Obesity" section in chapter 8.

Potential contributors to the obesity epidemic include people's difficulty with judging appropriate portion size and decreased daily activity. Over the past 20 to 30 years, a significant increase in average daily caloric consumption has occurred. Men are consuming, on average, an additional 168 to 268 calories per day, and women are consuming an additional 143 to 335 calories per day (CDC, 2004). Many factors have contributed to this increase including consumption of food away from home, particularly fast food, increased portion sizes, increased intake of sweetened beverages, and increased consumption of between-meal snacks. The amount of food that counts as a serving in each category is listed in table 4.2. If a person eats a larger amount than that listed in table 4.2, it counts as more than one serving. For example, an average restaurant portion of spaghetti counts as two to three servings on the food guide pyramid or MyPlate. One of the problems with weight control in the United States is the supersizing of food in restaurants and fast-food chains. Table 4.2 is a portion guide that can translate to our everyday eating habits. When the food guide pyramid lists a serving of a given food, this is what that serving should look like.

Food Labels

The Food and Drug Administration (FDA) regulates food labeling (see figure 4.6 on page 62). The Nutrition Labeling and Education Act of 1990 (NLEA) revamped the food label. The new food label design reflects current health concerns and makes them easier to understand. The consistent design allows consumers to compare nutritional values of similar products so that they can make sound nutritional decisions. The new label, titled Nutrition Facts, is an effort to simplify and encourage the use of nutritional information. Nutritional labeling is now mandatory for most packaged foods; the panel has been redesigned to describe similar serving sizes and nutrients. The terminology for nutrition content claims used on packaging has been standardized with specific FDA definitions such as low fat, fat free, and reduced calorie. Ingredient lists are required on

Table 4.2 Serving Sizes to Use With the Food Guide Pyramid

Food	Serving size guideline
Fruits	Tennis ball
Nonstarchy vegetables	Baseball
Natural carbohydrates (rice, pasta, cereal)	Your cupped hand
3 oz (90 g) of meat, fish, or poultry	Deck of playing cards
Pancakes or small waffle	Compact disc
1/2 cup raw veggies, cooked rice, pasta, or cut fruit	Rounded handful
1/4 cup dried fruit or nuts	Golf ball or large egg
1 tsp butter or peanut butter	End of your thumb

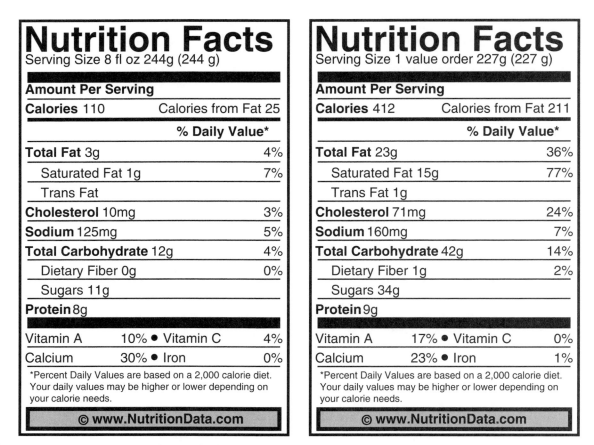

Nutrition Facts
Serving Size 8 fl oz 244g (244 g)

Amount Per Serving

Calories 110	Calories from Fat 25

	% Daily Value*
Total Fat 3g	4%
Saturated Fat 1g	7%
Trans Fat	
Cholesterol 10mg	3%
Sodium 125mg	5%
Total Carbohydrate 12g	4%
Dietary Fiber 0g	0%
Sugars 11g	
Protein 8g	

Vitamin A	10% • Vitamin C	4%
Calcium	30% • Iron	0%

*Percent Daily Values are based on a 2,000 calorie diet. Your daily values may be higher or lower depending on your calorie needs.

© www.NutritionData.com

Nutrition Facts
Serving Size 1 value order 227g (227 g)

Amount Per Serving

Calories 412	Calories from Fat 211

	% Daily Value*
Total Fat 23g	36%
Saturated Fat 15g	77%
Trans Fat 1g	
Cholesterol 71mg	24%
Sodium 160mg	7%
Total Carbohydrate 42g	14%
Dietary Fiber 1g	2%
Sugars 34g	
Protein 9g	

Vitamin A	17% • Vitamin C	0%
Calcium	23% • Iron	1%

*Percent Daily Values are based on a 2,000 calorie diet. Your daily values may be higher or lower depending on your calorie needs.

© www.NutritionData.com

Figure 4.6 The standard format for food labeling, as developed by the Food and Drug Administration. Standard food label formatting makes it easy to compare the nutritional value of a healthy dairy choice and a tasty dairy treat.

labels of all foods with more than one ingredient; the ingredients are listed in descending order of weight. Nutrition content claims differ from the Nutrition Facts label, which lists specific nutrient amounts. Together, nutrient content claims and the Nutrition Facts label help consumers compare one food with another and choose foods for a healthy diet.

Besides being able to consult food labels, people who shop in grocery stores will be more likely to find out whether the head of lettuce that they are buying was grown in Mexico or the United States. The country of origin labeling requires most food retailers to disclose where many types of meat, produce, and other food products come from. The goal of these rules is to make it easier for customers to know whether food was imported.

The FDA also standardized and established criteria for the health claims and nutrient content claims that appear on food labels. Under

the NLEA requirements, nutrition labeling is required for most foods. Labeling of meat and poultry products is regulated by the USDA. Voluntary nutrition information is also available for fish and for the 20 most frequently eaten raw fruits and vegetables. In addition, information is available for the 45 best-selling cuts of meat. This information is available to the stores to post through these programs. Most major grocery chains offer nutrition-based tours for public groups. Contact the local store manager to see whether this service is available in your area.

Under FDA regulations, food manufacturers are required to provide information about certain nutrients. Information on other nutrients can be provided on a voluntary basis. The sidebar shows a list of each. RDA amounts can't be used in food labeling because they're written specifically for specific age groups and genders. Food labels require something more generic that can be used across populations. The daily values (DV)

MANDATORY AND OPTIONAL NUTRIENT LISTINGS FOR A FOOD LABEL

1. Calories or total calories;
2. calories from fat;
3. calories from saturated fat (voluntary);
4. total fat;
5. saturated fat;
6. polyunsaturated fat (voluntary);
7. monounsaturated fat (voluntary);
8. cholesterol;
9. sodium;
10. potassium (voluntary);
11. total carbohydrate (including sugars (mono- and disaccharides), oligosaccharides, starch, fiber, and organic acids);
12. dietary fiber;
13. fiber (voluntary);
14. insoluble fiber (voluntary);
15. sugars;
16. sugar alcohol (voluntary);
17. other carbohydrate (voluntary);
18. protein; and
19. vitamins and minerals

Those nutrients that can be declared voluntarily must be declared when a nutrient content or health claim is made.

From, "Federal Register Advance Notice of Proposed Rulemaking (Food Labeling) 72 FR 62149 November 2, 2007: Revision of Reference Values and Mandatory Nutrients" [Federal Register: November 2, 2007 (Volume 72, Number 212)] [Page 62149-62175] From the Federal Register Online via GPO Access [wais.access.gpo.gov] [DOCID:fr02no07-16]

were established by the FDA for just this purpose. The daily values are based on a 2,000-calorie diet, which is an average intake. Of this 2,000-calorie intake, the daily values represent the following:

- ▶ Fat based on 25 to 30% of total calories
- ▶ No more than 10% from saturated fat
- ▶ Carbohydrate based on 50 to 60% of total calories

- ▶ At least half from complex carbohydrate, including at least 11.5 grams of fiber per 1,000 calories
- ▶ Protein based on 10 to 15% of calories

The DV reference diet of 2,000 calories represents less than 65 grams of fat, less than 20 grams of saturated fat, less than 300 milligrams of cholesterol, and less than 2,400 milligrams of sodium (FDA, 2008). Daily values is a new dietary reference term that will appear on the food label; it is made up of two sets of references, DRVs (daily reference values) and RDIs (reference daily intakes), based on the recommended dietary allowances for essential vitamins and minerals and, in selected groups, protein. The term *RDI* replaces the term *U.S. RDA*.

The FDA also regulates the claims that food manufacturers can make on their products, such as "low fat" or "light." Appendix B lists claims and the requirements that a food must meet before such claims can be put on product labels.

Dietary Guidelines

The USDA and USDHHS jointly collaborate to produce *Dietary Guidelines for Americans*, an overall set of guidelines for building a healthy, balanced lifestyle. These dietary guidelines are best used in conjunction with the food guide pyramid. The guidelines encourage moderation as well as variety in the diet. They also promote moderate intake of fat and cholesterol. Finally, they recommend moderate intake of sugar, sodium, and alcohol. If followed, these guidelines will minimize the risk of obesity and decrease risk for chronic disease in the future. Visit www.usda.gov for additional information.

To maintain body weight in a healthy range, people must balance calories from foods and beverages with the number of calories expended; those who attain this state are in **energy balance**. To reduce the risk of chronic disease in adulthood, people should engage in at least 30 minutes of moderate-intensity physical activity, above usual activity, at work or home on most days of the week. The CDC recommends that adolescents engage in at least 60 minutes of activity every day. To avoid a gradual weight gain over time, people should make small decreases in food and beverage calories and increase physical activity.

The surgeon general's report on physical activity and health offered these conclusions:

► All adolescents should be physically active daily, or nearly every day, as part of play, games, sports, work, transportation, recreation, physical education, or planned exercise, in the context of family, school, and community activities.

► Adolescents should engage in three or more sessions per week of activities that last 20 minutes or more at a time that require moderate to vigorous levels of exertion.

► Elementary school-aged children should accumulate at least 30 to 60 minutes of age-appropriate and developmentally appropriate physical activity on all or most days of the week.

► Children should not have extended periods of inactivity (www.health.gov/PAGuidelines/factsheetprof.aspx).

DIETARY GUIDELINES FOR AMERICANS

Aim for fitness
- Aim for a healthy weight.
- Be physically active each day.

Build a healthy base
- Let the pyramid guide your food choices.
- Choose a variety of grains daily, especially whole grains.
- Choose a variety of fruits and vegetables daily.
- Keep food safe to eat.

Choose sensibly
- Choose a diet that is low in saturated fat and cholesterol and moderate in total fat.
- Choose beverages and foods to moderate your intake of sugars.
- Choose and prepare foods with less salt.
- If you drink alcoholic beverages, do so in moderation.

From USDHHS and USDA.

Discretionary calorie allowance is the balance of calories remaining in a person's energy allowance after accounting for the calories needed to meet the recommended nutrient intakes. The discretionary calorie allowance may be used in selecting foods that are not nutrient dense, such as whole milk rather than reduced or fat-free milk, salad dressings, sugar, and butter. Such foods contain what are known as empty calories. Empty calories lack health-promoting nutrients and are often referred to as junk food.

There are six relevant dietary guidelines:

► Eat a variety of foods.
► Balance the food eaten with physical activity to maintain or improve body weight.
► Choose a diet with plenty of whole grains, vegetables, and fruits.
► Choose a diet low in fat, saturated fat, and cholesterol.
► Choose a diet moderate in sugars.
► Choose a diet moderate in salt and sodium.

CONSEQUENCES OF AN UNHEALTHY DIET

A lack of certain vitamins can cause deficiency diseases, and lack of certain minerals can cause other problems, such as brittle bones, anemia, or even irregular heartbeats. Taking in too much food overall, or too many high-calorie foods, can lead to obesity, which leads to a host of problems. The prevalence of obesity continues to be a health concern for adults, children, and adolescents in the United States. The rate of obesity raises concern because of its implications for Americans' health. Obesity raises the risk of many diseases and health conditions, including coronary heart disease; stroke; type 2 diabetes; cancer including endometrial, breast, and colon; hypertension; liver and gallbladder disease; sleep apnea and respiratory problems; osteoarthritis; and gynecological problems. According to the U.S. surgeon general's report *Overweight and Obesity: Health Consequences*, overweight children also have a higher rate of low self-esteem. Having a similarly unbalanced diet with all the calories coming from carbohydrate can lead to insulin resistance and type 2 diabetes.

The prolonged illness and disabilities associated with many chronic diseases also decrease the quality of life for millions of Americans. Much of the chronic disease burden is preventable.

When it comes to weight loss, we don't have to look far to find a fad diet promising fast results. But these diets can be unhealthy, can limit nutritional intake, and tend to fail or result in dangerous weight cycling. Some common diet types are listed in table 4.3.

Most of today's popular diets take advantage of people who are often willing to try anything to drop weight quickly. Unfortunately, although the quick fix may work for a short time, most people are not able to keep up with the diet's demands. People who use fad diets often gain back any weight that they initially lost. Numerous clues can help people avoid diets or diet products that promote empty promises of weight loss. In general, they should stay away from diets that are based on dramatically cutting back calories. The natural response of the body is to dump water,

so the weight loss is not a reduction in fat—it's only a loss of water. If the diet is based on claims that taking special pills, powders, or herbs will suppress appetite or block the absorption of fat, sugar, or carbohydrate, people should realize that no reliable, scientific research backs up these claims. Dieting in this way is especially risky for children and teens because we don't know much about how these supplements will affect growing bodies. If the diet requires spending a lot of money on pills, seminars, or prepackaged meals, it is probably too good to be true. Diets that completely cut out a needed food group or require eating only specific foods in certain combinations may not provide all the nutrients that are needed, especially when children are still growing. If a fad diet requires skipping meals or replacing meals with special drinks or food bars, nutritional levels may not be met and the enjoyment of sharing a meal with family and friends will disappear. The final red flags in regard to fad diets are any suggestion of losing more than 1 or

Table 4.3 Unhealthy, Fad Diets

Diet type	Some examples
Controlled carbohydrate	• Dr. Atkins' New Diet Revolution • The Carbohydrate Addict's Diet • Protein Power • Sugar Busters • The Zone
High carbohydrate and low fat	• Dr. Dean Ornish: Eat More, Weight Less • The Good Carbohydrate Revolution • The Pritkin Principle
Controlled portion sizes	• Dr. Shapiro's Picture Perfect Weight Loss • Volumetrics Weight Control Plan
Food combining	• Fit for Life • Suzanne Somers' Somersizing
Liquid diets	• Cambridge Diet • Slim-Fast
Diet pills and herbal remedies	• Dexatrim Natural • Hydroxycut • Metabolife 356
Other	• Eat Right for Your Type: The Blood Type Diet • Macrobiotics • Mayo Clinic Diet*

*Although many diet plans use this name, none of them were created by the Mayo Clinic nor are they approved by the Mayo Clinic. The Mayo Clinic Healthy Weight Pyramid is the only diet plan created by the Mayo Clinic.

2 pounds (.5 to 1 kg) per week, claims based on before and after photos, testimonials, or limits on food choices. The key is not a short-term dietary change but rather a lifestyle that includes healthy eating and balancing the calories consumed with the calories expended.

The health benefits of staying at a healthy weight are huge and well worth the effort. Being either overweight or underweight carries a variety of health risks. Being underweight (below the standard weight range for a given height) carries a variety of high-risk health factors including bone loss and osteoporosis, anemia and nutrient deficiencies, as well as amenorrhea. Other health risks for those underweight include having trouble fighting off disease and delayed wound healing. When people choose not to eat the proper number of calories, vulnerability to infection and disease increases. The warning signs that low body weight is becoming a problem include lethargy, depression, loss of lean body mass, and loose, elastic skin. Some people are thin because of a fast metabolism or genetics. Others are thin because they are not getting the calories and nutrients that their growing bodies need or they are exercising excessively to burn calories.

Research shows that good nutrition can help lower the risk for many chronic diseases. Research also suggests that not having breakfast can affect children's intellectual performance. Unhealthy eating habits that contribute to health problems tend to be established early in life; young people who have unhealthy habits tend to maintain these habits as they age.

One-third of all children born in 2000 or later will suffer from diabetes at some point in their lives; many others will face chronic obesity-related health problems like heart disease, high blood pressure, cancer, and asthma (*Let's Move*, 2010). On February 9, 2010, First Lady Michelle Obama announced the ambitious national goal of solving the challenge of childhood obesity. The nationwide campaign Let's Move is designed to help achieve a healthier generation of kids.

Because many children consume as many as half of their daily calories at school, good nutrition at school is more important than ever. This initiative includes a new commitment from school food suppliers to take steps to meet the Healthier U.S. School Challenge goals. The goal is to decrease the amount of sugar, fat, and salt in school meals; increase the amount of whole grains; and double the amount of produce served. The new legislation will allow the Department of Agriculture to create new standards for all foods in schools, including vending machine items, to give students healthier meal options. The new standards are expected to make popular foods healthier. Pizza can be made with whole-wheat crust and low-fat mozzarella, and hamburgers can be made with leaner meat. Vending machines can be stocked with less candy and fewer high-calorie sodas. These new guidelines will require all stakeholders to promote healthy eating behaviors.

Establishing healthy eating habits at a young age is critical to proper growth and development, including healthy bones, skin, and energy levels; and a lowered risk of dental cavities, eating disorders, malnutrition, and iron-deficiency anemia. Healthy eating habits also contribute to the likelihood that youth will continue to make healthy nutrition choices into adulthood.

There are no magic pills when it comes to maintaining an ideal diet. At the end of the day, it comes down to calories ingested being equal to calories expended. This concept is called energy balance. Calorie requirements, however, will increase during periods of growth, and this need must be accommodated as well. But if a person eats more than physiologically required, then that person will gain weight. One pound (.45 kg) of fat is equivalent to 3,500 kilocalories. An additional 10 calories per day over a person's daily needs can result in a gain of a pound over a year! Also, people should know that all calories are equal, no matter what food they were contained in. Low-fat diets will result in weight gain if they contain excessive calories.

Teachers can use many strategies to help children and young adults learn good eating habits. Nutrition-related activities with students should emphasize the following:

▶ Individual eating habits should respect family lifestyles.

▶ Begin the day with breakfast to provide energy and nutrients.

- Control calorie consumption by spacing meals throughout the course of the day.
- Most nutritional needs should be met with regular meals, supplemented by snacks.
- Find pleasure in food while being aware of the nutrient and caloric content in food.
- Practice balance, variety, and moderation.
- Enjoy food. Enjoy good health. Enjoy life.

The following Web sites provide additional information on nutrition:

- www.nutrition.gov—Comprehensive online resource for government-based nutrition information, including *Dietary Guidelines for Americans*, food labeling information, and the food guide pyramids
- www.eatright.org—Web site for the American Dietetic Association
- www.fda.gov/Food/Dietary Supplements/ default.htm—FDA information on supplements and food labeling
- www.fda.gov/Food/LabelingNutrition/ default.htm—Food labeling standards
- www.foodinsight.org—Nutrition and Food Safety Resources, the New Food Label Education Program
- www.fns.usda.gov—Nutrition education and information on an integrated, behavior-based, comprehensive plan for promoting the nutritional health of children
- www.health.gov/dietaryguidelines—*Dietary Guidelines for Americans*
- www.mypyramid.gov—Information on the food guide pyramid

Other nutrition sources include programs such as Power of Choice, which was developed by the U.S. Department of Health and Human Services, the Food and Drug Administration, and USDA's Food and Nutrition Service in 2003. It is intended for after-school program leaders working with young adolescents. For more information, see www.fns.usda.gov/tn/Resources/ power_of_choice.html.

SUMMARY

The most serious consequence of a person's poor diet is an ongoing failure to achieve his or her physical best. The diet provides both energy and building blocks for everyone, regardless of activity level. Building aerobic fitness is impossible without having sufficient energy to keep the heart rate elevated. Muscular strength and endurance require building new muscle tissue with nutrients. Good flexibility requires a healthy skeleton, also built up from nutrients. An ideal body composition clearly depends on an appropriate diet. Good diet alone cannot create fitness, and neither can activity alone. The interactions of physical activity and nutrition are important in the life of every person. People need physical activity as much as they need to have all 45 nutrients in their diets. A good diet optimizes physical activity and promotes health. Use the information in this chapter to teach students about these connections.

As Surgeon General Regina M. Benjamin said, "the real reward is invigorating, energizing, joyous health. It is a level of health that allows people to embrace each day and live their lives to the fullest without disease or disability."

Components of Health-Related Fitness

Part II covers the basic concepts and applications related to the components of health-related fitness for K through 12 programming. Each chapter defines a component of health-related fitness and provides teaching guidelines and training methods related to that component. Chapter 5 focuses on aerobic fitness. Updated information is provided throughout this part of the book, including, in this chapter, a new target heart rate zone formula. Chapter 6 focuses on muscular strength and endurance. Muscular fitness is often taught as two separate components with adults, but strength and endurance are combined in the Physical Best program because it is developmentally appropriate to do so with children in a physical education setting. Chapter 7 explores flexibility training for youth, and chapter 8 covers body composition education, measurement, and related issues as well as new Fitnessgram body composition standards.

Aerobic Fitness

Jan Bishop

Aerobic fitness is just one component of health-related fitness, but it is generally considered the most important physiological indicator of good health and physical condition. The many benefits of good aerobic fitness include those outlined in chapter 1.

A number of other terms are frequently used to describe this component of health-related fitness, such as *cardiorespiratory fitness*, *aerobic endurance*, *aerobic capacity*, *aerobic power*, *cardiorespiratory endurance*, *cardiovascular fitness*, and *cardiovascular endurance*. Throughout this chapter and text, the simpler term *aerobic fitness* is used.

Chapter Contents

To understand the concept of aerobic fitness (the ability to perform aerobic activities), it is important to understand the difference between aerobic activity and physical activity. Physical activity can be defined as any bodily movement that results in energy expenditure. Aerobic means "with oxygen"; therefore, aerobic activity is that which uses oxygen to produce energy for movement. These types of activities build aerobic fitness, which is "the ability to perform large muscle, dynamic, moderate-to-high intensity exercise for prolonged periods" (ACSM, 2010). Aerobic activities include distance running, swimming, and cross-country skiing. These activities are quite different from anaerobic activities such as push-ups and sprints. All aerobic activity is physical activity, but not all physical activity (e.g., a push-up) is aerobic.

To gain health benefits from aerobic activity, a person has to perform it at an appropriate intensity. There are two ways to assess aerobic intensity—in absolute or relative terms (USDHHS, 2008). An absolute measure refers to things like walking at 3 to 4 miles per hour (4.8 to 6.4 kph) or running a 12-minute mile (7 1/2-minute km). A relative measure determines intensity as a percentage of maximum heart rate, heart rate reserve, or aerobic capacity reserve. In the first case everyone works at a specified intensity, like a brisk walk. In the latter, the intensity is adjusted to the individual's level of fitness (i.e., using an individualized training heart rate zone). The advisory committee for the *2008 Physical Activity Guidelines for Americans* examined the relationship between health benefits and aerobic activity measured in both absolute and relative terms. Their goal was to translate scientific evidence concerning intensity into user-friendly guidelines. They concluded that guidelines expressed in accrued minutes of moderate- and vigorous-intensity activity would be easy to follow and would result in the achievement of substantial health benefits by those who followed them.

The portion of the *2008 Physical Activity Guidelines for Americans* that addresses guidelines for children and adolescents describes aerobic activities as "those in which young people rhythmically move their large muscles. Running, hopping, skipping, jumping rope, swimming, dancing, and bicycling are all examples of aerobic activities"

(USDHHS, 2008, p. 16). What is important to note is that children's normal movement activity is not prolonged. Children like to use intermittent activity with short rests. In recognition of the way that children tend to play, the guidelines for the aerobic activity of children and adolescents expand the definition to include "activities in short bursts, which may not technically be aerobic activities" (p. 16). By counting these "brief activities" the working definition of aerobic activity draws a bit closer to that of physical activity. Children commonly combine aerobic movement with muscle- and bone-building movement; just picture a youngster running around the playground, swinging across the monkey bars, jumping to the ground, and running again. In this context, aerobic fitness can be thought of as the ability to exercise or play for extended periods without getting tired.

In the remainder of this chapter, aerobic fitness guidelines will be discussed in terms of both physical activity appropriate to children and adolescents (ages 6–17) and aerobic activity defined in relative terms (i.e., heart rate, oxygen consumption) that is appropriate for high school students.

IMPORTANCE OF AEROBIC FITNESS

The importance of increased physical activity and enhanced fitness in youth cannot be overemphasized. In fact, *Healthy People 2010* (USDHHS, 2000a) lists physical activity as one of the nation's 10 leading health indicators, and two of the plan's objectives specifically target increased physical activity for youth. Objective 22-6 targets moderate physical activity, and the goal is to increase the proportion of adolescents who engage in moderate physical activity for at least 30 minutes on five or more days of the week. Objective 22-7 targets vigorous physical activity, striving to increase the proportion of adolescents who engage in vigorous physical activity that promotes aerobic fitness three or more days per week for 20 or more minutes per occasion.

The *2008 Physical Activity Guidelines for Americans* (USDHHS, 2008) calls for children and adolescents to do 60 minutes or more of physical activity a day, spending most of this time in either moderate- or vigorous-intensity aerobic physical activity and performing vigorous-intensity physical activity on at least three days a week. Muscle-strengthening and bone-strengthening activities should also be included as part of the recommendation that children and adolescents engage in 60 minutes of physical activity a day on three days of the week. For examples of aerobic, muscle-strengthening, and bone-strengthening physical activities, refer to table 3.1 in chapter 3.

Lack of physical activity during adolescence may have long-term health implications when people reach adulthood. There is a known increase in morbidity and mortality in adults attributable to chronic disease and sedentary lifestyles (USDHHS, 2000a). Research (Guo et al., 1994) also shows an association between overweight adolescents and an increased risk of being overweight as an adult; in addition, Janz et al. (2002) state that maintenance of physical fitness through puberty has favorable health benefits in later years. Further rationale for promoting increased physical activity during childhood stems from the *National Health and Nutrition Examination Survey, Phase I, 1988–1991* (McDowell et al., 1994). Data indicate that increased caloric intake is not solely responsible for the increased prevalence of overweight youth and that lack of physical activity may be a contributing factor. Many organizations, including the National Association for Sport and Physical Education (NASPE, 2004b), the Centers for Disease Control and Prevention (CDC, 2010), the American Academy of Pediatrics (AAP, 2000b), and the U.S. Department of Health and Human Services (USDHHS, 2008), advocate increasing childhood physical activity that will carry into adulthood, thereby reducing health problems associated with inactivity. This is where Physical Best can help provide students with the knowledge, skills, values, and confidence they need to engage in physical activity now and in the future through fun and enjoyable activities.

DEFINING AND MEASURING AEROBIC FITNESS

A person's level of aerobic fitness is contingent on the ability of the heart and lungs to circulate oxygen-rich blood to the exercising tissues, the ability of the muscle cells to extract and use the oxygen for energy production, and the ability of the circulatory system to return blood to the heart. The amount of oxygen that a person uses per minute is called oxygen consumption. For adults the criterion measure of aerobic fitness is **maximal oxygen consumption** ($\dot{V}O_2$max). This quantity is the maximum amount of oxygen that a person can use to produce energy during physical activity. During a laboratory test, oxygen consumption is measured while the individual exercises at increasingly higher workloads. At some point, despite an increase in workload, oxygen consumption does not increase; it has maxed out. In normal healthy adults $\dot{V}O_2$max generally increases with fitness and is therefore a good measure of aerobic fitness. A discussion on children and $\dot{V}O_2$max follows in the next section. Because laboratory $\dot{V}O_2$max tests are not practical for the public, it is fortunate that many valid and reliable field tests are available that can predict $\dot{V}O_2$max from submaximal aerobic fitness tests. Physical Best exclusively endorses Fitnessgram (developed by the Cooper Institute) and all related materials and products as the submaximal assessment instrument to estimate $\dot{V}O_2$max and aerobic fitness (see chapter 13). Teachers may choose the PACER (progressive aerobic cardiovascular endurance run), mile run, or the mile walk test depending on the age and ability of the student.

Although the Fitnessgram PACER test is recommended for all ages, it is the preferred test for participants in grades K through 3 and should be administered with an emphasis on having fun. Participation should be a pleasant experience. The PACER also serves as an excellent tool for teaching the concept of pacing for the mile run. An additional feature of Fitnessgram is the capability to compare results ($\dot{V}O_2$max estimates) among the three aerobic fitness tests. As you read and use the Fitnessgram test manual, note that the Cooper Institute (creators of Fitnessgram) uses the term *aerobic capacity* instead of *aerobic fitness*. As previously noted, however, the terms are often used interchangeably. Aerobic capacity is used in the test manual because this term refers more specifically to the volume of oxygen being consumed, whereas aerobic fitness refers to the amount of exercise that can be sustained using that oxygen.

For more information on the administration of the three aerobic tests, refer to the latest edition of the *Fitnessgram Test Administration Manual* by the Cooper Institute. For a full discussion concerning aerobic capacity and analysis of the three aerobic tests, refer to chapter 9 of the *Fitnessgram Reference Guide*. A free online copy can be found by going to the Web site www.fitnessgram.net and clicking on "Reference Guide" in the left-hand column.

Physical Best also supports the use of the Brockport Physical Fitness Test (BPFT) for people with disabilities. The BPFT is a health-related fitness assessment that can be easily customized through selection of any of its 27 items organized in three domains: aerobic function, body composition, and musculoskeletal function. The BPFT "may be used to identify the present level of performance, identify unique needs, and establish annual goals including short-term objectives" (Winnick 1999, p. 6). Therefore, this test can serve as a valuable tool not only for fitness testing but also for the development of an individualized education plan for students with disabilities. It is beyond the scope of this chapter to describe the BPFT in detail, but chapter 11 contains much information for assessing the fitness of people with disabilities. For more information, refer to the *Brockport Physical Fitness Test Manual* (Winnick & Short, 1999a).

TEACHING GUIDELINES FOR AEROBIC FITNESS

The concept of aerobic fitness can be taught to students of all ages, but the practice of aerobic training must take into consideration developmental differences. Children are not little adults; therefore, adult strategies of continuous exercise, use of the FITT guidelines, and interpretation of test results are not the same for children. The score that a student attains on an aerobic fitness test does not correlate well to the amount of aerobic activity that a child gets. Age, heredity, and maturation all play a role in aerobic capacity (aerobic fitness). Therefore, teachers should be careful *not to assume* that children with strong PACER or mile run scores are more active and that those with weaker scores are less active. For example, a child with the right genetics may be minimally active and still have a good score (Pangrazi & Corbin, 2008). Similarly, a person who has inherited a good memory may not have to practice much to spell words correctly, whereas an individual with poor memory functioning could practice a great deal and still not do well on a spelling test. An important difference is that with physical activity the act of doing it provides benefits; therefore, students accumulating appropriate amounts of regular moderate to vigorous activity (regardless of test scores) will benefit. Therefore, test scores, especially for elementary students, should be deemphasized and participation should be highlighted.

Even if adult training guidelines are applied, it is difficult to know how much of the increase in aerobic fitness as measured by $\dot{V}O_2$max (ml $\cdot$ kg^{-1} $\cdot$ min^{-1}) is due to training or simply to increases in body size and maturation. When body size and body scaling are used with $\dot{V}O_2$max measures, children have been found to have modest increases in aerobic fitness, about a third of that seen in adults (Rowland, 2005). When teaching children about aerobic fitness, teachers should keep in mind that genetics, developmental factors, body composition, and psychological factors like motivation as well as activity levels influence differences in performance on any aerobic fitness assessment. The goal of the Physical Best program is to promote noncompetitive, self-enhancing, and fun activities that encourage students to be physically active now and later, as adults (see sample activities in figure 5.1). Even if the relationship is not strong between increased physical activity and aerobic fitness in children (Rowland, 2005; Pangrazi & Corbin, 2008), the program aspires to promote active children to become active adults for whom aerobic training (following the FITT guidelines) yields improvements in aerobic fitness and enhanced health benefits. Parents, teachers, and coaches should encourage participation in a wide variety of enjoyable and available activities. In general, NASPE recommends sport sampling over sport specialization early in life (NASPE, 2010). There is some evidence to suggest that early sport specialization is the preferred approach in sports when elite performance is achieved before puberty (e.g., figure skating, gymnastics), but this research is sparse, and therefore some caution should be given before drawing conclu-

iStockphoto/Alberto Pomares

iStockphoto/Edwin Verin

Figure 5.1 Sample activities that can help students improve aerobic fitness.

sions (Carson, Blankenship, & Landers, in press; NASPE, 2010).

When preparing to teach students about physical activity and fitness, remember that the level and tempo of a child's play activity are characterized by alternating cycles of vigorous activity followed by a recovery period (Bailey et al., 1995; Corbin and Pangrazi, 2002). Plan multiple activities with rest periods to provide variety and to

parallel a child's natural play pattern. Circuit training provides an excellent challenge whereby children can independently explore movement, develop fundamental motor skills, and develop areas of health-related fitness. Circuits or station activities also provide opportunities for all children to be successful. Stations may be set up with various challenge levels, and students may explore and self-select activities to promote success. This type of activity removes the element of competition and the necessity to determine a winner and a loser of the activity. Many Physical Best activities use stations or are designed so that most children are active at the same time. Fitness concepts should be taught through physical activity and classroom lessons in which the number of inactive students is minimized, especially if the class meets only once or twice per week. Focus on a single concept each day rather than multiple concepts. You can teach the concept of venous return during the cool-down or simulate the circulatory system by using a jogging course in which the students act as blood traveling through the heart, arteries, or veins. Cross-discipline lessons and homework may serve as other avenues to teach fitness concepts.

DETERMINING HOW MUCH PHYSICAL ACTIVITY IS NEEDED

Aerobic fitness lessons should include segments in which teachers help students explore practical applications such as logging free-time aerobic fitness activities or lifestyle activities in a journal, learning to take their pulse, or organizing a school fitness night for families and friends. A school can also purchase the latest Fitnessgram software and teach students how to use the computer-based logging materials as well as the fitness assessments. This software can produce fitness reports that can be shared with parents or guardians and help document progress toward a goal. Be sure that students who are new to aerobic activity start slowly. The recommended approach is to increase a single variable (frequency, intensity, time, or type) gradually rather than increase all four variables. For the less-fit individual, it is better to increase time (duration) first instead of intensity. Children are less likely to become discouraged and more likely to adhere to an activity or exercise program if it does not cause extreme fatigue and soreness. Long periods of continuous vigorous activity are not recommended for children ages 6 through 12 unless chosen by the child and not prescribed by an adult (NASPE, 2004b).

To reduce the risk of injury or medical complications, work with the school nurse to determine which students have medical conditions that you should be aware of, such as orthopedic problems, asthma, epilepsy, diabetes, or other disabilities. Proper screening of your students will help you develop a well-rounded program that addresses the needs of all students, including those who should use extra caution when engaging in aerobic fitness activities.

AEROBIC FITNESS TRAINING PRINCIPLES

The training principles (progression, overload, specificity, individuality, and regularity) outlined in chapter 3 should be followed when developing aerobic fitness. These guidelines are especially helpful for older children, but Welk and Blair (2008) point out that "just because children CAN adapt to physical training does not mean they should be encouraged or required to do so" (p. 14). Postpubescent children will respond more favorably to training and conditioning than will younger prepubescent and pubescent children (Payne and Morrow, 1993). Rather than emphasize the adult exercise prescription model, the aim with children should be to foster and maintain a physically active lifestyle, as previously outlined. It is beyond the scope of this text to explain the physiological changes that affect aerobic fitness and performance in children during aerobic training. For more information on the trainability of children and endurance performance, refer to *Children's Exercise Physiology* (Rowland, 2005) or *Total Training for Young Champions* (Bompa, 2000).

Although the lifetime physical activity model provides guidelines for aerobic fitness training sufficient for good health, you may encounter students who want to achieve higher levels of fitness. Providing accurate and helpful information to assist interested students in reaching their aerobic fitness goals safely is important, but the five training principles are applicable only to older, postpubescent children. Table 5.1 provides information on how to apply the FITT guidelines for younger (5 to 12 years old) and adolescent (11 years old and older) children as well as older youth participating in athletics. Note that table 5.1 includes some overlap in age, allowing for changes in the guidelines based on individual developmental age, not chronological age.

Table 5.1 FITT Guidelines Applied to Aerobic Fitness

	Children (5–12 years)[a]	Adolescents (≥11 years)[b]	Middle and high school youth who participate in athletics[c]
Frequency	• Developmentally appropriate physical activity on all or most days of the week • Several bouts of physical activity lasting 15 min or more daily	• Daily or nearly every day • Three or more sessions per week	5 or 6 days per week
Intensity	• Mixture of moderate and vigorous intermittent activity • Moderate includes low-intensity games (hopscotch, foursquare), low-activity positions (goalie, outfielders), some chores, and yard work • Vigorous includes games involving running or chasing and playing sports (level 2 of activity pyramid)	• Moderate to vigorous activity. Maintaining a target heart rate is not expected at this level. • Rating of perceived exertion: 7–10 (Borg)[d], 1–3 (OMNI)[e]	• 60–90% heart rate max (MHR) or 50–85% heart rate reserve (HRR) • Rating of perceived exertion: 12–16 (Borg), 5–7 (OMNI)
Time	• Accumulation of at least 60 min, and up to several hours, of activity • Up to 50% of accumulated minutes should be accumulated in bouts of 15 min or more	• 30–60 min daily activity • 20 min or more in a single session	20–60 min
Type	• Variety of activities • Activities should be selected from the first three levels of the activity pyramid • Continuous activity should not be expected for most children	• Play, games, sports, work, transportation, recreation, physical education, or planned exercise in the context of family, school, and community activities • Brisk walking, jogging, stair climbing, basketball, racket sports, soccer, dance, lap swimming, skating, lawn mowing, and cycling	Activities that use large muscles and are used in a rhythmical fashion (e.g., brisk walking, jogging, stair climbing, basketball, racket sports, soccer, dance, lap swimming, skating, and cycling)

[a]National Association for Sport and Physical Education. (2004). *Physical activity for children: A statement of guidelines for children ages 5–12*, 2nd edition (Reston, VA: Author).

[b]Corbin, C .B., and Pangrazi, R.P. (2002). Physical activity for children: how much is enough? In G. J. Welk, R.J. Morrow, & H.B. Falls (Eds), *Fitnessgram Reference Guide* (p. 7 Internet Resource). Dallas, TX: The Cooper Institute.

[c]American College of Sports Medicine (2000). *ACSM's guidelines for exercise testing and prescription.* 6th Ed., Lippincott, Williams, and Wilkins: Philadelphia.

[d]Borg, G. (1998). *Borg's perceived exertion and pain scales* (Champaign, IL: Human Kinetics), 47.

[e]Robertson, R.J. (2004). *Perceived exertion for practitioners: Rating effort with the OMNI pictures system* (Champaign, IL: Human Kinetics), 141-150.

From National Association for Sport and Physical Education 2004; Corbin and Pangrazi 2002; American College of Sports Medicine 2000; Borg 1998.

MONITORING INTENSITY

An important question concerns how hard students should exercise. Teachers can use several methods to teach about and monitor the intensity of aerobic activity. Young children can be asked to place one hand on their heart and make a fist with their free hand every time they feel their heart beat. As the intensity of exercise increases they will feel and see (free hand) their heart speeding up. Older children can be taught to count their pulse (see "Taking the Pulse"), and high school students can learn how to calculate exercise within a target heart rate zone. In this way young children can link heart rate to the intensity of an activity, and older students can be taught that an increasing heart rate correlates with increasing oxygen consumption, which is the measure of aerobic capacity.

Two other methods of monitoring intensity are the talk test and ratings of perceived exertion (RPE). The talk test simply stipulates that your intensity is appropriate if you can talk but not sing. If you are too out of breath to talk the intensity is too high; if you can sing the intensity is too low. A rating of perceived exertion is an estimate of how hard or easy a person feels that she or he is working. Table 5.2 depicts the OMNI scales for rating perceived exertion for children (ages 8 through 15) and adults (ages 16 and older). These scales were developed using pictures of exertion as well as words and numbers. The pictures, provided in reproducible form in appendix A, are especially helpful with elementary and middle school children (see figure 5.2, *a* and *b*). This is because they may rate their level of perceived exer-

Table 5.2 Verbal Cues for OMNI RPE Scales

Adults	Children
Extremely easy = 0	Not tired at all = 0
Easy = 2	A little tired = 2
Somewhat easy = 4	Getting more tired = 4
Somewhat hard = 6	Tired = 6
Hard = 8	Really tired = 8
Extremely hard = 10	Very, very tired = 10

Reprinted, by permission, from V.H. Heyward, 2010, *Advanced fitness assessment and exercise prescription, 6th edition* (Champaign, IL: Human Kinetics), 69.

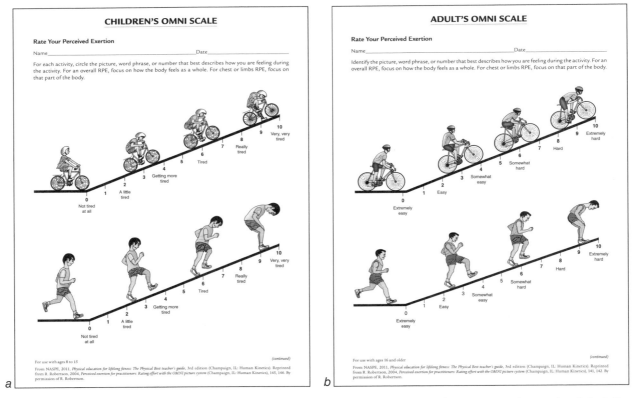

Figure 5.2 The *(a)* children's and *(b)* adult's OMNI RPE scales allow students to use the scale pictorially. Reproducible versions of these scales are available in appendix A.

Reprinted from R. Robertson, 2004, *Perceived exertion for practitioners: Rating effort with the OMNI pictures system* (Champaign, IL: Human Kinetics), 141, 142, 145, 146. By permission of R. Robertson.

tion more accurately by pointing to a picture than by selecting a number or word phrase. Note that the children's word phrases are different from the adult's phrases. The OMNI scales can be used to determine an RPE for the whole body, for the limbs, or for the chest, and are therefore useful for teaching about intensity in both aerobic and resistance exercise.

Taking the Pulse

To use heart rate as an estimate of aerobic intensity, students first need to learn how to take their pulse accurately. Two common sites used to count heart rate are the carotid artery (on the neck) and the radial artery (wrist, thumb side). First, teach students to locate the pulse by placing the first two fingers of the right hand lightly on the right side of the neck, below and to the right of the Adam's apple (figure 5.3a). The Adam's apple is not prominent in children, especially girls. In an alternate method, the children look straight ahead and place two fingers on the bone behind the bottom earlobe (mastoid process). They then gently press and slowly slide the fingers down and forward until they feel the heartbeat. The fingers will naturally follow the angle of the jaw and end up to the right of the Adam's apple. (K through 3 children may place a hand over the left side of the chest to feel the heartbeat.) Be sure that each student is capable of feeling his or her heart beating. Make sure that students do not press too hard or massage the neck because doing so will slow the heart rate; they should never palpate both arteries at the same time because reduced blood flow to the brain may cause them to faint. Teach older students to use the radial artery at the wrist by placing the first two fingers of either hand on the opposite wrist (palm facing up), just below the base of the thumb (figure 5.3b). Students should move their fingers around until they locate the pulse. Students should not use the thumb to

a *b*

Figure 5.3 Two methods of taking a pulse: (*a*) the carotid artery (neck) method and (*b*) the radial artery (wrist) method.

palpate the pulse because the thumb has a pulse in it and a double count may occur. When students are first learning to palpate the pulse, it is helpful to have them be active for a couple minutes so that the heartbeat is more pronounced.

Heartbeat is often counted for one minute when measuring resting heart rate; shorter time intervals are used to measure exercise heart rate. If the first heartbeat is counted while simultaneously starting the stopwatch, the first beat should be counted as zero. If the stopwatch is running, the first beat should be counted as one (Heyward, 2010). Students may either count their pulse for 6 seconds and multiply by 10 (simply add a zero to the number they counted), count for 10 seconds and multiply by 6 (see table 5.3), or count for 15 seconds and multiply by 4. Fitness professionals generally prefer the 10-second count because it tends to be the most accurate. To avoid having to multiply the 10-second count by 6, which can be difficult to do in your head, students can either refer to a chart (see table 5.3) or divide their TRHZ by 6 and use a range for beats per 10 seconds. For example, the range calculated earlier, 153 to 165 beats per minute, is 25 to 27 beats per 10 seconds.

Table 5.3 Heart Rate Based on a 10-Second Count

Beats per 10 seconds	Heart rate (bpm)	Beats per 10 seconds	Heart rate (bpm)
10	60	22	132
11	66	23	138
12	72	24	144
13	78	25	150
14	84	26	156
15	90	27	162
16	96	28	168
17	102	29	174
18	108	30	180
19	114	31	186
20	120	32	192
21	126	33	198

Target Heart Rate Zones

The target heart rate zone (THRZ) is a range of heart rates between which a person wants to work out to achieve optimal aerobic training. The low end of the zone is often referred to as the threshold of training. Two formulas, the maximum heart rate formula and the Karvonen (or heart rate reserve) formula can be used to determine a person's THRZ. To use these formulas, **maximal heart rate** (MHR) must first be calculated. There are two ways to do this, one newer than the other. Researchers have found some inherent difficulties in estimating MHR using the common formula (220 minus age) and subsequently calculating an exercise heart rate as a marker of training intensity in children. Children's maximal heart rates are age independent and generally range from 195 to 205 beats per minute; the range for maximal heart rate does not change with age until the late teens (Rowland, 2005).

Recent research (Tanaka, Monahan, and Seals, 2001) suggests a new formula for estimating maximal heart rate: $208 - (.7 \times age)$. Even newer research (Gellish et al., 2007) corroborates the previous formula with a slight change from 208 to 207, making the formula read $207 - (.7 \times age)$. The American College of Sports Medicine is endorsing this formula in their 8th edition of *Guidelines for Exercise Testing and Prescription* (ACSM, 2010). Although children were not used as participants in the development of the new formula, this procedure estimates maximal heart rates in children more in line with the range of 195 to 205 beats per minute reported by other researchers (Armstrong et al., 1991; Bailey et al., 1978; Cumming, Everatt, and Hastman, 1978; Rowland, 1996). Although the old formula was simpler to use, it generally overpredicted MHR in those 20 to 40 years of age and underpredicted MHR in those over 40 years of age (Tanaka, Monahan, and Seals, 2001). Although this new formula does not have a direct effect on school-age children, graduating seniors will move into that population within a couple of years.

Therefore, for high school students, the new formula, $MHR = 207 - (.7 \times age)$, should be used to calculate exercise heart rates. Younger children (ages 6 to 14 years) should not use exercise heart rate thresholds or zones; they should simply engage in activity following the previously discussed *2008 Physical Activity Guidelines* (USDHHS, 2008) and NASPE (2004b) guidelines for elementary school children or the guidelines for adolescents (Sallis & Patrick, 1994).

As mentioned, long periods of vigorous continuous activity are not considered age- and developmentally appropriate for children 6 to 12 years old unless the child self-selects the activity (NASPE, 2004b). High-intensity activity may discourage children from being active because exercising at this level is generally unpleasant. The emphasis for children should be on having fun and developing the locomotor skills necessary to succeed in more advanced activity or sport later in life. Malina (1996) suggests that activities performed in adulthood are based on locomotor and leisure skills learned early in a child's life. If a child is confident in the skills developed during childhood, she or he is more likely to continue those activities into adulthood. In addition, self-perception of competence declines as children get older (Jacobs et al., 2002), and children who underestimate their physical competence may discontinue participation in sport or may have low levels of physical achievement (Weiss & Horn, 1990). This information is important when working with children. Exercising at specified training heart rates or performing continuous high-intensity activity should be reserved for high school students.

For students beyond age 14, teachers may begin to introduce the calculation of target heart rates using the maximal heart rate formula or the heart rate reserve (HRR) method. For younger students, you can begin to teach concepts of intensity and heart rate monitoring by providing opportunities to compare resting heart rate with exercise heart rate, to learn basic anatomy of the cardiovascular and respiratory systems, and to learn how increased physical activity helps them play longer without getting tired. Reserve calculations and goals of meeting a specified target heart rate for high school students (or at least late teen years). Primary-grade students can begin to monitor their intensity levels by placing a hand over the heart before, during, and after moderate to vigorous physical activity; they can note the general speed of the heartbeat using terms such as slow, medium, and fast or turtle and race car. Students in the fourth through sixth grade can begin to locate the carotid and radial arteries to count heart rate, but they should not use target heart rate zones. Most students in seventh grade and up can be expected to calculate target heart rate values, but you should still avoid the use of target heart rate zones (THRZ) as requirements for participation in physical activities.

High school students can begin to use the THRZ to guide them in monitoring intensity of activity. Refer to tables 5.3 and 5.4 for selecting the appropriate percentage to monitor intensity. After intensity has been selected, begin by teaching the maximum heart rate method (Gellish et al., 2007), which is the simpler of the two methods of calculating the THRZ. To save class time, students can perform this calculation as a homework assignment. The second method, the Karvonen or heart rate reserve (HRR) method (ACSM, 2010; Gellish et al., 2007) takes into

Table 5.4 Progression of Activity Frequency, Intensity, and Time Based on Fitness Level

Low fitness	Marginal fitness		Good fitness
Frequency	3 days a week	3 to 5 days a week	3 to 6 days a week
Intensity			
Heart rate reserve (HRR)	40–50%	50–60%	60–85%
Maximum heart rate (max HR)	55–65%	65–75%	75–90%
Relative perceived exertion (RPE)	12–13 (Borg)[a], 5 (OMNI)[b]	13–14 (Borg), 5–6 (OMNI)	14–16 (Borg), 6–7 (OMNI)
Time	10–30 min	20–40 min	30–60 min

[a]Borg, G. (1998). *Borg's perceived exertion and pain scales* (Champaign, IL: Human Kinetics), 47.
[b]Robertson, R.J. (2004). *Perceived exertion for practitioners: Rating effort with the OMNI pictures system* (Champaign, IL: Human Kinetics).
From Corbin et al. 2004.

account the individual's resting heart rate. Refer to the section "Calculating Maximum Heart Rate and Target Heart Rate Zones for Middle or High School Students."

If teachers working with young children (6-14 years old) must make use of a target heart rate, they should use 85% of maximum heart rate max (MHR = 200 beats per minute) (Rowland, 1996). This is equal to approximately 170 beats per minute (T.W. Rowland, personal communication, December 2002). This heart rate provides a goal for students to attain but does not necessarily relate to the intensity necessary for fitness improvement. Rowland's *Children's Exercise Physiology* (2005) provides further explanation of the physiological changes and the high-intensity exercise required to elicit those changes in children. Remember that specifying target heart rates is not recommended for elementary-level children.

Using Heart Rate Monitors

Although heart rate monitors are not necessary, they are a popular and exciting way to teach students about aerobic fitness concepts. Heart rate monitors provide accurate information, whereas some students may have difficulty manually palpating the pulse, especially children below the fourth grade. If you are using heart rate monitors at the elementary level, make sure to use them for fun and for teaching aerobic fitness concepts, not for attaining a specified target heart rate. You may try activities such as asking students, "Who can get their heart rate to 140 beats per minute?" "150 beats per minute?" and so on. Follow the activity with a rest period. Then repeat the sequence using different heart rate goals. This routine provides short bursts of activity, is considered vigorous activity when higher heart rates are used, and provides a goal for elementary students to attain for brief periods. Heart rate monitors are also useful tools for teaching students of all ages about pacing. Students can run, try to guess their heart rates, and then check their estimates against the monitor. They can also learn pacing by trying to traverse a certain distance in a designated time. For example, jogging 1/8 mile (.2 km) in 1 minute is an 8-minute-per-mile (5 min per km) pace. Students can set the stopwatch on the HRM, jog, and then see whether they are close to a 1-minute

time. Using this self-testing, older students can try various pacing levels and see what pace keeps them in their target heart rate zone. At the middle and high school levels, monitors used to check calculated target heart rate or exercise intensity can help teach students about individualizing their aerobic fitness programs.

Using Pedometers

Pedometers are a fun and motivating way to challenge students to be more active. Both practitioners and researchers endorse the usefulness of pedometers for measuring and promoting physical activity (Beighle, Pangrazi, & Vincent, 2001; Tudor-Locke et. al., 2004; Cuddihy, Pangrazi, & Tomson, 2005). They provide an inexpensive, easy to obtain, objective measure of physical activity. This method is especially helpful when working with children because they often have difficulty discerning how much moderate to vigorous activity they perform. Increasing research is being done on pedometers. Although not all pedometers perform equally well, the research generally finds electronic pedometers to be reliable and valid indicators of physical activity (Crouter et al., 2003; Schneider, Crouter, & Bassett, 2004; Schneider, Crouter, Lukajic, & Bassett, 2003; Beets, Patton, & Edwards, 2005). The most accurate are Japanese made (Barfield, Rowe, & Michael, 2004; Tudor-Locke et al., 2008). Although the brand of pedometer may result in variations, pedometers tend to be an accurate means of assessing steps, less accurate at assessing distance, and even less accurate at assessing kilocalories (Crouter et al., 2003).

Distance is based on the number of steps taken and the stride length programmed into the pedometer; therefore, error can sneak in if stride length changes with the speed of a walk or run. Another issue worth noting is that pedometers tend to underestimate steps taken at a slow pace, around 2 miles per hour (54 m/min) (Crouter et al., 2003; Le Masurier et al., 2004). At a slow pace people may not produce enough vertical motion to trigger a step count (Beets et al., 2005; Crouter et al., 2003). Teachers who encourage their students to move briskly help ensure a more accurate step count. Young children or the elderly with less bounce in their steps may still lose steps, as will

CALCULATING MAXIMUM HEART RATE AND TARGET HEART RATE ZONES FOR MIDDLE OR HIGH SCHOOL STUDENTS

Maximum Heart Rate Method

The first step when using this method is to calculate the maximal heart rate (MHR) using the new formula: 207 − (.7 × age). Then, to calculate a target heart rate zone (THRZ), select a percentage between 55 or 60 to 90%. This becomes the threshold percentage for the calculation of target heart rate. Next, select a second percentage 10% higher than the threshold percentage. For example, a student who is 16 years old seeking a basic level of fitness (at 65–75% MHR) would find his or her THRZ as follows:

$$MHR = 207 - (.7 \times 16) = 195.8 \text{ or } 196$$

Calculate the THRZ by changing the selected percentages to decimals and multiplying them by the MHR:

$$.65 \times 196 = 127.4 \text{ or } 127$$

$$.75 \times 196 = 147$$

Rounded to the nearest whole number, this student's THRZ for maintaining or improving basic aerobic fitness is 127 to 147 heartbeats per minute.

Karvonen Method (Heart Rate Reserve [HRR])

This method takes into account an individual's fitness level and resting heart rate. For high school students, this method can be taught and used to demonstrate how intensity can be modified as fitness improves and resting heart rate decreases.

This method, also known as the **heart rate reserve** (HRR) method, involves multiple steps. HRR is calculated by subtracting resting heart rate from maximal heart rate. After this is completed, the student follows the same procedures in selecting two percentages, but the range of possible percentages is slightly different (50–85%) and the final step is to add back in resting heart rate. For example, the same 16-year-old student, with a resting heart rate of 70 and seeking a basic level of fitness (at 65–75% MHR) would find his or her THRZ as follows:

$$MHR = 207 - (.7 \times 16) = 195.8 \text{ or } 196$$

Calculate the THRZ by subtracting resting heart rate from maximal heart rate, and complete the following formula where HRR is heart rate reserve and RHR is resting heart rate. In this example, resting heart rate is 70 beats per minute.

$$HRR = [207 - (.7 \times AGE) - RHR] \text{ and THRZ is}$$
$$[([207 - (.7 \times AGE)] - RHR) \times \%] + RHR$$

$$HRR = [207 - (.7 \times 16) - 70] = 125.8$$

$$THRZ = [([207 - (.7 \times 16)] - 70) \times .65] + 70 = 151.77 \text{ or } 152$$

$$THRZ = [([207 - (.7 \times 16)] - 70) \times .75] + 70 = 164.35 \text{ or } 164$$

Rounded to the nearest whole number, this student's THRZ for maintaining or improving basic aerobic fitness is 152 to 164 heartbeats per minute.

---

those with unusual gait patterns. If a pedometer is ineffective with a gait pattern (or wheelchair), students can be paired and the count from the normal-gait student used for both.

One of the big questions is, How many steps are enough? A number of studies including both adults and children have been conducted in an attempt to link daily step counts to health benefits and recommended levels of physical activity. Because children are naturally more active than adults are, the adult standard of 10,000 steps (Hatano, 1993; Welk et al., 2000) may be low for them. To earn the Physical Activity Lifestyle

Award (PALA) using steps per day, the President's Council on Physical Fitness and Sport (2008b) requires girls to log at least 11,000 steps and boys at least 13,000 steps for five days for six weeks. These numbers are the result of studies examining activity patterns of youth with pedometers (Le Masurier et al., 2005; Vincent et al., 2003). Tudor-Locke and colleagues (2004) examined the relationship of steps per day to body mass index (BMI). They found that girls and boys ages 6 through 12 who accumulated 12,000 and 15,000 steps respectively tended to be under the international BMI standard for being overweight

PHYSICAL ACTIVITY LIFESTYLE AWARD (PALA)

The Physical Activity Lifestyle Award (PALA) was developed by the President's Council on Physical Fitness and Sport (PCPFS) with the purpose of motivating and rewarding people who regularly participate in physical activity. Achieving a specific level of physical fitness is not required. Thus, the PALA supports the goal of increasing the number of active healthy U.S. citizens. For more information go to www.presidentschallenge.org or call 800-258-8146.

or obese. Additional research is needed to address questions such as whether healthier children simply take more steps or whether taking a certain number of steps results in healthier children. Note that pedometers do not log physical activity done during activities such as biking and swimming.

To address individual differences, Pangrazi, Beighle, and Sidman (2003) suggest the following baseline and goal-setting approach. A baseline count is determined by wearing the pedometer for four days (children) or eight days (adults and adolescents) and determining the average number of steps per day. A 10% increase in steps is then calculated and added to the step goal amount every two weeks. The overall goal is to achieve about 4,000 to 6,000 steps above baseline. For example, a student whose baseline is 6,000 steps will increase this amount by 600 steps every two weeks until he or she reaches 10,000 to 12,000 steps per day.

Until recently one of the biggest drawbacks to pedometers was their inability to estimate intensity. One thousand walking steps was counted the same as 1,000 running steps despite an obvious difference in intensity. Newer pedometers allow students to collect the amount of time (minutes) they are active as well as the number of accumulated steps. Students can be taught to divide the total number of steps they take by the number of minutes they are active to obtain their steps per minute (SPM). Extending our example of 1,000 steps, a student could be performing 1,000 steps in 10 minutes (1,000/10 = 100 SPM)

or 1,000 steps in 20 minutes (1,000/20 = 50 SPM). The assumption is that the more steps a person takes per minute, the more intense the activity is. Information on adults is included in the following discussion because older high school students will soon want to know how to use pedometers as a method to track lifelong activity. For adults, moderate-intensity walking is approximately equal to at least 100 steps per minute (Marshall et al., 2009). To meet the current adult guideline of 150 minutes of moderate-intensity physical activity, the person could take 3,000 steps in 30 minutes or 1,000 steps in three 10-minute bouts (Marshall et al., 2009). Graser, Pangrazi, and Vincent (2009) tested 10- through 12-year-olds walking on a treadmill at moderate to vigorous walking paces and determined that a range of 120 to 140 SPM for both genders is a reasonable measure of moderate to vigorous physical activity (MVPA). Special populations such as those with high levels of body fat may benefit more by trying to improve their SPM count rather than using the 120 to 140 guideline. Pedometers with the steps per minute feature are an excellent way to teach all students about intensity, baseline recording, and goal setting.

The recommended location for the pedometer is at the waistline directly in line with the midpoint of the front of the thigh. But if abdominal fat or a loose waistband allows a spring-loaded pedometer to tilt forward 10 degrees or more, the step count will become less accurate and an alternative location may work better (Crouter, Schneider, & Bassett, 2005; Duncan et al., 2007). One solution for this problem is to have elastic belts that the pedometer can be placed on. This also solves the problem of fitting the pedometer clip over a waistband edge that is too thick. A student can also move the pedometer to the side or to the small of the back. Count steps and check the pedometer to see which location gives the most accurate count. In some cases moving the pedometer to the side or back has solved the problem of pedometer tilt, but then the student cannot read the pedometer independently. To test pedometer placement and accuracy, Cuddihy et al. (2005) recommend placing the pedometer on the waistband above the midpoint of the right thigh, walking 100 steps, and then checking the pedometer count. If the pedometer count is off by 3 or more steps, place the pedometer more to the right (slightly in front of or over the hip) and repeat the test. If the count is still off by 3 or more steps, place the pedometer on the waistband to the back or on an elastic belt. This test assumes that the pedometer is accurate within 3 steps when properly placed. Three styles of voice announcement pedometers for visually impaired students worked best when worn on the right side (Beets et al., 2007).

Pedometers are most effective when the teacher has an efficient method for handing them out, recording steps, and collecting them. If numbers are assigned ahead of time, students can come in, quickly pick up their pedometers from a storage unit, and use peers to get them on. Having students track steps on their own recording sheets is much quicker than having the teacher record all the steps. To prevent breakage, encourage the use of the safety leashes and have students put the pedometers on while kneeling or sitting down (at least in the beginning) so that dropping them is less likely to cause damage. Pedometers currently available offer a variety of tracking features including steps, distance, calories, continuous minute bouts, and total activity time. Select a pedometer type based on the reliability of the features used most. Then put them to use; many creative, instructional, and motivating lessons can be generated using pedometers (Lubans, Morgan, & Tudor-Locke, 2009; Pangrazi, Beighle, & Sidman, 2003, 2007).

CROSS-DISCIPLINE IDEAS

Many opportunities are available to use a cross-disciplinary approach when teaching aerobic fitness concepts. Collaboration with classroom teachers allows nonactive supporting activities to be taught in the classroom and physically active supporting activities to be taught during physical education. For example, math teachers can have students calculate the target heart rates (at the middle or high school level), and then students in physical education can practice moving in the target zone. Elementary students can be asked to keep track of, add up, and chart the number of minutes that they are active during physical education class, recess, and at home. Math students can predict the number of pedometer steps required to go a certain distance and then jog or walk the distance and compare the results.

In language arts, students can write about a physical activity in which they've engaged. Then

---

PULSE MATH

To promote interdisciplinary learning, you can easily create math problems based on calculating heart rate by having students count their pulse for various intervals. To add interest, make up problems such as the following:

1. Sun counted 35 heartbeats in 30 seconds. What is Sun's heart rate?

   60 seconds ÷ 30 seconds = 2

   So you multiply 35 heartbeats by 2:

   35 heartbeats × 2 = 70 heartbeats per minute

2. Deandre counted 27 heartbeats in 10 seconds. What is Deandre's heart rate?

   60 seconds ÷ 10 seconds = 6

   So you multiply 27 heartbeats by 6:

   27 heartbeats × 6 = 162 heartbeats per minute

3. Which person is more likely to be jogging, Sun or Deandre? (Deandre.) Which person is more likely to be sitting in class? (Sun.)

Because this is a practical way to integrate math across the curriculum, fourth-, fifth-, and sixth-grade classroom teachers may be willing to help you construct similar problems or may provide time in math class for students to learn and complete this type of work. Some students may also be able to design problems for themselves or peers to complete. These kinds of calculations, when presented creatively, may also provide an engaging activity for students who may be sitting out of physical education class for health reasons.

TEACHING TIP: TEACHING ABOUT AEROBIC FITNESS

Many students, particularly young children, will understand and monitor their heart rates more effectively when you provide some extra context. For example, you might use a metronome for teaching about heart rate. Students will better understand what 200 beats per minute sounds like.

Another fun method to reinforce how hard the heart works is to ask the students to calculate how many beats their hearts have made since birth. Figure out how many heartbeats occur per minute, then per hour, per day, per week, per year, and then years since birth. Encourage students to be as exact as their ages and abilities allow.

Carolyn Masterson, Associate Professor
Montclair State University
Upper Montclair, New Jersey

in physical education, they can convert poetry into movement. Science teachers can teach students how a drop of blood flows through the heart, lungs, and to the exercising muscles, and physical educators can have students move through a diagram of the heart drawn on the playground. Music teachers can teach about rhythm, and physical educators can have students create rhythmic aerobic routines. Geography and map reading can be integrated with orienteering. History can be recreated in a game. The possibilities are endless, and the rewards can be great as students experience practical applications and the integrated nature of knowledge. For more interdisciplinary ideas, consult the elementary and middle and secondary activity guides.

TRAINING METHODS FOR AEROBIC FITNESS

Three main training methods are used to maintain or increase aerobic fitness: continuous, interval, and circuit training. You must adjust application of these methods depending on the age, ability, and fitness level of each student. Building personal choice into each activity can do some of this individualizing for you. For example, offer a longer rest option during interval training or allow students to assist in the development of aerobic fitness circuits. Remember that students can monitor heart rates, but calculations and target heart rate zones should be used only for older students, as previously discussed.

Continuous Training

Continuous training is performing the same activity or exercise over an extended period. This style of activity is not common for children. **Continuous activity** is defined as "movement that lasts at least several minutes without rest periods" (NASPE, 2004b, 6). As stated previously, vigorous continuous activity is not recommended for children 6 to 12 years old, but some continuous moderate activity is appropriate (NASPE, 2004b). If you use continuous activity at the elementary level, build plenty of rest periods into the activity. Continuous activity of 3 to 5 minutes at moderate intensity may be the limit for primary grades or low-fit students, whereas 10 minutes may be a good limit for older (grades 3 through 5) elementary students. Twenty minutes or more of continuous activity, depending on fitness level and goals, is appropriate for students in middle school and high school. Table 5.1 provides information on using the FITT guidelines for youth of various ages.

For students at the high school level, calculating and monitoring exercise heart rate becomes important. At the middle school level, students can calculate heart rate but should not be required to maintain a set range. Activity at high intensity can become discouraging, so limit the time spent performing high-intensity activity, which is often more appropriate for training and conditioning athletes. Middle and high school students may use the adult model and calculate target heart rates or simply perform the activity at a pace at which they can comfortably converse.

To apply the principles of overload and progression, one can increase any of the components of the FITT principle (i.e., frequency, intensity, time, or type), but be careful of losing the enjoyment factor by increasing these variables too quickly. When a person is in the initial stages of an exercise program, it is recommended to increase duration first. After an individual has been exercising regularly for a month or more, the frequency, intensity, and time can be gradually adjusted upwards (ACSM, 2010). How to adjust the variable depends on the student; involve the student in goal setting and exercise planning. Active, low-organization games are fun ways to provide continuous physical activity. Teach games and activities that students will want to play in their free time. Middle and high school students may find that a mix of aerobic activities that sustain a target elevated heart rate for a designated period will be more enjoyable and therefore more beneficial to their overall fitness level.

Fartlek training is a modification of continuous training in which periods of increased intensity are interspersed with continuous activity over varying and natural terrain. The word *fartlek* comes from the Swedish word for "speed play," and the bursts of higher intensity exercise are not systematically controlled as they are in interval training. True fartlek training should be reserved for coaches and athletes and should not be used in physical education classes. This type of training (traversing over hills) develops technique, strength, muscular endurance, general aerobic endurance, and mental fitness (Greene & Pate, 1997); these benefits are not attributes that physical educators are trying to develop in the classroom. This training should be used only by coaches working with serious athletes who want to increase speed in a particular sport such as basketball. Despite the negative aspects of true fartlek training, a modified version of it may be used at the elementary level by placing stress on different muscle groups through frequent changes in level and direction (Virgilio, 1997). Figure 5.4 shows a sample fartlek training course appropriate for older, reasonably well-conditioned elementary students. A similar modified activity can be designed for older students especially if choice of intensity is built into the activity.

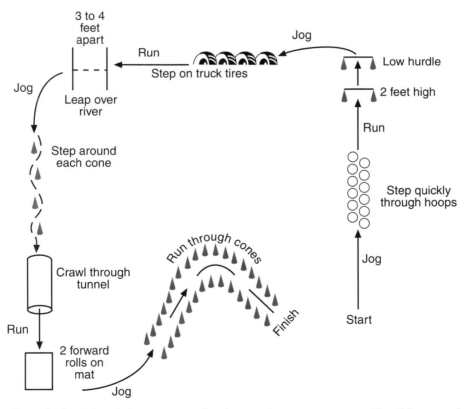

Figure 5.4 Sample fartlek training course. Students who use a course like this one should be older elementary age and reasonably well conditioned.

Adapted, by permission, from S. Virgilio, 1997, *Fitness education for children* (Champaign, IL: Human Kinetics), 149.

Interval Training

Interval training is based on the concept that more activity can be performed at higher exercise intensity with the same or even less fatigue compared with continuous training. This type of training involves alternating short bursts of activity with rest periods. Young children naturally engage in this type of activity; you must simply ensure that the students have a rest period between activity bursts. This type of training may also serve as an opportunity for older students to have a choice of how quickly the exercise period begins. After middle and high school students know how to palpate heart rate, you can have them count their preexercise heart rate and use that number to determine when the next activity begins. For this approach to be effective, you must limit the number of students at any one station. Otherwise, when a student's heart rate has decreased, signaling that it is time to move on, she or he must wait until a spot opens up at the next station.

Aerobic interval training involves alternating the intensity of an activity between the low and high ends of the aerobic zone without using rest intervals. Technically this is a form of fartlek training (speed play) rather than true interval training because it is continuous in nature. An example of this might be alternating medium- and fast-paced rope jumping. In an example of true intervals, the student would jump rope at a relatively high intensity for a short amount of time and then rest until the music restarted.

Start each station with the same number of students and plan equipment and space for three or four extra students per station. Most students will naturally want to move to the next station, especially if the activities are fun. Older students are capable of engaging in more structured interval training, but this should not be part of your physical education lesson. The trick is to make this type of training interesting. Leave running wind sprints for the track coach and have your students, for example, pass a soccer ball between partners, running as fast as they can downfield. Interval training can be designed to develop aerobic fitness by matching activity time (generally three to four minutes) with an equivalent rest interval (three to four minutes of rest) or by using one-half of the work period as the time interval for the rest period (one and a half to two minutes of rest).

Interval training is more than wind sprints. Here students jump rope to music that alternates between faster and slower tempos.

Circuit Training

Circuit training involves several different exercises or activities, allowing you to vary the intensity or type of activity as students move from station to station. Children naturally engage in this intermittent type of activity. Bailey et al. (1995) suggest that intermittent activity mixed with short rest periods is necessary for normal growth and development. You can also adjust intensity by changing the amount of time that each group spends at each station or the amount of rest or activity between stations (for instance, stretching between stations versus running once around the activity area). An example of circuit training appropriate for elementary-age children is shown in figure 5.5. Middle and high school students might use a similar setup that includes a variety of age-appropriate aerobic fitness activities through which they rotate in a timed cycle. Circuit training is an excellent way to create variety in aerobic fitness activity because the possible station combinations are endless.

LINE CHANGE

Virgilio (1997) offers a continuous aerobic fitness activity. This activity could also be considered a fartlek training activity (see the section "Continuous Training") because students may have to speed up temporarily to take over the lead.

Arrange students in straight lines of seven or eight, facing the same direction. Have them begin jogging or walking in any direction, staying in lines. At the signal, the last student in line jogs to the front to become the leader. Continue until everyone has had a chance to lead the line.

Reprinted, by permission, from S. Virgilio, 1997, *Fitness education for children* (Champaign, IL: Human Kinetics), 149.

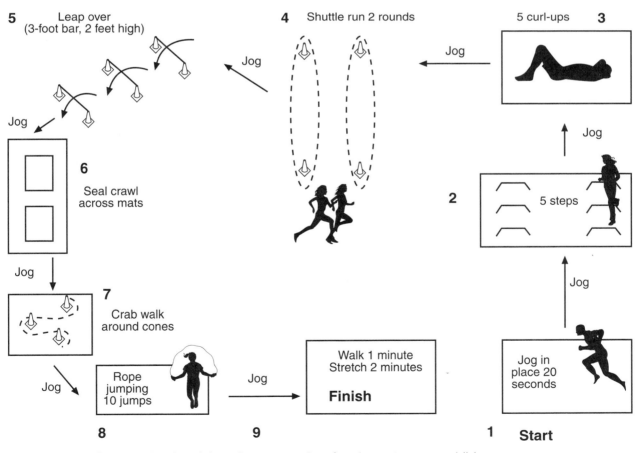

Figure 5.5 Sample circuit training plan appropriate for elementary-age children.

Reprinted, by permission, from S. Virgilio, 1997, *Fitness education for children* (Champaign, IL: Human Kinetics), 149.

STATION LEARNING AND EQUIPMENT

Stations arranged on a circuit (see figure 5.6) are a good way to stretch the equipment that you have a little further while also providing variety. For example, if you only have four stationary bikes, you can place these in one station on a circuit and divide the class into groups of four. The other stations can also feature aerobic fitness activities, such as rope jumping, step routines, and aerobic dance. If you have plenty of steps and jump ropes, arrange more than one station using each of these so that groups alternate activities. Here are some other tips for using stations effectively:

- Use stations as a review of previously learned skills.
- Design task cards that are grade and age appropriate—they are good motivators.
- Have students design the stations based on a particular theme or fitness component.
- Alternate intensity levels at the stations and alternate fitness components.

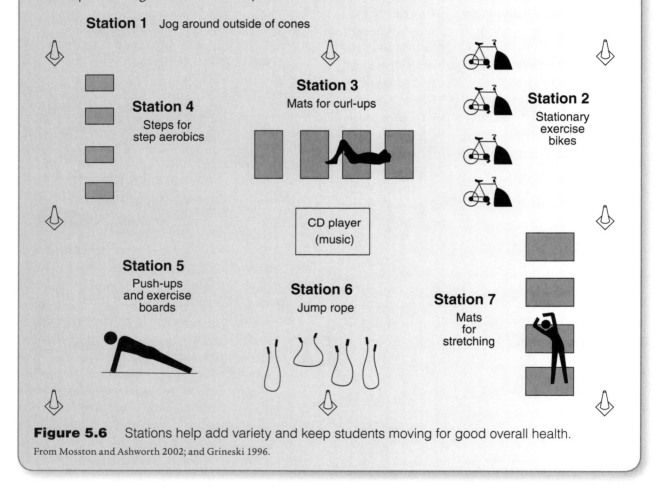

Figure 5.6 Stations help add variety and keep students moving for good overall health.

From Mosston and Ashworth 2002; and Grineski 1996.

Older elementary students and middle and high school students can even design the stations as a practical application of the fitness knowledge that they are learning. Like continuous training, circuit training can be aerobic in nature, and the individual's fitness level will dictate the intensity and duration of the activity. To keep the activity organized and moving quickly, consider using task cards and arrow signs to help facilitate the movement direction of the activities.

ADDRESSING MOTOR SKILLS THROUGH AEROBIC FITNESS ACTIVITIES

The importance of skill development should not be underestimated, especially at the elementary level. The *Physical Best Activity Guides* provide many opportunities to address motor skill development during aerobic fitness training to help make fitness activities more enjoyable and interesting. For example, "Aerobic Sports" in the *Physical Best Activity Guide: Elementary Level, Third Edition* rotates students through a variety of stations using sport skills.

Many activities could be modified to include a manipulative object or to vary the form of locomotion while developing aerobic fitness and sport skills. This approach demonstrates to students how aerobic fitness applies in the real world of physical activity. Address both health-related fitness and skill-related fitness whenever possible. Here are several specific ways to integrate motor skills with aerobic fitness activities:

- Aerobic circuit training using sport-specific skills at each station
- Obstacle courses
- Soccer keep-away
- Activities in the *Physical Best Activity Guides*— modified to include sport skills
- In-line skating
- Swimming relays

SAFETY GUIDELINES FOR AEROBIC FITNESS ACTIVITIES

Research has shown that children respond to exercise differently than adults do (Bar-Or, 1993, 1994; Zwiren, 1988; Rowland, 1996), and there are many issues to consider when helping children increase their aerobic fitness. As a teacher, you should keep the following information regarding physiological differences between adults and children in mind when manipulating the principles of training (Bar-Or, 1984; Rowland, 1996):

- Children produce more heat, relative to body size, at rest and during exercise (equal absolute workloads) than adults do.
- Children sweat less than adults do and therefore have difficulty using evaporation as a method of heat dissipation.
- Prepubertal children cannot sustain exercise in hot environments as compared with adults.
- Children fatigue sooner than adults do when exercising in the heat.
- Children are less economical and use more oxygen than adults do at any given submaximal exercise intensity.
- Children's heart rates are generally higher than those of adults at rest and across all levels of exercise.
- Children's maximal heart rates vary from 195 to 205, and large variability is present between individual subjects.
- Children have less efficient **ventilation** (volume of air moved) compared with adults.
- Children have higher breathing frequencies (bf) and lower **tidal volumes** (V_T), or volume of air either inhaled or exhaled in a normal resting breath, compared with adults.
- Children have higher pulmonary ventilation (breathing frequency × tidal volume) per liter of oxygen consumed during submaximal and maximal exercise.
- Children hyperventilate during exercise more than adults do.

Because of these physiological factors, you should build in frequent rest periods, especially for younger students, and provide water before, during, and after physical activity. Emphasize lifestyle activities and limit highly organized sport with high-intensity training to avoid injury. Avoid sessions in hot and humid weather with elementary children, and, using your best judgment, slow down or cancel the activity with middle and high school students. Although most students in your classes will handle aerobic fitness activities safely, you will encounter a few who will need special guidance and modified activities. Be sure that you know which students have any form of asthma,

Teach the overload and progression principles and FITT guidelines to students with special needs through carefully planned and modified activities.

orthopedic concerns, heart anomalies, diabetes, and the like. Not all these conditions will be obvious, so review school records, talk to the school nurse or classroom teachers, survey parents, and carefully follow school or district policies to ensure that you are fully informed. Ask for input on what each child in question can handle and seek advice on how to apply the overload and progression principles and FITT guidelines safely. If in doubt, obtain written parental permission to talk to the student's health care provider (see also chapter 11).

SUMMARY

Aerobic fitness activities can and should be enjoyable at every age. Young children thrive on intermittent, playful activities. Middle school students can start to stretch their aerobic endur-

ance but still should not be held to target heart rate zone criteria. High school students can learn how intensity is related to oxygen consumption, heart rate, and perceptions of exertion. The joy of aerobic movement can be sustained by teaching a wide variety of activities and allowing students to work at their own levels (see table 5.1). Using circuits that include a variety of stations is an effective way to accomplish this. Aerobic fitness can be combined with skill development and built into many activities already offered in the curriculum. Students can learn to assess their aerobic fitness using the PACER test, mile walk, or mile run. The ultimate goal is for students to find aerobic activities that they enjoy, develop a healthy activity pattern, and understand how to apply the FITT guidelines and other training principles to reach their personal aerobic fitness goals.

Muscular Strength and Endurance

Joe Deutsch

Chapter Contents

For the development of total fitness, a well-rounded health-related fitness program must include muscular strength and muscular endurance. The health benefits of muscular strength and endurance programs for adults are well documented, but little research is available on the health benefits for children. This lack of documented health-related benefits does not mean that children cannot improve muscular strength and endurance. When developing muscular fitness programs, remember that children are not little adults and that the adult model of weightlifting is not applicable to children. Many adults lift weights for reasons other than improved weightlifting performance, such as enhanced sport performance or prevention of muscular injury, but the research is inconsistent about whether these benefits apply to children. Youth strength-training experts (Faigenbaum and Westcott, 2009) suggest that children participating in youth sports programs need to do strength-developing activities before participation, much like adult preseason conditioning, to prevent injury and enhance skill development. Although these training and conditioning recommendations may be appropriate, the emphasis of physical education classes should be on creating positive experiences that focus on technique (see figure 6.1). This approach will enable children to carry these skills into their leisure (sport participation) activities. Children should set realistic goals based on their individual needs and should be thoroughly educated in the techniques and safety issues of resistance training. Basic definitions, potential health benefits, and teaching guidelines for safe and effective programs are presented. This chapter will provide an overview of a solid, scientifically proven approach to teaching the principles of muscular strength and endurance to students.

Figure 6.1 Sample activities that can help students improve muscular strength and endurance: (a) push-ups (strength), (b) pull-ups (strength), (c) using leg muscles to bounce while sitting on a ball (endurance), and (d) exercise tubing (strength and endurance).

DEFINITIONS OF MUSCULAR STRENGTH AND ENDURANCE CONCEPTS

To administer a safe and effective resistance-training program for children, teachers must develop an understanding of a variety of terms related to the development of muscular strength and muscular endurance. **Muscular strength** is the ability of a muscle or muscle group to exert maximal force against a resistance one time through the full range of motion. The emphasis on the full range of motion is important because any movement less than full range is counter-productive—strength or endurance gains occur only in the range of motion exercised. Muscular strength is often denoted as **1RM**, which stands for "**one-repetition maximum**." See the section "Estimating 1RM" later in this chapter for important developmentally appropriate practices related to determining training loads. **Muscular endurance** is the ability of a muscle or muscle group to exert a submaximal force repeatedly over a period of time.

TEACHING TIP: TEACHING ABOUT MUSCULAR STRENGTH

Elementary students need to learn how different weights feel. You should have various types and sizes (2 to 10 pounds [1 to 5 kg]) of weights available at a station so that the students can learn about using different weights and learn how each weight feels.

There is more than one way to do a push-up, but they all require keeping the back stable. Place a beanbag or tennis ball on the backs of students to help them understand the correct form of a push-up. Challenge the students to keep the beanbag or tennis ball on their backs, which will indicate good technique.

Carolyn Masterson, Associate Professor
Montclair State University
Upper Montclair, New Jersey

In the Physical Best program, muscular strength and muscular endurance are combined together as **muscular fitness**, because in practical application of activities and exercises they are difficult to separate, especially at the primary grade level. You will find that many Physical Best activities use the weight of the child's body as the resistance (see "Teaching Tip: Teaching About Muscular Strength").

A sound weight-training practice, for both children and adults, is to focus on good form and multiple repetitions (muscular endurance) before engaging in lifting heavier weights and performing fewer repetitions (muscular strength). No participant, child or adult, should engage in rapid repetitions in which momentum assists in the lifting process. Participants should use a six-second count, taking two or three seconds to lift the weight and three or four seconds to lower the weight, focusing on technique. Furthermore, children should not engage in lifting heavy weights (performing fewer than 6 repetitions). The general guideline is for children to perform 6 to 15 reps of an exercise to see strength changes. Studies indicate that single-set programs of 8 to 10 exercises, performing 6 to 15 repetitions, maximize strength increases in youth (AAP, 2001; Faigenbaum & Westcott, 2009). You may choose to label your lessons as muscular fitness instead of specifying muscular strength or muscular endurance.

Resistance training or strength training is a systematic, preplanned program using a variety of methods (e.g., a person's own body weight or tension bands) or equipment (e.g., machines or free weights) that progressively stresses the musculoskeletal system to improve muscular strength (ACSM, 2003; Faigenbaum, 2007; Faigenbaum & Westcott, 2009). On the other hand, **weightlifting** is considered a competitive sport involving maximal lifts, and further specification includes Olympic weightlifting using the snatch and the clean and jerk lifts (AAP, 2001). It is also ill advised for children to participate in **powerlifting** (a competitive sport involving the dead lift, the squat, and the bench press) or **bodybuilding**, in which muscle size, symmetry, and definition are judged (AAP, 2001). Children are not physiologically mature enough to see changes in muscle size, symmetry, or definition. The medical concerns about resistance training often stem from the confusion in terminology. Many people follow the adult model of training and conditioning, focusing on lifting as much weight as possible (1RM) and on weightlifting competitions. These practices are inappropriate for children. Multiple recommendations or position statements on resistance training exist that provide guidance in developing children's resistance-training programs (AAP, 2001; ACSM, 2009, 2006; Faigenbaum, 2003; Hass, Faigenbaum, & Franklin, 2001; NSCA, 2008). Authorities generally agree that resistance training or weight training is safe for children, but weightlifting, bodybuilding, and other competitions that focus on maximal lifts are not recommended. Throughout this text, the term *resistance training* will be used when referring to activities that develop muscular strength and muscular endurance because it encompasses a greater variety of activities and does not require the use of weights only.

BENEFITS OF RESISTANCE TRAINING

A variety of benefits are associated with resistance training. Many of these benefits are age related, and greater sport performance benefits are associated with postpubescent adolescents. Potential benefits of resistance training include the following:

- Increased muscular strength (Faigenbaum, 2003, 2007; NSCA, 2008)
- Increased **muscular power**, or ability to exert a force rapidly (Faigenbaum, 2003)
- Increased muscular endurance (Faigenbaum, 2003; Faigenbaum & Westcott, 2009; NSCA, 2008)
- Improvement in aerobic fitness using circuit weight training (Faigenbaum, 2003)
- Prevention of musculoskeletal injury (Faigenbaum, 2003; Faigenbaum & Westcott, 2009)
- Improved sport performance (Faigenbaum, 2003; Faigenbaum & Westcott, 2009)
- Reduced risk of fractures in adulthood (Karlsson et al., 2002)
- Enhanced bone development, in both bone strength and bone growth, during the skeletal growth period (Faigenbaum, 2003; Turner & Robling, 2003)

Postpubescent children achieve these benefits, plus many of the health benefits associated with adult resistance-training programs, including the following:

POSITION OF THE NATIONAL STRENGTH AND CONDITIONING ASSOCIATION ON YOUTH RESISTANCE TRAINING

This is the current 2009 position of the NSCA:

1. A properly designed and supervised resistance-training program is safe for children.
2. A properly designed and supervised resistance-training program can increase the strength of children.
3. A properly designed and supervised resistance-training program can help to enhance the motor fitness skills and sports performance of children.
4. A properly designed and supervised resistance-training program can help to prevent injuries in youth sports and recreational activities.
5. A properly designed and supervised resistance-training program can help to improve the psychosocial well-being of children.
6. A properly designed and supervised resistance-training program can enhance the overall health of children.

Reprinted, by permission, from A.D. Faigenbaum et al., 2009, "Youth resistance training: Updated position statement paper from the National Strength and Conditioning Association," *Journal of Strength and Conditioning Research* 23(Suppl 5): S60-S76.

- Improved blood lipid profile
- Improved body composition
- Improved mental health and well-being
- A more positive attitude toward lifetime physical activity (Faigenbaum, 2003)

Safety is a concern in any aspect of physical education and health-related physical fitness, but it is especially critical to follow the safety guidelines outlined later in this chapter. You should also seek additional training specific to working with children and adolescents in developing muscular strength and endurance in a safe and effective manner. Furthermore, use common sense when designing and implementing curricula and activities in this area, paying careful attention to the age, developmental readiness, ability, maturity, experience, and fitness of your students.

RESISTANCE-TRAINING CAUTIONS

Before they consider equipment and teaching ideas, physical educators must understand some of the cautions involved with resistance training, especially for the prepubescent child. The following program considerations should be reviewed before developing children's resistance training programs (Faigenbaum & Westcott, 2009).

- The child must be psychologically and physically ready to accept teaching or coaching instruction.
- There must be adequate supervision by instructors who know resistance-training concerns for children and special problems of prepubescent children. The ratio of teachers to students should be 1:5, or 1:10 with experienced teenage participants.
- Proper technique and safety for each lift must be emphasized.
- Caution must be used with machines that are not designed to fit children.
- Resistance training should not be an isolated component—it should be part of a comprehensive program to increase motor skills and fitness.

- The resistance-training program should be preceded by a warm-up and followed by a cool-down.
- Both **concentric contractions** (muscle shortens) and **eccentric contractions** (dynamic, muscle lengthens) should be included in the program.
- Full range of motion must be emphasized.

Besides these program considerations, the American Academy of Pediatrics also recommends that children and adolescents receive a medical evaluation to determine any underlying medical condition or orthopedic problem that may limit or prohibit participation in resistance training. These cautions should not deter teachers from incorporating resistance training in physical education class. With proper instruction and supervision, resistance training can be a fun and safe activity for all ages (Sullivan & Anderson, 2000).

> Age-specific training guidelines, program variations, and competent supervision will make resistance-training programs safe, effective, and fun for children. Instructors must understand the physical and emotional uniqueness of children and, in turn, children must appreciate the potential benefits and risks associated with resistance training. Although the needs, goals, and interests of children will continually change, resistance training should be considered a safe and effective component of youth fitness programs (Faigenbaum, 2007).

Although age-specific guidelines are provided through the FITT guidelines (see page 100 in this chapter) with resistance indicated by light to heavy weights, your program should accommodate the "training age" (i.e., resistance-training experience) of the child when developing resistance programs. This approach will allow younger, more experienced children to challenge themselves safely under proper instruction and supervision (using the progression and overload principles). Use the number of repetitions to determine the weight lifted, such that a child is performing 6 to 15 reps. This method eliminates the ambiguity of the "light" or "heavy" weight recommendations. When a child can lift 15 reps, then increase the weight by no more than 1 to 3 pounds (.5 to 1.5 kg) (Faigenbaum & Westcott, 2009).

TEACHING GUIDELINES FOR MUSCULAR STRENGTH AND ENDURANCE

Muscular fitness concepts and resistance-training sessions can be taught even if state-of-the-art equipment is not available. Surgical tubing or other resistance band material is inexpensive and readily available. In the primary grades, most children will be challenged using the weight of their own body, and for some children, this challenge carries through to the middle and high school level. Another idea is to collect cans of food and use them as small weights (they can later be donated to a local food bank). If the teacher or a parent is handy with a sewing machine, small saddlebags can be made to hold small weights, cans of food, or other items used for resistance training. The saddlebags can be draped over the extremities, and a child can individualize the program by selecting appropriate weights at each station. Balls can also be used that incorporate balance and strength. Partner-resistance exercises can be used if equipment is lacking. Many chil-

dren at the elementary level lack the emotional maturity to engage in formal resistance training, but they can perform the muscular strength and endurance activities from the *Physical Best Activity Guide: Elementary Level*. This guide provides appropriate muscular fitness activities for this level. Late elementary may be the first opportunity to introduce a more formal or comprehensive resistance-training program (Faigenbaum, 2003). Always take into account the participant's psychological and physical maturity when implementing resistance-training programs, although most guidelines use chronological age.

When purchasing equipment, focus on buying items that will meet the primary needs of the students. Most machine weights are not designed for the small size of children; therefore, resistance bands, dumbbells, medicine balls, or free weights may be a better choice of equipment. This recommendation does not come without caution, because the use of free weights poses additional safety concerns regarding proper form and spotting techniques. Most injuries involving youth resistance-training activities are related to improper lifting techniques, maximal lifts, or lack of qualified adult supervision (Faigenbaum, 2003); also, injury often occurs in exercise involving dead lifts, the bench press, or the overhead press. Remember that using traditional weight-training equipment represents only a small seg-

YOUTH RESISTANCE-TRAINING GUIDELINES

- Provide qualified instruction and supervision.
- Ensure that the exercise environment is safe and free of hazards.
- Begin each session with a 5- to 10-minute dynamic warm-up period.
- Start with one set of 10 to 15 repetitions with a moderate load on a variety of exercises. Progress to two or three sets of 6 to 15 repetitions depending on needs or goals.
- Increase the resistance gradually (5 to 10%) as strength improves.

- Focus on the correct exercise technique instead of the amount of weight lifted.
- Train two to three times per week on nonconsecutive days.
- Use individualized workout logs to monitor progress.
- Keep the program fresh and challenging by systematically varying the training program.

Adapted from A. Faigenbaum, 2007, "Resistance training for children and adolescents: Are there health outcomes?" *American Journal of Lifestyle Medicine* 1: 196.

ment of exercises and activities. Students should first manage their own body weight before lifting heavier weights. We have included many activities and exercises in the *Physical Best Activity Guides* that teach muscular strength and endurance concepts without requiring the use of a weight room.

PRINCIPLES OF TRAINING

The basic training principles presented in chapter 3 apply to resistance training, and teachers may use a variety of activities to improve muscular strength or endurance as long as these training principles are followed. Manipulating the mode of exercise, number of sets, number of repetitions, and amount of weight lifted is critical in the adult model, but recent research (Faigenbaum, Westcott, Loud, & Long, 1999) indicates that greater gains in strength occur in preadolescent youth (boys and girls) when doing approximately 14 reps (lifting moderate weight) in contrast to doing 7 reps (lifting heavier weight). As previously indicated, one **set** of 8 to 15 **repetitions** is appropriate for youth, and more sets may be added as youth improve and the goal moves from learning techniques to increasing **volume** as needed for training and conditioning for sport. This section provides a review of how the training principles from chapter 3 are specifically applied to resistance training.

Overload, Progression, Specificity, Individuality, and Regularity

The **overload principle**—placing greater-than-normal demands on the musculature of the body—suggests that people involved with activities designed to improve muscular strength or muscular endurance must increase their workload periodically throughout the course of the program. Specifically, overload requires increasing the resistance against the exercising muscles to a level greater than that used before. Increasing the number of repetitions provides another avenue to overload the muscle, but this type of overload develops muscular endurance, not muscular strength. Decreasing the rest interval between activities can be used as well as a com-

bination of these methods. Keep in mind that the increase must be appropriate for the age and fitness level of the students and that chronological age may not always be the best indicator for determining the amount of weight to be lifted or the number of repetitions to perform. These recommendations are slightly different from the exercise prescription for adults, and they yield a safe and effective method of increasing strength in children. Therefore, one to three sets of 6 to 15 repetitions is recommended. This protocol provides opportunities for children to succeed and appreciate what they have accomplished (Faigenbaum, 2003; Faigenbaum & Westcott, 2009).

The principle of **progression** refers to a gradual increase. It is a systematic approach to increasing the resistance and intensity of the activity. To avoid injury, however, students must understand appropriate progression and set goals accordingly. For example, as beginners, they should know that developing a good base for muscular fitness often entails using the weight of their own body first, followed by one to three sets of 6 to 15 repetitions. The resistance lifted begins with a weight that can be lifted 6 to 10 times (and not 11), and the number of repetitions is gradually increased to 15. Point out that adding only 1 to 3 pounds (.5 to 1.5 kg) at a time is safer and more realistic than increasing by an excessive amount (more than 3 pounds). Avoid increasing the load by more than 5 pounds (2.5 kg) under any circumstances. In some instances one component may be increased while the other components are actually decreased. For example, as intensity increases, volume will decrease, and vice versa. Make sure that you develop a plan of health-related fitness activities that will lead the student to an improved level of fitness in a safe but progressive manner. The *Physical Best Activity Guides* provide many activities that have been developed with this principle in mind.

The **specificity principle** states that the "training effects derived from an exercise program are specific to the exercise performed and muscles involved" (ACSM, 2009). For resistance training, specificity suggests that the activities selected should provide the outcome represented by the class objectives for the day (see the *Physical Best Activity Guides* for examples). The previously described principles of overload and progression provide the foundation for establishing specificity in the teaching plan.

The **regularity principle** states that activity must be performed on a regular basis to be effective, and that long periods of inactivity can lead to loss of benefits achieved during the training session. Engaging in muscular strength and endurance training two or three times per week is sufficient for a lifetime of good muscular health. Yet, as mentioned in chapter 5, teachers will most likely encounter students who want to achieve higher levels of fitness. The teacher is responsible for providing accurate and helpful information to assist interested students in reaching their muscular strength and endurance goals safely.

The **individuality principle** takes into account that each child has different goals for physical activity and muscular fitness, as well as different initial muscular fitness levels. For children, a variety of activities should be incorporated into a program, facilitating a broad range of skill development, including muscular fitness activities. This variety provides opportunity for all children to be successful and provides a baseline of motor skills for future development as the child matures and shows interest in specific sport activities.

FITT Guidelines

Guidelines for muscular fitness are based on policy statements or position statements from the American Academy of Pediatrics (2001) and the National Strength and Conditioning Association (2008). It is generally agreed that the frequency of resistance training should be two or three times per week. In examining exercise intensity, the recommendations are more complex and are related to stages of maturation. Table 6.1 summarizes the FITT (frequency, intensity, time, and type) guidelines based on age and current recommendations by the American Academy of Pediatrics, the American College of Sports Medicine, and the National Strength and Conditioning Association.

Childhood (prepubescence) is generally thought of as a period during which students should learn proper technique and use the weight of their own bodies. They then progress through to the postpubescent stage, when the adult model may be applied. Weight should always be added in small increments (1 to 3 pounds [5 to 1.5 kg]), and a range of 6 to 15 repetitions should be performed. The time, or duration, of resistance training should be at least 20 to 30 minutes or the time required to lift one to three sets, 6 to 15 repetitions, with rest periods based on the goal of the activity session.

Table 6.1 FITT Guidelines Applied to Muscular Fitness

Ages	9–11 years [a, b]	12–14 years [a, b]	15–16 years [a]	≥17 years[c]
Frequency	2 or 3 days/week	2 or 3 days/week	2 or 3 days/week	2 days/week
Intensity	Very light weight	Light weight	Moderate weight	Light to heavy weight (based on type selected)
Time	At least one set (may do two sets), 6–15 reps, at least 20–30 min	At least one set (may do three sets), 6–15 reps, at least 20–30 min	At least one set (may do three or four sets), 6–15 reps, at least 20–30 min	Minimum one set, 8–12 reps
Type	Major muscle groups, one exercise per muscle or muscle group	Major muscle groups, one exercise per muscle or muscle group	Major muscle groups, two exercises per muscle or muscle group	Major muscle groups, 8–10 exercises; select muscular strength, power, or endurance

[a]Modified from AAP (2001). "Strength training by children and adolescents (RE0048)." *Pediatrics*, 107(6): 1470–1472.

[b]Modified from Faigenbaum, A.D., 2007. Resistance training for children and adolescents: Are there health outcomes? *American Journal of Lifestyle* Medicine 1:190–200.

[c]Modified from American College of Sports Medicine, 2008, *ACSM's guidelines for exercise testing and prescription*, 6th ed. (Baltimore: Lippincott, Williams, and Wilkins).

Adapted from AAP 2001; Faigenbaum 2007; American College of Sports Medicine 2008.

A rest period of 2 or 3 minutes should be used for a strength session, whereas shorter periods of 90 seconds may be used for a muscular endurance or power session. Keep in mind that the child's anaerobic system is not fully developed, and feelings of light-headedness or nausea may result if the child is not allowed short rest periods while progressing through an endurance session.

Type refers to the kind of resistance training performed during the session, such as muscular strength, power, or endurance (see table 6.1). It may also refer to the variety of weight-training methods available such as tension bands, free weights, body weight, machine weights, or partner-resistance exercises.

Estimating 1RM

Extreme caution must be applied when discussing the concept of a one-repetition maximum (1RM). Children will naturally want to know how much weight they can lift and will want to challenge classmates to determine who is the strongest. Remember that safety precautions must be taught first and that the lifting of a 1RM should absolutely not be used to obtain a training intensity. Children should not be exposed to loads greater than 70 to 80% of an estimated 1RM or to explosive lifts using free weights during pre-puberty, puberty, and early postpuberty (Bompa & Carrera, 2005). Keep in mind that these suggestions apply to most children and most educational programs. In some instances among late postpubescent youth, with proper training and supervision, explosive lifting techniques may be taught. A variety of methods are used to estimate the 1RM, such as performing a 10RM and using a table to predict the 1RM (Baechle & Earle, 2008) or calculating a 1RM from a weight that is lifted no less than 6 and no more than 12 repetitions. For children, it is much simpler to use the range of 6 to 12 repetitions to estimate the 1RM versus determining a precise 10RM. Estimating a 1RM should be reserved for the postpubescent child (girls ages 13 to 18; boys ages 14 to 18) or those at the high school level.

To estimate a student's 1RM, consult table 6.2 on page 102. In the "Max reps (RM): 10/75% 1RM" column, first find the tested 10RM load; then read across the row to the "Max reps (RM):

1/100% 1RM" column to find the student's projected 1RM. For example, if a student's 10RM is 75 pounds (34 kg), the estimated 1RM is 100 pounds (45 kg) (Baechle and Earle, 2008).

Manipulating the Intensity of the Workout

A person can develop either muscular strength or muscular endurance with the same total load by manipulating the intensity of the workout. To develop muscular strength, increase intensity by increasing the weight lifted and reducing the number of reps (e.g., a student leg presses 100 pounds [45 kg] for 6 reps; the total load is 600 pounds [270 kg]). To develop muscular endurance, increase intensity by decreasing the weight lifted and increasing the number of reps (e.g., the student leg presses 50 pounds [23 kg] for 12 reps; total load is 600 pounds [270 kg]).

Speed of lifting also influences intensity (Faigenbaum & Westcott, 2009), but speed should not be introduced to children. Circuit training that involves multiple repetitions in a specified period should include activities that use the weight of the body, such as push-ups, curl-ups, or other activities not performed on machine weights or free weights. It is better to specify the number of repetitions to perform slowly and in the correct form rather than emphasize how many repetitions to complete in a 30-second time span (Bompa & Carrera, 2005). Be aware, especially with weight machines, that lifting too fast creates momentum that aids the lifting, thereby reducing intensity. The focus of resistance training for children should be on developing form and technique, and not on changing the intensity by varying the speed at which the weight is lifted. Lifting too fast (4 seconds or faster per rep) also increases the likelihood of injury. Faigenbaum and Westcott (2009) recommend 6-second reps (2 seconds of lifting and 4 seconds of lowering) but assert that 8-second reps (4 lifting and 4 lowering) to 14-second reps (10 lifting and 4 lowering) are also effective. Moderate to slow exercise speeds are recommended over fast lifting speeds for a variety of reasons, including longer periods of muscle tension, higher levels of muscle force, decreased levels of momentum, and decreased risk of injury (Faigenbaum & Westcott, 2009).

Table 6.2 Estimating 1RM and Training Loads

Max reps (RM)	1	2	3	4	5	6	7	8	9	10	12	15
% 1 RM	100	95	93	90	87	85	83	80	77	75	67	65
Load (lb or kg)	10	10	9	9	9	9	8	8	8	8	7	7
	20	19	19	18	17	17	17	16	15	15	13	13
	30	29	28	27	26	26	25	24	23	23	20	20
	40	38	37	36	35	34	33	32	31	30	27	26
	50	48	47	45	44	43	42	40	39	38	34	33
	60	57	56	54	52	51	50	48	46	45	40	39
	70	67	65	63	61	60	58	56	54	53	47	46
	80	76	74	72	70	68	66	64	62	60	54	52
	90	86	84	81	78	77	75	72	69	68	60	59
	100	95	93	90	87	85	83	80	77	75	67	65
	110	105	102	99	96	94	91	88	85	83	74	72
	120	114	112	108	104	102	100	96	92	90	80	78
	130	124	121	117	113	111	108	104	100	98	87	85
	140	133	130	126	122	119	116	112	108	105	94	91
	150	143	140	135	131	128	125	120	116	113	101	98
	160	152	149	144	139	136	133	128	123	120	107	104
	170	162	158	153	148	145	141	136	131	128	114	111
	180	171	167	162	157	153	149	144	139	135	121	117
	190	181	177	171	165	162	158	152	146	143	127	124
	200	190	186	180	174	170	166	160	154	150	134	130
	210	200	195	189	183	179	174	168	162	158	141	137
	220	209	205	198	191	187	183	176	169	165	147	143
	230	219	214	207	200	196	191	184	177	173	154	150
	240	228	223	216	209	204	199	192	185	180	161	156
	250	238	233	225	218	213	208	200	193	188	168	163
	260	247	242	234	226	221	206	208	200	195	174	169
	270	257	251	243	235	230	224	216	208	203	181	176
	280	266	260	252	244	238	232	224	216	210	188	182
	290	276	270	261	252	247	241	232	223	218	194	189

Reprinted, by permission, from NSCA, 2008, Resistance training, written by T.R. Baechle, R.W. Earle, and D. Wathem, 2008, *Essentials of strength training and conditioning*, 3rd ed., edited by T.R. Baechle and R.W. Earle (Champaign, IL: Human Kinetics), 397.

TRAINING METHODS FOR MUSCULAR STRENGTH AND ENDURANCE

According to the National Strength and Conditioning Association (NSCA, 2008), when guiding a student to progress from base development to intermediate to advanced development, a 5 to 10% increase in overall load is appropriate for most children. Beginning students, especially elementary students, should primarily engage in circuit training using their own body weight, partners, or light medicine balls, and the volume should be low and intensity very low (Bompa &

Carrera, 2005). Help each child begin slowly and then gradually increase frequency, intensity, or time according to individual needs and goals. Table 6.1 offers general progression guidelines based on age group. A training log such as the one shown in figure 6.2 can help a child see individual progress and feel a sense of accomplishment (see appendix A for a reproducible example).

Body-Weight Training

Although quantifying intensity is difficult, curl-ups, push-ups, and other body-weight exercises all help build muscular strength and endurance with little or no equipment. This type of resistance training is appropriate for the very young student (K–4) or the student who is just beginning resistance-training activity. Primary-grade students or those having difficulty with the curl-up or push-up should perform reverse curl-ups or simply perform the lowering phase of the push-up, holding this position. These activities can be presented in a fun and safe way, and they provide positive health-related benefits to the student. Add interest to them by playing music or creating games such as Around the World from

MUSCULAR STRENGTH AND ENDURANCE TRAINING LOG

Name_____ Date_____

Exercise	Set 1		Set 2		Set 3	
	Weight	Reps	Weight	Reps	Weight	Reps

From NASPE, 2011, *Physical education for lifelong fitness: The Physical Best teacher's guide*, 3rd edition (Champaign, IL: Human Kinetics). Adapted, by permission, from W. Kraemer and S. Fleck, 2005, *Strength training for young athletes*, 2nd ed. (Champaign, IL: Human Kinetics), 58.

Figure 6.2 Sample training log. A reproducible version of this form is available in appendix A.

Adapted, by permission, from W. Kraemer and S. Fleck, 2005, *Strength training for young athletes,* 2nd ed. (Champaign, IL: Human Kinetics), 58.

TRAINING RECOMMENDATIONS

If a child of any age begins a program with no previous experience, you should start the child at lower levels and move him or her to more advanced levels as exercise tolerance, skill, amount of training time, and understanding permit.

- Start slowly—single set, 10 to 15 repetitions, twice per week—allowing students to gain confidence.
- Gradually increase the overload to performing one to three sets, 6 to 15 repetitions, two or three times per week.
- Use 5 to 10% increases in training load (2 to 5 pounds [1 to 2.5 kg]) for most exercises.
- Emphasize full range of motion.
- Emphasize intrinsic enjoyment.

- Have students use personalized logs.
- Share personal success stories.
- Emphasize having fun.
- Incorporate variety in your classroom activities.
- Introduce new exercises.
- Change the training mode.
- Vary the number of sets and repetitions.
- Use multiple goals.
- Do not limit the goals to increasing muscular strength or endurance.
- Teach students about their bodies and safe lifting techniques; aim for development of positive attitudes toward physical activity.

Adapted, by permission, from A. Faigenbaum, 2003, "Youth resistance training," *PCPFS Research Digest* 4(3): 1-8; A. Faigenbaum and W.L. Westcott, 2009, *Youth strength training: Programs for health, fitness and sport* (Champaign, IL: Human Kinetics).

AROUND THE WORLD

Build upper-body strength and reinforce math skills with this activity. Divide students into groups of four to six. Have them each get into push-up position and form a circle with their feet in the center and their heads facing outward. Direct the students in each group to pass a beanbag from one person to the next around the circle. Have each group count the number of passes they can make in 30 seconds and then rest for 30 seconds. Conduct up to three 30-second rounds.

Reprinted from Hichwa 1998.

Right Fielders Are People Too (Hichwa, 1998). (See the sidebar "Around the World.")

Body-weight training is not only for young children. This form of exercise has the advantage of not requiring equipment, which means that it can be an inexpensive part of a muscular fitness training program throughout adulthood. Body-weight training is also less likely to cause injury—and it is the easiest program to take along on vacation! Teaching proper form for a variety of body-weight alternatives to students of all ages, even if your high school is lucky enough to have a state-of-the-art weight room, is recommended.

Ultimately, the goal is for students to take personal responsibility for health-related fitness. Students need to be provided with opportunities to plan and implement their personally designed programs.

Partner-Resisted Training

The partner-resisted training method is an extension of basic body-weight exercises. Although gauging the intensity of this type of training is difficult, this method is helpful when starting a program or living within a tight budget. Using either no equipment or simple equipment such as towels, cords, or elastic bands, partner-resistance exercises isolate individual muscles or muscle groups better than solo body-weight exercises do. Partner-resistance exercises are useful for all age groups from upper elementary grades through adulthood, but especially for those too small to fit standard weight machines (see figures 6.3

and 6.4 in the section "Partners as Resistance" for examples). When selecting partners, match height, weight, and strength levels as closely as possible to ensure safety and ease of working together. Encourage good communication and demand mature, safe behavior. Partners should also help each other maintain correct technique and high motivation by monitoring and encouraging each other.

Alternative Methods of Training

Resistance band training is appropriate for upper elementary and older students, and medicine ball training can be adapted to all ages, including primary-grade children using a variety of weighted balls. Band training involves using surgical tubing, rubber cords, or bands manufactured specifically for muscular strength and endurance training, such as the Exertube, Dyna Band, Flexi-Cord, or Thera-Band. Use thicker tubing for greater resistance and thinner tubing for less resistance. In addition, a student can adjust resistance by prestretching the cord more or less. Although a user cannot measure intensity precisely, this method is an inexpensive, effective way to expand your muscular fitness training program. An added advantage is that spotting is rarely required for such exercises. Figure 6.5 on page 106 in the section "Rubber Cord Standing Chest Press" shows an example of resistance band exercises.

Medicine balls can be purchased in various weights and sizes. Faigenbaum and Westcott (2009) suggest three benefits in using medicine balls in your program. First, this type of training uses dynamic movements that can be performed either slowly or rapidly. Second, the balls can be used to develop the upper body, lower body, and trunk using catching and throwing movements. The most important reason listed is to develop the core, which includes the abdominal muscles and the hip and lower-back musculature. Besides being an effective avenue of increasing muscular fitness in children, these methods of conditioning involve multiple students simultaneously participating and are relatively cheap to purchase (Westcott, 2003). Figure 6.6 on page 107 in the section "Medicine Ball Chest Pass" shows an example of an exercise that can be performed with a medicine ball.

PARTNERS AS RESISTANCE: ELBOW, FLEX, AND EXTEND

- **Position**: Partners stand facing each other, arms at sides, elbows bent to right angles, palms down.

- **Part 1**: Partner B places hands on top of partner A's hands and presses down. Partner A resists but allows elbows to extend until arm is straight. Rest for 10 seconds.

- **Return motion**: Partner A flexes elbow while partner B resists but allows elbows to bend to right angle in 10 counts. Rest for 10 seconds.

- **Reverse**: Partner B flexes elbows while partner A's hands are on top. Repeat the exercise.

Figure 6.3 Partners provide resistance in the elbow flex and extend exercise.

Reprinted, by permission, from K. McConnell, C.B. Corbin, and D. Dale, 2005, *Fitness for life activity and vocabulary cards,* 5th edition (Champaign, IL: Human Kinetics).

PARTNERS AS RESISTANCE: KNEE FLEX

- **Position**: Partner B lies face down on a bench or mat with knees hanging over the edge. If on a mat, partner B's left knee should be bent to a 45-degree angle. Partner A kneels at partner B's feet and loops a towel over partner B's left ankle with the ends downward. Keep towel pull perpendicular to the leg.

- **Part 1**: Partner A maintains resistance on the towel as partner B flexes the left knee as far as possible. Rest for 10 seconds and lower the leg.

- **Part 2**: Repeat with the right leg. Repeat again on each leg and rest again.

- **Reverse**: Change places and repeat all knee exercises.

Figure 6.4 Partners provide resistance in the knee flex exercise.

Reprinted, by permission, from K. McConnell, C.B. Corbin, and D. Dale, 2005, *Fitness for life activity and vocabulary cards,* 5th edition (Champaign, IL: Human Kinetics).

RUBBER CORD STANDING CHEST PRESS

Muscles

- Pectoralis major, anterior deltoid, triceps

Procedure

- Stand with your feet about shoulder-width apart and the rubber cord wrapped around the back of your shoulders.
- Grasp the ends of the cord firmly and place both hands (palms facing the floor) in front of your shoulders with your elbows flexed.
- Slowly straighten your elbows until you fully extend both arms. Then return to starting position and repeat.

Technique Tips

- Exhale during the pushing phase of the exercise and inhale during the return phase.
- Do not twist or arch your body.

Figure 6.5 Student performs a chest press using a resistance band.

Reprinted, by permission, from A. Faigenbaum and W. Westcott, 2009, *Youth strength training: Programs for health, fitness, and sport* (Champaign, IL: Human Kinetics), 103.

Kettle bells have been around for decades and have gained popularity again in recent years. These ball-shaped weights range in size and weight. The reason for the boost in popularity in recent years is that the training focuses on whole-body conditioning. Lifting and controlling a kettle bell forces the muscles in the entire body (especially the core) to contract together, building strength and stability at the same time. You must train your students to use kettle bells correctly; otherwise, serious injury could occur.

Stability balls are another way for students to develop muscular strength, endurance, and balance. A 45-centimeter ball accommodates prepubescent children's height and allows them to use the ball constructively. One exercise for each body part and three or four core stability exercises are considered appropriate for children between 8 and 12 years of age (Goldberg & Twist, 2007).

Weight Training

A program may use free or machine weights or both, depending on goals, equipment availability, and space in which to conduct a weight-training program. Introduce exercises one at a time by discussing the purpose of each one, demonstrating correct technique, and outlining ranges of appropriate weight loads, repetitions, and speed. In addition, relate these factors to intensity,

MEDICINE BALL CHEST PASS

Muscles

- Chest, arms

Procedure

- Stand erect while holding a medicine ball at chest level with both hands.
- Step forward and press the ball off your chest.

Technique Tips

- Exhale as you push the ball off your chest.
- Keep your torso erect after you release the ball. Do not lean forward.
- A partner can stand about 10 feet (3 m) away and catch the ball. Over time the students can increase the distance between partners. The greater the distance is, the greater the effort that is required.
- For variety, you can perform this exercise while kneeling on the floor. Keep your body straight as you push the ball off your chest.

Figure 6.6 Medicine ball chest pass.

Reprinted, by permission, from A. Faigenbaum and W. Westcott, 2009, *Youth strength training: Programs for health, fitness, and sport* (Champaign, IL: Human Kinetics), 117.

program goals, and individual goals. Follow the safety and health guidelines provided earlier in this chapter to ensure a safe and effective weight-training program. If weight training is in addition to or in place of other forms of training, teach students alternative exercises that target the same muscle or muscle group. Likewise, if a program relies heavily on machine use, demonstrate the corresponding free-weight exercises to broaden the chances that students will use the exercises outside of and after their school program. Figure 6.7*a* shows the biceps curl as performed on a machine, and figure 6.7*b* shows its free-weight alternative (see page 108). Most weight training using machine weights and barbells should be reserved for postpubescent children. Table 6.3 on page 109 provides suggestions that are appropriate exercises for the prepubescent child (Bompa &

Carrera, 2005). Appendix C contains illustrations of these exercises.

ADDRESSING MOTOR SKILLS THROUGH MUSCULAR STRENGTH AND ENDURANCE ACTIVITIES

Simply put, a strong, more enduring muscle can do what it's called on to do reliably and accurately. Therefore, increasing muscular strength and endurance can enhance performance. The National Strength and Conditioning Association (Faigenbaum, 2007) states that children cannot "play" themselves into shape, and that preseason

a   b

Figure 6.7   Biceps curl performed (*a*) on a machine and (*b*) with free weights.

and in-season training time should be supplemented with a resistance-training program to enhance sports and recreational activities. Most research in this area indicates that training adaptations are specific to the movement pattern, velocity of movement, contraction type, and contraction force (Faigenbaum, 2003). These fast movements (power) are generally contraindicated when weightlifting, but children can engage in plyometric exercises (hops, jumps, and throws) if intensity and volume are carefully monitored. Faigenbaum and Chu (2001) also suggest caution when using plyometric training. They strongly suggest a solid base of strength training before plyometric training and suggest beginning **plyometrics** using low-intensity drills.

You can have students perform motor skills to increase muscular strength and endurance. For example, young children enjoy playing tag games using various locomotor skills. These games increase the muscular endurance of the leg muscles. Students in the fourth grade and up may enjoy team-building activities that require arm strength to conquer, such as the circle of teamwork. This activity requires a group of students to stand in a circle, interlock their arms, and stretch the circle out by walking backward; then at the tightest point, the students simultaneously lean backward. Such activities help students see how specific strength-building activities (e.g., calisthenics and weightlifting) help a person enjoy real life. Students also see the practical ways that

Table 6.3 Muscular Fitness Exercises*

Exercise	Muscles worked
Dumbbell side raise	Shoulders
Dumbbell curl	Biceps
Dumbbell shoulder press	Shoulders, trapezius
Dumbbell fly	Chest, shoulders
Medicine ball chest throw	Shoulders, triceps
Medicine ball zigzag throw	Arms, shoulders
Medicine ball twist throw	Arms, trunk, oblique abdominals
Medicine ball forward overhead throw	Chest, shoulders, arms, abdominals
Medicine ball scoop throw	Ankles, knees, hip extensors, arms, shoulders, back
Abdominal crunch	Abdominals, hip flexors
Medicine ball back roll	Abdominals, hip flexors
Medicine ball side pass relay	Oblique abdominals, shoulders
Trunk twist	Oblique abdominals
Single-leg back raise	Hip extensors, spine
Chest raise and clap	Lower back
Seated back extension	Back, shoulders
Dodge the rope	Calves, knee extensors

*See appendix C for descriptions and photos of these exercises.

Adapted from T. Bompa, 2000, *Total training for young champions* (Champaign, IL: Human Kinetics), 115-123.

enjoyable activities build muscular strength and endurance. Students should be helped to see the connections among the many physical activities in their school program as well as among community-based physical activities.

SAFETY GUIDELINES FOR MUSCULAR STRENGTH AND ENDURANCE ACTIVITIES

In the past, many fitness and health experts, as well as parents, have feared that strength training is dangerous for children. They pointed to the possibility of harming bone development or stunting growth, but research does not support these fears—as long as the child strength-trains in a developmentally appropriate program that emphasizes safe limits and includes adequate adult supervision. The American College of Sports Medicine (2003) and the National Strength and Conditioning Association (2008) have all taken the position that weight training can benefit children if it is properly prescribed and supervised. Specifically, the NSCA asserts that strength can be improved through training even in the very young child and that strength training can begin at any age (NSCA, 2008). Such training includes using the child's body weight in calisthenics (such as curl-ups, push-ups, and the like) or performing high repetitions with light weights or resistance bands. Lifting maximal weights, however, should be delayed until all the long bones have finished growing at about 17 years of age (older in boys).

To determine the number of reps that a child should do per set, have the child count how many total reps (up to 15) he or she can do with correct form. Then use half of that number as the set size. When performing this set becomes easy, the child can work up to two sets and then three, applying the principles of progression and overload. Retest for maximum reps when performing three sets becomes too easy. Kraemer and Fleck (2005) recommend no less than two minutes of rest between weightlifting sets if strength is the goal, unless an older student (middle school and above) is ready for more specialized training, depending on maturity and fitness levels. Because cartilage is not as strong as bone, the **growth plates** (section of cartilage at the end of long bones in children) are an area that can be highly susceptible to injury. If children are taught how to strength-train properly and use appropriate training loads, the risk appears to be minimal (NSCA, 2008).

As previously stated, elementary prepubescent children should engage in circuit training using their own body weight, partners, or light medicine balls, and the volume should be low and intensity very low (Bompa & Carrera, 2005). If properly instructed and supervised, older elementary level children can use resistance bands and light free weights safely. Examples of exercises using

free weights and medicine balls are shown in figure 6.8, *a* through *c*. Make sure that students understand the safety issues involved in partner exercises and that no horse play will be tolerated. Students must also understand that they will not build the large muscles that some older postpubescent students and adults are capable of building. Physiologically speaking, this goal is simply not realistic. Middle and high school students can and should participate in resistive muscular strength and endurance activities that involve the use of free weights if they are able to do so. Activities do not need to be limited to dumbbell and barbell weight-room activities. Resistance bands, body-weight exercises, homemade equipment (e.g., plastic milk jugs filled with sand), and so on may provide more opportunities for greater simultaneous participation.

One of the most important safety considerations is to individualize the resistance-training program. In addition, encourage children to compete against themselves and not each other in terms of how much they can lift. The empha-

Figure 6.8 (*a*) Biceps curl using light free weights (tennis balls), (*b*) triceps extension using a free weight, and (*c*) front squat using a medicine ball.

sis should be on the amount of weight lifted 6 to 15 times and not on how much weight can be lifted in a single lift. For all children—kindergarten through high school seniors—setting realistic goals and focusing on correct technique are important safety precautions. To satisfy the competitive spirit in some children, Kraemer and Fleck (2005) suggest holding correct technique contests in which weight load plays no role in the final calculations (figure 6.9).

Finally, if the school has a weight room, ensure that it is set up so that traffic flows through it efficiently and that the space between stations is sufficient. Kraemer and Fleck (2005) recommend a minimum of 5 feet (150 cm) between machines and adequate room for free weights to be dropped suddenly if need be. If possible, use machines instead of free weights for overhead movements such as those required in the bench press; reserve the bench press for older high school students.

Always use spotters for all free-weight exercises, even though some light exercises may not require a spotter. Using a spotter is a good habit for students to develop, leaving no room for incorrect decisions regarding spotting. Students can work in pairs, spotting each other and monitoring correct technique.

Above all, to provide a safe and beneficial muscular fitness program for children, do not use a program designed for adults—even with adolescents. Modify and individualize progress slowly, and reassess the safety and effectiveness of the program frequently.

SUMMARY

By following the guidelines outlined in this chapter, students can be taught the importance of muscular strength and endurance training in safe and effective ways. Teachers must remember that the best way to keep each child safe is to build in individual choices and help each child set realistic goals. Never push a child to lift a heavier weight than he or she has trained for or to perform "just one more rep." Instead, motivate children to participate and progress by creating an enjoyable and supportive class atmosphere,

---

DUMBBELL PRESS TECHNIQUE

Resistance Used

Correct form is essential to avoid injury and get the most from the dumbbell press exercise. Start with a low weight and increase the resistance only if you can maintain proper technique.

Starting Position

Elbows are straight (dumbbells positioned straight above the shoulders); feet are flat on the floor or flat on the end of the bench; buttocks and shoulders touch bench; dumbbells face horizontal to the body (palms up).

Points available: 0-6
Points earned: _____

Lowering (Eccentric) Phase

Descent of dumbbells is controlled; elbows are out to the side; forearms are perpendicular to the floor. Dumbbells are lowered down and a little to the side until the elbows are slightly below the shoulders; roll the shoulder blades back and down like they are being pinched together and raise the chest; feet stay flat on the floor; head stays still.

Points available: 0-7
Points earned: _____

Up (Concentric) Phase

Elbows are out to the sides; both arms straighten at the same controlled speed; motion is smooth and continuous; elbows do not lock; shoulder blades do not rise off the bench; head stays still; feet stay flat on floor.

Points available: 0-9
Points earned: _____

Finishing Position

Same position as starting position.

Points available: 0-3
Points earned: _____

Total points available: 0-25
Total points earned: _____

Technique Tips

- Inhale as you lower the weights and exhale as you lift them.
- A spotter should be behind the lifter's head and should assist the lifter with getting the dumbbells into place and remove them when finished. Impress on young weight trainers the importance of having a spotter during the exercise because the lifter presses the dumbbells over the face, neck, and chest.
- Practice the timing and technique of this exercise using minimal (2- to 5-pound [1 to 2.5 kg]) dumbbells.
- Use only an amount of weight that allows you to maintain proper form and technique throughout the full range of motion.
- Avoid dropping dumbbells when finished. Muscles are under considerable tension and dropping them will release the tension rapidly, potentially causing injury.
- Let your back keep a natural arch so that you have minor gap between the bench and your lower back.

From NASPE, 2011, *Physical education for lifelong fitness: The Physical Best teacher's guide*, 3rd edition (Champaign, IL: Human Kinetics).

Figure 6.9 Correct technique is vital for weight training, so focus on technique during instruction and during assessment. A reproducible version of this form is available in appendix A.

TRAINING A STUDENT TO SPOT A PARTNER

The **spotting** techniques recommended by experts vary, but everyone in the weight-training community agrees on one important point: Proper spotting is vital to the overall safety of the person lifting the weight and the effectiveness of incorporating the FITT guidelines. Although this chapter is not geared specifically to weight training, but rather to health-related physical activity that suggests weight training merely as one of many methods, proper spotting must be used when training your students with resistive weights. Several good books on weight training that incorporate spotting techniques are available, in particular, *Weight Training: Steps to Success, Second Edition*, by Thomas Baechle and Barney Groves (1998).

rewarding effort and correct technique rather than physical prowess. The *Physical Best Activity Guides* offer a variety of age-appropriate muscular strength and endurance activities. Resistance training can be extremely interesting and rewarding. When selecting activities for students, keep in mind that the ultimate goal of health-related physical fitness education is to produce graduates who take personal responsibility for each area of health-related fitness as a way of life.

Flexibility

Brian Mosier

Students may have little or no knowledge of safe flexibility training. They may have learned much of what they do know (correct and incorrect knowledge) by mimicking role models at home or in sport or recreation settings. Teacher tasks should educate or reeducate students in safe and correct stretching techniques, as well as inform them about the many health-related benefits associated with good flexibility. Specifically, a well-designed flexibility program (following the principles of training described in chapter 3) aids in muscle relaxation; improves overall health-related fitness, posture, and body symmetry; may relieve muscle cramps and soreness; and reduces the risk of injury—all of which make physical activity of all types easier and safer to do (see figure 7.1 on page 114). In addition, stretching can relieve emotional stress, increase feelings of well-being, and help prepare the body to move from resting to exercising more smoothly. This chapter covers basic information regarding flexibility and stretching techniques that students should know before leaving your program. They can apply this information to achieve and maintain good flexibility for life.

Chapter Contents

a   *b*

Figure 7.1   Sample stretches that can help students improve flexibility.

DEFINITIONS OF FLEXIBILITY CONCEPTS

Flexibility is a term used to characterize the range of motion (ROM) of a single joint or a series of joints (ACSM, 2006a). Children may not understand the concept of joint movement through a full ROM, but they will understand how well they bend and twist. For younger learners, an activity such as "head, shoulders, knees, and toes" may be used to demonstrate bending and twisting at different levels. For older students, you can use Silly Putty to demonstrate flexibility by showing the children how it does not bend and stretch when it is cold in contrast to how it stretches and elongates (like muscles) when it is warm. Evaluating students on how well they can perform the Fitnessgram back-saver sit and reach or shoulder stretch will also teach the importance of flexibility.

Optimal flexibility allows a joint or group of joints to move freely and efficiently. Too much laxity or hypermobility in a joint is not healthy and may lead to injury. **Laxity** refers to the degree of abnormal motion of a given joint. Abnormal joint laxity means that the ligaments connecting bone to bone can no longer provide stability to the joint. **Hypermobility** refers to excess ROM at a joint (Heyward, 2002). Both conditions may predispose a person to injury. People with hypermobility should not be allowed to stretch into the extremes of ROM and should try to maintain as much joint stability as possible (ACSM, 2006b).

There are two types of flexibility. The first, **static flexibility**, relates to the range of motion about a joint with no emphasis on speed (Alter, 2004). The limits of a person's static flexibility are determined by his or her tolerance to the stretched position (Knudson, Magnusson, & McHugh, 2000). The second, **dynamic flexibility**, refers to the ability to use a range of joint movement in the performance of a physical activity at a normal or rapid speed (Alter, 2004). Dynamic flexibility exercises are commonly used in sport-specific movements. Dynamic flexibility does not involve a bouncing-type movement, which is characteristic of a ballistic stretch, but rather a controlled elongation of a specific muscle group (Faigenbaum & McFarland, 2007).

TYPES OF STRETCHING

Stretching is a method used to maintain or increase one's flexibility. There are many types of stretching. From a safety perspective, static stretching and controlled dynamic stretching should be emphasized in physical education instruction. Static stretching provides the greatest benefits while having the least negative effect with respect to injury. Experts now recognize dynamic stretching as a safe option to ballistic stretching. The most important aspect of dynamic stretching is to perform the movement in a controlled manner through the ROM (Corbin, Welk, Corbin, & Welk, 2009). Ballistic stretching should not be performed in physical education class. Knudson, Magnusson, and McHugh (2000) report that the ballistic movements may be related more to speed, coordination, strength, but not flexibility.

The types of stretching that foster flexibility are classified as follows (ACSM, 2006b):

- In the **active stretch (unassisted)**, the person stretching provides the force of the stretch and assistance comes only from the opposing (antagonist) muscle (e.g., trunk lift, as shown in figure 7.2 on page 116).

- In the **passive stretch (assisted)**, the person, a partner, gravity, or an implement provides the force of the stretch (see figure 7.3 on page 116).

- A **static stretch** is a slow, sustained stretch that is held for 10 to 30 seconds. The person stretches the muscular–tendon unit to the point where mild discomfort is felt and then backs off slightly, holding the stretch at a point just before discomfort occurs. This stretch is generally considered safe, and it does not rely on cooperation from a partner. In physical education classes, especially at the elementary level, this type of stretching is preferred. The advantages of static stretching include decreased possibility of exceeding the normal ROM and less muscle soreness (Fredette, 2001).

- **Ballistic stretching** involves moving quickly, bouncing, or using momentum to produce the stretch. Like PNF (see description later in list), it elicits muscle soreness (Fredette, 2001). This type of stretch is often viewed as necessary for sport movements and should be reserved for coaching or conditioning athletes and not used in general physical education classes. An example of ballistic stretching is bouncing down repeatedly to touch the toes.

- **Dynamic stretching**, not to be confused with ballistic stretching, involves moving parts of your body and gradually increasing ROM, speed of movement, or both. People tend to use the terms *dynamic* and *ballistic* interchangeably, but dynamic stretching is different from ballistic stretching in that it avoids the bouncy, jerky type of movement. Examples of dynamic stretches include controlled leg and arm swings that safely go through the student's ROM.

- **PNF (proprioceptive neuromuscular facilitation)** is a static stretch using combinations of the active and passive stretching techniques (see figure 7.4 on page 117). This specialized static stretch uses a contraction–relaxation combination of movements, "taking advantage of reflexes and neuromuscular principles to relax the muscles being stretched" (Knudson, Magnusson, & McHugh, 2000). PNF often yields the greatest improvements in flexibility. PNF has also been shown to be more difficult to teach and to perform, and to yield greater muscle soreness (Fredette, 2001). The greatest changes in ROM generally occur after the first repetition, and to achieve lasting changes in ROM, PNF stretching needs to be performed once or twice per week (Sharman, Cresswell, & Riek, 2006). This type of stretch should not be performed by children 6 to 10 years old, but it can be performed by pubescent or postpubescent students (Bompa, 2000) or those who have developed a solid base of training and are undergoing formal athletic conditioning with help from a qualified coach. A partner is usually required for PNF. Safety, proper instruction, and responsibility are key issues in performing this type of stretch; injury may result when children are not responsible, when they fail to listen to the cues of their partners (thereby forcing a stretch), or when they incorrectly perform a stretch.

Figure 7.2   Example of active stretching.

Figure 7.3   Example of passive stretching.

PNF GASTROCNEMIUS STRETCH

- Pull a towel toward you until you feel mild tension.
- Hold the towel in position and try to point the toes against the towel resistance for several seconds.
- Relax and then pull toward you again.

Figure 7.4 Example of PNF stretching.

Yogic stretching involves unique stretching maneuvers that are mainly static and focus primarily on the trunk musculature (ACSM, 2006b). This form of stretching originated from yoga, which is a form of abstract meditation and mental concentration that is approximately 3,000 years old (Sherman et al., 2005). Many forms of yoga have become frequently practiced in private studios and health and fitness clubs, and have been infused into K through 12 curriculums. Although achieving the union of mind, body, and spirit is difficult to evaluate, data have supported changes on a physical and psychological level. Yoga practice can result in decreased stress, improved strength, and improved flexibility over a relatively short period (Cowen & Adams, 2005). Care should be used when considering yogic stretching in physical education because some extreme asanas (postures) may lead to an increased chance of injury.

PHYSICAL BEST'S POSITION

Many experts caution that participants should perform at least five minutes of low-intensity aerobic fitness activity to warm muscles before performing any stretching. We recommend that teachers ensure that their students take this simple precaution before beginning flexibility activities (ACSM, 2006b).

BENEFITS OF FLEXIBILITY

The specificity principle states that the observed range of motion at each joint is specific to the flexibility exercises performed at each joint; therefore, the benefits that follow apply only to the muscles and joints used in a stretching program. Alter (2004) states the following benefits of increased flexibility:

▶ Decreased muscle tension and increased relaxation.

▶ Greater ease of movement.

▶ Improved coordination.

▶ Increased range of motion.

▶ Possibility of reduced injury risk (although normal flexibility is essential for good muscular fitness, greater than normal levels of flexibility fail to show a reduction in the risk of injury).

▶ Better body awareness and postural alignment.

▶ Improved circulation and air exchange.

▶ Smoother and easier contractions.

▶ May relieve muscle soreness.

▶ Prevention of low back pain and other spinal problems, if normal flexibility levels are maintained.

▶ Improved personal appearance and self-image.

▶ Improved development and maintenance of motor skills.

ATHLETIC PERFORMANCE AND FLEXIBILITY

Does increased flexibility improve athletic performance? The consensus appears to be that the performance benefits are not as great as once thought. Some evidence suggests that less static flexibility may actually benefit performance when it comes to running economy (Jones, 2002) and that static stretching before performing some muscular activities may lead to a decrease in strength and muscular performance (Nieman, 2008; Shrier, 2004). The performance-enhancing potential of static stretching is presently lacking (Thacker, Gilchrist, & Stroup, 2004). Therefore, children should perhaps perform controlled dynamic exercises during the warm-up period and static stretching during the cool-down period (Faigenbaum et al., 2005). Until more research confirms these recent findings, teachers should encourage their students to maintain normal flexibility and range of motion and should teach them the importance of a well-rounded fitness program that includes flexibility.

Flexibility is for everyone, and regardless of ability or disability, everyone can learn to stretch and benefit from improved range of motion. All these benefits contribute to the overall health and well-being of the individual and affirm the importance of including flexibility activities in your physical education daily lessons (see the *Physical Best Activity Guides* for specific examples).

FACTORS AFFECTING FLEXIBILITY

No matter what factors affect flexibility, most people can improve their flexibility through appropriate and regular stretching (at least two or three days per week). Keep in mind, however, that many factors influence the amount of flexibility observed or measured at each joint. Emphasize to students that irregular participation in a flexibility program also yields poor results. The old adage "Use it or lose it" applies here. The following are some factors that affect flexibility:

▶ *Muscle temperature* affects muscle elasticity, or the ability of the muscle to stretch beyond its normal resting length and then return to its prestretched length at the completion of the exercise.

▶ *Age and gender* affect flexibility. Children are generally more flexible than adults. In addition, some changes occur between the primary grades and high school—flexibility remains stable or gradually declines to about age 12 and then increases to peak flexibility at about ages 15 to 18 years old (Knudson, Magnusson, & McHugh, 2000). Females are generally more flexible than males (Alter, 2004). In addition, research shows that maintaining a good flexibility plan across the life span may limit or reduce the natural changes in elasticity and compliance of muscle tissue (ACSM, 2006b; Knudson, Magnusson, & McHugh, 2000).

▶ *Tissue interference*, such as excess body fat or well-developed musculature, is another factor that affects flexibility. This constraint may also include bone and joint limitations such as in the elbow joint where ROM beyond 180 degrees is limited by bone. Do not allow tissue interference to prevent your students from improving flexibility. High body fat is generally a result of inactivity, and the student with well-developed musculature as a limiting factor (usually not a factor until late high school, if at all) may simply be lacking a flexibility exercise program. These students, if taught, can develop and maintain adequate flexibility (Heyward, 2002).

▶ *Genetics* can have an effect on flexibility. Flexibility can be limited or excessive (hypermobility) because of a person's genetic makeup. Even so, the person must use the joints regularly to develop and maintain flexibility. If this is not done, the person's ROM may be adversely affected.

Other factors that may limit flexibility include pain, poor coordination and strength during active movement, and extensibility of the **muscular–tendon unit** (i.e., tension in muscles). Note that most of these limitations can be reversed and stated as benefits of flexibility (decreased pain after an injury, improved coordination, and reduced tension). Consider each limitation for each individual when designing a flexibility program (Alter, 2004; Knudson, Magnusson, & McHugh, 2000).

Although most of the limitations can be overcome in a well-designed, appropriately progressive flexibility program, pain should never be ignored, and limitations caused by bone or joint structures may require special attention and individualization. Certain diseases (e.g., muscular dystrophy and cerebral palsy) limit flexibility, and for many of these conditions, you should consult with an adapted physical educator or the child's physician to inquire about appropriate stretching activities.

TEACHING GUIDELINES FOR FLEXIBILITY

Flexibility is one of the five components of health-related fitness (Corbin, Welk, Corbin, & Welk, 2009). Flexibility should be taught as a separate form of fitness and not just incorporated into a warm-up or cool-down session. Flexibility training is an area of health-related fitness that improves rapidly. Anyone can learn to stretch correctly, and everyone can attain the benefits of improved flexibility. First, select the type of stretch that meets the needs of the lesson. Allow students to participate in selecting the various

flexibility exercises. The exercises may be completed in a warm-up or cool-down, or incorporated throughout the lesson (activities are available in the *Physical Best Activity Guides*). After you have completed proper instruction for a repertoire of exercises for the total body, you can use station cards, modify the warm-up or cool-down, or have students select the specific exercise to meet their individual goals.

In the physical education setting, the static stretch is generally preferred and considered among the safest methods for enhancing ROM. Recent studies (Faigenbaum et al., 2005, 2006) show benefits of adding controlled dynamic stretching into the curriculum. A program of planned stretches (like those shown in figure 7.5 on page 120) does not take much class time, and it is generally easy to ensure that each individual in a large group of students is performing them correctly.

Establish a regular schedule of flexibility fitness lessons and stretching in your classes; include definitions and basic concepts regarding the FITT guidelines and safety precautions. This approach will not only teach students the importance of stretching but also allow integration of flexibility concepts into all aspects of health-related fitness. This is also the time to explain the relationship between flexibility exercises performed in class and the back-saver sit-and-reach assessment, the shoulder stretch assessment, and the trunk extensor strength and flexibility assessment performed during fitness assessment. As with all areas of health-related fitness, conducting periodic assessments will let students know where they are and help them set goals on how to improve.

Just as in weight training, proper form and technique are important for flexibility training. Students who stretch improperly and place excess stress on their joints and connective tissues increase their risk of injury during activities designed to improve health and well-being. Also, emphasize that flexibility training, either with or without a partner, is no place for horseplay because injury may result. This caution is especially important when using PNF or partner stretching. Stress safety and slow, gradual, individualized progression when teaching children about flexibility (see the sidebar "Partner-Resisted Hamstring Stretch" and figure 7.6 on page 121).

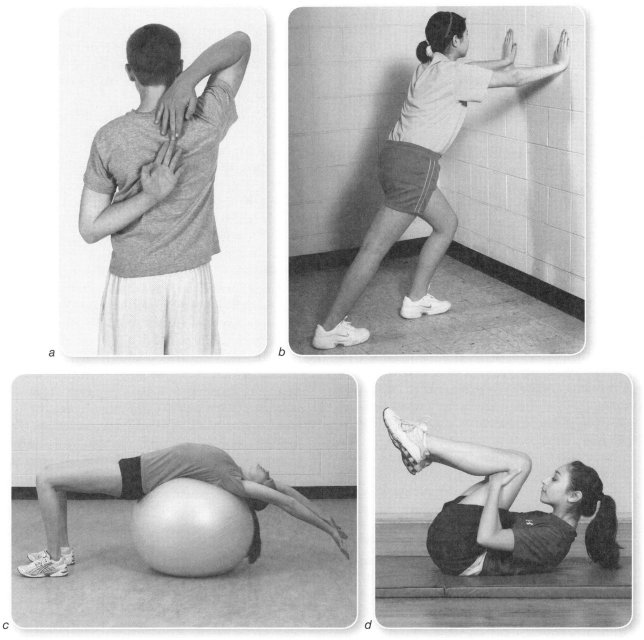

Figure 7.5 Examples of (*a* and *b*) static stretches and (*c* and *d*) dynamic stretches.

Never make flexibility training competitive; instead, as with muscular strength training, emphasize correct technique and personal bests.

Two major advantages of teaching flexibility are (1) that it does not require much equipment and (2) that many different areas can provide sufficient space for conducting the program. For example, students can stretch in a gymnasium, on a field, on the blacktop, in a classroom, or, if traffic is sparse, in a hallway. Outdoors mats or parachutes can be placed on the ground to protect clothing. Visual aids such as posters, task cards, and pictures of schoolmates performing stretches can help guide students working independently at stations. See appendix D for details about questionable exercise and their safer alternatives, complete with photos showing each. As a result of instructional time spent working on flexibility, students should understand the definition of flexibility, ways to stretch safely, the importance of maintaining flexibility across the life span, and the methods available to improve and assess flexibility.

PARTNER-RESISTED HAMSTRING STRETCH

Figure 7.6 Partners must slowly and safely work together to achieve a proper partner stretch.

1. The stretcher lies supine and lifts her thigh to flex her hip to 90 degrees with the knee bent.

2. The partner should stabilize the thigh in this position while the stretcher straightens the raised leg as far as possible, without pain. This action lengthens the hamstrings to the pain-free end of range. The straight leg should remain flat on the mat.

3. The partner can offer resistance to the isometric contraction of the hamstrings, at the same time making sure that the stretcher keeps her hips flat on the mat. The partner may need to work with the stretcher on body awareness until she is able to stabilize her hips properly before performing this stretch.

4. The partner directs the stretcher to begin slowly to attempt to push her heel toward the floor, bending the knee, which isometrically contracts the hamstrings.

5. After the isometric push, the stretcher relaxes and inhales deeply. During this time, she maintains the leg in the starting position.

Adapted, by permission, from R.E. McAtee and J. Charland, 1999, *Facilitated stretching*, 2nd ed. (Champaign, IL: Human Kinetics), 34.

PRINCIPLES OF TRAINING

All students should learn how to apply the principles of training to flexibility. These principles are discussed in chapter 3, as well as in each chapter related to the health-related fitness components. Applying these training principles helps students improve flexibility and implement the FITT guidelines (discussed later in the chapter) in their programs.

Overload, Progression, Specificity, Regularity, and Individuality

The principle of overload states that to adapt and improve flexibility, the muscular–tendon unit must be stretched until tension (point of mild discomfort) is felt; the person then backs off slightly and holds the stretch at a point just before discomfort occurs. The principle of progression calls for gradually increasing the amount of time that each stretch is held, starting for 10 seconds and building up to at least 30 seconds. Your students should not use the progression principle to increase the load (tension) placed on the muscle, because they should stretch a joint only through the limits of normal ROM (ACSM, 2006b). If they stretch to the point of mild discomfort and then back off slightly, they will overload the muscle at the proper tension. The stretch should feel tight, but not painful. Above all, dispel the "No pain, no gain" notion. Flexibility training should not be painful (see "Safety Guidelines for Flexibility Activities" later in this chapter). Specificity and regularity, as in other areas of health-related fitness, state that to increase flexibility of a particular area, a person must perform exercises for a specific muscle or muscle group and do it on a regular basis. The ACSM (2006a) recommends that flexibility exercises be done a minimum of two to three days per week and up to five to seven days per week. According to the regularity principle, any improvements in flexibility will be lost if the person stops performing flexibility exercises. As stated in other chapters that discuss the principles of training, each student should have individual goals based on need, physical limitations, or personal motivation.

FITT Guidelines

Table 7.1 provides information on how to manipulate time and type based on the FITT guidelines when performing stretching exercises (partner-assisted and PNF stretching). The recommended *frequency* for flexibility training is daily (two to three times per week minimum but preferably daily) to be able to attain the maximum benefits. Increasing the number of flexibility sessions per week from three to seven is also a method to increase the overload placed on the muscle. As previously mentioned, the *intensity* for all flexibility exercises should be to the point just before discomfort occurs (stretch to the point of slight discomfort and back off slightly). Intensity is an extremely important factor in a safe and effective flexibility-training program. A static stretch that goes beyond the point of mild discomfort (to pain) will not only decrease your students' desire to stretch but also increase the likelihood of injury. *Time* refers to how long the stretch is held. Recommendations range from 10 seconds through 1 minute. The American College of Sports Medicine (2006a) proposes that a stretch be held for a minimum of 10 seconds and progress to 30 seconds. (Note that a student

Table 7.1   FITT Guidelines Applied to Flexibility

	Guidelines
Frequency	Two to three days per week, preferably daily and after a warm-up to raise muscle temperature.
Intensity	Slow elongation of the muscle to the point of mild discomfort and back off slightly.
Time	Up to two to four stretches per muscle or muscle group. Hold each stretch for 10 to 30 seconds. Always warm up properly before stretching.
Type	The preferred stretch for the physical education class is controlled stretching for all muscles or muscle groups.

Adapted from Knudson, Magnusson, and McHugh 2000; American College of Sports Medicine 2006a.

should always begin holding a stretch for a short period and gradually progress to the 30-second period.) *Type* refers to the kind of stretching used to develop flexibility, such as static, PNF, partner, or dynamic stretches.

Before students begin any flexibility exercise, be sure to provide proper instruction and have students perform an active warm-up before stretching. Younger or less experienced students should learn the basic static stretches that increase flexibility of major muscle groups, whereas older or more experienced students may be ready for a greater variety of sport-specific stretches and advanced stretching techniques.

Bompa (2000) suggests laying a strong foundation of static stretches when children are 6 to 10 years of age, which he terms the initiation phase of training. He also suggests using various stages of maturation as a guide to indicate when it is appropriate to perform the three basic types of stretching (static, dynamic, and PNF). Remember that PNF and partner stretching require extensive instruction and mature, responsible students; these types of stretches may pose safety threats if not performed correctly.

Teach students to follow the FITT guidelines using controlled, steady stretching, holding each stretch only to the point of mild tension, not pain—regardless of what they have been told in the past. Students should be empowered to individualize each stretch, doing only what is comfortable for them, not what a classmate can do. Teach students that ballistic stretching is appropriate only in certain sport situations and then only if done correctly.

If a student is too flexible (displays hypermobility), has abnormal ROM (laxity), severely lacks flexibility, or has other unusual bone or joint structural limitations, and such an anomaly seems to cause serious performance or safety concerns, meet with the student and parents. Suggest that the parents and student visit a trained health care professional for further evaluation.

ADDRESSING MOTOR SKILLS THROUGH FLEXIBILITY ACTIVITIES

Naturally, a student who can move through a full range of motion (ROM) is more likely to be ready to learn and perform motor skills correctly. Likewise, a student with limited ROM will have a more difficult time mastering the same motor skill. The specificity principle applies here: Students who want to be able to punt a football or perform a high kick in soccer must have good hip and leg flexibility to be successful. Good flexibility, then, enhances motor skill development. Address motor skills through flexibility activities and vice versa by pointing out the connections between the stretches being taught and the motor skill activities that students practice in class. When students make the connection between flexibility and the physical activities that they are engaging in, they will be more likely to continue working on enhancing flexibility as a lifestyle choice.

If your students want to be able to punt a football or perform a high kick in martial arts, they must have good leg flexibility to be successful.

SAFETY GUIDELINES FOR FLEXIBILITY ACTIVITIES

Many safety issues relate to stretching in the physical education setting. Be aware of the previously discussed factors that may limit flexibility. Before stretching, students should complete a general whole-body warm-up. Those with physical disabilities may need to use a longer warm-up period to enhance joint mobility. For static stretching, students should use slow movements, holding each stretch at the point just before mild discomfort occurs (backing off slightly when discomfort is felt) for 10 to 30 seconds. For dynamic stretching, students should mimic movement from a specific sport or exercise in an exaggerated but controlled manner (ACSM, 2006b). By following these protocols, teachers allow students to individualize their efforts.

Other general rules that apply include making sure that students limit or avoid locking any joint when performing flexibility exercises. Advising student to maintain "soft knees" and "soft joints" can help them avoid any unnecessary overstretching of ligaments.

A second rule related to overstretching involves the issue of forcing a stretch. Require students to pay attention to their bodies regarding feelings of discomfort and pain. These feelings are signals that the student is forcing the stretch, going beyond the normal range of motion and possibly damaging ligaments.

A third rule is never to allow students to hyperflex (bend from the waist) or hyperextend the spine while stretching, because this action places undue stress on the intervertebral discs of the spine. Bending from the hips in a forward-flexed position is OK, but bending only from the waist is not. The compression of the discs of the lower back is one of the reasons that the back-saver sit-and-reach assessment was implemented. The forward-flexed position at the waist causes increased pressure on the discs. Stretching one leg at a time reduces the pressure. Similarly, hyperextension is not recommended because it compresses the discs. Going from a flexed position to extension is OK, but going beyond normal extension into hyperextension (bending backward) is not. Be aware that a physician in some instances may prescribe hyperextension exercises to rehabilitate the lower back, but most of the population should generally avoid this motion. The undue stress on the intervertebral discs is exacerbated if twisting or rotation is combined with hyperflexion or hyperextension. Although this motion may not present an immediate concern or injury, over time these actions may contribute to chronic degeneration of the discs and low-back pain as a person ages.

Contraindicated Exercises

Contraindicated exercises are those exercises that have been determined to be unsafe or to have the potential for increasing the risk of injury if people continue to incorporate them into their physical activity programs. An injury may not occur every time a contraindicated exercise is performed, but an injury may result over weeks or years of repeated microtrauma to the tissue. Several exercises (see appendix D for examples) should be avoided to reduce the risk of joint injury.

Hypermobility, joint laxity, and flexibility safety issues have been discussed previously. When a student performs an exercise that takes a joint well beyond its normal range of motion, such as in some **hyperflexion** or **hyperextension** exercises, the risk for development of joint laxity and possible injury increases (Corbin, Welk, Corbin, & Welk, 2009).

For these reasons, provide alternatives when designing your flexibility unit, keeping in mind the specificity principle and the availability of exercise prescriptions by medical personnel. Some sports demand extreme ROM, such as gymnastics, dancing, and certain positions such as baseball catcher, which requires the full squat. In these instances, it may be necessary to follow the medically prescribed exercise prescription and to teach dynamic, sport-specific flexibility exercises. If so, use extreme caution, active warm-ups, and static stretching after the muscles have been warmed up. Many of the exercises in appendix D are considered questionable or contraindicated for group exercise, such as that used in physical education classes. In many instances, teachers do not have the time or the expertise to prescribe exercises for special situations. Corbin et al. (2004) suggest that physical educators teach to the needs of the majority and include exercises that have the least negative effect while providing the most positive benefits. If alternative exercises are available to those that can possibly cause injury, it makes sense to use the alternative exercises for a safer, more effective program.

SUMMARY

Flexibility is just as important to health-related fitness as other components are, so resist the temptation to relegate it to warm-ups and cool-downs. When appropriate, feature it as the core activity of a lesson. This approach will allow time to demonstrate how important, relaxing, and pleasurable flexibility exercises can be. In addition, it is educational to make explicit connections for students between the stretches taught in class and the activities that they perform in and outside of class. See the chapter on flexibility in the *Physical Best Activity Guides* for model flexibility-training lessons. Refer to the principles of flexibility and the FITT formula to enhance students' performance in flexibility and other areas of the physical education curriculum. Good flexibility is crucial for a healthy range of motion, which in turn improves overall health-related fitness, posture, risk of injury, and enhances safety when engaging in physical activity. Remember that controlled stretching is most appropriate in a health-related physical fitness education program. Moreover, static stretching offers the safest type of flexibility training for the majority of students with the least negative effect. Addressing the appropriate types of stretching and providing students with examples and experiences of using different types of stretching can provide a lifelong tool for safely maintaining individual flexibility.

Body Composition

Scott Going and Melody Kyzer

Chapter Contents

Few physical educators would deny that teaching about body composition is one of the most sensitive areas of health-related fitness education. Cultural, social, and personal beliefs and attitudes make this a difficult topic, so the temptation to avoid the subject is great. But understanding body composition—including what affects it and what benefits are provided by a healthy body composition—is critical to overall health-related fitness. The current pediatric obesity epidemic, with its attendant health issues, especially in adolescents, underscores the importance of this topic. Although calculating exact body composition indicators with very young children is not important, these children still need to explore the related concepts and understand how an active lifestyle affects body composition. Older children need this information, too, as well as tools to monitor and affect body composition positively throughout life. This information is critical for the prevention of chronic disease.

TEACHING GUIDELINES FOR BODY COMPOSITION

Body composition is the amount of lean body mass (all tissues other than fat, such as bone, muscle, organs, and body fluids) and the amount of body fat, usually expressed in terms of percent body weight. Excess fat and a high fat-to-lean ratio present a health risk. Several common ways are available to gauge whether body composition is healthy, and a range of values indicates what constitutes a healthy percent body fat. Tables 8.1 and 8.2 identify recommended ranges for body fat (Cooper Institute, 2010).

To teach students about body composition in a sensitive and professional manner, you should be mindful of four main aspects:

▶ Project an attitude of acceptance toward individual differences and demand that students follow your lead with their peers.

▶ Respect each person's privacy (e.g., collect measures in private).

▶ Relate body composition to the other components of health-related fitness in meaningful ways.

▶ Acknowledge whether or not you can help a student who is over or under an appropriate body fat and refer the student or parents to professional help if clinically indicated.

Accepting Individual Differences

Teachers should avoid asserting that there are absolute indicators of good and poor health related to body composition. Remember that even experts cannot agree on how body composition is best measured and that the healthy range is wide. When teaching body composition, approach it as an individual and personal topic about which everyone should try to be compassionate. Never use a student as a positive or negative model of composition. In addition, explain to students that genetics plays a role in body composition (this topic is discussed in detail later in the chapter). Physical education teachers should

Table 8.1 Fitnessgram Body Composition Standards for Boys

Age	Percent body fat				Body mass index			
	Very lean	HFZ	NI—some risk	NI—high risk	Very lean	HFZ	NI—some risk	NI—high risk
5	≤8.8	8.9–18.8	18.9	≥27.0	≤13.8	13.9–16.7	16.8	≥17.5
6	≤8.4	8.5–18.8	18.9	≥27.0	≤13.7	13.8–16.9	17.0	≥17.8
7	≤8.2	8.3–18.8	18.9	≥27.0	≤13.7	13.8–17.3	17.4	≥18.3
8	≤8.3	8.4–18.8	18.9	≥27.0	≤13.8	13.9–17.8	17.9	≥19.0
9	≤8.6	8.7–20.6	20.7	≥30.1	≤14.0	14.1–18.5	18.6	≥19.9
10	≤8.8	8.9–22.4	22.5	≥33.2	≤14.2	14.3–18.9	19.0	≥20.8
11	≤8.7	8.8–23.6	23.7	≥35.4	≤14.5	14.6–19.7	19.8	≥21.8
12	≤8.3	8.4–23.6	23.7	≥35.9	≤15.0	15.1–20.5	20.6	≥22.7
13	≤7.7	7.8–22.8	22.9	≥35.0	≤15.4	15.5–21.3	21.4	≥23.6
14	≤7.0	7.1–21.3	21.4	≥33.2	≤16.0	16.1–22.1	22.2	≥24.5
15	≤6.5	6.6–20.1	20.2	≥31.5	≤16.5	16.6–22.9	23.0	≥25.3
16	≤6.4	6.5–20.1	20.2	≥31.6	≤17.1	17.2–23.7	23.8	≥26.0
17	≤6.6	6.7–20.9	21.0	≥33.0	≤17.7	17.8–24.4	24.5	≥26.7
>17	≤6.9	7.0–22.2	22.3	≥35.1	≤18.2	18.3–25.1	25.2	≥27.5

HFZ = healthy fitness zone.

NI = needs improvement.

From The Cooper Institute 2010.

Table 8.2 Fitnessgram Body Composition Standards for Girls

Age	Percent body fat				Body mass index			
	Very lean	HFZ	NI—some risk	NI—high risk	Very lean	HFZ	NI—some risk	NI—high risk
5	<9.7	9.8–20.8	20.9	>28.4	<13.5	13.6–16.7	16.8	>17.3
6	<9.8	9.9–20.8	20.9	>28.4	<13.4	13.5–17.0	17.1	>17.7
7	<10.0	10.1–20.8	20.9	>28.4	<13.4	13.5–17.5	17.6	>18.3
8	<10.4	10.5–20.8	20.9	>28.4	<13.5	13.6–18.2	18.3	>19.1
9	<10.9	10.8–22.6	22.7	>30.8	<13.7	13.8–18.9	19.0	>20.0
10	<11.5	11.6–24.3	24.4	>33.0	<14.0	14.1–19.5	19.6	>21.0
11	<12.1	12.2–25.7	25.8	>34.5	<14.4	14.5–20.4	20.5	>21.9
12	<12.6	12.7–26.7	26.8	>35.5	<14.8	14.9–21.2	21.3	>22.9
13	<13.3	13.4–27.7	27.8	>36.3	<15.3	15.4–22.0	22.1	>23.8
14	<13.9	14.0–28.5	28.6	>36.8	<15.8	15.9–22.8	22.9	>24.6
15	<14.5	14.6–29.1	29.2	>37.1	<16.3	16.4–23.5	23.6	>25.4
16	<15.2	15.3–29.7	29.8	>37.4	<16.8	16.9–24.1	24.2	>26.1
17	<15.8	15.9–30.4	30.5	>37.9	<17.2	17.3–24.6	24.7	>26.7
>17	<16.4	16.5–31.3	31.4	>38.6	<17.5	17.6–25.1	25.2	>27.2

HFZ = healthy fitness zone.

NI = needs improvement.

From The Cooper Institute 2010.

encourage students to find personal satisfaction with their overall health, wellness, and physical activity habits rather than struggle to measure up to a rigid standard or to cultural expectations. Remind students that "normal" comes in all shapes and sizes.

Respecting Privacy

Never publicize a student's measurements or percent body fat; in addition, be sure to secure the information where other students cannot access it. Also, be aware that students with a less-than-perfect body composition may be reluctant to be measured in front of their more physically fit peers. Conduct skinfold caliper assessment, weighing, and any other measuring in private as a voluntary activity. Ask another adult to help with assessment or with conducting the rest of the class while you are occupied with this procedure. Explain to students that body composition is a personal matter and that they should focus only on their own information. Check with a school

administrator regarding guidelines that may be in place. For example, parental permission may need to be obtained for skinfold assessment (or at least parent notification of upcoming assessment). Having another adult present during assessment to prevent harassment issues may also be prudent.

RELATING BODY COMPOSITION TO OTHER HEALTH-RELATED FITNESS COMPONENTS

As with any other component of health-related fitness, a person's body composition does not happen in isolation from the other components. Indeed, it is important to show students the connections among all health-related fitness components so that they can clearly see how their personal choices affect this area of health-related fitness. Although genetics, environment, and culture play significant roles in body composition, it can be modified with regular participation in activities designed to improve other fitness components (e.g., aerobic fitness activities and muscle-strengthening activities):

▶ Aerobic fitness—Aerobic activities burn calories.

▶ Muscular strength and endurance—Lean tissue with its high ratio of muscle burns (metabolizes) more calories at rest than adipose tissue does. Emphasize physical activity that follows the principles of training (chapter 3) to increase the likelihood of maintaining an appropriate body composition.

▶ Flexibility—A flexible body can better tolerate aerobic fitness and muscular strength and endurance activities. Yoga is one activity that can improve flexibility. People who practice yoga may be more aware of health and body issues and practice other health-enhancing activities such as healthy eating.

A thorough understanding of body composition, variables that affect it, and the benefits of a healthy body composition is critical to overall health-related fitness.

Strive to point out connections among physical activity, diet, and body composition related to daily life, recreational pursuits, and physical education activities. Emphasize, too, that a student who is overfat because of genetics can still greatly reduce health risks by being physically active even in the absence of significant changes in body weight and composition. Physical activity, even without calorie restriction, is effective in reducing a person's risk for chronic disease, regardless of the person's level of obesity (Ross, Freeman, & Janssen, 2000; USDHHS, 1996). Several studies have now shown that overfat people who exercise regularly are at no greater health risk than thin people who don't exercise (Haskell et al., 2007).

Strength Training and Body Composition Management

Strength training can be a valuable adjunct to a body composition management program. A weight-reduction program can cause loss of lean tissue (primary muscle) along with body fat. Strength training can prevent significant loss of lean body mass, which in turn prevents decreases in **resting energy expenditure (REE)**, the energy that the body uses at rest. Each additional pound (.5 kg) of muscle tissue can raise the REE by 35 kilocalories per day (Campbell et al., 1994), which over the course of a year is a significant contribution to total energy expenditure and weight control.

Students need to know that although resistance training burns calories, the effect is relatively small compared to that of aerobic exercise. They must also understand that it is physiologically impossible for muscle cells to turn into fat in the future, and vice versa (a common misconception). A combination of aerobic exercise and resistance training is best for body composition management.

METHODS OF MEASURING BODY COMPOSITION

Experts do not agree on the best method for measuring body composition. Elementary students should be taught the basic concepts of body composition and the variables that affect it, and middle and high school students should be taught

specific methods of assessing body composition and the pros and cons of each method.

Skinfold Caliper Assessment

Skinfold caliper assessment is a commonly used method for determining body composition in the physical education setting. It involves using **skinfold calipers** to take **skinfold** measurements at specific sites on the body (figure 8.1).

Skinfold caliper assessment is the most accurate way of measuring body composition generally available to the physical educator, and implementing it is relatively inexpensive. But to take accurate and reliable measurements, a tester must be well trained. Measuring takes a great deal of class time and teacher attention. Because this method involves touching a student, other sensitivities may arise. If teachers do not feel comfortable with or qualified to perform this assessment method, further training or arrangements

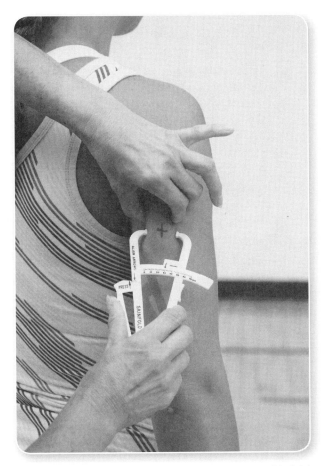

Figure 8.1 Using calipers to take an arm skinfold measurement.

TIPS FOR CONDUCTING SKINFOLD ASSESSMENT

Many teachers feel uncomfortable measuring percent body fat for a variety of reasons, including the following:

- A student may feel embarrassed by his or her assessment results.
- A teacher may be reluctant to touch students in any manner.
- Students may be reluctant to let teachers touch them in any manner.
- Training and practice are required to measure skinfolds accurately.

There are several methods you can use to address these concerns.

- Get the training and practice needed to take accurate measurements. NASPE-AAHPERD provides workshops and in-services on Physical Best and Fitnessgram assessment techniques (contact NASPE for details). Invite a qualified fitness instructor, university physical education instructor, school nurse, or certified athletic trainer to conduct this assessment.
- Teach older students to use the skinfold calipers. This approach allows them to assume responsibility, ensures the privacy of their results, and gives them the option to peer assess, working with a trusted friend. But be sensitive. If overweight children are in a class, having students measure each other (and possibly expose the overweight children to ridicule) may not be an option. Some calipers have a limited range that may preclude the measurement of larger folds, embarrassing the student being assessed. On the other hand, students should learn that people come in all different sizes and that all people should feel welcome and comfortable in physical activity settings. Regardless of positive habits, people are made differently.

- Focus on making students aware of the personal choices that all people make that affect their body composition. This information helps students set goals based on the process of a physically active and healthful lifestyle rather than the product. In addition, teach students that both too much and too little body fat can be harmful. If students are of the appropriate age, discuss eating disorders.
- Conduct skinfold assessment in a separate room if possible, assessing one student at a time. This protocol may relieve some of a student's discomfort with the situation.
- If touching a student may raise concerns, arrange to have a knowledgeable second adult attend the assessment. Also, Physical Best provides options for calculating body composition. Body mass index calculations can be used instead of skinfolds.

for more qualified personnel to help (perhaps someone from the physical education or athletic training department of a local university) should be sought. Specific guidelines for skinfold measurement administration and age-appropriate guidelines are published in the latest *Fitnessgram Test Administration Manual* by the Cooper Institute (see appendix E).

Body Mass Index

Although attention paid by the media to **body mass index (BMI)** has recently risen, this method of determining body composition is not new. BMI has been used as a measure of overweight and obesity in population studies for years. Federal agencies generally use this measure when reporting obesity statistics. In adults, the following definitions are used:

- ▶ Less than 18.5—underweight
- ▶ 18.5–25—optimal
- ▶ 25.1–29.9—overweight
- ▶ Over 30—obese
- ▶ Over 40—morbidly obese

The health risk (from excess weight) increases greatly with BMIs over 30 in adults. As BMI continues to rise, so does the health risk.

BMI is a ratio of weight to height. This mathematical formula correlates with body fat in the general population. BMI is a measure best used for postpubescent students. In children and adolescents, BMI standards are age and gender specific. Girls and boys mature at different ages and in different ways. As a result, the Centers for Disease Control and Prevention (CDC) has created age-specific BMI tables that allow for gender differences, growth spurts, and the changing relationship between BMI and body composition as boys and girls mature. These charts exist for children ages 2 through 20 (see figures E.1 and E.2 in appendix E). The CDC also has a pediatric BMI calculator available at http://apps.nccd.cdc.gov/dnpabmi. In children and adolescents (up to age 18) gender- and age-specific percentiles are used to define desirable ranges of BMI. Recommended standards are the following:

- Less than 5th percentile—underweight
- Greater than 85th to 94.9—overweight
- Greater than or equal to 95th—obese

The BMIs corresponding to CDC percentiles are based on national distributions of weight for height for boys and girls who were measured in the 1960s and 1970s before the onset of the childhood obesity epidemic. They are not necessarily equivalent with the HFZ BMIs from the Fitnessgram, which were developed using a different approach. Fitnessgram standards were based on health-related criteria (e.g., CVD risk factors) linked to desirable ranges of percent body fat. Past standards were derived from data from the Bogalusa Heart Study, a long-term study of the natural history of heart disease (Williams et al., 1992). More recently, measures of percent fat have become available from the National Health and Nutrition Examination Survey, the longest ongoing surveillance study with a nationwide sample of the U.S. population. For the first time, it was possible to derive standards for youth from a nationally representative sample with measures of body composition and disease risk factors.

The body composition standards shown in tables 8.1 and 8.2 were developed by determining the values of percent fat that best discriminated youth at risk for chronic disease from those with lower risk. These revised standards will be incorporated into the new Fitnessgram software (version 8.6) and reports. The corresponding BMI standards shown in tables 8.1 and 8.2 were derived by finding the BMI that best identified the various percent fat zones. BMIs that identify the very lean boys and girls are equivalent to the CDC-defined 5th percentile of age- and gender-specific BMI, the accepted definition for underweight.

BMI provides a quick body composition check that a person can self-administer. This method takes little class time and teacher attention and is easy for a student to use outside of a physical education program. Its primary disadvantage is that it oversimplifies the body composition picture because it does not distinguish lean mass from body fat. For example, two people at the

CALCULATING BMI

To calculate a person's BMI, simply divide weight in pounds by height in inches squared, and multiply that by 703.

BMI = (weight in pounds ÷ [height in inches × height in inches]) × 703

For example, a boy who weighs 150 pounds and is 5 feet, 5 inches tall would calculate his BMI as follows:

Step 1: BMI = (150lbs ÷ [65in × 65in]) × 703

Step 2: (150lbs ÷ 4,225in²) = 0.0355

Step 3: 0.0355 × 703 = 24.9

The boy's BMI is 24.9.

If you are using the metric system, divide the weight in kilograms by the height in meters squared.

BMI = weight in kilograms ÷ (height in meters × height in meters)

The same boy is 165 centimeters (1.65 m) tall and weighs 68 kilograms:

Step 1: BMI = 68kg ÷ (1.65m × 1.65m)

Step 2: BMI = 68kg ÷ 2.72m² = 24.9

The boy's BMI is 24.9.

PERCENT BODY FAT VERSUS BODY MASS INDEX

Body mass index (BMI) does not estimate percent fat, but merely gives an indication of the appropriateness of the weight relative to height (CIAR, 2004). The following example demonstrates how two students who fall into the healthy fitness zone (HFZ) based on body mass index calculations can have quite different levels of body fat. In this example, Jane's percent body fat is 35 and outside the HFZ, whereas Jeanette's percent body fat is 19 and in the HFZ.

Jane and Jeanette are both 16 years old, weigh 130 pounds (59 kg), and are 5 feet, 6 inches (168 cm) tall. Although both girls have the same body mass index (BMI), body composition assessments show that Jane is carrying approximately 45 pounds (20.4 kg) of fat, whereas Jeanette has only approximately 25 pounds (11.3 kg) of fat.

Jane's percent body fat is calculated as follows:

$$45lbs \div 130lbs = 0.35 \text{ (round to the nearest 100th) (metric: } 20.4kg \div 59kg = 0.35)$$

$$0.35 \times 100 = 35\% \text{ body fat}$$

Jane's BMI is calculated as follows:

$$(130lbs \div [66in]^2) \times 703$$

$$(130lbs \div 4,356in^2) \times 703$$

$$0.0298 \times 703 = 20.9$$

Or, using the metric formula:

$$59kg \div (1.68m)^2$$

$$59kg \div 2.82in^2 = 20.9$$

Jeanette's percent body fat is as follows:

$$25lbs \div 130lbs = 0.19 \text{ (rounded to the nearest 100th) (metric: } 11.3kg \div 59kg = 0.19)$$

$$0.19 \times 100 = 19\% \text{ body fat}$$

Jeanette's BMI is calculated as follows:

$$(130lbs \div [66in]^2) \times 703$$

$$(130lbs \div 4,356in^2) \times 703$$

$$0.0298 \times 703 = 20.9$$

Or, using the metric formula:

$$59kg \div (1.68m)^2$$

$$59kg \div 2.82m^2 = 20.9$$

So although height–weight charts and BMI may provide a general indication of health, they do not provide a measure of percent fat and therefore do not tell the complete story of body composition.

---

same BMI and fitness level may have different fat-to-lean mass ratios (based on genetic factors and differences in other components, such as bone size) and vastly different percentages of body fat (see "Percent Body Fat Versus Body Mass Index"). A person can be fit and healthy or unfit and unhealthy at levels of BMI that define underweight, overweight, and obesity. Even so, BMI gives people one indicator of health and wellness, and it has been used widely in epidemiological studies. When indicated, help students with BMIs at the extremes look for causes and solutions, and encourage them to complete a more accurate assessment of body composition.

To have postpubescent students calculate their own body mass index, use "Calculating BMI."

Height–Weight Chart

Height–weight charts were originally the creation of Louis Dublin, an actuary for the Metropolitan Life Insurance Company. These charts arose because insurance companies attempted to predict scientifically which clients were lower or higher risks to insure. As with BMI, height–weight charts are oversimplifications of body composition data because they do not take into account percent body fat. They should be used only as guidelines for appropriate weight ranges. Although using wall charts may make teaching progression simpler, this approach does not provide accurate results, and it has often led to public posting of comparisons of students' body compositions (something to be avoided at all costs). For examples of the Metropolitan Height–Weight charts, see www.nutritionclassroom.com/metropolitan_life_weight_tables.htm.

Waist-to-Hip Ratio

Because research has shown that the distribution of body fat relates to its adverse effects, scientists have investigated the correlation between waist-to-hip ratios and health risks. The findings indicate that being pear-shaped is better than being apple-shaped; that is, it is better to have excess weight on the hips and thighs than around the waist (Wickelgren, 1998). In fact, research indicates that excess abdominal fat giving an apple shape increases the risk for heart disease and diabetes later in life (Ziegler & Filer, 2000). Waist-to-hip ratio is a simple way to evaluate whether a person is pear- or apple-shaped. For example, a person with a waist measurement of 28 inches (71.1 cm) and a hip measurement of 38 inches (96.5 cm) would have a waist-to-hip ratio of 0.74 (28 ÷ 38 = 0.736, or 71.1 ÷ 96.5 = 0.736, rounded to the nearest hundredth). Ratios above 0.86 in women and 0.95 in men indicate a waist-to-hip ratio (and an apple shape) associated with higher levels of heart disease, diabetes, and cancer. These numbers have not been adjusted or validated for children, however, so the usefulness of this assessment is limited in the health-related physical fitness education program.

Although the concept of apples and pears is useful to explain fat distribution to children and youth, the waist-to-hip ratio can be difficult to interpret. For example, a ratio over 1.0 could occur because of a small waist or large hip circumference. Given this uncertainty, use of waist circumference alone, which is significantly associated with abdominal fat and adverse health risk, is becoming more common. The waist circumference alone may be a more useful and easily obtainable index in both adults and children (Katmarzyk et al., 2004). Accepted standards for youth, although not presently available, are being developed. Analyses with U.S. national data support the conclusion that children above the 90th percentile for age, gender, and ethnic background are at increased risk for obesity comorbidities (Fernandez et al., 2004).

A waist circumference above the 90th percentile can be used to refer a child for further screening until more definitive standards are derived.

Bioelectrical Impedance Analyzers

Bioelectrical impedance is an alternative, noninvasive technique requiring little skill to administer. This method is becoming a popular alternative to skinfold measures in the public schools for assessing body composition. Research has shown that fat-free mass (FFM) or percent body fat can be accurately predicted in children and adults using impedance (the errors are about the same as with skinfolds), provided that population-specific equations are used to estimate composition (Heyward & Wagner, 2004). A low-level electrical current (50 kilohertz) of different amplitudes (800 or 500 microamperes) is introduced into the body through four electrodes placed on the wrists and ankles. Alternative impedance instruments use a handheld device or a bathroom-scale-type instrument whereby the subject stands on two metal footpads to estimate body composition. Impedance is based on a simple premise that tissues containing a lot of water and electrolytes conduct electricity, whereas tissues storing a lot of fat are poor conductors of electricity. But the rapid administration and ease of use of this method does not come without some precautions. It is generally recommended that the manufacturer's general equations not be used, unless the population that you are assessing is a subgroup of the population in which the equation was validated and then cross-validated.

If you decide to use impedance instead of skinfold assessments to assess body composition, use the following recommendations:

▶ Purchase an impedance instrument that offers multiple equations, including equations for children.

▶ The alternative is to purchase an instrument that provides the user with the resistance, reactance, and impedance readings, to which you then apply an appropriate equation (Heyward & Wagner, 2004) based on the age, gender, and population that you are assessing.

- ▶ Standardize measurement protocol according to the manufacturer's recommendations.
- ▶ Avoid metal tables or other conductive surfaces.
- ▶ Ensure that the student's arms and legs are abducted slightly away from the trunk.
- ▶ Require the student to remove metal jewelry.
- ▶ Make sure that the student is well hydrated.
- ▶ Avoid assessment soon (less than two hours) after a meal or exercise.

Here are some suggested references to help select an equation:

- ▶ The best equation to use for white boys and girls ages 10 to 19 years is one developed by Houtkooper et al. (1992).
- ▶ For children under 10 years of age, use the equations of Lohman (1992) or Kushner et al. (1992).
- ▶ Race-specific equations have been developed for native Japanese boys (9 to 14 years old) and girls (9 to 15 years old) (Kim et al., 1993; Watanabe et al., 1993).
- ▶ Currently, no cross-validated impedance equations are available for American Indian, Asian American, black, or Hispanic children.

HELPING THE OVERFAT OR UNDERFAT STUDENT

Either through formal assessment or informal observations, you will identify students who appear to be over or under an appropriate percent body fat. As a physical educator, you should not attempt to treat serious problems such as eating disorders or extreme obesity; instead you should refer these students to their parents for professional help. The following sections discuss the symptoms and causes of obesity and eating disorders to help identify contributing factors.

Obesity

According to the Centers for Disease Control and Prevention, approximately 65% of all adults in the United States are overweight or obese. In addition, the percentage of youth who are overweight or obese has more than doubled in the last three decades. Current estimates are that between 15 and 20% of U.S. children aged 6 to 17 are overweight (Ogden, Carrol, Curtin, et al., 2010). Given these statistics, physical educators are likely to have overweight children in their classes. **Obesity** is defined as 120% of ideal body weight or greater or a BMI greater than 30 in adults. In children and

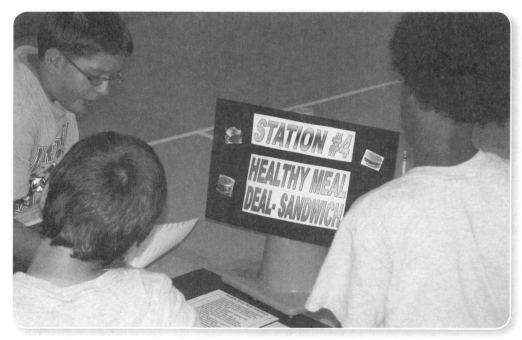

Restaurants and fast-food joints may provide a social haven for many of your students, but you must encourage them to order wisely and to consider the nutritional value (or lack thereof) of the food that they order.

adolescents (those younger than 18 years of age), a BMI equaling or exceeding the 95th percentile for their age and gender is defined as obesity, the adolescent equivalent of adult obesity. Obesity has three main contributing factors: genetics, diet, and physical activity. Keep this in mind when preparing lesson plans.

▶ Genetics—Research suggests that genetics contributes about 30% to a person's body weight (Zeigler & Filer, 1996). The genetic component is multiple: It determines metabolism, placement of excess fat (hips, arms, abdomen, and so on), effectiveness of the gastrointestinal tract, level of appetite, preferences for certain types of food such as sweets and salty snacks, and response to exercise. Many factors are involved, and the exact genes, their products, and the exact biochemical mechanisms are still being researched.

▶ Diet—The average American diet contains 14% more calories than it did 30 years ago (McDowell et al., 1994). Eating as few as nine and a half additional calories per day will result in 1 pound (.45 kg) of additional fat over a year. Americans are eating more meals away from home, as well as more fast food and fried food. The typical on-the-run American lifestyle leads to long days of snacking and lots of take-out. According to the CDC (2002, 2004), more than 60% of youth eat too much fat, and fewer than 20% eat the recommended five or more servings of fruits and vegetables on a daily basis. These poor eating habits developed during childhood may continue to be established throughout adulthood.

▶ Physical activity—Physical activity increases the body's use of calories, which aids in maintaining a normal weight and optimizing overall health. The level of physical activity continues to decrease in the United States. Despite the widely documented benefits of exercise, including better long-term health, improved body image, and less depression, more than 60% of American adults are sedentary. This inactivity is not limited to adults. More than 30% of youth ages 9 to 12 don't regularly engage in physical activity. Video games and television have replaced much of the after-school yard play. In addition, daily participation in high school physical education classes dropped from 42% in 1991 to 29% in 1999 (NCCDPHP, 2003).

TEACHING TIP

In addition to the many activities in the *Physical Best Activity Guides*, the following class application ideas for teaching nutritional concepts related to body composition can be used.

Use Teaching Models

Create class fat models to supplement lectures and stimulate class discussion. Obtain nutritional analysis information from local fast-food chains. The Web site www.fatcalories.com contains extensive information on fast-food nutritional content. Note that five grams of fat is equivalent to one teaspoon of Crisco or margarine. Label clear plastic cups with food type and add the proper amount of fat. This activity helps students visualize the actual fat content in their favorite fast-food items (see table 8.3 on page 138).

Journaling

Have students complete a dietary journal of all foods eaten in the previous 24 hours. Students should record how they felt (emotions), when they ate, and why they ate that particular item. The objective is to demonstrate how often people eat for reasons other than hunger and why they choose the foods that they do. (Food choices are often more about convenience, taste, and availability than making healthy choices. Although younger children may not get to choose their food daily, they do get some choice with school lunches and at restaurants.)

Find a Menu

Many restaurants will donate a menu if asked, and many more print take-out menus. Select the healthiest food items from local restaurants. These can then be used to have class discussions regarding the best menu choices.

Table 8.3 Nutritional Value of Popular Fast Foods

Food item	Calories	% calories from fat	Total fat (g)	Saturated fat (g)	Cholesterol (mg)	Protein (g)	Total carbo-hydrate (g)	Fiber (g)	Sugar (g)	Sodium (mg)	Calcium (% RDI)
McDonald's											
Hamburger	280	32%	10	4	30	12	35	2	7	560	20%
Cheese-burger	330	39%	14	6	45	15	35	2	7	800	25%
Quarter Pounder	420	45%	21	8	70	23	36	2	8	780	20%
Quarter Pounder With Cheese	530	51%	30	13	95	28	38	2	9	1,250	35%
Big Mac	580	52%	33	11	85	24	47	3	7	1,050	35%
Filet-O-Fish	470	51%	26	5	50	15	45	1	5	730	20%
McChicken	430	49%	23	4.5	45	14	41	3	6	840	20%
Chicken McNuggets (6 pieces)	310	58%	20	4	50	15	18	2	0	680	2%
French Fries (large)	540	43%	26	4.5	0	8	68	6	0	350	2%
Side Salad (no dressing)	15	0	0	0	0	1	3	1	1	10	2%
Grilled Chicken Bacon Ranch Salad (no dressing)	270	44%	13	5	75	28	11	3	4	830	15%
Ranch Dressing (1 pkg)	290	93%	30	4.5	20	1	4	0	3	530	4%
Low-Fat Balsamic Vinaigrette (1 pkg)	40	63%	3	0	0	0	4	0	3	730	*
Chocolate Triple Thick Shake (small)	430	26%	12	8	50	11	70	1	61	210	35%
Egg McMuffin	300	37%	12	5	235	18	29	2	3	840	30%
Bacon, Egg, & Cheese Biscuit	480	58%	31	10	250	21	31	1	3	1,360	15%

Food item	Calories	% calories from fat	Total fat (g)	Saturated fat (g)	Cholesterol (mg)	Protein (g)	Total carbo-hydrate (g)	Fiber (g)	Sugar (g)	Sodium (mg)	Calcium (% RDI)
Ham, Egg, & Cheese Bagel	550	36%	23	8	255	26	58	2	10	1,500	20%
Hot Cakes w/ margarine & syrup	600	25%	17	3	20	9	104	0	40	770	10%
Hash Browns	130	54%	8	1.5	0	1	14	1	0	330	*

*Contains less than 2% of the daily value.
Additional food items listed at www.mcdonalds.com/countries/usa/food/nutrition/categories/nutrition/index.html.

Pizza Hut											
Hand-Tossed Pizza, cheese, 1 slice	240	38%	10	5	10	12	28	2	1	650	20%
Personal Pan Pizza, pepperoni	620	40%	28	11	30	26	70	5	<2	1,430	30%
Meat Lover's Stuffed Crust, 1 slice	470	49%	25	11	50	22	40	3	2	1,430	25%
Veggie Lover's the Big New Yorker, 1 slice	480	42%	22	6	10	19	57	10	<10	1,410	25%
Thin 'N Crispy Pizza, cheese, 1 slice	200	80	9	5	10	10	22	2	1	590	20%
Mild Buffalo Wings, 5 pieces	200	110	12	3.5	150	23	<1	0	0	510	2%
Breadstick	130	35	4	1	0	3	20	1	1	170	NA
Breadstick Dipping Sauce	30	5	0.5	0	0	<1	5	<1	2	170	NA
Supreme Sandwich	640	250	28	10	28	34	62	4	7	2,150	30%

NA = not available.
Additional food items listed at www.pizzahut.com (click on "Nutritional Info").

Data from www.mcdonalds.com/countries/usa/food/nutrition/categories/nutrition/index.html and www.pizzahut.com.

Eating Disorders

At the opposite end of the spectrum are eating disorders. Although obesity is now the biggest nutritional problem among youths, physical educators cannot focus only on obesity. In fact, psychological and social pressures to look thin have driven some youngsters to the extremes of eating disorders, all of which pose serious health risks.

Three eating disorders are common in the school-age population: anorexia nervosa, bulimia, and binge eating. Physical educators and coaches must be able to recognize the warning signs of each. To help students achieve and maintain an ideal body composition, teach them the right combination of caloric intake, caloric expenditure, and behavioral skills. Stress that healthy people come in all shapes and sizes, and discuss the unrealistic images that are often portrayed in the media. Behavior modification includes the frequency of eating, the portion size of food, and commitment to an active lifestyle. If an eating disorder is suspected discuss this with the school nurse and refer the child and parents to an appropriate professional.

▶ **Anorexia nervosa** (see the sidebar "Warning Signs of Anorexia") is a serious and potentially fatal disease characterized by self-induced starvation and extreme weight loss. According to the National Eating Disorders Association (2003), anorexia nervosa has five primary symptoms:

- Refusal to maintain a normal body weight (although there is no clinically established cutoff, a weight loss to less than 85% of ideal body weight is considered at risk.)
- An intense fear of weight and of getting "fat."
- Feeling "fat" despite dramatic weight loss.
- Loss of periods.
- Extreme concern with body weight and appearance.

Approximately 95% of people with anorexia nervosa are female. Anorexia nervosa has some extremely negative health consequences, including an abnormally slow heart rate, a reduction in bone mass, hair loss, dry hair, and severe dehydration (which can result in kidney failure). People

---

WARNING SIGNS OF ANOREXIA

- Dramatic weight loss
- Preoccupation with weight, calories, and fat grams
- Refusal to eat certain foods, progressing to restrictions against whole categories of food
- Frequent comments about feeling fat or overweight despite dramatic weight loss
- Anxiety about getting fat
- Denial of hunger
- Development of food rituals (e.g., eating foods in certain orders, excessive chewing, rearranging food on a plate)
- Consistent excuses avoiding mealtimes or situations involving food
- Excessive, rigid exercise regimen (despite weather, fatigue, illness, or injury)—the need to burn off calories taken in
- Withdrawal from usual friends and activities
- Behaviors and attitudes indicating that weight loss, dieting, and control of food are becoming primary concerns

Reprinted, by permission, from the National Eating Disorders Foundation, 2001, *Warning signs of anorexia nervosa*. Available: http://www.nationaleatingdisorders.org.

---

with anorexia nervosa also experience growth of a downy layer of hair called **lanugo**. Its purpose is to help the body to keep warm. Of those with anorexia nervosa, statistics indicate that 5 to 20% will die.

▶ **Bulimia** (see the sidebar "Warning Signs of Bulimia") is a serious, potentially fatal eating disorder characterized by a destructive cycle of **bingeing** and **purging**. According to the National Eating Disorders Association, bulimia has three primary symptoms:

- Eating large quantities of food in short periods, or bingeing, typically in secret.
- Following these binges, performing a compensatory behavior to account for the caloric intake. This behavior may include

vomiting, laxative abuse, diuretic abuse, fasting, or compulsive exercise.

- Extreme concern with body weight and shape.

Estimates of the prevalence of bulimia vary, but between 1 and 5% of the U.S. population is affected. Estimates vary because bulimia can go undetected for long periods. Approximately 80% of bulimics are female. Unlike those with anorexia nervosa, most people with bulimia are at normal weight or even slightly above. Health consequences of bulimia include tooth decay, ulcers, electrolyte disturbances, and potential for gastric rupture.

▶ **Binge eating** (see "Warning Signs of Binge Eating") is a type of eating disorder not otherwise specified and is characterized by recurrent binge eating without the regular use of compensatory measures to counter the binge eating. According to the National Eating Disorders Foundation, some of the most significant health consequences of binge eating include

- high blood pressure,
- high cholesterol levels,
- heart disease,
- diabetes mellitus, and
- gallbladder disease.

The prevalence of binge eating is approximately 1 to 5% of the general population, and

---

WARNING SIGNS OF BULIMIA

- Evidence of binge eating, such as the existence of wrappers and containers indicating the consumption of large amounts of food
- Evidence of purging behaviors, including frequent trips to the bathroom after meals, signs or smells of vomiting, presence of wrappers or packages of laxatives or diuretics
- Excessive, rigid exercise regimen (despite weather, fatigue, illness, or injury)—the need to burn off calories taken in
- Unusual swelling of the cheeks or jaw area
- Calluses on the back of the hands and knuckles from self-induced vomiting
- Discoloration or staining of the teeth (from stomach acid in vomit)
- Creation of complex lifestyle schedules or rituals to make time for binge-and-purge sessions
- Withdrawal from usual friends and activities
- In general, behaviors and attitudes indicating that weight loss, dieting, and control of food are becoming primary concerns

---

WARNING SIGNS OF BINGE EATING

- Evidence of binge eating, including disappearance of large amounts of food in short periods of time or the existence of wrappers and containers indicating the consumption of large amounts of food
- Develops food rituals (e.g., eats only a particular food or food group [e.g., condiments], excessive chewing, doesn't allow foods to touch)
- Steals or hoards food in strange places
- Hides body with baggy clothes
- Creates lifestyle schedules or rituals to make time for binge sessions
- Skips meals or takes small portions of food at regular meals
- Has periods of uncontrolled, impulsive, or continuous eating beyond the point of feeling comfortably full
- Does not purge
- Engages in sporadic fasting or repetitive dieting
- Body weight varies from normal to mild, moderate, or severe obesity

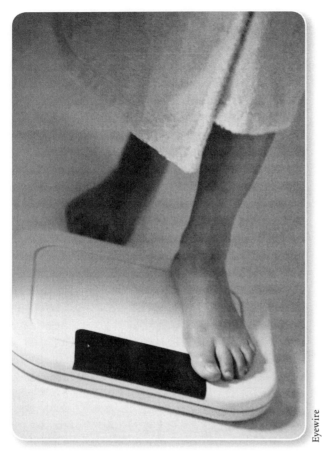

Eyewire

Appearance and body image are important to most teenagers. The extreme pressure to be thin can lead to problems with eating disorders such as anorexia.

CAUTION!

Although extreme **underweight** (less than 90% of ideal body weight) is a symptom of disordered eating, some children are simply genetically thin. Diagnosis of an eating disorder requires disordered body image perception in addition to unhealthy and dangerous eating habits.

---

it affects women slightly more often than men. Binge eating is often associated with symptoms of depression. People struggling with binge eating disorder often express distress, shame, and guilt over their eating behaviors.

People with binge eating disorder often eat an unusually large amount of food and feel out of control during the binges. Unlike bulimia or anorexia, binge eaters do not throw up their food, exercise a lot, or eat only small amounts of only certain foods. Because of this, binge eaters are often overweight or obese. People with binge eating disorder also may

- eat more quickly than usual during binge episodes,
- eat until they are uncomfortably full,
- eat when they are not hungry,
- eat alone because of embarrassment, and
- feel disgusted, depressed, or guilty after overeating.

About 2% of all adults in the United States (as many as 4 million Americans) have binge eating disorder.

Based on http://www.nationaleatingdisorders.org/nedaDir/files/documents/handouts/BingeED.pdf

Addressing the Problem

Use the following guidelines to approach the situation in a professional manner.

- Always maintain student and family privacy.
- Approach the student and parents diplomatically. Be sure to avoid making statements that they may perceive as accusatory.
- Respect parental wishes unless you believe, as in the case of suspected anorexia nervosa, that the child is in danger.
- Work with other school personnel, such as the school nurse and counselor, and seek written permission to share your observations with the child's health care worker. At the same time, seek advice on how to tailor the program to meet the child's needs. School districts have access to registered dietitians who may be able to tailor a meal plan for students with weight problems or eating disorders. Eating regular well-balanced meals throughout the day may decrease the urge to binge eat and help the student lose weight, if they are overweight, and improve body composition.
- Ensure that the physical education program is interesting and promotes physical activity as a lifestyle choice for all students. Avoid unreasonable expectations. For example,

obese children are more likely to maintain and therefore benefit from mild physical activity than from moderate to vigorous physical activity (USDHHS, 1999).

▶ Deal with less serious problems only; refer students with serious problems to a professional who is qualified to treat the problem.

SUMMARY

Although approaching body composition in the physical education setting can be a delicate matter, this element is just as important as any other health-related component of physical fitness. Handle body composition instruction professionally and effectively by focusing on how an active lifestyle positively affects body composition rather than overemphasizing assessment results. Connect this material to the other components of health-related fitness. Make assessment voluntary and respect each student's privacy. Finally, learn to recognize when a student's body composition is a serious health concern and refer such children to a qualified health care professional. Chapter 4, "Nutrition," will be helpful in teaching about body composition.

Curriculum and Teaching Methods

Part III provides an overview of curriculum development and teaching methods relevant to health-related fitness education, as well as information on including children of all abilities and backgrounds in the health-related fitness content. Basic program design principles, recommended core content, and activity selection are covered. Chapter 10 explores teaching styles, including utilizing cooperative learning, teaching strategies such as scheduling, the teaching environment, and teaching tools. Part III concludes with chapter 11, which focuses on the topic of inclusion. The chapter offers practical tips for including students with special needs. In addition, it addresses gender, culture, and ability.

Integrating Health-Related Physical Fitness Education Into the Curriculum

Bane McCracken

National physical education content standards define what a physically educated person is and provide a direction for programs. Quality physical education programs have a written curriculum that guides teachers by acting as a road map to accomplish specific outcomes and provide evidence of student progress. This chapter helps physical education teachers develop curricula that include health-related fitness instruction (NASPE standard 4) and promote developmentally appropriate physical lifestyles (NASPE standard 3).

Chapter Contents

There has been much discussion concerning what is and what is not a quality curriculum. For the purpose of this chapter a quality curriculum includes several elements:

▶ An overview that describes in general terms the goals of the program.

▶ A scope that indicates what is to be included in the curriculum. The scope could be a specific grade level, one middle school, an entire school system for grades K through 12, or even a state-level curriculum.

▶ Specific objectives aligned with the national standards.

▶ Assessment tools for every objective to provide evidence of student progress.

Physical Best is not a complete curriculum. Rather, it is a curriculum supplement that helps incorporate the teaching of health-related fitness into the traditional curriculum. The Physical Best materials, philosophy, and resources can be used to create a complete fitness curriculum model for a school or system. When discussing various curriculum models, Physical Best is many times used as an example of a fitness education model. But in this chapter, Physical Best is considered a curriculum supplement.

Discussion of curriculum development in this chapter may include other components of the physical education curriculum, but the focus will be on developing objectives for physical activity and health-related fitness.

CURRICULUM DEVELOPMENT

In an ideal situation, a local school agency has a coordinator of physical education who is in charge of curriculum development. To develop a physical education curriculum or refine an existing curriculum to include health-related fitness education, the coordinator assembles a curriculum team to write the curriculum. It is reviewed by all the teachers in the system, input is evaluated, and amendments are made. The curriculum is coordinated and sequenced for all grades K through 12. But in situations in which the school system does not have a coordinator, individual teachers may be delegated the responsibility of curriculum development.

Regardless of the situation, the initial considerations for writing a curriculum are scope and sequence, requirements and policies, appropriate skills or movement forms, and user friendliness.

Scope and Sequence

Program scope refers to the number and type of schools for which the curriculum is to be developed. The curriculum's programs may be for a single elementary school or all the schools in a city, county, or district school system. Having a scope that goes across all programmatic levels is advantageous. Developing physically educated students is difficult without coordinating the teaching of skills from one grade level to the next. The curriculum should be written for all schools in the system, but flexibility should be sufficient to allow schools to take advantage of local physical activity opportunities, especially in larger systems.

The curriculum sequence is the sequential presentation of skills and the coordination of skill development from one grade level and programmatic level to the next. An effective approach is to have all grade levels represented during the writing of a curriculum to provide for the smooth transition of skill development from one school to the next and for each grade level. It is especially important to make smooth transitions from one programmatic level to the next—K–2 to 3–5, 3–5 to middle school, and middle school to high school. Proper sequencing, assessment of individual skills, and good record keeping help teachers know where to begin at the beginning of the year, how to individualize instruction, and how to document improvement.

Local and State Requirements and Policies

According to the *Shape of the Nation Report: Status of Physical Education in the USA* (NASPE, 2006), all states have adopted or are in the process of adopting standards for physical education based on NASPE standards. These state standards along with state and local requirements and policies should provide the basis for developing a local curriculum. State and local school requirements and policies determine the students' opportunity to learn. Some school districts have excellent designated physical education facilities and equipment, and require daily physical education taught by a certified professional. Other schools may share a facility with the food service program and require only 30 minutes of physical education per week. Although setting high standards may be good practice, writing an impractical curriculum is not a good idea.

A limiting factor when developing a curriculum is time. The amount of time that students spend with their teachers determines what and how much can be accomplished. A curriculum for an elementary program based on delivery on one day each week will have different sequencing than a daily program. Programs in which teachers have limited time with their students must use creative means to help students meet outcomes. For example, providing equipment during recess, lunch, and before and after school allows students to practice the skills taught during physical education class. Regularly scheduled physical education homework provides additional learning opportunities, encourages students to break the habit of inactivity, and teaches students to take responsibility for their learning.

Few school systems provide adequate time during the school day for the students to practice and learn the skills taught in their classes. Requiring students to practice skills outside of the school day (physical education homework) helps develop good habits, increases learning, and helps students become physically active for life.

Effective homework assignment for physical education starts by spending more time providing quality instruction and less time playing games. After instruction, students should be challenged to practice at home and be required to demonstrate improvement during the next scheduled class. Parent and sibling involvement can be accomplished by using activity logs that require the signature of a responsible adult and by scheduling parents' nights and family fun nights at schools when parents are instructed on the importance of physical activity and how to monitor their child's progress. Middle and high school students can demonstrate progress using digital cameras, videos, and PowerPoint presentations that use before and after photos and video to demonstrate progress. During a high school golf unit, for example, students are filmed hitting golf balls during the first week of class. The students critique their swings and make a PowerPoint presentation that identifies flaws in technique. During the last week of the golf unit, students again film themselves and make a PowerPoint presentation that demonstrates how their practice resulted in better form.

Appropriate Movement Skills or Forms

For any curriculum to be sound, a physical educator must consider the developmental appropriateness of the selected content. **Developmentally appropriate activities** are those that are appropriate based on a student's developmental level, age, ability level, interests, and experience and knowledge. Appropriateness on a grade-level basis is an initial target. First, study the guidelines set by experts in the field, such as those developed by the National Association for Sport and Physical Education (NASPE). These guidelines include published documents such as the assessment series and the appropriate practices series, available through AAHPERD. Then use experience as the best teacher: Learn by trial and error what each particular group of students can handle. But remember that although developmental appropriateness is important, you must not overlook the age of the student for whom the content is being developed. For example, if a high school student lacks aerobic fitness, tag is not an appropriate activity to offer as a choice, but riding a stationary bike while reading a favorite magazine would be a good alternative based on the student's age and ability. Both activities will accomplish the same goal.

Content selection should occur along a continuum from completely childlike to as adultlike in nature as possible. Figure 9.1 on page 150 shows a sample continuum for aerobic fitness activities that proceed from childlike activities in the early grades to adultlike activities in high school.

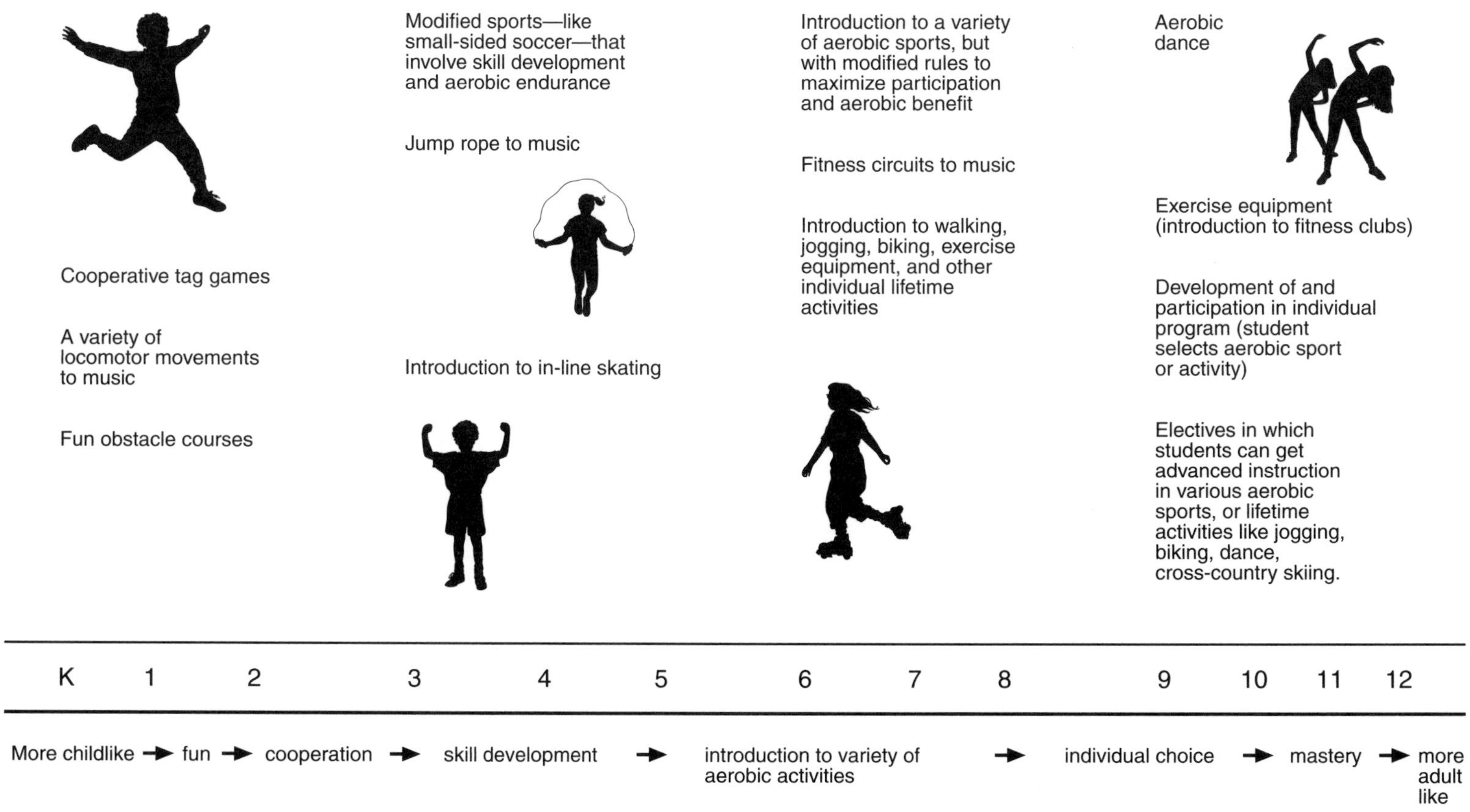

A variety of
locomotor movements
to music

Fun obstacle courses

Cooperative tag games

Modified sports—like
small-sided soccer—that
involve skill development
and aerobic endurance

Jump rope to music

Introduction to in-line skating

Introduction to a variety
of aerobic sports, but
with modified rules to
maximize participation
and aerobic benefit

Fitness circuits to music

Introduction to walking,
jogging, biking, exercise
equipment, and other
individual lifetime
activities

Aerobic
dance

Exercise equipment
(introduction to fitness clubs)

Development of and
participation in individual
program (student
selects aerobic sport
or activity)

Electives in which
students can get
advanced instruction
in various aerobic
sports, or lifetime
activities like jogging,
biking, dance,
cross-country skiing.

| K | 1 | 2 | 3 | 4 | 5 | 6 | 7 | 8 | 9 | 10 | 11 | 12 |

More childlike → fun → cooperation → skill development → introduction to variety of aerobic activities → individual choice → mastery → more adult like

Figure 9.1 Your activity selection should occur along a continuum that moves students from childlike to adultlike activities. This example describes a possible continuum for teaching aerobic fitness.

User Friendliness

A curriculum is meant to be used by the teachers. Too many times official documents are left in their shrink-wrap, stuck in a desk drawer, and never seen again. To make sure that teachers use the documents, keep them simple to use and easy to understand. A committee should develop a curriculum, and members of the staff should make up the majority of the group and do most of the writing.

RECOMMENDED CORE CONTENT FOR A HEALTH-RELATED FITNESS EDUCATION

A health-related fitness program teaches the basic training principles of health-related fitness, fitness safety, nutrition, fitness consumer awareness, and the benefits of physical activity. In addition, the program teaches that lifelong physical activity is individual and can be enjoyable. Because Physical Best aligns itself predominately with a fitness-based curriculum model, it is only logical that a set of core competencies and information should be included in the curriculum. At a minimum, a program should include the following content information:

▶ Basic knowledge of health-related fitness and physical activity principles and skills—Students need concrete knowledge about the principles of progression and overload as applied to each component of health-related fitness, including proper nutrition, safety, and the body's adaptation to exercise. Include training techniques specific to each component of health-related fitness. Pacing while running, for example, saves precious energy to go the distance. Thus, students need to learn to judge their effort and speed. Students should also master basic running biomechanics and other techniques (e.g., proper stretching and weight-lifting safety) to prevent injury, ensuring that they can participate safely and efficiently in the long term. Students must be able to identify and use specific strategies for measuring frequency, intensity, time, and type of their participation in

physical activity. Other relevant health-related fitness skills include the ability to monitor and interpret heart rates accurately and the ability to apply basic injury prevention and treatment strategies. Students should also be required to provide evidence of participating in physical activity or, for older students, employing a self-designed personal fitness plan.

▶ Consumer education—Students need to know the truth about fitness, weight control, and nutritional supplements and other products, especially how to discern fact from fiction in advertising. They also need experience comparison shopping for the fitness facilities, equipment, and activity opportunities that suit their interests and resources.

▶ Knowledge of the benefits of physical activity—Students need to know how they will benefit from physical activity today (e.g., look and feel better) and in the long term. Remember that youths don't relate well to problems that they might have at age 50 or 60. So although it's vital that they know this information, emphasize immediate benefits to maintain their interest.

▶ Understanding of the personal nature of fitness—Students need to know that they can find what works for them. Not everyone needs to do the same activities, but they do need some sort of physical activity to gain the health benefits. The curriculum should therefore emphasize the many choices available to be physically active.

▶ Knowledge that physical activity can be fun—The instruction should include lab or physical activity days for students to apply what they're learning in the classroom in an enjoyable learning environment. For example, some schools offer the course as two days per week in the classroom and three days per week in the physical activity setting.

The details of what to include in order to fulfill each component depend, of course, on your particular curriculum guidelines, student population, and school and community resources. In general, however, select activities that teach students to apply health-related fitness knowledge in real-life settings, that require higher-order thinking and problem solving, and that encourage students to take personal responsibility.

PHYSICAL EDUCATION CURRICULUM ANALYSIS TOOL (PECAT)

The National Centers for Disease Control and Prevention (CDC) and the National Association for Sport and Physical Education (NASPE) have used experts in the field of physical education to develop the PECAT. The purpose of the PECAT is to help school districts conduct a clear, complete, and consistent analysis of physical education curricula. The results of the PECAT can help school districts enhance and develop effective physical education curricula as well as refine existing curricula to include fitness education. The PECAT is available at no cost. Copies and further information can be obtained in several ways:

- Downloading from the CDC Web site: www.cdc.gov/HealthyYouth/PECAT
- Requesting by e-mail: CDC-INFO@cdc.gov
- Requesting by toll-free phone call: 800-CDC-INFO

Several trainings for using the PECAT have been conducted nationally, and more are scheduled. The PECAT is designed to analyze an existing curriculum, but it can also be used as a guide when developing a new curriculum. The PECAT has specific examples of lesson outcomes for all grade levels and all standards. The following are some examples of the PECAT recommendations for meeting NASPE standard 4:

Elementary K through 2

- Specific lessons about the response of the body to physical activity (e.g., increased heart rate, faster breathing, and sweating)
- Specific lessons about developing basic knowledge of the components of health-related fitness (e.g., cardiorespiratory, muscular endurance, muscular strength, flexibility, and body composition)
- Specific lessons that allow students to participate in vigorous, intermittent physical activity for short periods during physical education class

- Specific lessons about the concept of personal choices in physical activity and ways in which those physical activity choices contribute to physical fitness
- Specific instructions that clearly indicate the appropriate grade level at which each concept and activity related to physical fitness should be introduced and subsequently taught

From CDC 2006.

Elementary 3 through 5

- Specific lessons on self-assessment of physical fitness (e.g., a teaching activity using a criterion-referenced standard fitness test such as Fitnessgram for self-assessment of fitness)
- Specific lessons on the definition of the components of fitness and appropriate use of tools for assessing each fitness component (e.g., flexibility, body composition, muscular strength and endurance, and aerobic fitness)
- Specific lessons that allow students to participate in moderate to vigorous physical activity for longer periods without tiring
- Specific lessons that allow physical educators to teach the concept of interpreting fitness test results and choosing appropriate activities to improve each component of physical fitness
- Specific instructions that clearly indicate the appropriate grade level at which each concept and activity related to physical fitness should be introduced and subsequently taught

From CDC 2006.

Middle school 6 through 8

- Specific lessons on how to assess personal fitness status for each fitness component and use this information to develop individualized physical fitness goals with little help from the teacher
- Specific lessons on basic principles of training (e.g., overload, specificity) and how these principles can be used to improve a student's level of physical fitness
- Specific lessons that provide opportunities for students to participate in and effectively

monitor physical activities that improve each component of fitness

▶ Specific lessons that identify how each component of physical fitness is related to overall fitness

▶ Specific instructions that clearly indicate the appropriate grade level at which each concept and activity related to physical fitness should be introduced and subsequently taught

From CDC 2006.

High school 9 through 12

▶ Specific lessons on appropriate activities for each fitness component, as well as activities that will help students meet their personal fitness goals

▶ Specific lessons on basic exercise physiology concepts, such as the ability of the brain to send signals and receive them from muscles, the ability of the cardiorespiratory system to adapt to varying levels of intense physical activity, and the principles of training in preparing for competitive sports or recreational activities

▶ Specific lessons on age- and gender-appropriate health-related fitness standards and ways in which to monitor and interpret personal fitness data

▶ Specific lessons that allow students to develop a personal health-related fitness program, based on specific, individual goals

▶ Specific instructions that clearly indicate the appropriate grade level at which each concept and activity related to physical fitness should be introduced and subsequently applied to the development of a personalized fitness program

From CDC 2006.

Note that the examples provided of the PECAT lesson outcome recommendations are for NASPE standard 4 only and relate to developing a health-enhancing level of fitness. To find recommended lesson outcomes for all other standards, refer to the PECAT.

An educator can include health-related fitness education and physical activity sequentially in a physical education curriculum in two ways: as a stand-alone unit or by embedding fitness objectives into the teaching of skills. At the elementary level, students first learn to identify the physiological changes taking place because of physical activity. Later they learn to distinguish between moderate and vigorous activities and identify the components of fitness while learning basic movement skills. Elementary students may learn to compare the relative intensity levels of walking, skipping, jogging, and running while learning locomotor skills. Connecting push-ups, modified pull-ups, and curl-ups with muscular strength and endurance teaches student the components of fitness in a physically active way. For example, you might have first graders put their hands on their chests to feel their hearts beating fast and talk about how being active causes this to happen. Third graders might practice counting how many times they feel their hearts beat and discuss more specifically how this relates to physical activity. Fifth graders can be taught to find their pulse two different ways (wrist and carotid artery) or can use a heart rate monitor and then graph their rates based on various activities.

During the middle school years as students learn to apply the movement skills learned in elementary school to specific movement forms, they also learn the relative fitness benefits of these activities. Teachers may ask student to rank a variety of activities based on their relative fitness value or identify the fitness component best associated with a specific sport. During the middle school years students begin to experience the fitness guideline of FITT, progression, and overload. By the end of middle school students should understand that a brisk 30-minute walk may have more fitness benefits than 2 hours of softball. Seventh graders might be asked to monitor their heart rates for a week doing different activities, graph the results, and write a paper that compares the various rates and offers reasons for the differences. High school students might be asked to develop an exercise plan based on their target heart rates, carry out the plan, and record the results (which requires knowing how to take their own pulse). They might also write a paper or do research regarding the response of the heart to stress on the body.

Students' knowledge about health-related fitness should progress so that they understand how the activities they take part in affect their health.

The high school curriculum should have specific objectives that require students to demonstrate the skills, knowledge, and understandings needed to participate in a lifetime of physical activity. Fitness education objectives are addressed as a separate unit of study and during individual units of study. The objectives of a separate fitness education unit of study should require students to assess their personnel fitness and make lifetime plans for developing and maintaining a health-enhancing level of fitness. In this unit of study, students learn to exercise. In other units of study, students learn to use various training techniques to enhance performance and maintain a level of fitness that allows continued participation. Students may learn to use dumbbells to improve their tennis game and reduce the chance of developing tennis elbow. A volleyball

unit may include plyometrics to improve jumping, or stretching to address specific muscle groups used in volleyball.

PROGRAM DESIGN

Health-related physical fitness education focuses on having students assume progressively more responsibility for their own health, fitness, and well-being. Overall, the K through 12 program should build progressively toward the ultimate goal: producing members of society who take lifelong personal responsibility for engaging in health-related physical activity. When designing a curriculum, start at the end and work backward. What should students know and be able to do when they graduate from high school? An example of a high school curriculum goal may be to use cycling, tennis, volleyball, personal fitness, and golf as a means of establishing a physically active lifestyle. Movement activities should be separated into units, and a performance task should be developed for each activity. Performance tasks describe in a general way what the students should know and be able to do at the end of each unit. For example, a performance task for a tennis unit may require students to demonstrate the ability to participate in a local tennis event. A performance task for a cycling unit may require students to demonstrate the knowledge, skills, and understanding necessary to participate in a local cycling event.

Another way to think of designing developmentally appropriate content is to consider a diamond-shaped framework such as that shown in figure 9.2. Within the diamond curriculum framework, elementary-level students develop the basic skills and knowledge (both fitness and movement related) that they will ultimately need to be able to enjoy lifetime activities. Middle school students then use these skills to sample a variety of physical activities. This approach gives students the opportunity to form personal opinions about various activities and sports. High school students select a few physical activities in which to specialize and around which they may build personal physical activity plans. Building a foundation of basic skills in elementary school and developing proficiency in self-selected areas

National Standards and Guidelines

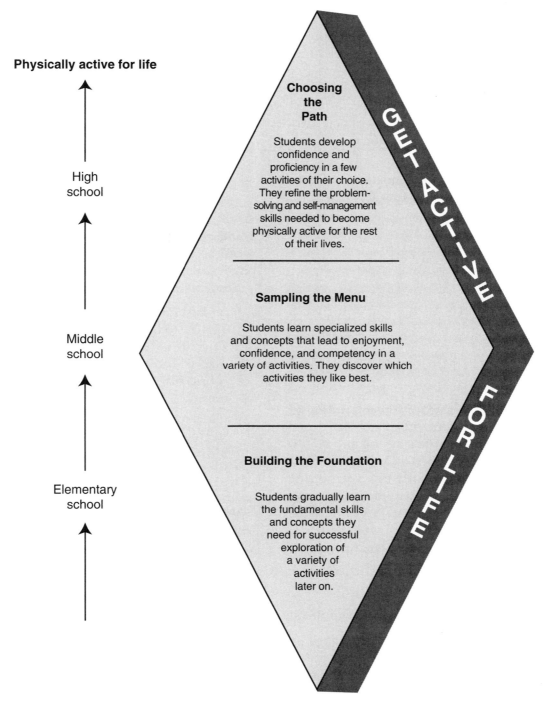

Physically active for life

High school

Middle school

Elementary school

Choosing the Path

Students develop confidence and proficiency in a few activities of their choice. They refine the problem-solving and self-management skills needed to become physically active for the rest of their lives.

Sampling the Menu

Students learn specialized skills and concepts that lead to enjoyment, confidence, and competency in a variety of activities. They discover which activities they like best.

Building the Foundation

Students gradually learn the fundamental skills and concepts they need for successful exploration of a variety of activities later on.

GET ACTIVE FOR LIFE

Figure 9.2   This diamond-shaped framework provides another way of describing a lifetime activity continuum.

Reprinted, by permission, from C. Himberg, 2003, *Teaching secondary physical education in the 21st century* (Champaign, IL: Human Kinetics), 19.

in high school forms a continuum that is likely to lead to positive adult health-related fitness behaviors.

The next step in writing a curriculum is to develop objectives that specifically describe the knowledge, skills, and understanding needed to accomplish the performance tasks. This goal can be achieved by referring to the NASPE standards for physical education and listing specific objectives for each standard. An example of objectives for a cycling unit aligned with national standards may include the following:

Standard 1 Demonstrate competency in motor skills and movement patterns needed to perform a variety of physical activities

Students will

- use mature form when mounting, dismounting, starting, stopping, breaking, shifting gears, pedaling, turning on a variety of surfaces, ascending, descending, doing track stands and wheel hops, and riding over obstacles; and
- perform basic bicycle maintenance and repairs.

Standard 2 Demonstrate understanding of movement concepts, principles, strategies, and tactics as they apply to the learning and performance of physical activities

Students will continually analyze cycling skills, develop and participate in activities to improve skills, and realize that improving skills increases enjoyment of cycling.

Standard 3 Participate regularly in physical activity

Students will

- research and compare cycling equipment availability and costs;
- always wear a bicycle helmet;
- locate on a map local, regional, and national cycling opportunities such as trails, designated areas, Rails to Trails, and American Discovery Trail;
- identify local, regional, and national cycling resources such as bike shops, clubs, American Cycling Federation, League of American Bicyclists, and so on; and

- maintain a physical activity log that documents participation in cycling activities in addition to physical education classes.

Standard 4 Achieve and maintain a health-enhancing level of fitness

Students will

- use cycling as a means of increasing physical activity opportunities and developing a health-enhancing level of physical activity; and
- assess personal fitness, analyze fitness benefits and requirements of cycling, and identify and document participation in activities to improve fitness and cycling performance.

Standard 5 Exhibit responsible personal and social behavior that respects self and others in physical activity settings

Students will

- understand and follow rules of the road as applied to cycling (cyclists follow the same rules as automobiles) by stopping at all marked intersections, riding on the right, riding single file, signaling intent, and so on; and
- understand and follow rules of the trail by staying on the trail, leaving no trace, obeying regulations, sharing the trail with others (including animals), and knowing their equipment and ability.

Standard 6 Value physical activity for health, enjoyment, challenge, self-expression, and social interaction

Students will use cycling as a means of creating opportunities for social interaction and personal enjoyment.

NATIONAL STANDARDS

A physical education curriculum that focuses only on skill development and teaches only competitive team sports is no longer appropriate. Today's physical education curricula must focus on fitness, teach authentic lifetime skills, and be standards based. Physical education programs that teach students the skills needed to make physical activity enjoyable over a lifetime include specific objectives that help students learn to be physically active and develop a health-enhancing level of fitness. Tables 9.1 through 9.3 list the standards set by the national governing bodies for physical education, health, and dance. The standards that are most strongly correlated with Physical Best are highlighted in bold. These standards are listed in the *Physical Best Activity Guides* to demonstrate the connection of each activity to the applicable standards.

Physical education teaches skills that make physical activity enjoyable over a lifetime. Physical education is not recess, it is not a recreation period, it is not where students go to get fit, and it should not be viewed as the student's physical activity opportunity. Physical education is where students go to learn. Students should be physically active because of what they learn in their physical education classes.

Table 9.1   National Standards for Physical Education

Standard 1	Demonstrates competency in motor skills and movement patterns needed to perform a variety of physical activities
Standard 2	Demonstrates understanding of movement concepts, principles, strategies, and tactics as they apply to the learning and performance of physical activities
Standard 3	**Participates regularly in physical activity**
Standard 4	**Achieves and maintains a health-enhancing level of physical fitness**
Standard 5	Exhibits responsible personal and social behavior that respects self and others in physical activity settings
Standard 6	Values physical activity for health, enjoyment, challenge, self-expression, or social interaction

Reprinted from NASPE 2004.

Table 9.2   National Health Education Standards

Standard 1	**Students will comprehend concepts related to health promotion and disease prevention.**
Standard 2	Students will demonstrate the ability to access valid health information and health-promoting products and services.
Standard 3	**Students will demonstrate the ability to practice health-enhancing behaviors and reduce health risks.**
Standard 4	Students will analyze the influence of culture, media, technology, and other factors on health.
Standard 5	Students will demonstrate the ability to use interpersonal communication skills to enhance health.
Standard 6	**Students will demonstrate the ability to use goal-setting and decision-making skills to enhance health.**
Standard 7	Students will demonstrate the ability to advocate for personal, family, and community health.

Reprinted from American Association of Health Education 1995.

Table 9.3   National Standards for Dance Education

Standard 1	Identifying and demonstrating movement elements and skills in performing dance
Standard 2	Understanding choreographic principles, processes, and structures
Standard 3	Understanding dance as a way to create and communicate meaning
Standard 4	Applying and demonstrating critical and creative thinking skills in dance
Standard 5	Demonstrating and understanding dance in various cultures and historical periods
Standard 6	**Making connections between dance and healthful living**
Standard 7	Making connections between dance and other disciplines

Reprinted from National Dance Association 1994.

An elementary curriculum must focus on learning basic movement skills (e.g., throwing and catching, striking, fleeing and dodging, volleying). During the middle school years the curriculum should offer the chance for students to learn basic skills in a variety of diverse activities that take advantage of local physical activity opportunities. These activities may include team sports, individual and dual competitive sports, individual noncompetitive activities, outdoor adventure activities, and rhythmic activities. Teachers should spend most of the class time teaching skills and only play games that have been modified to allow maximum participation and that match the students' skill levels.

High school years should allow students to choose from activities that they have found enjoyable during middle school and in which they wish to refine their skills and pursue for a lifetime.

A well-written physical education curriculum must include objectives that require students to develop and demonstrate a physically active lifestyle (standard 3). Participating in an activity only during class time does not meet this objective. Students should be participating in activities outside of class because of what they learn in class. If students are not participating in an activity that is included in the curriculum, we must ask ourselves why. To find the answer, we must analyze the content, instructional practices, and local policies.

Golf is an excellent example of a lifetime sport that can be appropriate to include in many middle and high school curricula, but it may not be suitable in economically depressed areas where most residents deem it too expensive. Volleyball is a popular activity found in many middle and high school curricula. But many students may dislike volleyball by the time they get to high school because the middle school instruction was ineffective, the curriculum was not properly sequenced, or too much time was spent playing the game and not enough time spent teaching the skills needed to make the game enjoyable.

Local policies are often found to be the biggest restricting factor. Although it is desirable to provide students a variety of choices, doing so may be impractical if not impossible in some circumstances, so selections may need to be limited. In such cases coordinating middle and high school curricula is especially important.

DEVELOPING A CURRICULUM TO PROMOTE LIFETIME FITNESS

During the first part of the 20th century, farmers lifted bales of hay, coal miners used picks and shovels, and factory workers manually produced their products. Housework was done by hand, lawns were mowed with push mowers, most children walked to school, and families played together instead of watching television. We didn't need to know about fitness because our lifestyles were active and we naturally developed a health-enhancing level of fitness.

During the second half of the 20th century our lifestyles became sedentary. When the *Surgeon General's Report on Physical Activity and Health* was published in 1996, it told us what we already knew: Physical activity is good for your health. By participating in regular moderate to vigorous physical activity, we develop a health-enhancing level of fitness. Quality physical education programs had already begun to change, and physical education began to focus on fitness. We realized that students needed to be able to recognize the fitness benefits of physical activity, understand the fitness requirements of specific activities, and learn to develop a plan to achieve and maintain a health-enhancing level of fitness. Many of our teachers were unprepared for the change. Our preparation did not include fitness. Therefore, many of us needed to find a resource that could help develop programs that teach students fitness and fitness concepts.

Now that we have had a while to adapt to the necessary changes in physical education focus, there are many resources available to us to help educators teach students to become active throughout their lives. Using the NASPE standards is one way to develop a curriculum that will help you to do this.

An example is the Stairway to Lifetime Fitness, developed by Corbin and Lindsey (2005) (see figure 9.3), which succinctly outlines the process through which teachers must guide students. Younger students are more likely to be on a lower, more dependent step. Conversely, older students need to be operating on a higher step (see table 9.4).

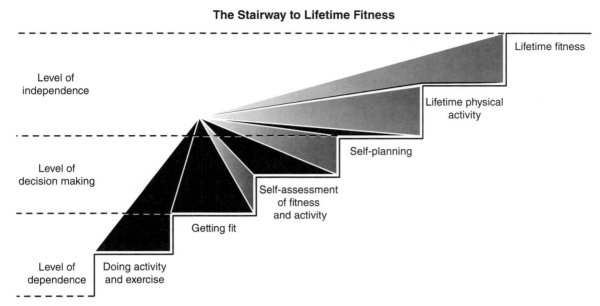

The Stairway to Lifetime Fitness

Level of independence

Level of decision making

Level of dependence

Lifetime fitness

Lifetime physical activity

Self-planning

Self-assessment of fitness and activity

Getting fit

Doing activity and exercise

Figure 9.3 The Stairway to Lifetime Fitness outlines the steps that teachers can use to guide students toward a lifetime of fitness.

Reprinted, by permission, from C. Corbin and R. Lindsey, 2005, *Fitness for life*, 5th ed. (Champaign, IL: Human Kinetics), 12.

Table 9.4 Sample Activity Progressions by Topic

	Primary (K–2)	Intermediate (3–5)	Middle school (6–8)	High school (9–12)
Corbin and Lindsey's Stairway to Lifetime Fitness (2005)	Step 1—Doing regular exercise	Step 2—Achieving physical fitness	Step 3—Personal exercise patterns	Step 4—Self-evaluation Step 5—Problem solving and decision making
Heart rate	Place hand on heart before and after vigorous activity and compare HR	Count pulse; learn math to find HR based on partial count	Practice math to find HR based on partial count; graph HR monitor data; assess effort based on graphed data	Design workouts based on knowledge of HR and THRZ
Running	Learn correct stride; run in low-organization games	Analyze running strides of peers using rubric; design low-organization games that incorporate a high amount of running	Teach peers to run more efficiently; report on how running efficiently helps a person succeed in a favorite sport	Design interval workouts that alternate high- and low-intensity effort as determined by HR; make the workout fun for a friend to do
Upper-body strength training	Play on the monkey bars on the playground	Play fun push-up games (see Hichwa, 1998); learn tubing exercises	Learn more tubing exercises; design games that increase muscular strength without equipment	Learn how to lift weights safely; design a personal weight-training program; explore community options for weight training and do cost analysis

A well-written curriculum includes lessons that teach students to be physically active outside of their physical education classes. For example, elementary curricula should include specific lessons that help students distinguish between moderate and vigorous physical activity, choose specific forms of physical activity outside of class, monitor physical activity intensity levels, and document outside-of-class physical activity. Middle school students may be required to document outside-of-class physical activity and develop physical activity plans based on the results of fitness assessment. High school students should document outside-of-class participation as part of a unit of study, research equipment sources, and develop budgets for physical activity pursuits. During a golf unit, students may be required to play a round of golf or participate in a local tournament during a tennis unit, and a bicycle unit may include after-school group rides.

Students can be assigned to research physical activity resources to make connections between what they learn in class and physical activity resources outside the school environment. Doing research on clubs and organizations such as League of American Bicyclists, Trout Unlimited, the YMCA, United States Golf and Tennis Associations help students identify physical activity resources. Local chapters of these physical activity organizations have regularly scheduled meetings, and many of these organizations have youth development programs to recruit new members. Attending a local chapter meeting of Trout Unlimited may result in a lifetime interest in fishing.

Preparing Students for Fitness Beyond School

Exercising without an understanding of fitness concepts and using poor technique makes exercise drudgery. Many people begin the New Year by making a resolution to start exercising and get back in shape, resulting in membership increases at fitness centers during January. Unfortunately, many fail to make immediate progress, and fatigue and injury result instead. Fitness center participation returns to normal in only a few weeks as people become discouraged and stop exercising. Developing an understanding of

exercise skills, principles, and strategies should be part of a quality health-related physical education curriculum. A physically educated person should be able to exercise efficiently and use exercise as a means of maintaining a health-enhancing level of fitness.

The object of health-related physical fitness education is to teach students how to achieve and maintain a health-enhancing level of fitness throughout their lives. To do this, students need to understand the fitness benefits of physical activity, identify the fitness requirements of selected movement forms, and develop fitness plans to improve performance that allow for continued participation.

Fitness education is integrated and clearly addressed in a curriculum that is aligned with all national standards for physical education. Students learn more than movement skills. In a cycling unit, for example, students learn to make plans to be physically active and to use cycling as a means of developing a health-enhancing level of fitness. The units for other movement forms would use the same design and include specific objectives that require students to demonstrate using golf, tennis, and volleyball as a means of maintaining a health-enhancing level of fitness and outside-of-class participation.

Teaching Activities for Lifelong Fitness

Participation in any of the typical sport activities taught in a physical education setting takes time to keep up after the person is outside the school system. Often the responsibilities that come with maturity do not allow for frequent trips to the golf course, tennis courts, or bike path. Poor weather can reduce the opportunities for participation. When the opportunity for enjoyable recreation is limited, other measures need to be used to maintain health-enhancing level of fitness. Teachers must incorporate activities and health lessons within their curriculum that will help students continue to pursue their lifelong fitness goals after they are out of school.

As students move from middle to high school, you should select activities that are relevant to them both now and in their futures. Show students what is available for young adults in their community. Are there bike paths, volleyball leagues, cross-country skiing, walking paths, and health clubs? Take field trips to introduce students to the many options available. Have community members (e.g., health fitness instructors, league directors, running club leaders, sport facility owners, and the like) come to class to demonstrate new activities and tell students how they can get involved. Assign homework that relates to the real world, such as consumer education assignments. Or have them select the health club that they would join as an adult and write a paper about why they chose the particular club. In short, the older the students are, the more authentic the activities should be.

Most forms of physical activity have some fitness benefits. Playing a round of golf and riding in a golf cart, however, offers limited fitness benefits. Riding instead of walking does not raise pulse rates and does little to improve aerobic fitness and maintain a health-enhancing level of fitness. Yoga and tai chi are great for developing flexibility but produce limited cardiovascular benefits. Walking and hiking generate excellent cardiovascular benefits but may not develop sufficient muscular strength to prevent injuries and enhance enjoyment.

So beyond being introduced to activities and community outlets for lifelong activity opportunities, students must learn what benefits come from such activities. Understanding the relative fitness benefits of specific physical activities helps students realize that participation in a variety of movement forms is necessary to develop and maintain a health-enhancing level of fitness. The golf enthusiast needs to know that walking instead of riding in a cart will greatly improve the fitness benefits of golf, and participating in yoga may improve the person's golf game by improving flexibility. Hikers will find that weight training increases enjoyment by making it easier to carry a backpack and reducing fatigue. Understanding the relative fitness benefits of selected movement forms helps students realize that no single activity can develop and maintain all components of fitness. Participation in a variety of activities is necessary to address all components of fitness and develop and maintain a balanced, health-enhancing level of fitness.

Identifying the fitness requirements of specific movement forms can help students learn how to

continue participation throughout their lifespan and make physical activity more enjoyable. Cross-country skiing is a fun physically active pursuit that produces excellent fitness benefits. Going on a winter cross-country skiing vacation can be great fun for those who are fit for skiing. By identifying the fitness requirements of a movement form such as cross-country skiing, students learn to focus on the fitness components needed to prepare for participation and select activities that help improve fitness for skiing. Cross-country skiing requires a high level of aerobic fitness and muscular endurance. Students should be able to identify other forms of cardiovascular activities, such as swimming, that can help improve their readiness for cross-country skiing.

Understanding the fitness benefits and fitness requirements of selected movement forms can help students develop a lifelong fitness plan. Students should learn how to improve performance by developing and participating in activity-specific training programs. Most top professional athletes participate in training programs that lengthen their careers and improve performance. When students research successful professional athletes such as Brett Favre and Keri Walsh-Jennings, they will see the importance of sports-specific training and can use those examples to develop their own programs. Students can learn that participation in activities such as softball has little aerobic fitness benefit and does not by itself develop a health-enhancing level of fitness.

Participating in activities such as walking, jogging, or swimming complement softball and should be part of a well-rounded fitness plan. Other activities such as weight training can strengthen muscles used in softball and improve performance, and yoga will improve flexibility and reduce the chance of injury.

FITNESS FOR LIFE

The lifetime personal fitness program that is most used nationwide is *Fitness for Life*, created by Charles Corbin and Ruth Lindsey. Fitness for Life courses and programs complement Physical Best and are also fully integrated with Physical Best and Fitnessgram, sharing the same HELP philosophy (see the sidebar "HELP Philosophy" on page 10). Physical Best sets the foundation leading up to such courses and programs, and reinforces the lifetime fitness skills and concepts needed after these courses and programs are completed.

Fitness for Life is a comprehensive K through 12 program designed to help students take responsibility for their own activity, fitness, and health and to prepare them to be physically active and healthy throughout their adult lives. This standards-based program has been carefully articulated following a pedagogically sound scope and sequence to enhance student learning and progress. This program, published by Human Kinetics, includes a variety of resources. For more information on Fitness for Life, visit www.fitnessforlife.org or www.HumanKinetics.com or call 800-747-4457.

DETERMINING UNIT- OR GRADE-LEVEL OUTCOMES

A good way to begin developing unit outcomes is to develop a performance task that describes what a student should be able to do at the conclusion of the unit. A performance task for a hiking and backpacking unit may be to be able to hike the Appalachian Trail. This does not mean that the students actually hike the Appalachian Trail, but they must demonstrate that they have the skills, knowledge, and understanding necessary to complete the task if they so choose. Outcomes are then created for each standard.

Hiking and backpacking outcomes for standard 3 may include locating the Appalachian Trail and other National Scenic and Historic Trails, planning and participating in a local hike or overnight campout, developing a budget, researching

local regulations, applying for permits, and so on.

Outcomes for standard 4 may include developing a training program to hike 20 miles (32 km) per day carrying a 60-pound (27 kg) backpack, analyzing diet, and calculating and comparing calories burned while hiking with and without a backpack.

Developing performance tasks for each grade level also helps to maintain appropriate sequencing of objectives from one grade level to another and provides a means of documenting student progress. An example of sequential performance tasks and learning outcomes, as well as grade-level objectives for standards 3 and 4 for volleyball, are listed in table 9.5. After the performance task has been established, objectives for each standard and grade level are written to guide student learning.

SUMMARY

A quality physical education curriculum provides the framework for students to learn the necessary health-related physical fitness education concepts. It integrates motor skills and physical activity in a developmentally appropriate K through 12 progression as well as other subject areas to create a well-balanced, meaningful approach. The programs produce students who view physical activity as a worthwhile, pleasurable, and lifelong endeavor. Students discover where their physical activity interests lie and learn how to design and implement a personal health-related fitness plan that suits their individual needs and situations. A well-designed and expertly implemented curriculum can inspire and empower students to lead physically active lives.

Table 9.5 Sample Volleyball Performance Objectives

Grade level	Performance task and learning outcomes	Standard 3 objectives	Standard 4 objectives
6th	Participates in modified volleyball games using beach balls, reduced numbers, smaller court, lower net, and relaxed rules during physical education classes and practices volley skills during other school-related volleyball opportunities	• Practices volleyball skills during PE classes • Practices volleyball skills during recess and other opportunities during the school day	Identifies fitness benefits of volleyball
7th	Participates in modified volleyball games using lightweight practice balls, reduced numbers, and smaller court during physical education classes and during other school-related volleyball opportunities	• Practices volleyball skills during PE classes • Practices volleyball skills during recess and other opportunities during the school day • Documents participation in volleyball-related activities	Identifies fitness requirements of volleyball
8th	Participates in modified volleyball games using smaller numbers and court size during physical education classes, during other school-related volleyball opportunities, and outside of school volleyball opportunities	• Practices volleyball skills during PE classes • Practices volleyball skills during recess and other opportunities during the school day • Documents participation in modified games of volleyball outside of the school setting	Identifies and participates in activities that improve volleyball performance and improve fitness for volleyball
High school	Participates in semicompetitive volleyball games during physical education classes and other school-sponsored volleyball opportunities and seek to participate in local volleyball opportunities outside of the school setting	Documents participation in organized volleyball games outside of the school setting	Develops a lifetime fitness plan that includes regular participation in volleyball

Teaching Styles and Strategies

Diane Tunnell

Teaching is to the teacher as cooking is to the chef. There are recipes to be followed, but as all great chefs know, the unique ingredients and the creativity of the chef are what make a great meal. Teaching can be seen in the same light. It is a combination of many ingredients, and the teacher makes wise decisions about how to blend those ingredients to achieve a particular outcome.

The recipe for excellence in teaching calls for the teacher to understand that each student possesses unique abilities and aptitudes. The teacher must be able to blend student characteristics, instructional (teaching) styles or strategies, the environment where the learning is to take place, and his or her personality characteristics to come up with a winning recipe that allows each student to experience success. Just as the chef does not rely on one outstanding recipe to meet all the varied tastes of his or her clients, the teacher cannot rely on just one method of imparting knowledge to all of his or her students. Therefore, an excellent teacher, like the excellent chef, has a variety of recipes to maximize student learning and assure that all the desired outcomes are achieved.

A teaching style is only one aspect of teaching. Before any teaching style can be implemented several other factors must be considered: the content to be taught, the capability of the physical environment to carry out certain styles, the time allotted or necessary for style implementation, the amount of allocated class time, the teacher's personal style, and most important the students themselves. Across the nation, school demographics are changing, so instructional practices must be modified to meet the challenges of a more diverse population. As teaching styles and strategies are presented throughout this chapter, consider the factors mentioned to see whether that particular style matches program objectives, content, and students' developmental levels. Also, consider what modifications can be made to allow a match between teaching style and each lesson. No one teaching style has been demonstrated to enhance learning for all students, and each style has unique outcomes. Using a variety of teaching styles appropriately will ensure that the needs of all students are met. The main goal is for all students to experience success in the movement environment.

PREPARING THE ENVIRONMENT

Success in education is defined as student achievement. Several factors influence the success of a lesson. Did the student learn what was planned by the conclusion of the lesson? Did the student achieve the objectives set at the beginning of the lesson? The ultimate goal of teaching is student learning. The environment where physical activity is taught plays an important role in establishing the tone for student learning. Although some environmental factors cannot be modified, such as size of the playing fields, teachers can design a learning arena that is inviting, encouraging, and safe.

Create an attractive learning environment. Craft bright and interesting bulletin boards and other wall displays that teach. Integrate work and action pictures of your students. Have visual aids to set up as attractive focal points during a lesson such as models of the human heart, a skeleton, an oversized rubber band to represent a muscle stretching, or attractive posters that highlight the bones or muscles that you are studying that week. For younger students you might have a cardboard skeleton that you begin putting together as you study the anatomy of the body.

Displays will enhance student learning, especially if the materials are available for them to see close up or examine personally during a lesson. Students, parents, and other volunteers can help generate these displays. Consider asking the art teacher to integrate this as a special project into his or her class.

Incorporate music. Music is an excellent avenue to enhance the learning environment. Music can welcome students, signal station changes, and provide a background that invites participation. Incorporating music with a good beat and tempo can also be used to help develop kinesthetic awareness of the body in motion and spatial awareness. Music helps students integrate multisensory skills that are necessary to accomplish all physical activities. Within the bounds of good taste, allow students to bring music from home (screen before using in class).

Provide a safe environment. A safe environment provides a foundation for learning. No one can learn about or enjoy physical activity if he or she is afraid. Physical safety includes an environment free of debris, hazards, and other unsafe situations. Make sure that activity areas, locker rooms, and classrooms are clean, freshly painted, and safe. Teach students specific safety information. Remind students often about safety concerns, and practice emergency procedures.

An attractive learning environment will help students engage in the topics being taught within the classroom.

Keeping Students Actively Involved

Students contribute to a successful learning environment. No matter how upbeat and attractive the classroom environment is, the students will play a big part. Here are some tips that teachers can use to help keep students involved.

► At the beginning of each semester or year, dedicate several days to having students participate in team building or cooperative activities to help increase student involvement. Design activities that provide opportunities for students to work with their classmates to achieve specific outcomes and learn leadership skills.

► Students live in the here and now, and relevant tasks and activities can provide the connection between learning in the movement setting and the world outside of school. Having students make choices about what they want to learn influences student participation. Mandated curriculum outcomes can usually be accomplished in many ways; let students share in these decisions.

► To enhance learning and provide meaning when teaching students to develop active life-

styles, have them locate services or avenues in the community where they can participate outside of the school environment.

► Provide open gym or playgrounds before and after school to allow extra time to experiment and apply what has been learned in the movement setting. Often in a class setting too much information is presented at one time, thus reducing actual practice time. Offering additional time either before school, after school, or during the lunch break will allow students to achieve greater proficiency, which may carry over throughout life.

► Communicate by interacting with as many students as possible during each class session using positive and constructive verbal and nonverbal communication. Students are acutely aware of body language and the tone of statements. By showing a genuine interest in your students, they are more likely to respond by working a little harder, resulting in greater participation. If the student does not understand the task, go over the basic steps in a nonthreatening manner. For example, you may say, "Serena, let's try that skill again, only this time concentrate on keeping your elbows straight instead of bent" instead of saying, "Serena, why can't you remember that I said to keep your elbows straight!"

▶ Involve yourself in the lesson. Don't be the teacher that just tells the students what to do; involve yourself, when appropriate, by joining in the activity. Play a few minutes with each group; show them how it is done.

▶ Design or modify activities to suit the age, experience, and ability of the students participating. If the class is practicing push-ups and several students have insufficient upper-body strength to perform a full body push-up, allow them to perform a modified push-up or wall push-up. At the other end of the spectrum, provide enhanced activities for students who are ready to move forward. Those who can easily perform full body push-ups could attempt to perform triceps push-ups (bringing the arms close to the body instead of shoulder-width apart), perform fingertip push-ups (using just the fingers instead of the entire palm), or perform a clap between push-ups.

▶ When teaching new activities, some students may be reluctant to participate for a variety of reasons; they may perceive themselves as less skilled and be afraid of failure and embarrassment, or their experiences with learning new skills may have been negative. Give students the opportunity to watch before participating. Reassurance from the teacher along with a belief that students can succeed will help them overcome apprehension.

Equipment

Having enough equipment is helpful in maximizing physical activity. A good point to remember is that no one improves health-related fitness while waiting in a line to be active.

▶ Set up equipment and test audiovisual equipment and computer programs before class begins.

▶ Make sure that equipment is in good working order by inspecting it at least once a month.

▶ Secure exercise equipment such as treadmills and stationary bikes so that they cannot be used without adult supervision.

▶ Design a procedure for transporting and distributing equipment.

▶ Assign squad leaders, specific students, or student assistants to pass out and return equipment.

Here are some ideas that might help eliminate or reduce equipment shortages:

▶ Contact community members for donations of quality used equipment (as a tax deduction, of course). Local health and fitness clubs may be willing to donate a portion of their retired equipment to schools to enhance a fitness room.

▶ Scour garage sales and classified ads to purchase quality used treadmills, elliptical machines, rowing machines, weight benches, dumbbells, stability balls, or stationary bikes for a fraction of the original cost.

▶ Parents may be willing to donate used equipment.

▶ Consider having the school or a qualified individual make some equipment. An example might be dot agility mats. This piece of equipment is easy to replicate at about a third of the cost of a remanufactured mat. The mat is constructed of heavy nonslip rubber in a square that comes in various sizes, often a 24-inch or 36-inch (60 or 90 cm) square (size is based on audience), that has five dots marked on it with permanent marker (see figure 10.1).

▶ Pool resources with other schools (both financial and equipment). Several schools can collaborate to buy equipment and then design a rotation system for usage.

▶ Host fund-raising projects to help purchase equipment, if the school allows such activity.

▶ Another way to gain equipment is by writing and applying for grants. Money is available at the state and federal levels. NASPE's Web site contains a section on grant writing and the availability of grant money (www.aahperd.org/naspe).

Figure 10.1   A dot agility mat.

TEACHING STYLES

Teaching can greatly affect student interest and enjoyment—and therefore student attitudes toward physical activity—so using a variety of teaching styles is necessary. Just as the chef uses a variety of ingredients, the excellent teacher uses an array of styles and strategies to enhance student learning. Depending on the style or strategy chosen, passive learning can be turned into active learning.

Teaching styles and strategies refer to the type of interaction between the student and the teacher. It ranges on a continuum from basic, direct instruction to student-initiated learning, in which the teacher serves as a facilitator and the student has increased responsibility for learning.

A Continuum of Teaching

Mosston and Ashworth (2002) have defined 11 teaching styles along a continuum from direct instruction (teacher initiated) to indirect instruction (self-teaching). Each of these styles can

enhance health-related physical fitness education. The continuum approach is an excellent avenue for helping students to gain knowledge. During the initial phase of teaching health-related fitness, students will benefit from a direct approach. As they mature and gain knowledge, skills, and experience, teaching from a more student-centered approach supports independent learning and allows students to have more personal responsibility for their own physical activity choices.

Mosston and Ashworth's (2002) identified teaching styles include command (direct), practice, reciprocal, self-check, inclusion, guided discovery, convergent discovery, divergent production, learner designed, learner initiated, and self-teaching. Although teaching styles form a continuum from teacher-directed to student-initiated learning, they are not implemented in a linear manner. Using both the command (direct) and practice styles at the same time would be ineffective when content is new and students lack the understanding needed to work independently. For example, a particular protocol determines success for curl-ups performed for Fitnessgram. Using direct instruction, teachers provide students with correct information. On the other hand, after students have learned the basics of a particular routine, allowing them the autonomy to refine, enhance, or modify the routine using a more independent learning style is appropriate. As students develop responsible behaviors, they will likely make better selections concerning their future health.

Command (direct).   Teachers are the decision makers. Students do the same thing at the same time. This style is appropriate for teaching new skills and for managing a class that needs a high degree of structure. Direct teaching is also appropriate when task sequencing is essential and when deviating from the sequence is not permitted, as in teaching how to perform CPR. Direct teaching is appropriate for delivering some lecture information essential to success before students perform the task. Other topics that might be taught effectively using direct instruction include calculating resting heart rate and recording data on a graph to determine which exercise resulted in higher heart rates.

TEACHING TIP: VARYING YOUR TEACHING STYLE

Most effective teachers have a variety of teaching styles in their repertoires. Different classes, skills, and concepts will benefit from teachers' use of different styles, although finding which styles produce the most learning in various situations is a challenge. The better grasp teachers have of the different styles, the more likely they will be to try to use them. Teaching might be compared to carpentry. If teachers have only a hammer and a saw in their tool belts, they will be limited in the kind of work they can do. Likewise, if a teacher has only two teaching styles in his or her repertoire, there will be a limited possibility of reaching all students—and limiting their opportunity to learn.

Catherine Himberg, Professor of Physical Education

    California State University
    Chico, California

From Himberg, Hutchinson, and Rousell 2003.

Practice. Teachers decide what to teach, demonstrate or use task sheets to introduce the skill, mandate the amount of time that students will practice, and circulate among students, giving them feedback. Students determine the number of practice trials and the order in which they will practice skills (if more than one is part of the lesson). This style is often used in a physical education setting, and although it is valuable, it should not be overused. This style is appropriate for teaching a new skill and for skill refinement; compared with the command style, it affords students more latitude about how much practice they think they need. For example, high school students might be asked to bring their heart rates into their target heart rate zones, but they are free to choose from four different activities. Another example includes having students participate at stations performing different exercises presented on a task card that offers differing intensity levels (e.g., push-ups: choose either regular, modified, or wall.).

Reciprocal. Students are provided with opportunities to become more independent. Tasks are designed for students to work collaboratively (usually in pairs or groups of three) and provide feedback about each other's performance. Each group of students is supplied a task sheet that has the specific instructions and roles that they are to perform. A student is either the observer or the performer. This style is used primarily for refinement. Social interaction is an important aspect of reciprocal teaching. This style is also an excellent avenue for accomplishing standard 5 of the National Standards for Physical Education as outlined by NASPE: exhibiting responsible personal and social behavior that respects self and others in physical activity settings. The teacher's role is not to correct performance but to monitor student interactions and to encourage the observers to give positive, quality feedback to the performers. This style allows students to become more actively involved in their own learning, which can result in greater understanding. An example of this style is preparing students to take a Fitnessgram assessment. Students can practice the individual tests with a partner or small group. Each member of the group can provide information and motivation.

Self-check. As in the reciprocal style, students are involved in evaluating their own performance. The teacher determines the tasks to be completed. Criteria sheets are used to assess the quality of performance. Each student performs the tasks and provides his or her own feedback by completing the sheet. This style is appropriate for refining skills and building self-reliance. This style also is designed to be used with tasks that can be self-monitored. The self-check style works well for physical activity homework assignments. For example, ask students to log aerobic fitness activity time performed outside of class. Students select appropriate activities and monitor their progress.

Inclusion. Teacher-designed tasks provide students with choice through options. This style helps the teacher individualize lessons. Students choose a particular difficulty level at which to perform. Responsibility for learning is placed with the student. Students choose when to move to a more difficult level of performance. Students develop responsibility for their own health. For example, when students are performing rope jumping, they have the choice of the type of jump (skip or two feet) to be performed or the pace (regular or double time). When working on muscular strength and endurance, they can choose between using dumbbells of various weight (given certain parameters) or dynabands of various tensile strength. For younger students you can set up cones of three different heights and let them choose the height to practice skier jumps, thus working on muscular endurance. Expectations must be clear so that students know that they are expected to increase the difficulty.

Guided discovery. In this style, the teacher is working to enhance not only the physical abilities of students but also their critical-thinking skills. The teacher determines the task and then designs a sequence of questions or problems that will lead students to one right answer. The teacher guides the students but does not give them the answer. Student success depends on the teacher's ability to arrange the task in a logical sequence. This style helps students become active participants in the learning process. An example of a guided discovery has students write a report that answers the following questions:

- ▶ Can you identify a jogging or in-line skating route starting from school or home that allows you to jog or skate for 20 minutes? In this example, students might have to try several routes to find one that meets the criteria.
- ▶ What should you wear? How might your clothing change with the time of day and weather?
- ▶ What safety issues will you have to consider? Do these change with the time of day or weather?

Another example of the guided discovery style might be to have students perform three different activities (jumping rope, jogging, in-line skating) for a designated time using heart rate monitors and recording the results. After they finish all the activities, have them determine which one helped them reach and maintain their target heart rate the best and which one they liked the best. They will likely discover that the one they enjoyed the most produced the best results.

An example of a guided discovery assignment might be assigning students to write a report that answers a question such as "What safety concerns should you address when in-line skating or jogging in your neighborhood?"

For younger students, have them find the answer to the following question: Which activity, from the choices given, makes your heart beat the fastest? Allow students to try three or four different activities such as jumping rope, skipping around the gym, jogging in place, or crawling from one cone to another to answer this question.

Convergent discovery. Students are provided with a problem that has one answer. They go through the discovery process to converge on the answer, and the teacher facilitates the process. Students are encouraged to become independent, critical thinkers using trial and error.

For example, high school students can complete a report on what it would take to begin participating in a beneficial aerobic fitness activity. Another example poses the question, "What effect does gaining or losing weight (body fat) have on your heart rate?" Students experiment by performing several tasks, adding or subtracting more weight during the activity for each trial until they reach the answer. Students can increase or decrease the resistance, using any of the following: hand weights, ankle weights, books, or medicine balls.

Divergent production. An open-ended problem is presented to students to solve. This style is appropriate for students who are ready to work independently. For example, pose a particular situation to students: "You have broken your ankle, but you want to maintain good aerobic fitness while wearing your cast." They must devise an aerobic fitness plan to meet this challenge. Younger students might develop a routine that includes three locomotor movements that they can perform at a moderate level of physical activity.

Gardner's Theory of Multiple Intelligences

Implementing a variety of teaching styles is just one part of providing a positive learning experience. Another important consideration is how students learn. Students have different learning styles. Acknowledging and addressing students' learning styles provides another strategy to ensure successful student learning. People use three basic senses in learning how to perform physical activity: auditory (hearing), visual (seeing), and kinesthetic (doing). When teachers prepare lessons that incorporate strategies that address individual learning styles, student learning is enhanced. **Gardner's theory of multiple intelligences** (1983, 1993) asserts that because each person learns and produces best through various avenues, students need to have opportunities to develop weak avenues and excel through strong avenues.

An example in developing a lesson using multiple intelligences is to take a health-related fitness concept and use the process of concept mapping to see how to incorporate the different intelligences. The effect of this approach will be more student involvement that results in student learning. Here is an example of how a teacher might teach the concept of aerobic fitness using the eight different intelligences:

- Bodily-kinesthetic intelligence (learn by doing; physical learning)—Perform any movement or activity to aid in understanding aerobic fitness.
- Spatial intelligence (pictures)—Perform locomotor activities using task cards with pictures.
- Interpersonal intelligence (social; cooperative)—Perform any physical activity in groups or pairs for greater motivation.
- Musical intelligence (music or beat; rhythmic movement)—Skip rope to the beat of music.
- Logical-mathematical intelligence (numbers expert)—Count the number of heartbeats in one minute.
- Intrapersonal intelligence (self-learning; reflecting individual)—Perform two types of aerobic exercise and measure heart rate to compare benefits of each.
- Naturalistic intelligence (environmentalist)—Design a walking or jogging route in your neighborhood.
- Linguistic intelligence (word smart)—Explain why our hearts beat fast when we exercise.

The *Physical Best Activity Guides* combine health-related fitness concepts, using a variety of instructional styles and strategies in physically challenging and fun activities. "Frantic Ball" in the *Elementary Activity Guide* is an example of an activity that combines mathematical, spatial, and kinesthetic intelligence. "Body Composition Survivor" is a secondary-level activity that incorporates linguistic, cooperative, kinesthetic, and guided discovery. Using station activities provides an effective way to incorporate the practice instructional style, linguistic intelligence, and health-related fitness concepts. As students move from station to station performing the designated activity, task cards are posted with relevant concepts. Students must read and accomplish the task with their groups. At the end of class they can write in their journals or discuss the concept presented. The activity "Health Quest" found in the *Middle and High School Activity Guide* is a good illustration of this concept. It stresses the importance of aerobic fitness as students perform a variety of different activities. An example for elementary students is "Muscle Hustle," which stresses the importance of muscular strength and endurance.

Incorporating a variety of styles and intelligences may strengthen a student's understanding of a concept or activity, thus increasing learning. Remember the Chinese proverb that says, "I hear and I forget. I see and I remember. I do and I understand."

Bodily-kinesthetic intelligence. Bodily-kinesthetic intelligence is a natural fit for physical activity leading toward health-related fitness. Moving to learn isn't just for the gymnasium! People strong in bodily-kinesthetic intelligence solve problems or create with their bodies. These individuals like to experience the action, or feel the way that the body reacts in certain circumstances.

To address this intelligence, younger students will enjoy miming actions (e.g., actions of a muscle extending or flexing), crafts that reinforce concepts (e.g., a valentine promising yourself to eat more heart healthy), a hands-on science lesson (e.g., capillary action shown by dropping colored water on a good brand of paper towel), drama (e.g., act out oxygen exchange in the lungs), and other creative movement.

Movement-based curriculum models are an excellent avenue to enhance and incorporate this intelligence. This curriculum model is organized around themes involving the body and its interrelationship with space, time, effort, and flow. An example that combines a health-related concept within a movement base curriculum theme would be to have the students practice push-ups with a partner. Have them do push-ups in unison. Another example would be to have students move at different paces (slow, medium, and fast) or different levels (low, medium, and high) to determine which makes the heart beat faster.

This approach also works on body movement and spatial relationship. Middle or high school students might be asked to create a video for

teaching elementary students about health-related fitness. Another way to use this intelligence is to have students design and implement a personal fitness plan. Hand weights, ankle weights, balance boards, or step boxes can be used to assist students in achieving better muscular development. Bodily-kinesthetic intelligence epitomizes the essence of a physical-educated person.

Spatial intelligence. Spatial intelligence is the understanding of how objects are oriented in space. A strong sense of direction and the ability to visualize end products accurately are suggestive of this intelligence. Incorporate teacher and student demonstrations as much as possible. Students can demonstrate a particular skill or analyze each other's running technique. The group activity "Knots" is an example of using this intelligence.

Students use critical thinking, problem solving, and cooperation skills to unravel the knot of hands.

Students form a circle and place both hands in the center. Students walk to the center and all join hands with other students across from them, forming a tangled mess or "knot." Then students must try to untie the knot without letting go of hands. This will involve students stepping over, crawling under, and moving around one another. All students must work cooperatively and determine how to solve the problem in the space provided. They must conceptualize the spatial aspects (LeFevre, 2002).

On a more cognitive level, students can create charts, graphs, diagrams, and three-dimensional models. This activity works well for charting heart rates, recording weight-training progress, and logging physical activity. Another aspect is to have students perform activities blindfolded to get the feel of an activity from a different perspective.

Interpersonal intelligence. Interpersonal intelligence is the ability to understand and relate well to others. People with this type of intelligence are often interested in group brainstorming, cooperative activities, peer tutoring, simulations, and community-based activities. Students could work in small groups to develop an aerobic fitness circuit, brainstorm solutions to problems as a class or in small groups, or use simulations to teach real-world interpersonal skills. For instance, ask, "How would you spend $100 in this community to participate in physical activity?" Have students collect data on the cost of facilities, equipment, and so on as homework and then work in small groups to help each other make wise and satisfying choices. Train students to participate as peer tutors or volunteers in the community on a health-related fitness service project (e.g., leading active games at a day care center).

Musical intelligence. Musical intelligence is the ability to interpret, transform, and express musical forms. Using raps, chants, songs, rhythms, and musical concepts is the ideal way to reach students that tend to learn in this manner.

Music and movement are highly integrated. Give students opportunities to experiment with music and its relationship to health-related fitness. Music can also be used to enliven and set the pace for physical activities. Students can enhance presentations through rap, chants, and songs.

Logical-mathematical intelligence. Logical-mathematical intelligence suggests a strong ability to reason and use numbers effectively. People who excel in this area seem to relate most problems back to a number problem or puzzle. These individuals also like to engage in problem-solving tasks and critical-thinking activities. In a physical environment setting, students can use this intelligence in a variety of ways to help understand certain health-related concepts.

Middle or high school students can be challenged to solve health-related fitness problems such as calculating target heart rate zones, the percentage of fat calories (kilocalories) found in a particular food, energy expenditure related to climbing a flight of stairs, or the number of kilocalories expended walking versus running a mile. Elementary students can create movement sequences and patterns for jump rope, which includes counting skill repetitions while developing muscular strength and endurance or aerobic fitness. This form of intelligence can also be combined with spatial intelligence in an activity. You can ask students how far it is from point A to point B and how many steps it will take them if they walk, run, skip, or hop. Then have them find the solution through participation.

Intrapersonal intelligence. People who tend to be more intrinsically motivated, self-reflecting, self-reliant, and independent excel in intrapersonal intelligence. Minimal motivation is needed for these individuals to accomplish a task. Accomplishing goals seem easier because of their ability to self-reflect. These students prefer to learn through making personal connections, participating in self-paced activities, and setting goals.

A health-related physical fitness education program should guide students toward becoming more independent. For example, self-testing and reflective journal writing opportunities help students make personal connections to the information. Fitness stations with a variety of tasks or levels encourage the development of intrapersonal intelligence. For instance, students could participate at a jump rope station where they choose between three types of jumping—forward, backward, or criss-cross. Another example would have students time themselves to see how many push-up they can accomplish in 15, 30, or 45 seconds.

Younger students just developing reading skills would have pictures at the station to help them perform the appropriate activity. Older students can research and try out various physical activities that they find interesting. Self-paced activities and learning centers, where students have the option of challenging themselves, can also be provided.

Naturalistic intelligence. Activities that involve our environment or that relate to our natural surroundings enhance naturalistic intelligence. People strong in naturalistic intelligence like to be outdoors and learn through analogies to the environment. This intelligence can be addressed by using themes from nature as well as stories and poems about nature to encourage movement experiences that develop health-related physical fitness. For example, performing the crab walk, bear walk, and seal crawl helps young children study movement in nature while developing muscular strength and endurance. At the middle or high school level, science teachers can be solicited to create a study of how plants and animals live at high altitudes and what the human physiological implications are for exercising at high altitudes (e.g., What adaptations have plants and animals made at high altitude? What are the acute changes that humans face when performing at high altitudes? What are the chronic adaptations to high altitude?). All students, regardless of age, can also consider the value of physical activity in natural settings, such as hiking, canoeing, and rafting.

An adventure-based curriculum is an excellent choice to augment this intelligence. Entire grades can be taken to a natural setting (outdoor recreational camps) to teach integrated content including social studies, science, math, and physical education. These students are provided opportunities to participate in hiking, canoeing, orienteering, and rock climbing.

Adventure-based activities such as hiking and canoeing help children study movement in nature while developing muscular strength and endurance.

Linguistic intelligence. Linguistic intelligence involves using words effectively; these students can be classified as "word smart." Of interest to these students are opportunities to read, tell stories, debate, perform writing activities, and participate in group discussions. Addressing this intelligence would include activities such as keeping a written log of their participation in health-related physical fitness education activities. Combining linguistic intelligence with musical intelligence provides students with opportunities to perform physical activity to poems, raps, and routines that they create. Another avenue for incorporating this intelligence includes keeping a journal that describes what they learned or how to apply what they learned during daily activities. Developing a fitness plan using the FITT principle is another example of linguistic intelligence. Adjusting the directions and responses to make activities developmentally appropriate allows younger students to participate in similar activities.

Cooperative Learning

Cooperative learning occurs when students work together to complete a specified task or achieve a certain goal. It places the responsibility for learning on the student and promotes a more active learning environment. The versatility of this style allows it to integrate multiple intelligences, and it has the potential to incorporate all three learning domains. The physical environment is an ideal setting for cooperative learning to take place because students must work in teams or small groups to perform many of the traditional physical education activities. Cooperative learning is also an excellent way to help students become more involved in health-related activities because they work in groups rather than as isolated individuals. Peers can encourage each other to work harder or provide leadership to assist those who are struggling.

Jigsawing is an example of cooperative learning. Each member of a team is given a particular assignment to complete; each team member then brings back her product and places her piece of the "puzzle" with other team members' pieces to form a complete picture. The sidebar "Jigsawing Assignment" provides an example of how students can use the jigsaw strategy in a physical education environment. Students are provided with opportunities to be responsible for their own learning. Cognitive, psychomotor, and affective learning domains are addressed through cooperative-learning strategies. Teachers serve as facilitators and provide the students with instructional feedback.

Another benefit of cooperative learning is its motivating qualities. Students are free to work with friends, problem solve, and interact with a variety of people.

ENHANCING HEALTH-RELATED FITNESS IN THE CLASSROOM SETTING

The classroom setting can be an opportune place to discuss content from physiology and psychology, exercise principles, and goal-setting techniques, although teaching health-related fitness need not be relegated to the classroom setting. Developing cognitive understanding ensures that students will receive a comprehensive health-related fitness education.

Planning

1. Create classroom lessons that complement the existing curriculum. Teach health-related fitness lessons that reinforce concepts learned during participation through physical activity. Students should be actively engaged in activities that create opportunities to develop responsibility for their own learning. The teaching styles presented earlier in this chapter can be used in the classroom setting.

2. Organize lessons according to health-related fitness concepts.

3. Link what students learn in the classroom with the physical environment.

The following are examples of content that can be used in the classroom setting:

Healthy heart statement. Younger students can create several model hearts that are accompanied by a specific statement highlighting ways to stay heart healthy. Several laminated heart pieces are given to a group of three to five students. Each piece represents a part of a complete heart that the students will piece together. After completing the model, the students can discuss the statements.

JIGSAWING ASSIGNMENT

Unit: health-related fitness components

Jigsawing Instructions

1. Divide students into groups of four and either assign each member a fitness component or allow them to assign themselves a fitness component.

2. Give team members three to five activities that will enhance specific fitness components. If time allows, have students design or locate the activities themselves.

3. All members regroup and design three or four warm-up routines that include all four components of fitness.

4. Be certain to have the appropriate materials on hand.

5. Another approach is to assign the first part of this assignment as homework and then devote one class period to the group portion.

6. Then you can have the group lead the class in the warm-up routines for the next couple of weeks.

Example Jigsawing Activity: Move, Move, Move

For this activity have good four-count rhythm music. Step aerobics music will work well.

1. Divide students into groups of four or fewer.

2. Give each group a particular movement that they must perform and have them practice their movement for a short period to the beat of the music. For example:

- Group one: jump in one spot eight times.
- Group two: hop on left foot four times; hop on right foot four times.
- Group three: do feet-only jumping jacks four times (each jack counts as two).

3. Then regroup students so that the new groups have one person from each of the original groups representing a different movement.

4. Then have them combine their movements to form a new routine or movement sequence.

5. Allow them to practice their routine.

6. Have each group perform their routine for the entire class.

Make the movement developmentally appropriate for the age level. For younger students use pictures with words to describe their movement; with older elementary students just the words should suffice. You could also allow them to design their own four- to eight-count movements.

Example Jigsawing Activity: Aerobic Routine

After students have had several days performing aerobics or step aerobics, let them design their own routine to teach to the class.

Place students into groups of three to five and give each of them a particular component of an aerobic routine to design. Then have them come together and put the routine to music.

One student designs the warm-up segment; two or three students design the aerobic segment, and one student designs the cool-down segment.

Adapted from Rink 1998.

Interpreting heart rate data. Middle and high school students can calculate their resting heart rates and target heart rate zones (see chapter 5), chart heart rates in graph form, log workout results, and calculate averages.

Fitness plans. Older students can take on the role of fitness expert advisor for a newspaper or magazine. Create several fictitious letters that are sent to the fitness expert advisors for advice. After students have written their responses, have

them post their responses or read them aloud in class and discuss. Here are some examples: (1) I am a pitcher for my team and I want to make my arms stronger so that I can throw harder. What can I do to accomplish this? (2) I want to make my varsity sport team next year but I am not very strong. What exercises or activities can I do to help me gain overall strength and run faster?

Treating injuries. Naturally, preventing injuries is the way to go, but students need to understand that injuries can occur even when they are careful. Contact the American Red Cross or the National Safety Council for more information on basic first aid and cardiopulmonary resuscitation (CPR). Recommended injury treatment topics to be covered include the following: heat- and cold-related problems (heat stress, heat exhaustion, hypothermia, and hyperthermia); fluid intake (dehydration); sunburn and skin protection; and the role of nutrition in reducing injuries and improving overall health and fitness (see chapter 4).

Becoming a good fitness consumer. In this age of advertising blitzes, cable shopping networks, and Internet surfing, being a good fitness consumer is essential. Students need to know how to comparison shop to get the most for their money when paying for equipment, supplies, and services. Learning how to discern when a product isn't worth the container it comes in is an important skill. The following are suggestions for consumer education activities that can be adapted to fit students' ages and abilities:

▶ Ask students to compare vitamin supplement claims with the research and then make recommendations to their classmates based on their findings. (Have the class discuss whether they agree or not.)

▶ Direct students to bring in an advertisement for a fad diet or a piece of exercise equipment that promises miracle results. Have them report (orally or in writing) on whether the claim is true and why or why not.

▶ Discuss what might make an advertisement effective (e.g., flashy, quick bites of information, enthusiastic claims, and so on). Have small groups of students develop magazine ads or act out TV commercials that advertise the benefits of a health-related fitness activity or practice (e.g., drinking plenty of water before, during, and after exercise; playing an active game instead of watching TV; and the like).

▶ Take a field trip to a local sports equipment store. Have students prepare specific questions to ask about equipment that interests them. Ask the salespeople to help the students compare the features of similar products. Then for homework, have each student choose one of the products and explain in writing why it was the best buy for his or her needs.

Logging physical activity data. The classroom is an ideal setting for teaching students how to develop appropriate goals and physical activity logs. Emphasis can be placed on accurately recording data. If students have access to a computer lab they can record their fitness score using Fitnessgram and their activity logs using Activitygram. Students can be shown how to use generic programs such as Microsoft Excel to keep physical activity logs or design a physical activity calendar. Calendars can also include goals and specific activities that emphasize the overload principle. Students can use spreadsheet programs and computerized logbooks for running and other aerobic activities. Help students understand the connections between the results that they have recorded and changes in their physical activities and health-related fitness scores. Students can use the written records to create new goals based on their success.

Setting goals. The classroom setting provides opportunities to explain the purpose and mechanisms of goal setting (chapter 2). Sample class activities include the following:

▶ Help a fictional person set appropriate goals (e.g., How might a teenager build upper-body strength so that she or he can climb the climbing wall? A person wants to improve body composition. What are realistic ways in which he or she can reach this goal?).

▶ Students work with a friend to help each other set realistic goals and plan activities to reach the goals in one health-related fitness area. Instruct them to think of incentives that they can offer each other (e.g., "If we both follow our plan, we'll buy those new outfits," or "We'll walk to the mall together so that we can talk while we exercise").

▶ Brainstorm reasons why people might not stick to their physical activity plans until they reach their goals. Then choose one problem and list ways to overcome it.

Give younger students a handout to work on that includes a list of specific activities. Ask them how many of each activity they think they can do in a certain time (15 seconds, 30 seconds, and so on). Then have them perform the activity and write their actual number completed. Conclude by having them circle the final number if they accomplished their initial goal or place an X over the final number if they did not. Discuss goal expectations. Recording sheets can be used during the year to help students see their progress. This is also good lead-up practice for designing personal fitness plans.

Designing a personal health-related fitness plan. Primary-grade students can begin to make choices about how they will reach personal goals in each component of health-related fitness. Material is divided into small pieces so that students can understand and apply what they have learned. How much information is presented depends on students' developmental level. *The Physical Best Activity Guides* provide examples of developmentally appropriate activities that focus on specific components of health-related fitness.

Effective personal health-related fitness plans change as students change. Illustrate this point through examples of personal health-related fitness plans. Showing how goals are selected and reset after successful achievement is an important component. Students can begin to understand the process of tailoring a program to fit their current needs.

THE HOMEWORK CONCEPT

Many states have physical education standards that include specific outcomes in the cognitive, psychomotor, and affective domains. To achieve these standards, teachers include homework that moves physical activity and fitness development outside the gymnasium and into the home and community. Homework allows students to explore a topic; allows a cross-curricular approach; allows a variety of strategies to be incorporated; and can increase communication between parents, students, and the school.

Homework assignments should be purposeful.

▶ Incorporate actual physical activity as a homework assignment or a portion of the assignment. If students design a health and physical activity calendar, make certain that

they include activity as part of the calendar (see figure 10.2 on page 180).

▶ Make sure that homework assignments are connected to current lessons so that students can apply what they have learned in the classroom to the real world. Students live in the here and now, so keeping homework connected to current lessons keeps their experiences relevant.

▶ Homework can increase family involvement. Opportunities to link families and schools together are beneficial for all involved. Physical activity participation can be increased, communication avenues can be opened, and stronger family relationships can be developed.

The variety and type of possible homework assignments are numerous. They can be as simple as completing a worksheet or as comprehensive as developing a portfolio. Kindergartners as well as seniors in high school can do homework. The key is designing the appropriate assignment. Much of the information described in the preceding section (as topics for the classroom setting) could be modified to present as homework for students, thus allowing more class time for actual activity.

EXTENDING PHYSICAL ACTIVITY TIME

The amount of time that physical educators have with their students varies widely from state to state, school to school, and level to level. Regardless of how frequently you see your students, take advantage of strategies that can extend physical activity time beyond the walls of the gymnasium. The goal is to get students into the habit of being physically active on their own; keeping activities personally enjoyable is important so that students don't view these extra activities as drudgery. Adapt the following suggestions to fit students' age ranges and school facilities. These ideas should serve as extensions of physical education, not replacements. In other words, they are meant to enhance what is taught during physical education class. Administrators and colleagues must understand this perspective and not use outside class physical activity as a reason to reduce physical education programs.

SAMPLE HOMEWORK ASSIGNMENTS

These are examples of either a reflection or closure activity or a simple homework assignment for your students to complete.

Sport Reporting

Students attend a sporting event at their school. They watch the event, paying attention to the types of health- and skill-related components that the athletes need to perform the activity effectively. After the event the students identify the health- and skill-related fitness components they observed during the game using examples.

Interview

Students interview family members regarding their physical activity habits and write up a summary of the interview.

Brain Power

Students design crossword puzzles or word finds for their peers using health-related fitness terms.

Question for the Day

Design a question that will cause students to reflect on the day's lesson. For example, when teaching a unit on golf, you might ask, "Which of the health-related fitness components can you maintain or improve through regular participation in golf?"

Research Paper

Students pick a successful athlete and locate information about the workout regimen that the athlete uses or used to stay on top of his or her game physically and emotionally.

Active Andy and Suzy Slug

An example of an assignment for primary students might begin by having a discussion about what it means to be active and what activities they can do at home or after school to stay active. Reproduce pictures of children being either active or not active and send them home with the students. Ask them to draw a happy face beside the pictures that show kids being active and a sad face beside those being inactive.

Health Calendar

Have students design a calendar that celebrates physical education, fitness, and being healthy. The calendar can cover a week, two weeks, or a month (teacher's choice). The students should plan activities to do during that time and log their success. Figure 10.2 is one such calendar that was designed to celebrate National Physical Education Week, which is always the first week of May.

MAY						
Sunday	Monday	Tuesday	Wednesday	Thursday	Friday	Saturday
1	2	3	4	5	6	7
	No television or video games today. Go outside and do something physical.	Jump rope for at least 15 minutes today.	Take a 20-to 30-minute walk around the park or neighborhood today; go with a friend or walk the dog.	While watching your favorite television program, do sitting exercises such as crunches, push-ups, stretching, leg raises, biceps curls; and so on.	Ride your bike for 30 minutes. Tell a parent where you are going. Follow the laws of the road. Be safe!	

Figure 10.2 Keeping calendars is a motivating way to help students track and plan the frequency of their participation in physical activity.

▶ Fitness breaks—Physical activity can be accumulated throughout the day in short bouts, making this an increasingly popular and beneficial option. Classroom teachers can be asked to support increases in physical activity time. The trained and certified physical educator must train them to conduct these breaks. Provide information regarding the value of physical activity on students' classroom behavior, such as the fact that exercise increases blood flow to the brain and thus helps people think better. You may want to offer a 5-minute summary of several possible activities at each staff meeting Some ideas for classroom teachers would be to have students take a 5- to 10-minute dance break during which lively music is played and students continually move. Changing the music to a slower tempo can quiet the students. One idea is to have students cool down through a meditation-type activity. Another idea, weather permitting, is to take the students to the playground and have them perform a variety of locomotor movements in a designated space for at least 10 minutes. Many resources on the Internet provide simple break activities that require no specialized equipment.

▶ Recess—Ensure that students have ample equipment to perform physical activity. Student input is beneficial. Activities taught during physical education can frequently be used during recess.

▶ Lunchtime—Lunchtime free play is simply a longer recess in most schools, but it can be much more. The physical education teacher can be available as a personal fitness consultant or can train student volunteers to conduct fun fitness activities.

▶ Intramurals—These physical activity programs are conducted between teams of students or individual students from the same school. Adapt a program to augment the fitness curriculum. Ensure that the program is fun and welcoming to all who wish to participate. Consider having students keep track of minutes of activity or calculate calories burned as a way of keeping the focus on activity and fitness. Consider allowing students to add points for using encouraging words to classmates to keep the focus on social development and fun.

▶ Before-, during-, and after-school programs—Create a new program or enhance an existing program. Train others such as parents, senior volunteers, or child care workers to assist in these programs. Start a fitness club and offer incentives for participating.

▶ Home-based activities—Send home assignments for the entire family to participate in such as "The Family Health Minute." Present a specific health topic to your students and have them go home and discuss the information with (or explain it to) their families. Try to get them to set aside a few minutes two or three times a week. Provide new information each time or offer one topic with various subtopics. Have students create ways to be physically active while watching television. For example, during a commercial break a family could participate in an activity challenge. Each member performs 5 curl-ups during one commercial or hops on one foot 10 times during the commercial. Another idea is to work on flexibility by performing various stretches during a commercial. Commercials tend to run in 15- and 30-second frames, so that interval would be an appropriate time to hold a stretch. Families could also have some hand weights close by and perform various upper-body movements (lateral raises, front raises, biceps curls) during commercials.

▶ Community events—Family nights, health fairs, and Jump Rope or Hoops for Heart events (American Heart Association and AAHPERD) involve the wider community, from parents and siblings to senior citizens. Such events not only help students become more fit and healthy but also provide publicity for your program.

TECHNOLOGY

Podcasting, text messaging, iPods, DVDs—technological advances continue to occur. But what are the implications of technology for a health-related fitness education program? Using technology in the classroom is a strategy that can enhance teaching health-related physical fitness by increasing student motivation, morale, and confidence. Because today's students far surpass many teachers in their knowledge of technology (from text messaging to video productions), it is helpful to incorporate technology into learning about health-related physical fitness. According to Hayes and Silbermann (2007), "Between their popularity and their efficient delivery of information, video games may help enhance student' motivation, understanding and performance in sport."

Hardware. DVDs, computers, and video equipment can greatly enhance the teaching of health-related fitness concepts. DVDs about health-related fitness topics, such as the functioning of the cardiorespiratory system, training principles, false advertising, and many other areas can be used to enhance understanding. Students can use computers to download, analyze, graph, and store heart rate monitor data. Students can use the Internet to research health-related fitness topics or encourage "fitness pals" in other schools through e-mail. Students can be divided into small groups to develop health-related fitness reports and then videotape a newscast to share with peers or younger students. Some schools are equipped with in-house TV and radio stations that may be available for that purpose.

Handheld computers allow easier recording of data and decrease the need for pen and pencil. Teachers can conduct fitness testing and simply record the results on their handheld devices. The results can later be downloaded to the departmental or school computer for single-student analysis or report generation. LCD projectors can be used to enlarge objectives, daily activities, and closure questions to poster size and to assist in ensuring that instruction is focused and intentional.

Software. Fitnessgram software not only provides teachers with functions such as the ability to print out reports and keep information organized but also provides a mode through which individual students (using passwords) can keep track of their own progress in health-related fitness. Another feature is the Activitygram, which allows teachers and students to monitor activity levels. Electronic portfolios are an excellent way to track student progress throughout their school years or to have students design their own portfolios and track their progress.

Video games have been around for a long time and have been deemed a significant factor in causing youth to have a more sedentary lifestyle. In response, computer companies have introduced interactive video games designed to engage players physically. These games are more than just animated exercise; many have built in assessments and scoring systems based on skill performance, as well as heart rate monitors (Trout & Christie, 2007). Several sport product companies are now marketing dance or agility programs that allow students to improve health-related fitness by watching a video and replicating the moves on specially designed electronic carpets. Dance Dance Revolution is one such product. Wii Fit is one of the more recent programs that have a multitude of activities to help improve health-related fitness.

Equipment. Heart rate monitors can provide valuable information to both teachers and students. Students learn how to monitor their heart rates during aerobic workouts. Exercise heart rate zones, recovery heart rates, and resting heart rates provide needed information during periods of vigorous physical activity. Simple one- and two-function monitors can provide feedback to students. Sophisticated multifunction models are capable of programming individual heart rate information that can be downloaded to a computer.

Pedometers are another form of technology that students can use to monitor their physical activity levels inside and outside of the physical education setting. Pedometers vary from simple one-function varieties to multifunction varieties.

A number of products are available that conduct body composition evaluations. Some work like a handheld device that allows the user to download the results. Others require the user to record the information physically on paper and transfer it to a computer.

Programmable exercise equipment such as treadmills, elliptical machines, stair climbers, and weight machines have evolved within the last few years to include recording mechanisms for heart rate and heart rate target zones.

Internet. Delivery of instruction is enhanced with the use of resources housed on the Internet such as video clips, Web casts, geocaching, and many other new applications. A teacher can design Web quests that require students to locate information from a variety of educational Web sites. MyPyramid.gov is an excellent site for student to find information about a variety of health-related fitness activities.

The use of technology with a physical education curriculum, such as heart monitors and pedometers, can help students learn to monitor their physical activity and apply it to their activity outside of the classroom.

Using technology for inclusion. Technology has the capability to help all students be more physically active and learn about health-related fitness. Students with and without disabilities have powered up for learning. Technology has also provided new ways to promote the inclusion of students with a variety of disabilities (see chapter 11 for more information about inclusion).

Purchasing Technology

Before deciding to purchase new technology, consider these points:

▶ Resist the impulse to go out and buy immediately. Instead, try to borrow the item from a colleague or conduct some research to determine whether the item matches the student population. Consider asking the sales representative to loan the equipment for a time.

▶ Does this piece of technology or software assist students in reaching program outcomes? Do not always rely on the company's brochure and demonstrations. Instead, log on to the Internet and search for reviews of the equipment. Try to discover whether the equipment will be outdated within a couple of years and how sustainable the equipment is and at what cost.

▶ Grants can be used to assist in the purchase of health-related fitness technology. The National Association for Sport and Physical Activity (NASPE) has a Web page that identifies funding sources for physical education and related programs (www.aahperd.org/NASPE/grants).

▶ Technology can help teach, but it is no substitute for teaching. Technology products can easily become expensive toys. Make sure that each item is educationally sound for students and your program.

"Physical educators are in the business of promoting lifetime physical activity . . ." and if "interactive video games appear to be an effective tool in that quest . . ." (Trout & Christie, 2007, p. 45), then let's put them to good use.

SUMMARY

Health-related physical fitness education programs can be enhanced by creating an effective learning environment. By incorporating the principles described in this chapter, you can encourage students to pursue lifelong health-related fitness activities.

Create a fun and active learning environment, use appropriate teaching styles, and apply Gardner's theory of multiple intelligences to individualize programs to meet students' needs. Select a variety of developmentally appropriate learning experiences by ensuring that each is sequential, fun, safe, and inclusive.

Extend physical activity time by incorporating fitness breaks into the day for students. Make recess at the elementary level productive. Teach students activities that they can use during that time. Provide homework activities and assignments that reinforce what is being taught in the gymnasium. Involve family members in homework assignments. The more involved that families become, the greater the chance is that students will incorporate regular physical activity into their lives.

Although Physical Best promotes the principle of integrating health-related fitness knowledge into actual physical activities, sharing this information in depth in a classroom setting is effective at times. Incorporate technology into health-related fitness education. Let students move in the classroom; interested and actively engaged students learn more.

Including Everyone

Joni Morrison and Ginny Popiolek

Inclusion refers to the process of teaching students with disabilities together with their typically developing peers, using appropriate support systems that they otherwise would have received in a segregated setting. Although this chapter explores that concept in depth, it also looks at how to meet the needs of every student, regardless of gender, cultural or ethnic background, or ability level (whether or not a student has been identified as having a disability). In the Physical Best program, **inclusion** refers to the process of creating a learning environment that is open to and effective for all students whose needs and abilities fall outside the general range of those for children of similar age or whose cultural or religious beliefs differ from that of the majority group. In short, inclusion means that all students are included in an appropriate manner, so that all can reach their maximum potential.

RELEVANT LAWS

Although inclusion is the general trend in education and society (and the ethical philosophy to adopt), it is not mandated by law. The law mandates only the least restrictive environment (LRE) and civil rights. In the process of aligning with the No Child Left Behind Act Public Law 105-17, the Individuals with Disabilities Education Act (IDEA) was amended and signed into law in 2004. The provisions of this act became effective in 2005. These amendments continue to identify the curriculum content area of physical education for people with disabilities. This legislation identifies physical education as a curriculum area that is available to all children with disabilities. Least restrictive environment (LRE) mandates that students with disabilities are to be educated with their nondisabled peers to the maximum extent possible. The federal regulation states, "Physical Education services, specially designed if necessary, must be made available to every child with a disability receiving a free and appropriate public education." Figure 11.1 shows a continuum of placement options available to students with disabilities. Note that children with disabilities can move up and down the continuum based on their unique needs. Although some would advocate total inclusion at all times, physical educators should keep the intent of the law in mind and work to provide a quality program for children with disabilities regardless of their particular placement option.

The Individuals with Disabilities Education Act (IDEA) sought to change the status quo and integrate students with special needs to the fullest extent possible, based on each individual's needs and abilities. Educators began learning to focus first on what a person *could* do, rather than on what he or she *could not* do. In a similar vein, Title IX of the Education Amendments of 1972 prohibited discrimination based on gender and spelled out how public institutions should ensure an individual's civil rights regardless of gender. The Americans with Disabilities Act (ADA) has broadened the scope of inclusion and integra-

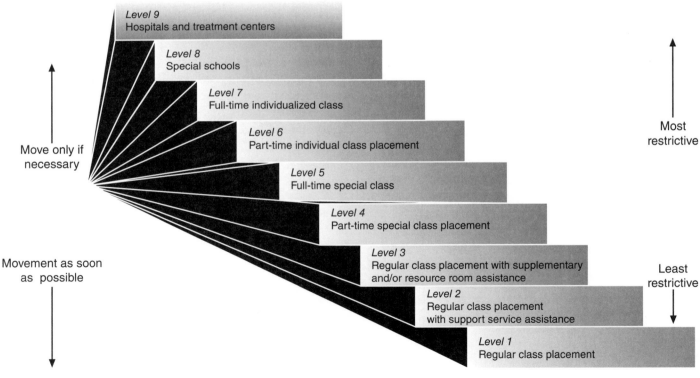

Figure 11.1 The continuum of placements for providing the least restrictive environment.

Adapted, by permission, from J. Winnick, 2010, *Adapted physical education and sport*, 5th ed. (Champaign, IL: Human Kinetics), 24.

tion by defining a disability as any individual characteristic that significantly impairs a major life activity.

Along with other civil rights legislation, this branch of law has created an acute awareness of the rights and needs of the individual. Aside from legal issues, however, offering a learning environment in which all students feel welcome and successful, achieve to the best of their abilities, and learn from diversity is simply the ethical action to take. Diversity is part of our society, and teachers should simulate the society in which students will function as adults as closely as possible—and model appropriate behavior toward those who appear, at least on the surface, to be unlike themselves.

BENEFITS OF INCLUSION

All students can benefit from true inclusion— from experiencing the diversity of society, from learning from those who appear to be unlike themselves, and from opportunities to find common ground despite differences. Inclusion allows students from other cultures to see a model of cultural inclusiveness that may positively influence their reactions to other cultures in the future, that validates their own culture, and that facilitates their own learning within the majority culture. Students with disabilities benefit from having peer models and greater opportunity to participate in physical activity. Peer tutoring is an appropriate and effective strategy to provide meaningful practice and high levels of motor activity. It also assists in maximizing active learning time (Lieberman & Houston-Wilson, 2002). All students benefit from being part of the problem solving that goes into being inclusive. Inclusion benefits both the child with a disability and students without disabilities. The hope is that these interactions will break down barriers and lead to acceptance and friendships between the two groups. Ultimately, programs benefit because they are more effective for all students as they work together toward the goal of developing positive lifelong physical activity behaviors.

All children should learn to participate together in physical activities no matter what their ability level. Adults work, recreate, and exercise side by side with people of varying abilities. Learning together at an early age prepares students for better cooperation later in life.

INCLUDING STUDENTS WHO DON'T SEEM TO FIT IN

I was working with a group of teenagers, many of whom seldom dressed appropriately for physical activity and were considered by other instructors as misfits. Instead of the prescribed activities, I introduced games analysis. We used leftover, abandoned, and broken equipment, such as broken bats and partially deflated balls. We also used as much other equipment as possible (e.g., more than four bases, lots of balls of different sizes and shapes, large discarded orange cones from a local construction site). Gradually, as they embraced the idea of changing games, they invented a baseball-like game. To this day I don't understand all aspects of their game—but they did!

The game involved eight bases; a player could run in any order he or she chose; more than one person could be on a single base at the same time; three teams competed simultaneously; and batters selected not only the type of pitch but also the type of ball to be pitched. It was a crazy game, but it wasn't long before every player was thoroughly engaged in the process of games modification, wearing appropriate attire, and creating and completing related homework assignments. Through games analysis, ownership of the program had shifted to the players.

Text is reprinted from G.S.D. Morris and J. Steihl, 1998, *Changing kids' games,* 2nd ed. (Champaign, IL: Human Kinetics), 41-42.

METHODS OF INCLUSION

What does all this mean for a health-related physical fitness education program? When programs include students who fall below the expected range of skill and ability, the answers include further individualizing based on each student's needs, modifying the activity for all students, and collaborating with peer tutors, parents, other volunteers, and colleagues.

An example of modifying an activity for all students is to allow students to choose which assessment of aerobic fitness they prefer to practice and perform. That way students with a disability can choose the assessment that allows them to use their abilities to their fullest, such as a blind student who chooses to perform the step test independently instead of the mile run, which would require the help of an assistant (AAALF–AAHPERD, 1995). A student with lower-body paralysis may need the activity to be changed completely, because she or he may benefit more from assessing for the upper-body strength and endurance needed to power a wheelchair and get into and out of a wheelchair (AAALF–AAHPERD, 1995).

The Brockport Physical Fitness Test (BPFT) is an assessment tool used for children with varying disabilities. The health-related fitness components addressed through instruction as well as assessment can be modified by using 27 test items that address aerobic functioning, body composition, and musculoskeletal functioning (muscular strength and endurance and flexibility or range of motion). The results of this assessment can give instructors the needed information to address students' specific instructional needs. (More information may be obtained in chapter 13.)

Adaptations to Meet Unique Needs

Changing an activity for everyone means that more students are actively engaged in the activity (both students who need special consideration and those who don't). Activities can be adapted in several ways to meet the needs of all students. Whenever a student with special needs is being evaluated regarding adaptations for physical activity programs, the following safety protocols should be implemented:

- ▶ Review of the student's records
- ▶ Conference with parents
- ▶ Possible contraindications (e.g., for scoliosis, repeated bending; or for autism, large noisy areas for instruction)
- ▶ Appropriate class size and instructional support
- ▶ Instructional environment
- ▶ Instructional strategies

After collecting the necessary information from the safety protocol, this information should be

DISABILITIES AWARENESS FIELD DAYS

Teachers at Western Union Elementary School (Waxhaw, North Carolina) wanted to increase students' understanding and acceptance of children with disabilities. The children began learning about various disabilities at the beginning of the school year to prepare them to get the most out of a two-day field event. Just before the field days, students were briefed about the activities and their purpose, and they were reminded that they would be hosting special guests. This meeting helped students understand that the events were for understanding what persons with disabilities *can* do, not to make fun of them. Students also raised money for the Special Olympics in a "Run for the Gold" event held the day before the main event began.

On the first day of the main event, third through fifth graders participated in six indoor activities: An Easter Seals Society representative explained the proper etiquette and preferred language to use when speaking to or about persons with disabilities; a teacher with a hearing impairment shared her daily life experiences; students taped their fingers together, splinted their arms, and so on, to simulate physical impairment; students wore glasses covered to varying degrees to simulate visual impairments; students wore socks on their hands and tried to perform fine motor tasks to simulate learning difficulties of people with mental handicaps; and students tried to speak with a marshmallow in their mouth to simulate speech impairment. Students were also encouraged to process what they had learned through various art and writing activities. Meanwhile, preschool through second graders enjoyed six outdoor activities (what was simulated appears in parentheses): charades (nonverbal communication); sit-down basketball (wheelchair basketball); nondominant hand beanbag throw (physical impairments such as cerebral palsy); floor volleyball (physical impairments experienced by persons with amputations and paralysis); and silent 100-yard (m) dash (hearing impairment). A member of the Tarwheels (a North Carolina wheelchair basketball team) also displayed his talents and spoke of never giving up. A parent of a child with a visual impairment shared the child's successes in judo and track and field. On the second day, the two age groups followed the reverse schedule.

Reprinted, by permission, from M. Jobe, 1998, "Disabilities awareness field days," *Journal of Teaching Elementary Physical Education* 9(1): 10-11.

organized onto an inclusion profile sheet (see figure 11.2 on page 190).

After the necessary information has been collected to support the individual's needs, consideration is given to four areas that cover various attributes of the teaching and learning environment (Lieberman & Houston-Wilson, 2002). See table 11.1 on page 191 for a list of questions to ask. Begin to develop specific instructional modifications based on curricular needs. Table 11.2 on page 192 provides examples of modifications based on specific instructional themes. Many of these modifications can and should be used throughout the instructional day. The adjustments made to instruction for children with disabilities are often used for children both with and without disabilities at all grade levels.

The sidebar "Including Pablo" on page 194 shows creative ways to adapt a high school weight-training class to be more inclusive. Use questioning strategies and opportunities in class to have students modify the games, drills, and activities to meet the needs of everyone. These extensions and refinements of lessons will develop a positive classroom environment. *Physical Best Activity Guides* offer inclusion tips for each activity. The tips represent a variety of student needs that physical educators may encounter. Many ideas can be easily transferred from one activity to another.

Teaching Strategies

Several teaching strategies can be effectively used to teach students physical and motor activities in physical education. These strategies include the multilevel approach and task analysis. In the multilevel approach, all students work on the same targeted areas (e.g., flexibility), but each student works toward goals appropriate for his or her abilities. For example, fourth graders without

---

INCLUSION PROFILE

Student's name _____

Student's date of birth _____ Classroom teacher _____

Disability code _____ Medications _____

Physical education goals and objectives: _____

_____

_____

_____

_____

Medical information or medical contraindications: _____

_____

_____

_____

Behavior management plan: _____

_____

_____

_____

Activity adaptations: _____

_____

_____

_____

Related service providers; (OT, PT, S/L, hearing, vision, and so on): _____

_____

_____

_____

_____

Locker room accomodations: _____

_____

_____

_____

From NASPE, 2011, *Physical education for lifelong fitness: The Physical Best teacher's guide*, 3rd edition (Champaign, IL: Human Kinetics).

Figure 11.2 Teachers should organize and store information about students in a record such as the inclusion profile sheet. A reproducible version of the student profile sheet is available in appendix A.

disabilities might explore stretches specific to an area of physical activity interest. At the same time, students with mild disabilities might focus on learning a new stretch, and students with severe disabilities might work on mastering one stretch without bouncing. Plan an activity for each level and decide which level is appropriate for which students so that the entire class is actively involved in learning. Figure 11.3 shows a sample form that may be used to assess the level of assistance that a person with a disability needs to perform a curl-up. Note that the task has been broken down into its component parts in a process known as **task analysis**. A person may need a task to be broken down more or less, depending on his or her disability. A score reflecting percentage of independence can then be calculated, giving you valuable information about the level and type of support that must be provided for the student. Developing a plan to increase independence will

---

CURL-UP ASSESSMENT

Name _____ Date _____

Directions

Circle the level of assistance that the person requires to perform the task. Total each level of assistance column and place the subtotals in the sum of scores row. Total the sum of scores row and place the score in the person's total score achieved row. Determine the percentage independence score based on the chart. Place number of repetitions in the product score row.

Key to Levels of Assistance

IND = Independent—the person is able to perform the task without assistance.

PPA = Partial physical assistance—the person needs some assistance to perform the task.

TPA = Total physical assistance—the person needs assistance to perform the entire task.

Curl-up	IND	PPA	TPA
1. Lie on back with knees bent	3	2	1
2. Place feet flat on the floor with legs slightly apart	3	2	1
3. Place arms straight, parallel to the trunk	3	2	1
4. Rest palms of hands on the mat with fingers stretched out	3	2	1
5. Rest head on partner's hands	3	2	1
6. Curl body in a forward position	3	2	1
7. Curl back down until head touches partner's hand	3	2	1
Sum of scores			
Total score achieved			
Total possible points	21		
Percentage independence score			
Product score			

Percentage of independence

7/21 = 33%	12/21 = 57%	17/21 = 80%
8/21 = 38%	13/21 = 61%	18/21 = 85%
9/21 = 42%	14/21 = 66%	19/21 = 90%
10/21 = 47%	15/21 = 71%	20/21 = 95%
11/21 = 52%	16/21 = 76%	21/21 = 100%

From NASPE, 2011, *Physical education for lifelong fitness: The Physical Best teacher's guide*, 3rd edition (Champaign, IL: Human Kinetics). Reprinted, by permission, from AAHPERD, 1995, *Physical best and individuals with disabilities: A handbook for inclusion in fitness programs* (Champaign, IL: Human Kinetics), 100.

Figure 11.3 Teachers can use paperwork such as the Curl-Up Assessment form to help them determine the level of help students with special needs will require for certain activities. A reproducible version of the Curl-Up Assessment form is available in appendix A.

Reprinted, by permission, from J. Winnick and F. Short, 1999, *The Brockport physical fitness test manual* (Champaign, IL: Human Kinetics), 131.

enhance the development of the fitness abilities of the participants (Houston-Wilson, 1995).

Collaboration

To include students with disabilities in physical education, a network of support systems must be in place. The ideas presented here can be used in the regular class setting or in expanded opportunities, such as before- and after-school programs. These can be optional opportunities or chances to help students who are experiencing difficulties catch up.

Collaboration can include many people, including peer tutors, parent and community service volunteers, paraprofessionals, and consultants. Choose the type of collaborator based on the student's needs, available resources, and the

Table 11.1 Teaching Considerations for Developing Activities

Teaching areas	Question	Answer
Instruction	What modality is optimum to maximize comprehension of instruction?	Students often benefit from a visual demonstration while receiving verbal directions.
	What supports need to be in place to assist with instruction (e.g., communication system, staff, and so on)?	Consider the need for supports such as adapted equipment, technology, communication systems (e.g., Mayer-Johnson symbols), or staff.
Rules	Do the rules allow everyone to participate and maintain the integrity of the game?	During a basketball game, a student with special needs may take three steps without dribbling before a violation.
	Can everyone understand the rules?	Complicated rules such as offsides are omitted or simplified to assist with comprehension.
	Do the rules provide a safe environment for everyone?	A student in a wheelchair is provided a buddy to assist with throwing and catching and to create a safety circle around the wheelchair.
Environment	Is the size of the area appropriate to the students and the activity?	A large multipurpose gymnasium has a line of cones down midcourt to create a smaller area in which to work. This might be done when instructing a small first-grade class that has a child with autism included for physical education.
	Are areas of instruction clearly delineated?	An inclusive second-grade class is taught in a fenced area because a child who has a tendency to run off is in the class.
	Does noise, temperature, air quality, or lighting in the area compromise the ability of students to participate?	The custodian at the school has the grass cut at night so that students with allergies and asthma can participate in the outdoor physical education classes.
Equipment	Is the equipment such that all students can participate or are modifications used to ensure total participation?	Jump ropes are modified; the ropes are cut in half for those who aren't able to get their feet off the ground. Beeper balls or Velcro balls and mitts are used.
	Is the equipment developmentally appropriate?	Students who are included in high school programs are participating in developmentally appropriate activities and are not throwing beanbags at a target.
	Is the equipment safe for all students (e.g., latex)?	Nonlatex equipment is provided.

individualized education plan (IEP) or 504 plan (discussed later in this chapter).

To determine the type of help that a student may need, consult with the student's direct service providers, such as classroom teachers and adapted physical education specialists as well as the occupational therapist, physical therapist, speech and language therapist, and other related service providers. All relevant information for each student must be collected before implementing a student's program. Medical and behavioral needs of some students can be overwhelming.

Information received through collaboration will have a direct influence on the quality of instruction and physical activity for that student. After consulting with other professionals organize the collected information into the student profile sheets. For many students, this profile sheet can be vital in the process of ensuring safety and success (see figure 11.2).

Teaching assistants and volunteers must be properly trained. They need to know how to help a student, how to avoid doing any harm (physical or emotional), and when to call for assistance.

Table 11.2 Thematic Inclusion Modifications

Equipment	Instruction	Environment
Throwing and catching		
• Footprints • Nerf ball • Poly spots • Textured ball • Hoops or large target • Beep or other auditory signal • Carpet squares • Contrasting color • Sequence pictures • Yarn ball • Balloon • Various weight • Velcro glove • Various size • Suspended object • Scarves • Deck rings • Ball with tail • Nonrolling ball • Ball on string • Slo-mo ball • Koosh ball • Bubbles • Scoops • Velcro vest	• Picture cues • Small group • Task cards • Peer tutor • Guided discovery • Mirroring • Visual or oral prompts • Peer tutor • Task variations • Problem solving • Physical assistance • Increase time for task • Positive reinforcement • Mayer-Johnson symbols • Parallel activities • Partner activities • Demonstrate or model activity • Transition schedule	• Clearly marked boundaries • Appropriate space for assistive mobility • Suspended targets (elastic rope) • Minimize visual clutter • Shorten distances • Remove obstacles in space • Place equipment at height accessible to student's needs
Striking skills		
• Footprints • Bean bags • Poly spots • Textured balls • Hoops for large targets • Beep or other auditory signals • Carpet squares • Contrasting color • Sequence pictures • Yarn • Balloons • Various weight • Velcro gloves • Suspended objects • Large shuttle or birdie • Balzac • Tee or large cone • Wider nets and courts • Short and large implements • Larger bat or racket • Deflated balls	• Picture cues • Partner work • Task cards • Visual aids • Guided discovery • Mirroring • Physical assistance • Peer tutor • Verbal command • Problem solving • Increase time for task • Small group • Positive reinforcement • Vary distances • Brighter lighting • Hand over hand • Mayer-Johnson symbols • Closer bases • Parallel activities • Simplify patterns • Disregard time limits • Modify grasps • Allow batter to sit • Transition schedule	• Clearly marked boundaries • Decrease distraction • Preferential placement to teacher • Appropriate space for assistive mobility • Minimize visual clutter • Allow student to sit • Modify station area • Success oriented • Place equipment at height accessible to student's needs
Fitness		
• Dyna bands • Modified jump ropes • Lighter weights	• Picture cues • Posted rules • Task cards	• Appropriate space for assistive mobility • Physical assistance

Equipment	Instruction	Environment
Fitness		
• Towels • Heart rate monitors • Pedometers • Insta Pulse bar • Therapy ball • Nonweighted bar • Small hand weights with Velcro • Small wedge or mats	• Visual aids • Guided discovery • Mirroring • Physical assistance • Peer tutor • Increase time for task • Small group • Positive reinforcement • Buddy system • Mayer-Johnson symbols • Daily take-home calendar • Brockport assessment • Modified log sheets • Transition schedule	• Decrease distractions • Success oriented • Place equipment at height accessible to student's needs
Integrated movement		
• Wedge mat • Tunnels • Hoops • Ramps • Floor beam • Wider beams • Bells on rope • Larger bases • Heavier rope • Balance board • Tape lines • Long jump ropes • Shakers • Chinese jump ropes • Soft-side flying discs • Half hoops • Various balls • Contrasting color for bases • Modified jump ropes	• Picture cues • Modified rules • Task cards • Visual aids • Guided discovery • Mirroring • Physical assistance • Peer tutor • Verbal command • Small group • Increase time for task • Tandem run • Positive reinforcement • Cognitive cues • Shorten base path • Simplified dance • Specific task in game • Reduce tempo • Mayer-Johnson symbols • Goal setting • Reduce number of steps • Transition schedule	• Appropriate space for assistive mobility • Physical assistance • Success oriented • Modified obstacle course • Minimize visual clutter • Clearly defined boundaries
Group initiatives		
• Pilo Polo sticks • Task cards • Cup stacking • Card deck • Bean bags • Deck rings • Rubber chickens or pigs • Picture cards • Long and short ropes • Parachute • Carpet squares • Buddy walkers • Poly spots • Scooter boards • Wands • Noodles • Hula hoops • Suspended targets	• Picture cues • Partner activities • Task cards • Visual aids • Guided discovery • Mirroring • Physical assistance • Peer tutor • Verbal command • Small group • Increase time for task • Modified rules • Positive reinforcement • Adapt play area • Mark positions on field • Group participation • Mayer-Johnson symbols • Transition schedule	• Clearly defined boundaries • Decrease distraction • Preferential placement to teacher • Appropriate space for assistive mobility • Physical assistance • Minimize visual clutter • Success oriented • Place equipment at height accessible to student's needs

Reprinted, by permission, from Harford County Public School.

INCLUDING PABLO

The 10th-grade weight-training class at Centerville High School had several students who had been identified as having a disability. One student's name was Pablo; he was nonambulatory and moved in a manual wheelchair. Pablo had been in school with many of the students in the class, but it had been a long time since they had seen him out of his wheelchair. Most of the time Pablo had participated in physical education by being the referee, keeping score, being an extra person on the team, or participating in an alternative activity on the side of the gymnasium. All the students liked Pablo and interacted with him, but they were unsure of what he was capable of doing physically.

During the first week of school, an adapted physical education teacher came to the class to work with Pablo. She created a weight-training sheet similar to the one used by the class, but it listed Pablo's activities and the weight and number of repetitions that he was to complete specifically marked. The adapted physical education teacher asked for volunteers to be Pablo's weight-training buddy. She explained that the buddy would be working at the same machine as Pablo to help him if he needed it but that the buddy would have time to complete his own workout. The buddies would rotate so that Pablo and the buddies would have a chance to work with other people. The adapted physical education teacher talked to the buddies and Pablo. She asked Pablo to demonstrate how he could independently transfer to the various weight-room equipment but would need help to set the pins for the weight amount. Everyone in the class was excited that Pablo was able to transfer out of his chair; it had been a long time since they had seen him out of his wheelchair while participating in physical activity. They also realized how important weight training was for Pablo. This class would help him develop strength so that he could continue to get out of his wheelchair independently.

The buddies soon became unnecessary for Pablo because everyone in the class helped with anything Pablo needed, and he needed very little. The students were happy to have Pablo as part of their class and included in activities. The adapted physical education teacher stopped by the weight-training class periodically to see how Pablo was doing. Everyone in the class told her how well Pablo was doing and whether he was improving.

This story was taken from an adapted physical education teacher who provided consultative adapted physical education in Maryland.

Time must be taken to develop a specific training program for these people before using them in the physical activity setting. Discussing the student's basic needs and abilities (while ensuring privacy) and simulating learning situations are good ways to provide training. Include these professionals in collaborative team meetings. Students with severe disabilities need assistants who are professionally trained by those qualified to do so.

MAJOR AREAS IN WHICH TO ENSURE INCLUSION

People with disabilities generally display the same physiological responses to exercise found in nondisabled persons, although factors such as heat dissipation and heart rate responses may be different. To ensure an inclusive learning environment, the following must be addressed: students with special needs, gender, culture, and ability levels outside the norm.

Students With Special Needs

Each student with special needs should come to class with either a 504 plan or an individualized education plan (IEP). An IEP lists a student's present level of performance, identifies attainable annual goals and objectives, includes clear instructions on how much time the child will spend in regular physical education class and with what support services, and identifies the level and purpose of support services. Although being part of an IEP team is time consuming, this process is vital to student learning and must receive proper attention.

Based on the IEP or 504 plan, curriculum and teaching methods are developed to meet the student's interests. Direct and repeated contact with involved special services staff, parents, and medical personnel must be made. Working with an adapted physical education teacher to ensure that the student receives the instruction that he or she needs is recommended. When designing health-related fitness plans for students with disabilities, keep the following in mind (adapted from DePauw, 1996):

▶ Individuals with disabilities generally display the same physiological responses to exercise found in nondisabled persons. (Some people with disabilities do not respond in the same way as those without disabilities; for example, heat dissipation and heart rate response may be different for a person with a spinal cord injury. Ask the family to consult with their physician.)

▶ Although specific disabilities may affect the intensity, duration, frequency, and type of exercise, people with disabilities can benefit from training, including improving their performances.

▶ Wheelchairs can be adjusted or modified (by those qualified to do so) to improve physical activity performance.

▶ Athletes in wheelchairs play basketball, tennis, and many other sports.

Use this information to ensure that students with disabilities are included in class activities to the greatest extent possible.

When deciding how best to teach an individual with a disability, focus on the individual rather than the disability. In other words, refrain from making automatic judgments about a person's condition. Look at what each child *can* do instead of assuming that he or she cannot do an activity.

Gender Inclusion

If you separate genders for activities, ensure that the activities are reasonably equivalent and not stereotypical. *Physical Best* recommends that genders not be separated at the elementary level. Try to avoid doing so at the middle and high school levels as well. Both genders can do many activities together to reach the physical education standards. Choose activities for a purpose (e.g., meeting the national standards), not simply because they have traditionally been used. Some

> ### DEVELOPING A RESPECTFUL ENVIRONMENT
>
> Craft (1994) suggests the following for teaching appropriate inclusive behavior to children without disabilities:
>
> - Do not allow students to show disrespectful behavior toward anyone.
> - Let students know that it's OK for anyone to make mistakes—including you.
> - Help students understand that people often tease or put down others because they feel insecure, are scared of others' differences, or are unsure of their own abilities.
> - Teach students to ask questions about differences in a positive manner; this approach helps to combat ignorance.
> - Have positive role models with disabilities share how they enjoy physical activity.
>
> This list of suggestions can encourage children to be more inclusive in regard to culture, gender, and race as well.

professionals say that in rare cases privacy, size and strength differences, and safety require some temporary gender separation at the middle and high school levels. But keep in mind that goal-based curriculums have a plethora of choice. Therefore, focus on the idea that activity choices are not an end in themselves. View activities as strategies for reaching program goals.

For adults most physical activity opportunities are not gender segregated. Men and women participate side by side in health clubs, biking and running clubs, dancing (a great activity to build aerobic fitness), wall climbing, in-line skating, and most other physical activities. In many communities, the most popular adult sports are coed softball and coed volleyball.

Students need to experience equal opportunity within each lesson as well. Research has suggested that educators tend to favor boys inadvertently. In physical education, for example, boys are more likely to give and receive positive specific feedback or specific corrective feedback (e.g., "I noticed how evenly you paced your mile run," or "Push

COEDUCATION CLASSES AND PHYSICAL EDUCATION

One of the most widely debated areas of equity in physical education is coeducational classes. In today's society, most teachers would never think of segregating students by ethnicity, but some still have a hard time having students from different gender groups in the same classes. Segregated classes prevent boys and girls from interacting with one another and learning how to work and play together. Segregation by gender limits opportunities for boys and girls to reconsider their stereotypical assumptions in the physical domain.

Placing boys and girls in the same physical education class is only the first step toward providing students with the opportunity to examine their preconceived ideas about the opposite gender (see figure 11.4). The figure that follows shows six steps to equity. Not every teacher needs to pass through all six steps, but you should be able to identify the step that you currently occupy. Step 6 is complete equity, including opportunities for both genders to demonstrate skills, answer questions, receive feedback, and feel respect from the teacher and other students. It also includes an environment in which the teacher uses inclusive language (referring to the class as "students" instead of "you guys") and avoids using stereotypical phrases (e.g., "You throw like a girl").

As you progress through steps 2 through 5, continually reflect on your teaching behaviors. When boys and girls appear not to be working well together, examine the learning environment and determine what might be causing the problem. Often I hear physical educators state that the boys won't let the girls touch the ball. Sometimes, the physical educator states that a girl must touch the ball before the team can score. When I question the teacher about whether all the boys in her class refuse to share, she typically responds, "No, it's a few aggressive boys." This response tells me that the situation has little to do with coeducational physical education because the same boys are also preventing other boys from touching the ball. The remedy is either to make a rule that everyone must touch the ball, or better yet, to reduce the size of the teams so that everyone on the team must be involved for the team to be successful. Requiring that a girl must touch the ball before scoring sends the message that girls need special treatment, which only serves to reinforce the stereotype that girls are not as competent as boys (Mohnsen, 1997).

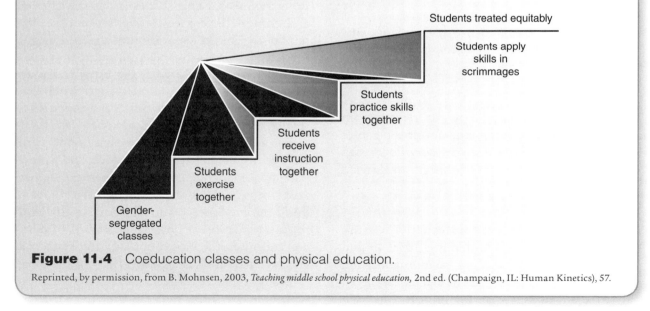

Figure 11.4 Coeducation classes and physical education.

Reprinted, by permission, from B. Mohnsen, 2003, *Teaching middle school physical education*, 2nd ed. (Champaign, IL: Human Kinetics), 57.

off with your toes more"). Girls are more likely to be passive observers and to receive general feedback (e.g., "Good job," or "Try again"). Boys are also more likely to be pushed to complete a task, whereas girls may be allowed to quit (Cohen, 1993; Hutchinson, 1995; Sadker & Sadker, 1995).

TEACHING TIP: THE EDUCATIONAL VALUE OF GENDER INCLUSION

If the purpose of physical education is to teach lifelong physical activity, then having coeducational classes is a real-world setting. When taking a fitness-based approach in class, students learn that a person does not have to be at a high level of skill to enjoy and participate in an activity with others. Placing students in situations that provide the opportunity to learn how to cooperate and involve all their teammates, regardless of gender, leads them toward positive attitudes about themselves, others, and physical activity. Giving our students opportunities to learn social skills through activities is what sets our discipline apart from others.

Connie Harris

2008 NASPE District Teacher of the Year
Eastern District High School
Westlake High School
Waldorf, Maryland

GENDER EQUITY CHECKLIST FOR PHYSICAL EDUCATION

- Is the curriculum gender inclusive?
- Do students participate in gender-integrated classes?
- Are teaching styles varied to accommodate different learning styles and preferences?
- Is gender-inclusive language used?
- Do instructional materials portray both genders as active participants in a variety of activities?
- Is equal attention given to boys and girls during classroom practices such as questioning, demonstration, and feedback?
- Are local community resources used to help erode gender barriers to sport participation?
- Is time consistently reserved for gender dialogue?
- Are there high expectations for both boys and girls?
- Is gender equity a pervasive schoolwide goal?

Reprinted, by permission, from L. Nilges, 1996, "Ingredients for a gender equitable physical education program," *Journal of Teaching Elementary Physical Education* 7(5):28-29.

One way to monitor instruction for gender bias is to videotape teaching episodes. Watching the recording and scoring the type of feedback given to boys and girls can highlight instructional patterns. If access to videotaping equipment is not available, a colleague or other trained observer could assess instructional behaviors. Figure 11.5 on page 198 shows a sample tally sheet.

Another way to fight gender bias is to ensure that visual aids include representation of both genders participating on equal, nonstereotypical terms. Invite guest speakers who have crossed gender lines to play sports. Expose students to a variety of activities that develop health-related fitness, regardless of gender.

Cultural Inclusion

Cultural influences can greatly affect what a person is interested in learning and doing. Because helping students learn what physical activity is enjoyable for them is an important part of health-related physical fitness education, being sensitive in this area is essential. Develop a survey to help determine student interests. You can then incorporate this information into program plans. Lowry (1995) writes, "If students believe that their opinions and perspectives are valued and used, then you have taken the first step in setting up a culturally sensitive environment." These basic steps can be taken in tandem with teachers of other subjects to help make health-related physical fitness education curriculum more culturally inclusive. Try to incorporate the physical activities, games, holidays and traditions, and music of other cultures. Incorporation of these culturally linked activities validates different ethnic backgrounds, provides a link to each student, and promotes acceptance and understanding for all students in the class.

Banks (1988) suggests that teachers consider three areas when they plan their lessons and overall programs:

▶ Integrate content—Use activities from other cultures to achieve program goals. For example, an active game from another country can be just as good for developing aerobic fitness as a familiar game.

▶ Plan how to reduce prejudice—Plan awareness activities that facilitate understanding among cultures, such as discussing different ways of dressing for exercise, based on cultural differences.

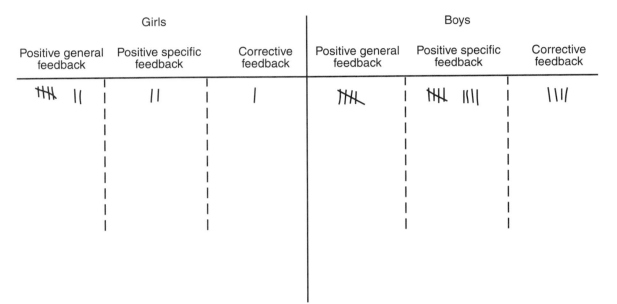

Girls			Boys		
Positive general feedback	Positive specific feedback	Corrective feedback	Positive general feedback	Positive specific feedback	Corrective feedback
⊪⊪ ‖	‖			⊪⊪	⊪⊪ ‖‖	\\‖/

Figure 11.5 Sample tally sheet.

Reprinted, by permission, from L. Nilges, 1996, "Ingredients for a gender equitable physical education program," *Journal of Teaching Elementary Physical Education* 7(5):28-29.

The use of fun games can help students of different cultures adjust to their new surroundings.

▶ Employ culturally responsive pedagogy—Respect differences and learn the history and meaning behind traditions and values.

Ask students and parents from various cultural backgrounds to share their beliefs and any individual requests with you. This process will further sensitize people to the philosophies and

---

TEACHING THE LIMITED ENGLISH OR NON-ENGLISH-SPEAKING STUDENT IN PHYSICAL EDUCATION

A student who doesn't speak English as his or her first language can succeed in and enjoy physical education. The following may help such a student:

- Assign an English-speaking buddy to help the student in physical education class. If possible, choose someone who speaks the same language as the non-English-speaking student (Mohnsen, 2003).

- Physically move a student through a skill to help him or her comprehend what is expected.

- Use gestures and other visual aids, such as toy people and small balls (Mohnsen, 2003).

- Use facial expressions and voice inflections to emphasize points.

- Remember to speak slowly and enunciate clearly (Mohnsen, 2003).

- Emphasize with the student the key word or phrase of the target skill and have the student's buddy do so as well.

- Encourage the student to repeat the **cue words** or phrases as he or she executes the skill to aid in learning the vocabulary that goes with the actions.

- Learn some of the important words and phrases from the child's native language.

Reprinted, by permission, from B. Pettifor, 1999, *Physical education methods for classroom teachers* (Champaign, IL: Human Kinetics), 259.

---

sociological issues that may affect physical education learning and fitness attitudes. Finally, respect diversity in cultural values. For example, gender equity may be an offensive concept in certain cultures, so respect the different expectations for girls and boys within each culture. Provide equal opportunity for all. Discuss other options with the student and her or his parents if religious or cultural beliefs are not supported. Involve a school counselor or administrator in discussions. If religious beliefs mandate that girls not wear shorts, discuss appropriate alternatives with the family and determine alternatives to address clothing for participating in physical activity (e.g., culottes, which look like a skirt, but function like shorts; Mohnsen, 1997). Keep in mind that not everyone in a class has to dress alike to be able to benefit from physical activity. Providing choices helps build on cultural diversity rather than trying to eliminate it.

Ability Inclusion

Students who are challenged (but not classified as having a disability) or extremely talented deserve inclusion, too.

Physically Elite Children

Although Sara, who can run a mile (1.6 km) in less than six minutes, or Jimmy, who can do 150 curl-ups, may not need much of your attention, don't neglect these students. You may find that the physically elite make good peer tutors. Placing them in this role will keep them interested in your program and may help them build social skills. But do not have them tutor so much that their own needs go unmet or that other students sense favoritism. In addition, challenge the physically gifted students in your classes to explore advanced participation in physical activity. By challenging these students, you can help those who might otherwise be bored (and, as a result, disrupt class) become assets to the class. For example, you might have a physically elite high school student read a book on becoming a personal trainer and then let the student serve as an assistant by helping other students during class. You might also arrange for this student to interview a personal trainer at a local health club (and have the student write a report). Show interest in such students' extracurricular sport activities and have them share their experiences with the rest of the class. Encourage independence and fitness gains in middle and high school students by encouraging them to use health-related fitness training principles to challenge themselves continually.

Physically Awkward Children

Wall (1982) defines the physically awkward child as one "without known neuromuscular problems who [fails] to perform . . . motor skills with proficiency." Don't assume that a physically awkward child will outgrow the problem on his or her own; many do not (Schincariol, 1994). Such children tend to become discouraged and consequently drop out of physical activity never to return, which only compounds their problems.

Students should be screened for motor skill delays by administering an assessment of motor proficiency (Schincariol, 1994). For example, the Test of Gross Motor Development (Ulrich, 2000) may provide useful information. Consult with an adapted physical education specialist and the child's parents to individualize the child's physical education program (Schincariol, 1994).

Physically awkward children need remedial help in the form of extra practice time, instruction, and encouragement (Schincariol, 1994). These students, like those with special needs, may need one-on-one help. Arrange for such students to work with a trained volunteer, teacher's aide, or peer tutor.

Create learning situations in which children who are physically awkward can learn, succeed, and have fun. Provide opportunities for students to learn the value and benefits of physical activity. Offering choices and variety is especially critical to enticing physically awkward students to persist in physical activity. For example, in conducting a fitness circuit with a jump rope station, offer the choice of doing step aerobics (step up and step down) to those who are unable to jump rope. This approach allows students to participate in an activity when their lack of motor skills might otherwise prevent them from getting a good workout.

TEACHING TIP: REACHING STUDENTS WHO ARE AFRAID TO TRY

Ben came up to me after the first class and quietly, but in a serious tone, said, "Mr. Hichwa, that was a good talk, but, you know, I don't do gym." Ben informed me that he was cut from his fourth-grade travel soccer team, his physical educational experience in the elementary school was far from positive, and he did not intend to expose himself to further failure or ridicule in the sixth grade. I thanked Ben for being so forthright and suggested that he come to our next class as an observer, which he agreed to do. At the end of that class, I asked him whether he thought that he could feel comfortable taking part in future class activities. Because I took the time to listen to him, showed respect for his concerns, and gave him time to feel comfortable in his new environment, Ben agreed to give it a try! Throughout the year, Ben tried his best, participated fully, and eventually learned to enjoy the many challenges.

At the beginning of sixth grade, Clare was very tall for her age, fairly heavy, and extremely clumsy. She would go through the motions, but even encouragement from her peers was construed as a personal affront and caused her great anguish. But by making developmentally appropriate changes, the activities became less threatening. Clare started to experience a little success, and her self-concept began to rise. She excelled at the problem-solving initiatives and slowly gained respect from the other students. Her running times improved as she participated more enthusiastically; she didn't feel inadequate when competing with herself and enjoyed monitoring her progress. By eighth grade, Clare felt confident enough to demonstrate the layup shot in basketball!

John Hichwa, Educational Consultant

1993 NASPE Middle School Physical Education Teacher of the Year

Redding, Connecticut

From J. Hichwa 1998.

Low-Fit or Obese Children

Poor fitness and obesity levels have many causes. Examples include lack of physical activity, diet, socioeconomic influences, and sedentary lifestyles created through technological advancements. Physical educators must be able to help motivate students to strive for greater levels of physical activity that can result in improved fitness. Assuming that these conditions arise from laziness is often a misconception. More likely, younger obese or low-fit students have higher workload levels than more-fit students. Embarrassment and fear of failure may prevent low-fit and obese students from wanting to participate.

For these children, a first step should be to have percent body fat measurements taken to determine the severity of the problem (see the latest *Fitnessgram Test Administration Manual*). Follow up with assurance through the family doctor that disease, health disorders, or hereditary problems are not the cause of the student's problems. Maintaining a student's privacy and respecting the family's wishes are high priorities. Consider holding a parent–teacher–student conference expressing concern and a desire to help. If medical conditions are involved, work with the family doctor and parents to establish parameters for the student's participation in class. Middle and high school students may benefit from sharing their negative experiences and personal concerns regarding physical activity and body composition. A private conference with you or a journal-writing opportunity that allows students to air their feelings may lead to improved attitudes toward appropriate physical activity.

After medical concerns have been ruled out, work with the student and family to set appropriate goals and design an individualized fitness plan, emphasizing fun and variety. Obese students may also need nutritional guidance. Stressing the benefits of mild exercise can be an important step toward increasing physical activity. Students should have an opportunity to set an individual pace within each activity. Encouraging the entire family to become more active can help increase the student's total physical activity time. Reinforce achievements by having students chart progress.

Teachers must be sensitive to the issues that affect overweight or obese students. Physical activity sessions must be positive experiences for everyone. Some guidelines include the following:

- Treat pupils as individuals, not comparing and contrasting them.
- Encourage a range of physical activities, including non-weight-bearing exercises, such as swimming, exercise in water, and cycling.
- Encourage low-impact activities, such as walking, and provide low-impact alternatives (such as marching) to high-impact exercises (such as jogging).
- Schedule rest periods to allow recovery from activity.
- Ensure correct exercise technique to minimize the risk of injury.
- Permit a choice of exercise clothing that reduces embarrassment.
- Ensure the wearing of supportive footwear during weight-bearing activities, and use soft surfaces rather than hard surfaces (such as concrete), where possible.
- Provide differentiated tasks to cater to a wide range of abilities, including low-level, easier tasks.
- Be aware of potential problems, such as breathing difficulties, movement restriction, edema (fluid retention resulting in swelling), chafing, excessive sweating, and discomfort during exercise.
- Encourage routine activity around the home and school.
- Where possible, provide opportunities for overweight and obese children to be active in a private, rather than a public, context.
- Enable obese children to follow an individually designed exercise program, based on their particular needs and capabilities.
- Encourage guidance and support from school, family, and friends.
- Always provide positive feedback and constant encouragement.

Adapted, by permission, from J.P. Harris and J.P. Elbourn, 1997, *Teaching health-related exercise at key stages 1 and 2* (Champaign, IL: Human Kinetics), 27.

Other Health Concerns— Asthma

Other health concerns may affect a student's ability or willingness to participate fully in the classroom. Asthma is a common example. People who have asthma are susceptible to narrowing of the airways, which makes breathing difficult. This narrowing can be brought on by a number of factors (such as irritants, allergens, weather changes, viral infections, emotions, and exercise). The factors differ among people and may vary over time.

Exercise-induced asthma may occur during or after exercise. The usual symptoms are wheezing, coughing, tightness of the chest, and breathlessness. Regular physical activity, however, has specific benefits for students with asthma (such as decreased frequency and severity of attacks and reduction in medication) over and above the benefits that it has for children in general; therefore, students with asthma should be encouraged to be active and should be integrated as fully as possible into physical education lessons and sporting activities. Students with asthma should be able to participate in activities alongside their peers with minimal adaptation. A student is most likely to experience exercise-induced asthma when performing continuous aerobic exercise at a relatively moderate intensity for more than six minutes in cold, dry air (for example, cross country running). Appendix F contains a "Student Asthma Action Card" that you can use to document your students' information.

Although you should treat each student individually, you should observe these general recommendations when students exercise:

- Encourage the use of an inhaler 5 to 10 minutes before exercise.
- Encourage students to have a spare inhaler readily available for use.
- A student arriving for activity with airway constriction should be excused from participation for that session.
- Allow a gradual warm-up of at least 10 minutes.
- Permit and encourage intermittent bursts of activity interspersed with reduced intensity exercise.

- Permit lower intensity (easier) activity.
- Encourage swimming—people with asthma more easily tolerate the environmental temperature and humidity of an indoor pool.
- In cold, dry weather, encourage the wearing of a scarf or exercise face mask over the mouth and nose in the open air.
- Encourage breathing through the nose during light exercise—this method warms and humidifies the air.
- Do not permit students with asthma to exercise when they have a cold or viral infection.
- Where possible, advise students with severe asthma to avoid exercise during the coldest parts of the day (usually early morning and evening) and in times of high pollution.
- If symptoms occur, ask the student to stop exercising and encourage him or her to use an inhaler and to rest until recovery is complete.
- In the case of an asthma attack, send for medical help, contact the student's parents, give medicine promptly and correctly, remain calm, encourage slow breathing, and ensure that the child is comfortable.

Reprinted, by permission, from J.P. Harris and J.P. Elbourn, 1997, *Teaching health-related exercise at key stages 1 and 2* (Champaign, IL: Human Kinetics), 25-27.

Nothing prevents most students with mild to moderate asthma from participating in a range of physical activities with minimal difficulty if they take appropriate precautions before and during exercise.

A WORD ABOUT INHALERS

Although students with asthma should be encouraged to participate in physical education as fully as possible, awareness of possible limitations is important. Students should have free and easy access to their inhalers. Schools should not keep asthma medication in a central store. Teachers who are better informed are more able to help students with asthma lead a normal life.

Adapted, by permission, from J.P. Harris and J.P. Elbourn, 1997, *Teaching health-related exercise at key stages 1 and 2* (Champaign, IL: Human Kinetics), 25-27.

SUMMARY

Inclusion in health-related physical fitness education means making it possible for all students to succeed in and enjoy physical activity. Thus, inclusion helps students meet the ultimate goal of becoming adults who value and pursue physical activity as a way of life. At the same time, inclusion can teach other students valuable life lessons: social skills, cultural respect, and the feeling that limitations are often unfairly assigned by those with limited visions of what people can do and be. To be inclusive (as opposed to simply going through the motions), teachers must make a commitment to plan and implement an inclusive program. Collaboration with both school and nonschool personnel makes the task of inclusion easier and ensures that the necessary input is available to tailor the program to the needs of all students.

Foundations of Assessment in Health-Related Fitness and Physical Activity

iStockphoto/Chris Schmidt

Part IV provides an overview of assessment issues related to health-related fitness and physical activity. Basic assessment principles, their relationship to health-related fitness, knowledge, self-responsibility, and attitudes are discussed. Chapter 12 relates the foundation for assessment—the National Standards for Physical Education—to health-related fitness and physical activity. Recommendations for selecting assessment tools, applying them, and using assessments to shape program planning are included. Chapter 13 explores appropriate methods for fitness assessment and physical activity assessment, and offers guidelines for assessing and sharing results in effective and helpful ways. Chapter 14 concludes this section on assessment with concrete suggestions for using the appropriate tools to assess cognitive, personal responsibility, and affective domains. Applying the concepts and suggestions found in this part will help create a program that challenges each student to develop positive lifelong physical fitness habits.

Principles of Assessment

Celia Regimbal

In the real world, personal trainers do not assign letter grades after working with clients. Typically, clients' expectations include a fitness assessment followed by the development and explanation of a personalized plan that will help them attain a higher fitness level. The same should be true for today's physical education teacher. Students should expect to participate in a health-related fitness assessment, and then, based on the results, be advised on the best course of action.

Chapter Contents

Assigning a grade to fitness scores does little to influence a student's physical activity level. In an ideal setting, all students would receive a detailed report on their current fitness status each grading period. Based on that report, each student would be assisted in developing an individualized fitness plan that meets preestablished goals. Information based on an individual's fitness assessment can be provided using assessments designed to help students develop and achieve health-related fitness goals.

Grading and assessment are not the same; they have different purposes. **Assessment** is a continuous collection and interpretation of information of student performance. Teachers and students are informed through assessment. **Grades** are a product based on previous performance. A grade is summative. This chapter will present examples of appropriate strategies for using assessment and eventually assigning grades.

ASSESSMENT

Student assessment is a high-stakes event. Assessment outcomes are often equated to a teacher's effectiveness in all subjects, including physical education. Many states and school districts have adopted the national physical education standards developed by the National Association for Sport and Physical Education (NASPE). These standards are used to guide content selection to meet students' unique needs. Standard 4, "achieves and maintains a health-enhancing level of physical fitness," is assessed using formalized assessments such as Fitnessgram. In addition, fitness assessment results are used to establish the effectiveness of a physical education program. Many states such as California and Texas publicly report the results of the Fitnessgram, and other states use aggregate fitness scores in school report cards (e.g., West Virginia and South Carolina).

Scores on fitness assessments evaluate only students' current fitness levels. Scores may indicate that change is needed but not specify how or what to change. Fitness scores are similar to an individual's blood pressure results; just knowing the score does not necessarily influence future results. Being active is what leads to better health-related fitness. Assessment should be used as a diagnostic tool. As a result of the assessment out-comes, teachers and students can work together to develop and provide the tools for maintaining or developing fitness outcomes. Assessment can be used to help frame the focus needed to develop health-related fitness.

Traditional assessment in physical education often takes the form of rules assessments (e.g., for specific games and sports), skill assessments, and informal teacher observation. Traditional forms of assessment have their place in physical education but are often time consuming and lack a clear relationship to learning outcomes. **Alternative assessment** involves using tools such as portfolios, journals, and role playing to collect evidence about student learning and achievement of program objectives.

Alternative assessment is often used interchangeably with *authentic assessment*. Authentic assessment takes place in a setting that represents or replicates the real world. Authentic assessment also includes consideration of the context of the activity, and it is more likely to assess a student's ability to perform or demonstrate knowledge in a game or real-life setting (Lacy & Hastad, 2005). Applied specifically to physical education, developmentally appropriate authentic assessment includes individual assessments of students as they move and participate in a variety of activities. Comparisons should be made by examining the student's progress since the previous assessment and by examining benchmarks of growth and maturation, not by using a single assessment score (summative evaluation) or the performance of other students in the class (norm-referenced assessment).

Authentic assessment in physical education can include counting daily steps using a pedometer or measuring heart rate at the beginning and end of an activity period and then reflecting on the change. In activity settings students can use rubrics to complete partner assessments during game play as a helpful way to integrate peer assessment throughout a unit.

Assessment using heart rate monitors and pedometers can help students develop an understanding of intensity, resting heart rate, and recovery times. Together students and the teacher can create an exertion chart that reflects the collective experience of the class. Based on the OMNI RPE scale of 0 to 10, a rating of 0 could represent little effort with no change in respiration and a small change in heart rate, perhaps 10 to 20 beats per minute. A rating of 10 could represent "Don't ask me to do one more thing until I catch my breath!" (See table 5.2 and the accompanying text on page 78 for information about the OMNI RPE scale.) Information from a pedometer can be used to track the increased number of steps that a student can take before feeling tired or how many more steps the student can take in the same amount of time. These examples show how students can use assessment to notice their improvement in areas of health-related fitness. Teachers can also use a handheld or desktop computer to record students' scores. Students can use the printed information as a guide to set personal goals as well as include this information in their journals or portfolios.

Authentic assessment in health-related physical fitness education should teach and motivate students to increase physical activity in a way that will affect their overall health and wellness. Assessing student performance during activities or during play can provide valuable information. The simple act of observing a child as she or he climbs a ladder, performs locomotor movements, or executes specific health-related fitness activities such as those found in the *Physical Best Activity Guides* can be used to develop a health-related fitness focus that is personally informative.

National Standards and Assessment

The Physical Best program is aligned with the national physical education standards. Standards-based content development guides teachers' selection of developmentally appropriate activities that enable students to accomplish specific outcomes. Psychomotor, cognitive, and affective objectives guide the outcomes of selected activities. NASPE's national standard 4, "Achieves and maintains a health-enhancing level of physical fitness," specifically addresses the area of personal fitness. When developing content, teachers may ask, "What is the appropriate age for fitness assessment to begin? What type of aerobic assessment should be administered? How many curl-ups represent the healthy fitness zone for a high school student? What are the physiological indicators of vigorous physical activity? How does a student learn to self-assess and establish achievable health-related fitness goals?" These and many other questions are addressed in chapter 2 as well as in the NASPE Assessment Series and the *Physical Best Activity Guides*.

Importance of Assessment

Assessment can provide the information needed to support student achievement. Assessment is both formative and summative. Formative assessment is conducted during a period of instruction (e.g., unit, semester, and so on.). Typically, this type of assessment provides information about student mastery and helps guide content development. Formative assessment can be done at the start of the school year to determine students' developmental levels. This activity can direct content selection and development to address specific student needs. Formative assessment can also help to determine instructional effectiveness relative to the achievement of student outcomes. Summative assessment is conducted at the end of an instructional period and typically combines numerous measures to provide a final unit or course grade. Summative assessment can be used as a diagnostic tool for assessing students' health-related fitness levels.

Assessment provides numerous useful outcomes:

- Opportunities to focus on individual student's outcomes
- Opportunities to address the components of health-related fitness
- Specific feedback to guide each student's personal goal setting by addressing how the components of health-related fitness can be improved through specific activities and exercises
- Feedback on the teacher's effectiveness
- Feedback on overall program effectiveness
- Important feedback about student instructional needs
- Information to guide future planning
- Information for parents about the fitness status of their children and what can be done to improve or maintain that fitness

▶ Subject matter credibility in the minds of administrators, students, and parents

The Physical Best program focuses on a holistic approach to developing all three learning domains. According to NASPE (2004a, 11), "The goal of physical education is to develop physically educated individuals who have the knowledge, skills, and confidence to enjoy a lifetime of healthful physical activity." The **psychomotor domain** refers to skills and motor or movement patterns. This domain is commonly assessed during drills, skill assessments, and gamelike activities. **Health-related fitness** is changed through participation in physical activities. Formative assessment tools can include measuring moderate and vigorous activity using heart rate monitors and step counts using pedometers. The **cognitive domain** refers to knowledge about concepts related to sport, games and fitness, rules, procedures, safety, and critical elements. Knowledge and understanding is most often assessed through written assessments, oral presentations, or final projects. Alternative assessments such as journals, developing fitness routines, role playing, and peer assessment activities can be used to document students' cognitive learning outcomes. The **affective domain** refers to the attitudes and values that a student has toward and during physical activity. Although more difficult to measure, affective behaviors can be assessed through journals, rubrics, questionnaires, and systematic observation of student behaviors, including relating to others and compliance with classroom standards and rules.

Both formal and informal assessments are important to a quality physical education program, and they can be used for assessing learning in various domains. Informal assessment can be recurring and understood through the feedback loop: Teachers observe performance and provide feedback to encourage students. This feedback can either assist in correcting performance or offer information that refines performance. Informal assessment is an important teaching strategy because it provides a quick appraisal of student learning. Typically, students receive informal assessment feedback during teacher or peer observations of practice, but they can also use self-assessment skills to self-evaluate

EXAMPLES OF LEARNING DOMAIN OBJECTIVES

Psychomotor Assessment

- The student is able to do a modified push-up with direction from the teacher.
- The student is able to sustain moderate physical activity for the physical education class period.

Cognitive Assessment

- The student can describe the components of health-related physical fitness.
- The student names one activity that contributes to a healthy lifestyle.
- The student identifies changes in the body that result from participation in vigorous physical activities.

Affective Assessment

- The student voluntarily responds to an invitation to participate in the fitness activity.
- The student participates in health-related fitness activities designed to improve or maintain aerobic fitness, muscular strength and endurance, flexibility, and body composition, both inside and outside of school.

Adapted from Moore 2006.

performance. Self-assessment allows students to practice strategies that they can use outside of the physical education classroom. Informal assessment takes less time and can be helpful for making decisions regarding pacing, selection of appropriate teaching strategies, or content modification.

Formal assessment is a more precise measure of student learning and results in recorded data that are often necessary to document final grades. Formal assessments can include teacher or student checklists, task sheets, fitness rubrics, student logs, portfolios, and Activitygram and Fitnessgram printouts. These examples demonstrate the standardized, teacher-conducted nature of formal assessment.

Choosing What to Assess

Health-related fitness assessment includes both cognitive and psychomotor domains. Cognitive assessment measures students' knowledge and understanding. Content areas include fitness concepts and principles, goal setting, and self-assessment. Cognitive assessment in health-related fitness includes assessing students' understanding of the importance of stretching and their knowledge of safe stretching activities. Other examples include having students explain why they should avoid ballistic stretching or how long they should hold a stretch.

Cognitive domain assessment can actively engage students in learning. Many examples of combining cognitive development with physical activity can be found in the *Physical Best Activity Guides*. Using the stretching example, the activity could be as simple as asking a question about how far to stretch or about which muscles and joints are affected by the stretch while students are engaged in stretching activities. Questions are an informal means of checking for understanding and provide no written record. Although questions do provide effective information, formal assessment strategies offer permanent documentation of student understanding. Authentic cognitive assessments include gathering information about students' abilities to perform such tasks as taking their heart rates and using pedometers to report on their physical activity levels. A stretching cognitive assessment could include identifying appropriate flexibility exercises for a specific activity. Appropriate knowledge can help students choose safe and enjoyable activities. Assessing students in all three domains helps develop a holistic approach to teaching and learning about physical education.

Psychomotor domain assessment is addressed frequently in physical education. Assessment in this domain involves examining the physical application of skills and strategies. Continuing with the stretching example, psychomotor assessment would include measuring how far students can stretch, or more specifically, the range of motion of selected joints of the body. One example would be using the back-saver sit-and-reach assessment.

Affective domain assessment is perhaps the most difficult and abstract area to assess, but it is a powerful tool for motivating students to

The back-saver sit-and-reach assessment is one method available for assessing a student's health-related fitness.

participate in a lifetime of physical activity. Affective assessment measures a student's feelings and attitude toward physical activity. Assessing the affective domain related to stretching could involve finding out how stretching makes a student feel. Do students feel more competent because their flexibility improved, or do they feel empowered because they know how to stretch correctly? To complete the stretching example, learning how often a student stretches when performing strenuous activity out of class reflects the student's attitudes and values toward stretching. Participation is the behavior that reflects the student's affect or feelings, and it should not be graded separately or without an examination of the factors that lead to participation levels.

Frequent formal and informal assessment should be viewed as an essential part of teaching because it provides teachers and students with information that may motivate students to develop regular physical activity habits. Determining whether assessment tasks can be performed in an authentic setting is important.

Recommended Assessment Tools

A variety of assessment strategies are available that will gather accurate information about a student's progress. A student might find one form of assessment easier to perform and interpret than others because of individual strengths. Providing a balance of the types of assessment tools used gives students a chance to excel in a variety of ways and giving students multiple opportunities to understand what they have learned can be motivating.

Each assessment strategy is designed to be developmentally appropriate as well as reliable and valid. Assessment is designed to answer the question, "Is the student moving toward the ultimate goals of a health-related physical fitness education program?"

Rubrics

A **rubric** is a scoring tool that identifies the criteria used for judging student performance (Lund & Kirk, 2010). Rubrics range in complexity from checklists to tools that are holistic in nature and can be used to assess skills, attitudes, and knowl-

edge. A checklist rubric might list certain skills—for example, "Runs tall, leans slightly forward" or "Offers encouragement and support to teammates"—and include a blank where a check mark or smiley face is placed if the skill is performed correctly. A rubric might also be analytic, whereby the skills are assigned point levels, perhaps from 1 to 5 for "Never" to "Always," or for more qualitative descriptions of levels of play. Finally, rubrics may be holistic, containing paragraphs written to describe various levels of performance. Each paragraph includes several different dimensions and traits (psychomotor, health-related fitness, affective, and cognitive) and is aligned with a point value or level number.

Well-designed rubrics inform students about expectations for the quality of work necessary to reach the standard or achieve a specific grade. Teachers, students, and peers can use rubrics to score or evaluate the information gathered by most of the assessment tools that we describe in this chapter. A rubric can also double as a task sheet to keep students focused on critical elements or knowledge concepts during class, or as an observation checklist to guide feedback given by teachers and peers. In addition, rubrics serve as a means of standardizing assessment, regardless of who uses them. This approach is one way to minimize subjectivity among different observers. Thus, being able to create and use effective rubrics is a vital teaching and assessment skill (see figure 12.1).

Several Web sites with examples of rubrics are available to assist teachers in the design of rubrics: www.pecentral.org; www.pelinks4u.org; www.rubistar.4teachers.org; www.teach-nology.com; http://school.discoveryeducation.com; www.rubrics4teachers.com.

Observations

Teacher observation is an important component in both student learning and classroom management. By circulating among students who are engaged in physical activities that integrate and apply health-related fitness concepts, teachers can gain information regarding individual student performance. Observation is an important part of being able to adjust lessons. For example, many students may be having trouble finding the proper physical location to measure heart rate. Based on

ASSESSING KNOWLEDGE OF CALCULATING AND USING HEART RATE RUBRIC

Student's name _____ Date _____

Score _____ Class _____

Target component	Score 1 point	Score 2 points
Can demonstrate sites at which to count the pulse	Knows one site	Knows two sites
Understands how heart rate information indicates intensity	Some understanding	Clearly understands
Can accurately count the pulse for a fraction of a minute and then accurately calculate heartbeats per minute with a calculator	Sometimes	Most of the time
Can describe ways and reasons to increase or decrease heart rate	Some understanding	Clearly understands

From NASPE, 2011, *Physical education for lifelong fitness: The Physical Best teacher's guide*, 3rd edition (Champaign, IL: Human Kinetics).

Figure 12.1 Example of a rubric to assess knowledge of calculating and using heart rate. A reproducible version of this rubric is available in appendix A.

this, the teacher stops observation activity and provides clarification.

Recording student performance with video is an observation technique that can help assess students. A number of companies offer software applications for the analysis of movement. The following sites provide information: www.dartfish.com, www.allsportsystems.com, and www.sports-motion.com. Periodically videotaping students provides opportunities for students, teachers, and parents to view performance levels. Students should understand that personal assessment is completed to provide information regarding important content areas and growth in performance. The information gained can be used to develop individual fitness plans through physical activity as well as increase understanding and improve performance. Peer assessments can also provide students with opportunities to use their knowledge and understanding of the components of fitness as they apply principles of training to develop plans to improve health-related fitness for the members of their group.

Self- or peer assessment using video can be included as a specific station during circuit training. Using video and a rubric to assess student performance provides greater accuracy in the observation of critical elements, behaviors, or events (Lacy & Hastad, 2005). Note, however, that informal teacher observation alone is not considered an adequate assessment practice. To provide useful, specific feedback to students, teachers need to implement formal, standardized strategies that go beyond observing student performance.

Journal and Log Entries

Journal and log entries provide a way to integrate writing into the physical education curriculum. Writing assessments can be used to determine students' level of understanding. Application of content can also be determined through journals and logs. **Logs** provide a baseline record of behaviors and help form the basis for setting personal goals related to physical activity frequency, intensity, duration, or type. Although logs can contain brief reflections on performance, they are mainly used to record participation data. For example, students log the dates and times of each aerobic fitness activity that they participate in outside of physical education. Heart rate before, during, and after each activity is recorded and analyzed. Student reflection based on log entries can be used to explain the relationship between heart rate levels and aerobic fitness development in a student journal.

A **journal** can include a written record that discusses how the student feels after each activity. Students are encouraged to discuss their successes. Journals are usually designed not only as records but also as reflections. Reflection is a type of journal entry that involves thinking about the learning process itself to help improve performance and attitude (Melograno, 2006). Combining logging and reflective journaling gives students the opportunity to review their progress, which often motivates them to continue being physically active. Students need to be taught how to set up effective logs and journals such as those shown in figures 12.2 and 12.3 on page 214.

FAMILY CHORES STEP LOG

Chore	Guardian	Guardian	Child	Child	Average chore step count
Sweeping					
Dusting					
Raking					
Washing windows					
Doing laundry					
Mowing the grass					
Individual total					

From NASPE, 2011, *Physical education for lifelong fitness: The Physical Best teacher's guide*, 3rd edition (Champaign, IL: Human Kinetics). Adapted, by permission, from R. Pangrazi, A. Beighle, and C. Sidman, 2007, *Pedometer power: 67 lessons for K-12*, 2nd ed. (Champaign, IL: Human Kinetics), 152.

Figure 12.2 This sample log sheet shows how a family can track their steps using a pedometer. A reproducible version of the Family Chores Step Log is available in appendix A.

Adapted, by permission, from R. Pangrazi, A. Beighle, and C. Sidman, 2007, *Pedometer power: 67 lessons for K-12,* 2nd ed. (Champaign, IL: Human Kinetics), 152.

Reflection develops with guidance and practice. Students should be encouraged to reflect on likes and dislikes as well as positive and negative feelings about participation. Younger students can begin by logging their activities using a program such as Activitygram. The program is easy and fun to use, and recording information as homework may draw parents into the assignment. Older students should be encouraged to react or reflect on the activities using teacher-developed prompts initially and then move to self-selected reflection content as they become more accustomed to writing reflectively.

Examples of logs can be found in NASPE's Teacher's Toolbox at www.pecentral.org. Alternatively, use www.rubistar.4teachers.org and make up your own, or search "activity logs" for a wide selection of possibilities.

Assessing reflective journal entries focuses on the students' understanding of the assignment. Although students can be assessed on other areas of a school curriculum, such as spelling and grammar, the focus is on applying and understanding physical education content. Remember that when students share their feelings there are no correct answers, only degrees of thoroughness and thoughtfulness. In figure 12.4 NASPE offers sample criteria and scoring guidelines for journal entries made during an adventure educa-

Turn a log into a reflective journal. Examine the Family Chores Step Log. Reflect on the log with respect to the concepts of FITT. Your reflection should consider these questions:

1. During the course of the day, which family member had the most steps? Which family member had the least?

2. Explain why you believe that the person with the most steps was more active.

3. Do you believe that the person who had the most steps is active enough to stay healthy? Why or why not?

4. In comparison to _____ (family member), why do you think that you had fewer steps?

5. Can you think of ways to increase the number of steps you had on any of the days that you were lower? Describe the strategies you would choose.

6. On which days were you most active? What did you do differently on the active days compared with the less active days?

7. Did you meet your daily goals for time?

8. Did you meet your weekly goals for frequency?

Figure 12.3 Sample reflective journal entry questions.

GROUP WORK CAN BE CHALLENGING

Assessing both the group's and each individual's performance can be challenging, and designing the rubrics for group projects is difficult. At the beginning of each project, students should be made aware of the criteria by which the project will be judged. Simply sharing the rubrics used for assessment is helpful. Then consider allowing groups and individuals to assess themselves and each other, alongside the teacher's official assessment. For example, if three group members each privately rate the fourth group member poorly, this appraisal may support your conclusions regarding this student. But be careful! These issues can be touchy. The skillful teacher will work to ensure that the student is not embarrassed but is instead helped and encouraged to practice the targeted activity. Developing a supportive and open teaching environment is the key to getting the best work out of everyone. Discussing any large discrepancies with those involved can be a valuable teaching technique. Using an individual accountability tool, such as a journal entry or quiz, can also help.

tion experience (e.g., ropes course, wall climbing, and the like).

Chapter 14 provides additional examples of using logs and journals to assess both the affective domain and cognitive knowledge. *Moving Into the Future: National Standards for Physical Education* (NASPE, 2004) also offers good examples and guidelines.

Student Projects

Student projects can include multiple assignments that encourage individuals, partners, or small groups to apply basic physical education knowledge in real-life settings. With teacher guidance, a student or group of students can explore an activity of interest, set goals, plan how to achieve those goals, and then strive for achievement (Melograno, 2006). For example, students can investigate how muscular strength and endurance enhance performance in a particular sport. Students then formulate, assess, and report (orally or in a journal) on the content they found that enhances performance. Projects tend to be cross-curricular in nature, bringing together content and skills developed within several subject areas. A rubric can be developed to assess each part of the project.

RUBRIC FOR SCORING JOURNAL ENTRIES

Scoring guidelines for journal entries

4—Exemplary: Expresses feelings of personal participation and about sharing it with friends

3—Acceptable: Identifies feelings of personal participation

2—Needs improvement: Has difficulty expressing feelings about participation

1—Unacceptable: Does not make journal entries

Criteria for assessing journal entries	Rating			
Analyzes and expresses feelings about physical activity	4	3	2	1
Identifies evidence of success, challenge, and enjoyment present in the activity	4	3	2	1
Explains the challenge that adventure activities provide	4	3	2	1
Describes the positive effects that friends and companions bring to this experience	4	3	2	1

Figure 12.4   Criteria and scoring for reflective journal entries during an adventure education experience.

Adapted from NASPE 2004.

NASPE (2004) offers the following guidelines for developing and using projects effectively.

▶ Use a variety of teaching styles.

▶ Start with small projects in the early grades to prepare them for more complex projects later.

▶ Explain criteria for assessment and scoring procedures at the beginning of the project.

▶ Have others also score the project, for example, community experts or colleagues in other disciplines.

▶ Pilot test any major project before using the results as a basis for promotion or graduation.

▶ Use this opportunity to individualize your program to meet each student's needs.

▶ Design a scoring rubric for each part of the project.

Based on *Moving Into the Future: National Standards for Physical Education* [2004] with permission from the National Association for Sport and Physical Education [NASPE], 1900 Association Drive, Reston, VA 20191-1599.

Cooperation with peers is essential for success. This interdependence builds social skills as well as health-related fitness skills. For example, a group works together to design a training circuit to enhance health-related fitness components. Then they oversee the circuit while another group performs the activities.

Group projects are assessed on both the overall group product and individual performance. Rubrics can be developed to assess the group's efforts, and each individual can also turn in a journal entry. The *Physical Best Activity Guides* provide many suggestions for both individual and group projects in health-related physical fitness education.

Health-Related Fitness Assessments

Fitness assessments, such as Fitnessgram (developed by the Cooper Institute and endorsed by NASPE), provide standardized methods for assessing each area of health-related fitness (see figure 12.5). As part of an authentic assessment approach, the assessment results can be used to help students plan how to maintain or improve each health-related fitness component. Students are taught how to perform fitness assessments independently or with a partner. These self-assessment opportunities are vital to preparing

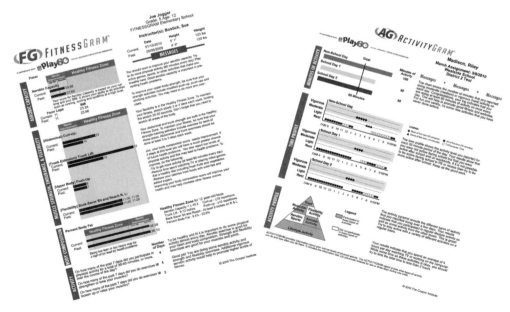

Figure 12.5 Fitnessgram and Activitygram provide students with individualized reports based on their fitness assessment scores.

Reprinted, by permission, from The Cooper Institute, 2010, *Fitnessgram/Activitygram test administration manual*, 5th ed. (Champaign, IL: Human Kinetics), 68.

students for designing their own health-related fitness programs. Students can be assessed more formally at the end of each academic year. The purpose of formal assessment is often to report fitness outcomes to state educational institutions. Results garnered from individual and partner assessment can be used by students to set individual goals. Teachers can also use the assessment results to evaluate physical education programs.

Written Forms of Assessment

Often we think of written assessments as objective tests (e.g., true/false, matching) or essays. While these tests do measure some levels of student learning, authentic written assessment provides a more thorough and integrated understanding. In addition to student journals and logs, students can develop fitness training programs for themselves or another. Projects that include research and development can also be developed. These can include, but are not limited to, magazine articles, videotaped instructions for a weight training program, or pictures of appropriate or inappropriate exercises. Authentic assessments critique students' levels of understanding as well as integration and application.

Discussions

Student discussions can provide teachers with a wealth of information. Assessment techniques can be brief, like conducting a check for understanding while stretching (overlapping), or more thorough, like interviewing students while they are participating in stations for circuit training. Interviewing students at a station during the circuit, pausing during a lesson, or providing opportunities for whole-class discussion can be effective tools for collecting information on student understanding. Student discussions are guided by objectives that state clear learning outcomes. Questions are planned and clearly focus on predetermined student learning outcomes. Summarizing the discussion at the end of a lesson can provide closure as well as make effective use of time during cool-down activities (again, overlapping).

The following can provide effective strategies for class discussions (adapted from Woods, 1997):

▶ Wait at least three seconds before calling on a student. This interval provides all students with time and motivation to ponder the question.

▶ Ask one individual or group to provide an answer and then have the rest of the students raise their hands if they agree with the answer.

▶ Have everyone respond orally at the same time on a specific signal. This approach can also be done nonverbally by having students signal thumbs-up or thumbs-down for true or false and yes or no.

▶ Direct partners to share their answers with each other. They can then raise their hands when they believe that the teacher has stated the correct answer (verbal multiple choice).

▶ Questioning should be quick and to the point to maintain class momentum.

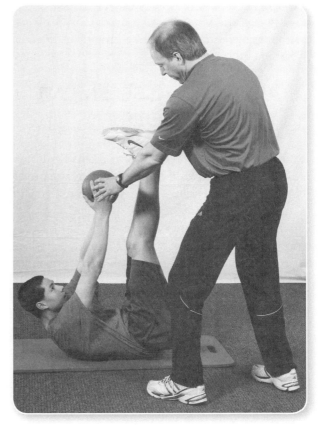

A brief discussion with a student at a circuit station can provide a quick assessment.

Discussions are quick, paperwork free, and especially helpful in assessing students who find written communication difficult (Woods, 1997).

Polls

Student polls can provide some of the same information as discussions but use less time. Posing questions and having students "vote" in response provides quick information from all students. Older students can secretly mark a ballot, whereas younger students might enjoy participating in a poker chip survey (Graham, 2008), in which they place one of two colors of poker chips to indicate yes or no, true or false, disagree or agree, and so on. Students can cast their votes on the way out of class. Results of a poll can be used as a group assessment to help plan and refine lessons as well as provide a point of review for ensuing lessons. One effective use of polling is to ask the students, at the conclusion of a lesson, to raise their hands if they enjoyed the activity or to give a thumbs-up if they would like to play the game again in class. Polling is a quick and efficient way to assess general group enjoyment, and it avoids singling out students by requiring them to provide individual responses.

APPLYING ASSESSMENT TOOLS

Standard 4 of the National Standards for Physical Education (NASPE, 2004) states that a physically educated student "achieves and maintains a health-enhancing level of physical fitness." Furthermore, students are expected to "become more skilled in their ability to plan, perform, and monitor physical activities appropriate for developing physical fitness." Tools that work well for self- and peer assessment are discussed in the following section.

Self-Assessment

Teaching students how to monitor their own progress, or **self-assess**, is an important key to reaching the ultimate goal of producing adults who know how to design appropriate physical activity programs for themselves. Self-assessment also helps students focus on performance progress rather than product, because they understand the critical elements (process components) better, which in turn improves performance standards and achievement. Earlier in this chapter discussion included using rubrics, journals, and logs to monitor student progress and assess fitness levels. Journals and logs can also be used to hold students accountable. The following sample journal assignments provide students an opportunity to reflect on their learning and check for understanding:

- "Help your friend..." Have students describe in writing how to do a particular health-related fitness activity safely (or have younger students make appropriate selections from a pair or series of pictures that show correct or incorrect performances).
- Record feelings. Have students record how they feel physically and emotionally after physical education class and other physical activity.
- Record performance. Have students record the number of times that they performed a health-related activity, such as each stretch, by making check marks. Young children might enjoy recording a smiley face or frowning face next to each check mark to indicate how they felt about each performance.
- Analyze performance. Have students record how well they thought they did on different activities and what exactly they will work on to improve their performances.

Peer Assessment

Peer assessment has students analyze each other's performance. This activity is an important part of developing physical, cognitive, and social skills. Analyzing others' performances helps students focus on the key parts of what they need to learn, thus reinforcing their learning. Most students need repeated instruction to assess their peers properly. Rubrics can be used to identify specific criteria to be used in the process of peer assessment.

Students work together in pairs or small groups to analyze each other's performances. Students use the same rubrics for peer assessment that they use for self-assessment. Students must be taught specific strategies for giving helpful feedback. Role-playing acceptable peer assessment behaviors can be helpful.

When daily peer and self-assessment occurs, students learn more, retain more of what they learn, perform more accurately, and are more accountable. Using multiple peer and self-assessments improves student understanding, retention, and accuracy of data collection and recording (Lund & Kirk, 2010).

Using Portfolios for Student Assessment

Ongoing informal assessment, such as day-to-day observations and peer and self-assessment, should periodically be supported with formal assessments. For example, self- and peer assessments such as rubrics and class assignments can be combined to create a more complete and authentic picture of each student's progress in a portfolio (see sidebar). A portfolio provides a ready reference for assessment, grading, and parent–teacher conferences.

PORTFOLIO MANAGEMENT

Assessing student portfolios can be time consuming, but teachers can develop a manageable plan for reviewing portfolios.

- First, determine the purpose for using the portfolio.
- Obtain or have students or volunteers make sturdy portfolios. Use a traditional three-hole folder, a folded piece of 12-by-18-inch (30 by 45 cm) construction paper with pockets added, a flat box, a hanging file, or another appropriate container. Another practical means of creating portfolios is to use computers. Creating Web sites or other electronic recordings of documents, videos, and projects is becoming easy and practical in school settings.
- Store portfolios by class in milk crates, portable hanging file boxes, or larger bins. At the elementary level, try to have the classroom teacher store the container and bring it to each physical education class.
- Train students to file their own papers or to file papers for younger students (but maintain confidentiality). Color coding by class or grade level can help. Establishing class management procedures for filing papers helps, too.
- If electronic portfolios are used, asking the technology teacher or homeroom teacher for help serves the purpose of practicing technology skills while creating a physical education portfolio.
- Establish protocols for passing out and collecting portfolios.
- Periodically, select or have students select representative pieces from their assessment activities to retain in their portfolios. This process leaves fewer bits and pieces for you to sort through. Designate how many pieces to select, taking the time to discuss what creates a good cross-section of items. Stamping each one with a message such as "Completed on Time" indicates that this piece of the portfolio will not be used as part of the student's assessment, reduces paperwork, and still provides student accountability. When pieces of the portfolio are designated after the work is completed, students will be motivated to try their best on each assignment.
- Staple or glue certain ongoing assessments, such as a fitness assessment record sheet, onto the front or back cover of each portfolio.
- Decide whether to staple in several sheets of paper to form journals inside each portfolio, use a separate notebook for journals, or add individual sheets to portfolios with journal entries as they are written.

A well-designed **portfolio** is a collection of tools that help teachers assess each student. Portfolios may be presented as a three-hole folder, a hanging file, or even as an electronic document saved on a DVD or Web site. Because portfolios highlight student progress, they are a powerful way to build students' self-efficacy. Self-efficacy fosters students' beliefs that they have the ability to learn and the competence to participate.

What should be included in a portfolio? A variety of assignments and assessments form a complete picture of each student's progress and achievements. Both informal and formal assessments such as periodic fitness assessment results; rubrics that reflect affective, cognitive, and physical development; journal entries; video clips; and projects can be included. Older students can select their own portfolio pieces (based on predetermined criteria).

Portfolios can go with students from grade to grade and school to school, making it possible to monitor long-term progress. In this regard, electronic portfolios are efficient and simple to move. Portfolios can also be a tool for monitoring program effectiveness in terms of delivering a sequentially designed curriculum.

GRADING AND REPORTING STUDENT PROGRESS

Assessing and grading have distinctly different purposes. Assessment tells teachers and students how they are improving or what they need to work on with respect to specific program objectives or standards. A grade is a single summative or composite symbol or score that becomes a permanent record of student achievement, and it must be representative of achievement of all program objectives (Lacy & Hastad, 2003). If a single grade must be provided it should represent a compilation of many assessments and measurements of improvement—not a limited or single assessment of student status. Lacy and Hastad (2003) also caution that teachers must be sensitive to the effect of grades on youth and that the grades must be tied to the school's procedures for issuing grades. An acceptable relationship between assessing and grading must be developed before grading begins.

Determining a fair and balanced single grade is without a doubt one of the most difficult aspects of the assessment process. Although fitness maintenance is a prominent program objective (i.e., NASPE standard 4: Achieves and maintains a health-enhancing level of physical fitness), the criterion used to evaluate fitness involves assessing a variety of components and crosses over several standards. With respect to grading and fitness assessment, it is appropriate to focus on providing clear and accurate feedback regarding individual goals and student achievement of those goals. Encouraging students to self-assess is recommended. If a composite or single grade is required by the school district, teachers are encouraged to provide alternative and helpful fitness feedback, such as individual Fitnessgram reports attached to the composite grade. This approach will help students understand the process of achieving and maintaining healthful levels. Grades should not be given based primarily on achievement of specific fitness scores. This type of grading can discourage students from continuing to be physically active.

For teachers who are looking for ways to include fitness outcomes in a composite grade, some possible solutions include the following:

▶ Providing a separate outcome or score for health-related fitness. Many teachers provide separate physical education grades that allow them to specify student performance in separate domains; this method could also be used to report health-related fitness performance.

▶ Listing health-related fitness outcomes along with specific motor skill performances in a physical education report card.

▶ Sending home individual Fitnessgram or Activitygram printouts when formative assessments are completed.

Performance feedback on fitness content should do the following:

▶ Help students understand where they can improve

▶ Help teachers recognize whether students are meeting program objectives and content standards

- ▶ Promote the health-related physical fitness education program to the school and community
- ▶ Justify the ongoing need for health-related physical fitness education in the curriculum

Sharing Information With Students and Parents

Share assessment feedback with students and parents. Use a balance of assessment tools across all domains to assess each student. Present knowledge assessment alongside affective fitness and motor skill assessments. This approach will help both students and parents see how knowledge enhances physical development.

Emphasize intrinsic over extrinsic motivators. Affective assessment data must be handled in a sensitive manner so that students will feel comfortable and communicate honestly.

Parent–teacher conferences are an excellent way to share information. Interaction with the parents or guardians provides the chance to convey information in a positive and caring manner. Conferences can be used to brainstorm ways to help the student and to find physical activity that the family enjoys. This element can be important in developing a program that has value to students and their families.

Set up teacher–student conferences as part of an activity circuit so that goals can be based on feedback and the student's personal objectives.

USING ASSESSMENTS FOR PROGRAM PLANNING

A central reason for regular assessment is to use the information to tailor programs that meet individual student needs. Assessment should not result in diminished activity time. Lectures have their place in a health-related physical fitness education program, yet the goal is to keep students as physically active as possible. Students can learn through doing. If students are having trouble learning how to pace themselves while running the mile, design an active game that teaches this concept to make the connection

more explicit. Remember that students enjoy moving. If students do not enjoy physical activity they are less likely to pursue it as a lifestyle choice. Including a variety of movement forms in addition to health-related fitness and sport activities—for example, dance, outdoor pursuits, and adventure programming—can spark interest in physical activity in otherwise reluctant students.

Motivating Through Assessment

Knowing how to be physically active for life is not enough: Students must want to pursue a physically active lifestyle. Giving students the responsibility for tracking their own progress is highly motivating (Hellison, 2003). Avoid comparisons among students. Instead, focus on helping students set goals for personal improvement so that they are more likely to feel successful each time they participate in physical activity. Even a very young child can set a simple goal, such as playing physically active games after school three times a week instead of watching television.

Goals should be set based on current personal health-related fitness levels, feelings of self-efficacy, knowledge of the FITT guidelines and training principles, access to various types of programs and activities, and the purposes that you have established for setting goals.

To guide self-assessment and goal setting, set benchmarks (i.e., the healthy fitness zones) by which students can monitor their own progress (see chapter 2). This process makes students more accountable for their own learning and progress. This approach is in keeping with the philosophy of helping students move from depending on your guidance to pursuing health-related fitness independently as a way of life.

Specifically, students may be motivated by carefully monitoring self-recorded progress toward goals that they set with their teacher. For this to occur, sufficient time must be given to allow for progress. Focus on small steps toward improvement or toward the goal. The small steps that can be seen in the student's own writing are the most motivating. These become fuel for developing a sense of competence. (Refer to chapter 2 for goal-setting strategies and guidelines.)

SUMMARY

To be authentic, assessment in physical education must allow students to demonstrate, in real-life settings, that they are moving toward the goal of becoming physically active adults. Physical education programs should motivate students to apply motor skills, knowledge, and approaches, including fitness knowledge, in the real world. Within the context of motivation, teachers should separate health-related fitness assessment from the grading system in physical education, and they should provide specific feedback using alternative methods that inform students about progress toward personal goals and strategies to achieve them. This chapter differentiated assessment from grading, provided suggestions about what and how to assess student learning, and suggested assessment tools to do so. In addition, differences between traditional and authentic, formative and summative, and formal and informal assessment were delineated. Chapters 13 and 14 elaborate on some of the tools discussed in this chapter and their application to assessing the health-related fitness, knowledge, and affective areas.

Chapter Contents

Assessing Health-Related Fitness and Physical Activity

Mary Jo Sariscsany

Helping students become physically active for a lifetime is a primary goal of physical education programs. Chapter 13 addresses specific strategies for assessing health-related fitness and physical activity levels within physical education and outside of school. Fitness assessment and curricular programs frequently reflect an emphasis on health-related fitness components as recommended in state and national standards. Student assessment often includes preassessments to establish a starting point to base personal goals for improving specific areas of health-related fitness. Fitness assessment has continued to develop. Historically, emphasis was placed on skill- or sport-related fitness (e.g., speed as measured by the student's 100-meter run time, power as measured by the standing long jump). Students' scores were compared with those of other students (normative scoring), leading many students to perceive themselves as unfit. Conversely, some students were able to achieve good scores primarily because of their genetic makeup, giving them a false picture of their present fitness levels.

Activities should be designed to allow all students degrees of success.

Effective health-related fitness assessments are not used to compare students with each other; they are used as a means to communicate each person's level of fitness. Appropriate health-related fitness assessment includes a variety of physical fitness tests designed to measure aerobic fitness, body composition, muscle strength, muscular endurance, and flexibility. Scores achieved using appropriate forms of fitness assessment can be used to establish personal goals that allow students to attain a level of fitness associated with good health. Personal goals rather than peer competition are the focus, allowing students to experience feelings of success based on their own levels of achievement.

GUIDELINES FOR APPROPRIATE HEALTH-RELATED FITNESS ASSESSMENT

Fitness assessment includes both process and product measurements that document students' progress toward good health and disease prevention. Fitness assessment is an integral piece of the overall curriculum. The following guidelines can be used to connect assessment to the overall physical education program:

▶ Students have opportunities to demonstrate behaviors that they need to create their own effective physical activity opportunities throughout life.

▶ Self-assessment helps make health-related fitness concepts essential content of the curriculum.

▶ Self-assessment individualizes instruction and sequence of learning.

▶ Students are provided with practical experiences that build confidence in their ability to seek improvement.

▶ Students understand how assessment and goal setting are integrated into lifestyle changes.

Teach and have students practice proper procedures for conducting health-related fitness assessment. Table 13.1 shows a continuum from teacher-controlled assessment to student self-assessment (along with the goals at each stage in the continuum).

As students develop their understanding and skills, they become more independent. The ultimate goal is to produce adults who can conduct their own health-related assessments in the context of self-designed physical activity programs. Elementary students will require a higher degree of direct teacher supervision. Students in middle

Table 13.1 Continuum for Moving Students From Teacher-Directed Assessment to Self-Assessment

	Format	Goal
1	Teacher-directed, self-testing practice	To familiarize students with testing procedures
2	Formal, teacher-administered testing	To provide accurate baseline data
	Goal setting	To focus training efforts
	Physical activity	To reach goals
3	Informal self-testing, checked by peer	To compare to baseline data, to provide more testing practice, and to ensure accuracy
	Reset goals (if necessary)	To focus future efforts
	Physical activity	To reach goals
4	Informal self-testing	To self-monitor progress, to provide more testing practice
	Reset goals (if necessary)	To focus future efforts
	Physical activity	To reach goals
5	Formal self-testing, checked by teacher	To ensure accurate current data
	Reset goals (if necessary)	To focus future efforts
	Physical activity	To reach goals
6	Formal self-testing, not checked	To monitor progress independently

school will likely be capable of cycling through the first three steps (teacher-directed self-assessment practice; formal, teacher-administered assessment; and informal self-checks). High school students should be able to progress to formal self-assessment. Remember that goal setting and physical activity are important steps after the initial self-assessment and will help perpetuate a continuous cycle that includes assessment, goal setting, and participation in physical activity.

FITNESSGRAM

Fitnessgram physical fitness assessment (Cooper Institute, 2007) is a comprehensive tool used to assess aerobic fitness, body composition, muscle strength, muscular endurance, and flexibility. Appropriate uses for Fitnessgram can be found in the sidebar on page 226. Fitnessgram uses **criterion-referenced health standards** or standards associated with good health. Scientific information is used to determine the amount of fitness needed to meet minimum health levels. Fitnessgram uses a **healthy fitness zone** (HFZ) to designate the range of fitness scores associated with good health. The healthy fitness zone is based on criterion-referenced standards because

they represent the age- and gender-appropriate fitness levels that a child needs for good health. **Normative standards** (e.g., percentiles) provide comparisons relative to other youth in a group but do not provide information concerning how the values relate to individual health (Corbin & Pangrazi, 2008).

The acronym HELP is used to describe the philosophy of Fitnessgram (see the sidebar "HELP Philosophy" on page 10). The Fitnessgram is designed for personal fitness self-assessment, institutional assessment, parental reporting, and personal tracking. Self-assessment is the focus of the Fitnessgram. Students should be taught how to evaluate and interpret their scores. Students can then use their scores to plan personal programs. Students can be helped to interpret their results and to develop programs for improvement and maintenance based on scores relative to the HFZ, which reflects fitness levels required for good health. Scores that fall below the HFZs are categorized as "Needs improvement" to indicate that students need to bring their scores into the healthy fitness zone.

As part of the Fitnessgram report students receive scores and interpretations of the scores as well as individualized recommendations to help them improve in the areas where their scores fell below the HFZ (see figure 12.5 on page 216). Feedback that is immediate and based on personal health-related fitness scores provides information that can help students understand how their scores relate to the achievement of a healthy lifestyle. Reinforcement statements regarding their healthy behaviors also encourage students to continue their positive behaviors.

Developmentally appropriate health-related fitness assessment conducted in a sound physical education program helps teach students how to be fit and healthy throughout their lifespan. Moreover, it provides a snapshot of each student's current fitness level, allowing both teachers and students to plan for improvement.

Activitygram

The **Activitygram** portion of Fitnessgram helps students understand how activity behaviors outside of school contribute to personal health and wellness. Activitygram was designed to help students self-monitor their physical activity patterns. Students can see how active they truly are,

APPROPRIATE USES FOR FITNESSGRAM

- Personal assessment to help students evaluate their level of health-related fitness
- Institutional assessment to allow teachers to view group data (for curriculum development)
- Personal-best assessment to allow individual students to determine performance levels privately
- Teaching students about criterion-referenced health standards and the types of activities needed to reach them
- Helping students track fitness results over time (in portfolios, for example)
- Document that Fitnessgram is being administered in schools and that student self-assessments are being tracked over time

From The Cooper Institute 2008.

and this information can provide students with information to set goals for their activity plans. By self-managing their activity levels students begin to learn skills that are essential to lifetime physical activity adherence (Dale & Corbin, 2000). Students are encouraged to think of the assessments as lifestyle assessments rather than school-based tests.

Physical activity assessments were added to Fitnessgram to emphasize to students the importance of developing lifetime habits of regular physical activity. Although students' fitness is important, they cannot maintain it unless they remain physically active. The Activitygram assessment is a recall of the student's physical activity, based on a validated physical activity instrument known as the Previous Day Physical Activity Recall (PDPAR; Weston, Petosa, & Pate 1997). In the assessment, the student reports his or her activity levels for each 30-minute block of time during the day. The format uses a three-day recall consisting of two school days and one nonschool day.

The software provides detailed information about the student's activity habits and prescriptive feedback about how active she or he should be. Students should begin using the Activitygram program in the fifth grade.

Preparing for Student Assessment Using Fitnessgram

Fitnessgram can be a positive experience for students. Being ready to administer fitness assessments makes the entire process flow more smoothly. The following suggestions will help streamline the process of administering Fitnessgram.

1. Prepare students—Allow two to six weeks for students to practice each item and increase their fitness levels. Administering Fitnessgram at the very beginning of the school year may lead to muscle soreness and discouragement. In addition, misleading follow-up results may occur because students improve rapidly after they get used to the procedures.

2. Read all instructions carefully—These are located in the latest version of the *Fitnessgram/ Activitygram Test Administration Manual*.

3. Collect the necessary equipment—Obtain the equipment needed and ensure that it is working properly. Sources of equipment are listed in the *Fitnessgram/Activitygram Test Administration Manual*.

4. Prepare record-keeping forms—Reproduce necessary forms (see the latest version of the *Fitnessgram/Activitygram Test Administration Manual*). Record student names as appropriate, depending on the form that you use. Some teachers may choose to use hand-held electronic devices to record student performances. The limitation to this is that students are not responsible for their own record management, which is an important consideration when deciding how to record fitness assessments.

5. Organize assessment stations—create a circuit, such as that shown in figure 13.1. Be sure that the setup allows you and the students to flow easily from one station to the next. In addition, locate the stations so that you can see all students, making adequate supervision easier. Make sure that forms, pencils, and clipboards are available at each station to allow students to record their results.

6. Organize students—Decide in advance how to group students and which group will begin at which station.

7. Maximize instruction—Plan fitness assessment along with other activities to continue the learning process and keep all students active.

Adapted, by permission, from The Cooper Institute, 2007, *Fitnessgram/ Activitygram test administration manual,* 4th ed. (Champaign, IL: Human Kinetics).

In addition, to help increase validity and reliability, practice administering Fitnessgram to a small group of students or colleagues before assessing on a larger scale.

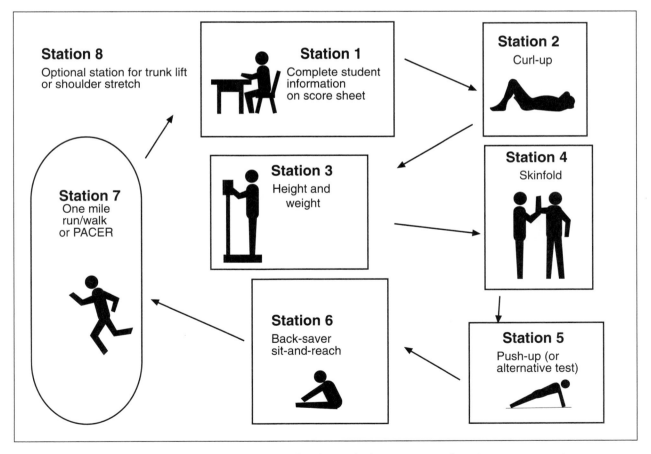

Figure 13.1   Creating a fitness assessment circuit can help you streamline the assessment process.

Involving Students

Most people learn best by doing. To develop students who can self-direct their own physically active lifestyles, they must be involved in each part of fitness assessment. Students become more willing to accept responsibility when they begin to understand the purpose of fitness assessment and relate their scores to what they do and do not do. Teachers can help students develop their personal responsibility skills using the following steps:

▶ Teach students proper procedures and provide opportunities to practice self- and peer assessment.

▶ Students regularly assess themselves on individual components of fitness, remembering that completing all Fitnessgram assessment components at the same time is not always necessary.

▶ Provide students with multiple opportunities to learn self-assessment procedures.

▶ Have students keep logs of their results to assist them in planning personal fitness improvement plans.

▶ Provide students with guidance and feedback that allows them to practice goal setting for each of the health-related fitness components.

Students can enter their own scores using Fitnessgram and establish goals relating to their results. The Fitnessgram software is simple enough that most students can enter their own scores. If elementary or middle school students need help entering scores, parents and high school students can be asked to assist.

Effective Practice

For optimal performance, students need to practice each item repeatedly. Practice ensures that the results are based on differences in fitness rather than on knowledge about how to perform the assessments. The following are simple suggestions for developing effective practice opportunities:

▶ Discuss and demonstrate the correct techniques (critical elements) involved in each assessment item. Deliver this information in multiple forms: posters, listed critical steps in word or picture form, or checklists of assessment steps for self- and peer checking.

▶ Have students practice with a friend. Provide rubrics for students to use during this practice so that partners can provide feedback on technique as well as motivational support. Repeated practice will help ensure success.

▶ Have assessment stations available during class time for students to self-assess on a regular basis.

▶ Encourage students to give their best effort when they practice the assessment.

▶ Assign fitness homework that involves parents.

▶ Focus on personal improvement and carefully guard student privacy. Fitness assessment is not a competitive sport. Student performances should never be compared with that of another student, and judging student effort is not acceptable.

▶ Teach through assessment by explaining the concepts behind each assessment and discussing results with students.

▶ Encourage parents to volunteer to help assess and record scores so that assessment day proceeds smoothly. Besides facilitating the assessment procedures, parent or guardian volunteers develop a clear understanding of fitness assessment.

Students can benefit from practice and self-assessment. Multiple practice sessions provide students with opportunities to understand fitness concepts and develop personal goals to improve their fitness. Practice settings provide student-friendly opportunities that focus on personal improvement.

Assessment Protocols

Fitnessgram protocols are thoroughly detailed in the test manual. Training students how to administer the protocols is essential to developing a student-centered environment that provides opportunities for students to take personal responsibility for their fitness development. The following strategies can increase student adherence to proper protocols, help students become more skillful at self- and peer-assessment, and help make fitness assessment a positive experience for both teacher and students:

▶ Explain and practice the protocols and purposes to students over multiple days. Students need to practice, practice, practice. This information is reviewed again on assessment days.

▶ Use the same information posters, rubrics, or task cards (listing the critical elements or common errors) used during practice sessions.

▶ Place drawings or diagrams depicting correct form and common errors at each station.

▶ Announce assessment days in advance. Unannounced fitness assessment can lead to negative attitudes toward both fitness and physical activity. If preparation and practice are sufficient, anxiety will decrease. Encouragement can motivate students to do their best.

▶ Postpone fitness assessment if the environment is too hot or too cold. Encourage students to dress appropriately. Provide water before, during, and after strenuous assessments, such as the PACER or one-mile run.

TEACHING TIP: SPREADING OUT FITNESS ASSESSMENTS

Instead of administering an entire fitness assessment battery at one time, teachers can incorporate fitness assessment with other units and activities throughout the school year. Specifically, assessing various health-related fitness components when the assessments match the concepts that the students are studying helps connect assessment to their lives. Students will be more motivated to self-assess because they see the connections between concepts, class activities, and assessment. This approach saves time because teaching concepts, relating assessment to each concept, and having students practice self-assessment all at once connects the related dots. This method can be more beneficial than conducting a formal assessment session.

Laura Borsdorf, Professor

Exercise and Sport Science Department
Ursinus College, Collegeville, Pennsylvania

Appropriate practice is essential if student fitness scores are to be valid and reliable. The more students practice the assessments, the more comfortable they become with how Fitnessgram is administered.

TAILORING HEALTH-RELATED FITNESS ASSESSMENT

Fitnessgram is designed to meet the needs of a diverse range of student abilities, which can be matched using alternative assessment items. For example, the PACER can be used in place of the mile run. Students have a wide range of aerobic fitness, and those who are less fit often stop running long after the more aerobically fit students have completed the mile run. This scenario could result in the less-fit youth feeling extremely self-conscious. The PACER assessment will have students stopping at various times, and those who are more aerobically fit will finish last. Thus, the students with lower fitness levels are far less likely to be spotlighted. In addition, the PACER provides opportunities for goal setting in a user-friendly way that students can relate to. Younger students may find it easier to envision improving their PACER scores by one or two laps than achieving an intangible time improvement for the one-mile run.

Space is usually not an issue with the PACER, but those who have smaller instructional spaces have the 15-meter PACER as an option. Note, however, that because of increased fatigue from making more stops and turns, the 15-meter PACER should be used only by elementary students. Staggered starts for the mile run can camouflage to a degree those students who run slower. Another idea is to have students of similar ability run in small groups together, at different times or on different days. Ideally, the students would choose which aerobic assessment they prefer, not only increasing their autonomy but also motivating them to do their best.

Elementary and Inexperienced Students

Elementary and less experienced students need to practice individual Fitnessgram assessment items under supervision. The goal is to expose younger students to the various assessment items. Because physical fitness is not strongly linked to physical activity in young children, Fitnessgram is recommended as formal assessment for those in the fifth grade and beyond. Younger students should practice so that they become familiar with the various parts of physical fitness and self-assessment, but scores should not be recorded. Standards of performance are not reliable before fourth grade. Personal fitness assessment is a major reason for using the Fitnessgram assessment. Students are taught to interpret their scores and interpret and understand the meaning of results. Younger students are not capable of using higher-order thinking skills to interpret their scores. Pairing older students with younger or inexperienced students can provide needed guidance and motivation.

Consider introducing, teaching, and practicing each assessment item before official assessment day. You can begin integrating one assessment item into each instructional unit. For example, focusing on flexibility (e.g., back-saver sit-and-reach assessment item) would be appropriate during an educational gymnastics unit. During a three-week unit on Ultimate Frisbee, the health-related fitness focus can be on aerobic capacity and heart rate recovery time. This approach helps students become familiar with each assessment item and teaches them how each health-related fitness component relates to an applied setting.

Middle and High School Students

Older students should be given increased responsibility for personal assessment with adequate supervision. Overdirecting students sends the message that they may not be able to assess themselves or their peers independently. When properly trained in the protocols for assessing health-related fitness, middle and high school students can often display responsible and mature behavior. Each student must have complete understanding of the purpose behind health-related fitness as well as respect for the privacy of their peers. Careful consideration must be given to the maturity and knowledge of each student. Teachers become facilitators and supervise the assessment environment. Providing students

opportunities to control the assessment environment reinforces the concept that students need to take personal responsibility for assessing and maintaining their personal health and fitness.

Reluctant or Overanxious Students

Some students may have had poor fitness assessment experiences in the past or may be more reserved and private than others. Reluctance and anxiety are common emotions in every assessment situation, but positive fitness assessment environments can help prevent these emotions from developing further. A key to reducing these behaviors is to have students practice each assessment item frequently over an extended period in a relaxed and safe atmosphere. Offering students a choice of assessment items that measure the same component, such as the PACER, the one-mile run, or the walk test for assessing aerobic fitness (for middle or high school students) may also help put students at ease. Student privacy regarding assessment scores must be ensured. Treating student feelings in a sensitive manner and reassuring students that personal achievement is the focus of the program will help create a positive environment. Students will gain a lot from self-assessment practice but will gain little from being forced to perform in formal assessments, and negative feelings toward physical activity could result.

Students With Disabilities

In general, the definitions, components, assessment items, and standards of health-related fitness used for students with disabilities should be the same as those used for students without disabilities (Lacy & Hastad, 2007). Fitnessgram can be modified for students with disabilities. Information on how to do this can be found in chapter 4 in the section "Considerations for Testing Special Populations" of the *Fitnessgram/Activitygram Test Administration Manual*. As a complement to Fitnessgram, the Brockport Physical Fitness Test also assesses the health-related fitness of people with disabilities (Winnick & Short, 1999).

The Brockport tests are specifically designed to assess the physical fitness of individuals with

Fitness assessment for students with disabilities should measure the student's ability to function in everyday activities and should take into account the student's interests.

a wide range of physical and mental disabilities and were developed through Project Target, a research study funded by the U.S. Department of Education. The Brockport Physical Fitness Test (BPFT) is a health-related, criterion-referenced assessment of fitness for children ages 10 through 17 that includes 27 assessment items specific to the areas of aerobic functioning, body composition, and musculoskeletal functioning. Many of these assessment items can be used as alternative items for standard health-related fitness assessments. Always review each student's IEP and consult with related service providers such as physical therapists, occupational therapists, and speech and language therapists to know the medical background of any student with a disability.

The Brockport Physical Fitness Test resources include the following:

- The *Brockport Physical Fitness Test Manual*
- The *Brockport Physical Fitness Training Guide*

- The *Brockport Physical Fitness Test Administration Video*
- The Fitness Challenge software

For more information or to order the Brockport Physical Fitness Test Kit or materials, contact Human Kinetics at 800-747-4457 or www. HumanKinetics.com.

When an individualized fitness program for a student with disabilities is designed, keep in mind that a major reason for fitness assessment should be to measure a person's ability to function in everyday activities. Look at each individual, assess needs and limitations, and design alternatives to bypass those limitations. Take into account a person's interests as well. For example, if a person in a wheelchair would like to be able to play wheelchair basketball more proficiently and with greater stamina, the fitness program should work to enhance the person's abilities in this area. Fitness assessment should then discern whether the person is making progress in areas relevant to enjoying this interest. Personalization of the assessment is encouraged. Teachers can identify each student's health-related concerns, and then together the teacher and student can select areas to be assessed and which assessment items to use (Winnick, 2005).

For more detailed guidelines on how to integrate personalized fitness assessments for people with disabilities, see chapter 11.

USING HEALTH-RELATED FITNESS RESULTS APPROPRIATELY

Health-related fitness results provide important information regarding student health. Both student and parents should be given a copy of the results that includes clear interpretations of the results and suggestions for improvement or maintenance in each area assessed. Parents and students should know why the assessments are administered. Students need to know both why and how the results will be used to establish goals and fitness plans for future achievement. Students and parents must also understand that the health-related fitness scores will not be used for grading.

Sharing Results With Students and Parents

Discuss and explain the reasons for the assessments and the meanings behind the results. With students, this discussion can be part of a set induction at the beginning of the lesson. Before assessment, parents should be notified by a letter that explains the philosophy, approach, and use of the results. Reassure both students and parents that student privacy will be respected. Share the actual forms used to record and interpret the assessment results (the relevant forms are provided in the *Fitnessgram/Activitygram Test Administration Manual* and software). A parent night that introduces the assessment protocols will help set the stage for clear and productive communication before and after assessment.

Blank Fitnessgram forms can be used to review the purpose and meaning of the assessment items and results. Distribute individual report forms privately, such as in a sealed envelope or during a student–teacher or parent–teacher conference. Setting up a station on a physical activity circuit at which you privately discuss assessment results while the rest of the student's group participates in an activity can also provide privacy.

Along with assessment results and interpretations, information and guidance can be given to each student about how to improve health. Help the student set realistic goals during this time (see chapter 2).

Grading

Fitness assessment results should not be used as a basis for grades. Lund and Kirk (2010) summarize the appropriate use of health-related fitness assessment:

> Unless results of fitness testing are used to improve student learning, testing should not be done. Additionally, the Physical Education Content Standards call for students to use this information to develop personal fitness improvement programs (NASPE, 2004). Performance-based assessment might call for students to create such a plan based on the analysis of personal fitness test results and knowledge of what optimal levels of fitness should be, causing students to use fitness results in a manner that would be helpful to them as adults. (p. 15)

Expanding on this concept, grades can be based on age-appropriate abilities to self-assess and interpret assessment results, as well as on written assessments of knowledge of fitness concepts and principles. Assignments relating to the process of how to set goals and plan personal programs are also excellent tasks to grade and include in the summative grade report.

Such emphases help students become adults who are physically active for life in self-designed, enjoyable fitness programs. In contrast, grades based solely on assessment results are likely to discourage students from continuing to be physically active after they leave your program. If you give credit for showing improvement in fitness assessment scores, remember that improvements will come in smaller increments for students who have already achieved a high level of fitness, so your grading system should not penalize high-fit students. Consider reporting the accomplishment of fitness goals as the measure of success and the achievement of a health-enhancing level of physical activity as the basis for feedback to parents. Many teachers send home a grade for physical education and attach a separate Fitnessgram report as the feedback related to health-related fitness. This method requires no extra work and is a more authentic and appropriate means to report student assessment results and health.

Planning

To be part of authentic assessment, fitness testing must provide feedback that helps shape a health-related physical fitness education program. Health-related fitness results can be used to help both teachers and students plan for future learning and fitness gains. For example, if students are making little or no progress in muscular strength and endurance, activities that enhance these areas can be designed and increased. More mature students can be involved in problem-solving tasks related to their personal fitness scores. Encourage students to set specific process-oriented goals related to the targeted areas, such as "I will do upper-body weight training two to three times per week on nonconsecutive days, and each week I will increase the number of push-ups I do by at least one repetition until I reach my healthy fitness zone. I will then continue to do this to maintain upper-body strength in the healthy fitness zone." Goal setting will help students tailor their personal fitness programs to their specific needs. Teachers check in with students regularly to monitor progress and provide suggestions for modifications.

Fitnessgram is an excellent health-related fitness assessment battery that provides up-to-date and sensitive health-related assessments and is easy to implement. The information in this chapter can help teachers plan, conduct, and follow up on fitness assessments that teach students what they need to know to participate throughout their lives in effective, personally designed fitness programs and physical activities.

GUIDELINES FOR APPROPRIATE PHYSICAL ACTIVITY ASSESSMENT

Many teachers report grading students on effort and participation. This practice lacks reliability and consistency because students may have widely varying physical fitness assessment results yet be applying similar levels of effort. In fact, students who are obese or less fit must exert greater effort to accomplish even simple movement (such as walking) than students who are already fit or who possess greater muscular strength.

Effort infers how hard a student tries. Although putting forth effort or trying hard is a highly valued characteristic in a competitive society, the appropriate benchmark for assessment is the authentic assessment and quantification of physical activity frequency, intensity, time, and type that contribute to attainment of the HFZ in each assessment or component area. Pedometers are an effective way to monitor the total amount of physical activity (e.g., walking, running, skipping) performed daily. Many pedometers measure steps and physical activity time. These measurements provide students with accurate information for goal setting. Personalized scores can be used to establish meaningful goals. Achieving these goals can be motivating. Effort is often directly related to motivational level, and motivation is best enhanced by creating a safe learning environment and successful experiences.

The goal of a quality physical education program is to develop a lifelong pattern of physical activity. But when it comes to health-related fitness measures, scores today do not necessarily indicate long-term results. The fifth grader born with the right genes might score well on the one-mile run without much effort, whereas a classmate might make a great effort but still record a poor time. But if the student with the good mile run time eventually becomes a couch potato and the student with the poor time continues to spend time participating in a variety of activities, the latter student will likely live a healthier life.

Ultimately, physical educators want a nation of physically active, healthy citizens, not a nation of ex-athletes who follow a couple of years of excellent fitness levels with 50 years of TV watching that result in declining health, high medical bills, and poor productivity. Reward time or persistence in physical activity, because that is what will, in the long term, result in lifelong health and fitness.

Encourage results, as well as time spent in physical activity. The Fitnessgram criteria help teachers obtain appropriate results for a broad range of students. In addition, consider the following: Did the student with the best one-mile run time in class spend as much time in a target heart rate zone as the student who took longer to complete the same distance? Challenge the high-achieving students to do even better, to set improved time and distance goals. Challenge each student to be his or her individual physical best, and reward physical activity time.

STRATEGIES FOR ASSESSING PHYSICAL ACTIVITY

Effective strategies for assessing physical activity link fitness concepts such as overload to the activity. Students may appear to be active when you are casually observing them, but closer assessment of activity data is necessary to determine whether students are truly applying the fitness principles of overload, intensity, and specificity to progress toward lifetime health-related fitness goals.

Logs and Journals

Logging physical activity information in a table, chart, or journal provides evidence of total time spent in physical activity. Time alone, however, does not necessarily demonstrate appropriate activity levels. Perceived exertion can be used by students to reflect how strenuous their physical activity bouts made them feel. Using a 0-to-10 perceived exertion scale gives students a good idea of the intensity level and provides them with information to change their activity levels to reach desired outcomes. (See table 5.2 and the accompanying text on page 78 for information about the OMNI RPE scale.) Teach students that their personal feelings of effort are important, not how they compare with other students. Use

the following strategies to gain student physical activity information:

▶ Teach students to use the perceived exertion scale so that they can record this data in their logs or journals.

▶ Graph intensity levels with duration of activities. Encourage students who do not demonstrate changes over time to examine their goals and revise strategies.

▶ Incorporate technology by having students use heart rate monitors and pedometers. Record indicators of intensity such as heart rate or steps over time.

▶ Involve parents or guardians by having them sign off on their child's log or journal periodically.

Heart Rate Monitors

According to Kirkpatrick and Birnbaum (1997), students can use **heart rate monitors** to assess physical activity intensity levels more accurately as well as gain individualized feedback. Heart rate monitors can be used as a self-assessment of aerobic fitness. For example, a high school student may use the information from a heart rate monitor to determine that his or her heart rate is below the target heart rate during moderate walking. Learning that he or she can no longer elevate the heart rate into the target heart rate zone by walking fast, this student would be encouraged to choose a more intense level of activity. The student can determine how intensity need to be adjusted to perform more vigorous aerobic fitness activity, such as jogging or using in-line skates, to participate in the target heart rate zone.

Target heart rate zones are not effectively used for younger children (elementary through middle school), but heart rate monitors can still provide an avenue to motivate young students. Younger students can examine resting heart rate before an activity and then compare the difference between exercise heart rate and resting heart rate.

Younger students can play a version of heart rate bingo (Kirkpatrick & Birnbaum, 1997). Bingo cards are developed with a wide range of anticipated resting and exercise heart rates. Each student has a card, or one can be developed for the whole class. A free space is included on the card where the student's resting heart rate is recorded. At the end of an activity, students find their exercise heart rate and record the heart rate on either the class bingo card or their personal bingo cards.

Students keep track of their exercise heart rate each day and begin to fill their cards. When a student gets a bingo by filling in a row, column, or diagonal, he or she turns in the card to receive a reward. Rewards can include items such as being an exercise leader or getting to choose a class activity. If a class bingo card is used, the class scores a bingo and they get to choose the next class activity from a list or choose other incentives.

Pedometers

Pedometers can provide authentic evaluation of daily physical activity (Pangrazi, Beighle & Sidman, 2007). **Pedometers** can be used as motivational tools to provide feedback on the duration (distance) or intensity (distance over time) of the physical activity. Rowlands and Eston (2005) concluded that 8- to 10-year-old girls who accumulated 13,000 steps and boys who accumulated 12,000 steps per day engaged in sufficient amounts of physical activity to meet the 60-minute standard for a health-enhancing level of activity. Step counts, however, vary greatly from day to day. Monitoring weekly steps rather than daily steps can help prevent feelings of failure. To begin, have students keep track of their daily steps in a journal and average the first three days. They will begin their walking program and set personal goals from this baseline. Work up to the long-range goals established by the President's Challenge of 11,000 steps per day for girls (ages 6–17) and 13,000 steps per day for boys (ages 6–17). Children can also encourage parents to set

daily step goals (adults should get 10,000 steps per day, or 12,000 steps if weight loss is a personal goal); this may increase family activity outside of school time. Refer to table 13.2 to assist students in setting step goals.

Pedometers may report steps, distance, calories burned, time spent exercising, or heart rate averaged over time. The simplest ones count steps only. Some have the capacity to adjust stride length. For an average adult, 10,000 steps is approximately 3 miles (5 km), but this distance will be different for children. Teachers can instruct students about how to determine the number of steps per mile or kilometer. To find the number of steps in a mile, mark off 100 feet and have students count the number of steps that they take in that distance. Find the distance between two heel strikes, or **stride length**, by dividing 100 feet by the number of steps taken. Then divide 5,280 feet by the stride length to estimate the student's steps per mile. Likewise, to find the number of steps in a kilometer, mark off 30 meters and have students count the number of steps that they take in that distance. Find the distance between two heel strikes, or stride length, by dividing 30 meters by the number of steps taken. Then divide 1,000 meters by the stride length to estimate the student's steps per kilometer. Providing the formula and task to the math teacher is an excellent strategy to share content across the curriculum and to inform other teachers about quality physical education at the same time.

Combining the recording of steps with heart rate is an ideal format for combining the concepts of time (distance traveled) with intensity. Increasing either the number of steps or the heart rate provides the overload needed for appropriate progressions to enhance aerobic fitness.

Table 13.2 Setting Step Goals

Start point	Goal	How to reach goal	Time needed
Less than 2,500 steps	5,000 steps/day	Increase 250 steps/day	10–20 days
2,501–5,000 steps	7,500 steps/day	Increase 300 steps/day	8–16 days
5,001–7,500 steps	10,000 steps/day	Increase 400 steps/day	6–12 days
7,501–10,000 steps	12,500 steps/day	Increase 500 steps/day	5–10 days
10,001–12,501 steps	15,000 steps/day	Increase 500 steps/day	5–10 days

From Sportline's Guide to Walking (Sportline, Inc, Campbell, CA)

USING PHYSICAL ACTIVITY ASSESSMENT RESULTS

Many questions arise about how to use participation or physical activity data. Should a minimum out-of-school physical activity participation level for a grade (e.g., three hours per week is an A) be set? What should happen if the child's family or day care situation makes engaging in physical activity outside of school difficult? Should a student who cannot yet run properly but who is trying hard to learn be held responsible? How should the teacher evaluate the child who participates in many extracurricular activities but does not keep a journal up to date and is unable to quantify the activity levels accurately? The following information can be used to deal with common dilemmas in ways that encourage rather than discourage physical activity.

Sharing Information With Students and Parents

Sending home current Fitnessgram and Activitygram printouts provides information that links assessment to strategies and goals for each child. Parents or guardians can also learn what they need to know to be able to help their children accomplish personal goals. These tactics help individualize approaches. Teachers can help students set goals based on feedback and the student's personal objectives (see chapters 2 and 12). Brainstorming with the family to find ways to increase physical activity increases communication. Using Fitnessgram reports and goal setting can help parents or guardians become advocates for quality physical education.

Grading

Students should be rewarded and praised for the achievement of physical activity goals as well as progress toward goals. Use a variety of assessment tools to support student grades. Frequency, intensity, time, and type can be quantified and evaluated effectively through the review of student reflection, achievement of goals, records of intensity and duration of activity, and portfolios. A broad scope of components should make up the final course grades.

SUMMARY

When teachers authentically assess physical fitness and physical activity, students can begin to see that fitness and physical activity are related. Each area can be used to monitor students' health-related physical fitness and reduce risk factors. Involving students in recording time, duration, intensity, and type of physical activity can encourage self-assessment. Visual recordings of daily physical activity may help students make decisions to change unhealthy behaviors. Students are encouraged to use effective strategies for adopting healthy habits.

Assessing the Cognitive and Affective Domains

Christina Sinclair and Sandra Nelson

In quality physical education programs teachers systematically teach and assess in the cognitive, affective, and physical domains using a variety of assessments (NASPE, 2008). To help physical educators provide quality physical education, chapter 13 examined best practices for assessing health-related fitness in the physical domain by presenting information on fitness assessment. This chapter highlights assessment of health-related fitness in the cognitive domain as well as personal responsibility and attitudes in the affective domain including ideas for assessing in each domain, ways to align assessment with the National Association for Sport and Physical Education (NASPE) standards, and useful tools for assessing in each domain.

Chapter Contents

COGNITIVE AND AFFECTIVE DOMAINS

Assessment of student learning is one of the greatest challenges that physical educators face today (Gallo, Sheehy, Patton, & Griffin, 2006). Traditionally, physical education teachers assessed using skill and perhaps fitness assessments (the physical domain) but did not always consider the cognitive and affective domains. As presented in chapter 12 the **cognitive domain** refers to knowledge about concepts related to sport, games and fitness, rules, procedures, safety, and critical elements, whereas the **affective domain** refers to attitudes and values that a student has toward and during physical activity. These two domains are often less familiar to physical educators, so assessment of these areas often seems a daunting and even scary task. The benefits of assessing what students know and can do in relation to the cognitive and affective domains should not be overlooked as an opportunity to increase the likelihood that students will increase and maintain physical activity levels. For example, people who are educated about physical fitness and experience positive feelings about physical activity will more likely become lifelong movers. Therefore, physical educators must become skillful at creating and implementing quality cognitive and affective assessments. Chapter 14 is designed to serve as a guide for developing and implementing quality cognitive and affective assessments.

Physical Best enables students to learn along the full continuum of the cognitive domain. Lessons include learning through the simplest form (knowledge, comprehension, application) of the cognitive domain hierarchy as well as the most complex domains (analysis, synthesis, and evaluation).

For example, activities demand that students list and define (knowledge), compute and discuss (comprehension), apply and calculate (application), analyze and differentiate (analysis), design and manage (synthesis), and evaluate and appraise (evaluation).

Physical Best also enables students to learn along the full continuum of the affective domain. Activities include learning through the simplest form (receiving, responding, valuing) of the affective domain hierarchy through the most complex (organization, characterization).

For example, Physical Best activities demand that students recognize and realize (receiving), to cooperate and examine (responding), to value and accept (valuing), to discriminate and order (organization), and to internalize and verify (characterization).

Physical Best promotes cognitive and affective learning by engaging students in real life and experiences. Students become independent learners who have the ability to be responsible for their own health-related fitness and learning. Because Physical Best includes important learning objectives in both the cognitive and affective domains, the use of assessment to determine how well such objectives are met is critical.

HEALTH-RELATED FITNESS KNOWLEDGE: THE COGNITIVE DOMAIN

When teaching and learning about health-related fitness the cognitive domain includes understanding components of health-related fitness, basic training principles, and nutrition as a means to develop a healthier lifestyle. This understanding is a crucial component of quality physical education programs for many reasons:

▶ Knowledge of physical fitness and personal exercise behavior are related. People tend to make a personal investment in activities that have meaning (Carron, Hausenblas, & Estabrooks, 2003).

▶ Understanding the science behind health-related physical fitness activities prepares students to sort fact from fiction when reading advertisements for quick weight-loss plans or new miracle exercise equipment.

▶ Knowing how to exercise, such as by performing appropriate stretching, using correct strength-training techniques, and maintaining proper hydration, prepares students to benefit from physical activity while being safe.

▶ Knowledgeable students are better prepared to make informed decisions in starting and maintaining physical activity programs.

As a result physical educators must create and implement cognitive assessments as a means to determine how well students understand and can apply components of health-related fitness, basic training principles, and nutrition. Consider the following examples:

Aerobic Fitness

▶ Show the concept of progression in a FITT workout plan to meet a personal goal set for the next PACER assessment.

▶ In small groups, design activity stations using a variety of games or activities and then demonstrate how to vary the intensity at each station.

Muscular Fitness

▶ Cut out or draw a picture of an activity that uses muscular fitness.

▶ Use the FITT principle to create a muscular fitness workout designed to meet a personal goal on the next push-up or curl-up assessment.

Flexibility

▶ After the teacher names a muscle, demonstrate an appropriate stretch for that muscle.

▶ Define intensity as it relates to flexibility. Next, explain how to monitor intensity when stretching.

Nutrition and Body Composition

▶ Go to www.mypyramid.gov and find the my pyramid tracker feature.

▶ Analyze food intake as well as physical activity habits to set and monitor physical activity and nutrition goals.

This list is not inclusive by any means, but it includes a variety of ideas for assessing each health-related fitness component. Additional assessment ideas are presented at the end of each Physical Best activity in both *Physical Best Activity Guide: Elementary Level, Third Edition* and *Physical Best Activity Guide: Middle and High School Level, Third Edition*.

Assessing NASPE Standards and Health-Related Fitness Knowledge

The cognitive domain aligns with NASPE content standard 2 (NASPE, 2004a): "A physically educated person demonstrates understanding of movement concepts, principles, strategies and tactics as they apply to the learning and performance of physical activities" (p. IV). This standard encompasses understanding basic training principles, and nutrition. In grades K through 2 assessment of this standard could include asking students to identify which activities build gradually on others for a warm-up and which descend in intensity for a cool-down (see figure 14.1). Students in kindergarten through second grade

Figure 14.1 Sample cognitive formative assessment that aligns with NASPE content standard 2 and is designed to determine the extent to which K through 2 children can identify activities for a proper warm-up and cool-down. A reproducible version of this form is available in appendix A.

can be asked to circle, draw, or shade pictures to check for cognitive understanding if reading or writing ability is limited. Figure 14.2 can be used to assess concepts taught in "Powerball Hunt" in *Physical Best Activity Guide: Elementary Level, Third Edition*. Figure 14.2 is an assessment designed for students in grades 3 through 5 to self-assess their heart rates to monitor the intensity of activities. This assessment can be used to determine student understanding of concepts like those taught in lesson 3.11, Jumping Frenzy, in *Physical Best Activity Guide: Elementary Level, Third Edition*.

At the secondary level, assessment of NASPE content standard 2 includes measuring students' understanding of the basic training principles such as intensity and time. Figure 14.3 is an example of an exit slip that measures students understanding of intensity and time.

The cognitive domain also aligns with aspects of NASPE content standard 4, which states, "A physically educated person achieves and maintains a health enhancing level of physical fitness" (NASPE, 2004a, p. IV). At the elementary level, assessment of standard 4 includes measuring awareness of fitness components. An example of this is the exit slip in figure 14.4, which assesses a child's ability to identify aerobic activities. At the middle school level, assessment of standard 4 should include making sure that students have a greater understanding of the fitness components, the way each is developed and maintained, and the importance of each in overall fitness. The goal-setting worksheet in figure 14.5 was designed to help students set and reach fitness goals based on Fitnessgram results. At the high school level, assessments may include measuring how well students develop personal fitness programs. For detailed guidelines on developing and assessing personal fitness plans, we encourage you to use *Fitness for Life* (Corbin & Lindsey, 2005).

Figure 14.2 Sample cognitive formative assessment designed to help children determine intensity levels using heart rate. This assessment aligns with NASPE content standard 2. A reproducible version of this form is available in appendix A.

Figure 14.3 Sample cognitive assessment that aligns with NASPE content standard 2 and is designed to measure students' understanding of intensity and time as they apply to the FITT principle. A reproducible version of this form is available in appendix A.

Bloom's Taxonomy and Cognitive Assessment

Bloom's taxonomy (Huitt, 2004) has traditionally served as a guide for designing behavioral instructional objectives that require the use of higher-order thinking skills (see table 14.1 on page 242). For example, each Physical Best lesson includes instructional objectives or purposes that may require students to list and define (knowledge), compute and discuss (comprehension), apply and calculate (application), analyze and differentiate (analysis), design and manage (synthesis), or evaluate and appraise (evaluation). To measure the extent to which such instructional objectives were met, quality assessments must be designed that align with instructional objectives. Therefore, Bloom's taxonomy is also a useful guide for developing cognitive assessments that create opportunities for students to use higher-order

thinking skills. For example, creation of a brochure or multimedia project that teaches others about a health-related fitness concept requires students to synthesize information by taking what they know to design something new. Additionally, asking students to interpret Fitnessgram scores and then identify strengths and areas for improvement would require analysis of personal fitness.

THE AFFECTIVE DOMAIN

When teaching and learning about health-related fitness, the affective domain includes helping students develop positive feelings, attitudes, values, and social behaviors in physical activity settings as a means to develop a healthier lifestyle, which is another crucial component of quality physical education programs. Therefore, teachers must address affective goals in their programs, because students may be skilled and even knowledgeable

Figure 14.4 Cognitive assessment designed to determine whether students can correctly identify aerobic activities. This assessment aligns with NASPE content standard 4. A reproducible version of this form is available in appendix A.

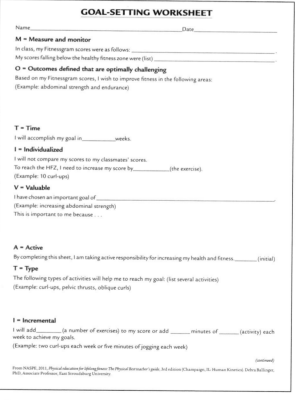

Figure 14.5 After Fitnessgram scores are determined, students can use this assessment to reflect on their scores and set personal fitness goals. A reproducible version of this form is available in appendix A.

Table 14.1 Taxonomy of the Cognitive Domain

Level	Definition	Sample verbs
Knowledge	Student recalls or recognizes information, ideas, and principles in the approximate form in which they were learned.	• Write • List • Label • Name • State • Define
Comprehension	Student translates, comprehends, or interprets information based on prior learning.	• Explain • Summarize • Paraphrase • Describe • Illustrate
Application	Student selects, transfers, and uses data and principles to complete a problem or task with a minimum of direction.	• Use • Compute • Solve • Demonstrate • Apply • Construct
Analysis	Student distinguishes, classifies, and relates the assumptions, hypotheses, evidence, or structure of a statement or question.	• Analyze • Categorize • Compare • Contrast • Separate
Synthesis	Student originates, integrates, and combines ideas into a product, plan, or proposal that is new to him or her.	• Create • Design • Hypothesize • Invent • Develop
Evaluation	Student appraises, assesses, or critiques on a basis of specific standards and criteria.	• Judge • Recommend • Critique • Justify

Adapted from W. Huitt, 2004, *Bloom et al.'s taxonomy of the cognitive domain.* (Valdosta, GA: Valdosta State University). By permission of W. Huitt. Available: http://www.edpsycinteractive.org/topics/cogsys/bloom.html.

and still choose not to participate (Rink, 2010). To increase the likelihood that students will choose to participate in meaningful ways that move them closer to independence on Corbin and Lindsey's Stairway to Lifetime Fitness (figure 9.3) and closer to mature levels of personal responsibility for their own physical activity (Hellison, 2003), physical educators must

▶ encourage all children to experience the satisfaction and joy that can result from learning about and participating regularly in physical activity (NASPE, 2008), and

▶ intentionally design activities that allow children opportunities to work together to develop social skills and responsible behavior (NASPE, 2008).

Assessing NASPE Standards and the Affective Domain

The affective domain aligns with NASPE content standard 5 (NASPE, 2004): "A physically educated person exhibits responsible personal and social behavior that respects self and others in physical activity settings" (p. IV). This standard includes helping students achieve self-initiated behaviors that promote personal and group success in activity settings. When focusing on health-related fitness, one way to meet this standard is to climb the Stairway to Lifetime Fitness (Corbin & Lindsey, 2005). As students climb the stairway the goal is to move from a level of dependence to a level of independence, allowing them to make responsible decisions about their lifetime physical activity (Corbin & Lindsey, 2005). At the elementary level students depend on others such as parents and teachers for their physical activity opportunities;

therefore, at this stage standard 5 encompasses children's understanding of activity-specific safe practices, rules, procedures, and etiquette and their learning to play alone and with diverse groups. The teacher observation assessment example in figure 14.6 aligns well with standard 5. It can be used to observe and provide feedback on how well children cooperate by taking turns and sharing equipment.

Although middle school students also depend on parents and teachers for their physical activity opportunities, standard 5 at this stage has students beginning to seek more independence from adults and having increased ability to effectively work alone and with diverse groups. The exit slip example in figure 14.7 aligns with

TEACHER OBSERVATION

Student's name_____ Date_____

Goal: Is self-directed while cooperating and showing compassion for others in small group work.
Relationship to standards: NASPE content standard 5.
Cooperation—willingly worked with the group to accomplish the task.
Self-direction—was focused and worked to complete the task without direct supervision.
Compassion—showed respect and concern for the feelings of others in the group even if their ideas were different from his or hers.

1—needs more work   2—sometimes   3—mastered

Group 1	Cooperation	Self-direction	Compassion

From NASPE, 2011, *Physical education for lifelong fitness: The Physical Best teacher's guide*, 3rd edition (Champaign, IL: Human Kinetics).

Figure 14.6 Teacher observation of affective behaviors during group fitness activities can provide valuable feedback to students and inform teaching practice. A reproducible version of this form is available in appendix A.

AFFECTIVE SELF-ASSESSMENT

Name_____ Date_____

Goal: Remains on task without close teacher monitoring and helps a partner.
Relationship to standards: NASPE content standard 5.

1. Today I tried hard even if the teacher was not looking.   Yes   I need to work on this
2. I helped my partner today   Yes   I need to work on this
3. One thing I said or did to help my partner was _____

From NASPE, 2011, *Physical education for lifelong fitness: The Physical Best teacher's guide*, 3rd edition (Champaign, IL: Human Kinetics).

Figure 14.7 Accepting responsibility for personal fitness is an integral part of learning to become physically active. This exit slip could be used after students work together to practice one or more Fitnessgram assessments. It is designed to allow students to self-reflect on how well they remained on task without close teacher monitoring and helped a partner. A reproducible version of this form is available in appendix A.

standard 5 by asking students to reflect on their ability to stay on task and help a partner. The peer assessment in figure 14.8 could also be used with middle school students. At the high school level students move further from dependence on others for their own physical activity opportunities and therefore begin to make responsible choices to maintain their own physical activity level while appreciating the influences of age, disability, gender, race, ethnicity, socioeconomic status, and culture. The journal stem example in figure 14.9 aligns with standard 5 and asks students to reflect on reasons for their participation during a free-choice period.

Hellison's levels of personal and social responsibility also align with standard 5 and can be used to guide development of program goals as a means to help teach students to take responsibility for their own development and contribute to the well-being of others (Hellison, 2003).

Hellison defines these levels of personal and social responsibility:

▸ Level IV, caring—Students at level IV, besides respecting others, participating, and being self-directed, are motivated to extend their sense of responsibility beyond themselves by cooperating, giving support, showing concern, and helping.

▸ Level III, self-direction—Students at level III not only show respect and participation but also are able to work without direct supervision. They can identify their own needs and begin to plan and carry out their physical education programs.

▸ Level II, participation—Students at level II not only show at least minimal respect for others but also willingly play, accept challenges, practice motor skills, and train for fitness under the teacher's supervision.

Figure 14.8 This assessment creates an opportunity for peers to provide one another with appropriate feedback on how well they follow all safety guidelines while performing basic yoga poses. A reproducible version of this form is available in appendix A.

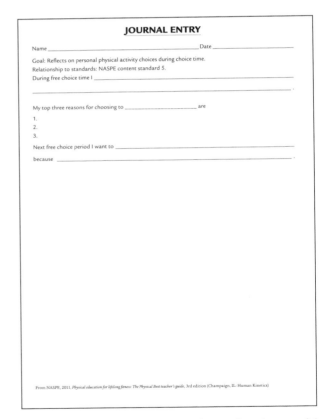

Figure 14.9 This sample journal entry would provide evidence of student reflection on personal physical activity choices during choice time. A reproducible version of this form is available in appendix A.

- Level I, respect—Students at level I may not participate in daily activities or show much mastery or improvement, but they are able to control their behavior enough that they don't interfere with the other students' right to learn or the teacher's right to teach. They do this without much prompting by the teacher and without constant supervision.
- Level zero, irresponsibility—Students who operate at level zero make excuses, blame others for their behavior, and deny personal responsibility for what they do or fail to do.

Reprinted, by permission, from D. Hellison, 2003, *Teaching responsibility through physical activity,* 2nd ed. (Champaign, IL: Human Kinetics), 28.

Physical Best activities create opportunities for students to practice using these levels of personal and social responsibility. Figures 14.6, 14.7, 14.9, and 14.11 were developed based on Hellison's levels and could be used with any number of Physical Best activities. Each of these assessments is a way for students to reflect on their responsibility level with feedback from the teacher.

The affective domain also aligns with NASPE content standard 6 (NASPE, 2004a): "A physically educated person values physical activity for health, enjoyment, challenge, self-expression, and/or social interaction" (p. IV). The goal of this standard is for students to develop awareness of the intrinsic values and benefits of participation in personally meaningful physical activity. Students should be encouraged to enjoy movement activities and see them as a way to gain competence, take on challenges, and interact socially. Because of these intrinsic benefits of participation, they will more likely pursue lifelong activity to meet their own health-related fitness needs (NASPE, 2004a). The exit slip in figure 14.10 aligns with standard 6 and is a way to help elementary school children begin to identify their emotions toward physical activity. The analytic rubric in figure 14.11 also meets standard 6 and allows middle

AFFECTIVE EXIT SLIP

Name ______________________ Date ______________

Goal: Identifies feelings associated with participation in physical activities.
Relationship to standards: NASPE content standard 6.

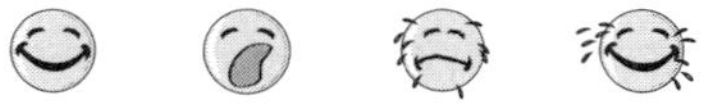

Today's activities in physical education made me feel
I felt this way because
____
____
____

From NASPE, 2011, *Physical education for lifelong fitness: The Physical Best teacher's guide*, 3rd edition (Champaign, IL: Human Kinetics).

Figure 14.10 Pictures and word stems can be used to help students identify feelings associated with participation in physical activities. A reproducible version of this form is available in appendix A.

AFFECTIVE ANALYTIC RUBRIC

Name ______________________ Date ______________

Goal: Seeks challenging experiences in physical education.
Relationship to standards: NASPE content standard 6.

How much did you challenge yourself today in class?

3—I challenged myself the whole time by trying new things even if they seemed hard.
2—I challenged myself part of the time by trying some of the new things we learned.
1—I need to work on challenging myself and would like help.

Next time I want to see whether I can _______________________________
____.

From NASPE, 2011, *Physical education for lifelong fitness: The Physical Best teacher's guide*, 3rd edition (Champaign, IL: Human Kinetics).

Figure 14.11 This assessment can be used during any fitness or skill development lesson to determine whether students seek challenging experiences in physical education. A reproducible version of this form is available in appendix A.

school students to reflect on how much they are challenging themselves in physical education. The last example, figure 14.12, can be used with middle and high school students as part of a physical fitness journal in which students record their performance on fitness assessments and their personal thoughts and feelings. Again, the focus of this type of assessment is less about the outcomes than it is about students' reflections about their involvement.

TOOLS FOR ASSESSING THE COGNITIVE AND AFFECTIVE DOMAINS

This section introduces a variety of standards-based assessment options designed to align with the cognitive and affective domains. The types

of assessment presented can be used on a regular basis to measure the extent to which students use higher order thinking skills relative to health-related fitness concepts, basic training principles and nutrition, and their contribution to a healthy lifestyle. Also included in this section are assessments designed to help determine student feelings, attitudes, values, and social behaviors in physical activity settings.

Teacher, peer, and self-observations. Although described previously in chapter 12 as a means for recording student performance in the psychomotor domain, teacher observations can also be used to check for observable affective behaviors such as cooperation, initiative, and compassion. To help improve their upper-body strength, students may learn a variety of push-up variations and then be asked to develop a push-up routine with a small group, much like the Mission Push-Up Possible activity in *Physical Best Activity Guide: Middle and High School Levels, Third Edition*. This activity creates a perfect opportunity to use the teacher observation sheet in figure 14.6 on page 243 to assess students' ability to be self-directed while cooperating and showing compassion for others in small-group work. For example, as students begin working in groups to develop push-up variation routines, the teacher rotates around the activity space not only to facilitate activity but also to watch and rate students on how well they cooperate by showing a willingness to work with the group to accomplish the task, demonstrate self-direction by staying focused and working to complete the task without direct supervision, and show compassion by respecting the feelings of others in the group even if someone else's ideas were different from their own. As mentioned in chapter 12 instruction should occur before the assessment to teach students about cooperation, self-direction, and compassion before assessing these behaviors.

Peer observations can be used much the same way as a teacher observation. Students can be assigned a secret fitness pal and then watch him or her throughout a lesson. Students would rate their partners and give them feedback on how well they followed safety guidelines while rotating to yoga stations. The peer observation sheet in figure 14.7 on page 243 could be used to help

FITNESS JOURNAL

Name _____   Date _____

	I wish I could . . .	I predict that . . .	I feel good about . . .	My fears are . . .
Before my fitness preassessments Date _____				
After my fitness preassessments Date _____				
One month after my fitness program Date _____				
Two months after my fitness program Date _____				
Three months after my fitness program Date _____				

From NASPE, 2011, *Physical education for lifelong fitness: The Physical Best teacher's guide*, 3rd edition (Champaign, IL: Human Kinetics). Reprinted, by permission, from V. Melograno, 1998, *Professional and student portfolios for physical education* (Champaign, IL: Human Kinetics), 128.

Figure 14.12 Students can use this assessment to express thoughts and feelings related to progress on their personal fitness goals. A reproducible version of this form is available in appendix A.

Reprinted, by permission, from V. Melograno, 1998, *Professional and student portfolios for physical education* (Champaign, IL: Human Kinetics), 128.

students give feedback to each other on following safety guidelines. Students can also be asked to self-assess their own affective behaviors and then set a goal for the next lesson.

Less formal check-ins. Less formal assessments can also be valuable ways to assess in the cognitive and affective domains. For example, a teacher can say to elementary children, "While staying in your own personal space, show me what you look like when you do your favorite aerobic fitness activity; now show me your favorite muscular fitness activity."

Asking students to show thumbs up, middle, or down is another effective form of informal assessment that can require students to self-assess in the affective domain. For example, many Physical Best activities require students to cooperate in small groups; therefore, students could self-reflect on how well they shared equipment and took turns. A teacher could say something like, "One of our goals today was to share equipment and take turns. You have five seconds to think about how well you did both of these things. When I say, 'Go,' show me a thumbs up if you shared and took turns the whole time, show me a thumb in the middle if you did this sometimes but need to get better, or show me a thumb down if you never shared or took turns today. Ready? Go!" Secondary students can indicate how well they helped spot a weight-training partner throughout a workout by showing the teacher a thumb up, middle, or down.

Another quick way for students to reflect and self-asses their affective behavior is to post Hellison's levels by the gym door and ask students to touch the level of responsibility that they plan to use as they enter the gym. Then as students leave they should also touch which level they think they achieved in class. This type of reflection can be used for individual goal-setting assessment.

Discussions. Chapter 12 provides effective strategies for conducting oral class discussion as a form of assessment. The content of such discussions can include questions centered on important fitness concepts. An example of this might involve putting students in groups of three and then asking each group to discuss the relationship between body composition and nutrition. Groups could then share ideas with the class. Discussions can also encourage students to share how they feel about an activity at the end of a lesson and can help teachers assess attitude and motivation. Ask students questions such as the following:

- How do you feel about running the mile?
- How do you feel about stretching at home while watching TV?
- How do you feel about continuing to design ball games that help increase aerobic fitness?
- How do you feel about today's activity?

An additional form of discussion not previously mentioned is a written questionnaire that teachers can assign as homework, such as the one shown in figure 14.13, which is appropriate for upper elementary students. Follow up by reviewing student answers and discussing results with students in a future lesson. Consider making

THINKING ABOUT PHYSICAL FITNESS AND ACTIVITIES

Name ______________________ Date ______________

1. I would rather exercise or play sports than watch TV.	Yes	No	
2. People who exercise regularly seem to have a lot of fun doing it.	Yes	No	
3. In school, I look forward to attending physical education class.	Yes	No	
4. During physical education class at school, I usually work up a sweat.	Yes	No	
5. When I grow up, I will probably be too busy to stay physically fit.	Yes	No	
6. How do you feel about your ability to strike a ball with a racket?	☺	😐	☹
7. How do you feel about your ability to kick a ball hard and hit a target?	☺	😐	☹
8. How do you feel about your ability to run a long distance without stopping?	☺	😐	☹
9. How do you feel about your ability to play many different games and sports?	☺	😐	☹
10. How do you feel about your ability to participate in gymnastics?	☺	😐	☹
11. How do you feel about your ability to participate in dance?	☺	😐	☹

From NASPE, 2011, *Physical education for lifelong fitness: The Physical Best teacher's guide*, 3rd edition (Champaign, IL: Human Kinetics). Reprinted, by permission, from G. Graham, 2008, *Teaching children physical education*, 3rd ed. (Champaign, IL: Human Kinetics), 159, 208.

Figure 14.13 Discussion can begin from written questions that you assign as homework, such as this questionnaire. A reproducible version of this figure is available in appendix A.

Reprinted, by permission, from G. Graham, 2008, *Teaching children physical education,* 3rd ed. (Champaign, IL: Human Kinetics), 208.

such questionnaires anonymous to increase the likelihood that students will be completely honest.

Role plays.   Chapter 12 lists role plays as one of many effective alternative assessments. Specific to the cognitive domain, role playing is a useful way to assess whether students can apply fitness knowledge. Role playing simulates real-life situations, giving students valuable practice. Cognitive assessment that teaches is an efficient and effective way to use precious class time. Set up role-play situations that call for students to demonstrate competence in a real-life context. The following are examples of role-play challenges:

▶ Students practice how to teach a younger student or partner to run correctly as pace changes. Students demonstrate knowledge of the components of a good running stride as a means to increase their aerobic fitness. Students work with a partner on the concept of pacing while listening to various pieces of music that incorporate different tempos.

▶ Students demonstrate two ways to take a pulse.

▶ In small groups, one student teaches three safe stretches to the rest of the group and explains what makes them safe.

▶ Each student pretends that a partner has sprained an ankle. The student demonstrates how to help the partner treat the injury safely following the RICES guidelines (rest, ice, compression, elevation, support).

▶ A student takes the role of a famous local athlete. Other students interview this person to find out what the person has done to improve his or her athletic achievement (adapted from NASPE, 1995).

Role playing is also a dynamic way to monitor attitude and motivation. Have groups of students act out how they feel about an activity or how they might change another person's opinion about physical activity. First, have groups brainstorm possible actions and statements among themselves. Next, have each group act out their ideas for the rest of the class. Then, discuss as a class which statements and actions are most likely to be helpful in a real-life situation. Ask students for

suggestions of other issues that they would like to explore in this way.

Written assessments.   Written tests still have a place as a valid assessment tool, as long as they are not overemphasized or overvalued. Design written assessments to parallel what is taught and particularly to match the level of cognitive complexity at which content is taught. Doing this helps you cover important cognitive objectives and allows collection of data that supports what each student knows. Carefully choose the format (e.g., objective assessments—multiple-choice, true–false; subjective assessments—short-answer, essay) that best fits the content being taught and the ages and abilities of the students being assessed. Consider take-home assessments and computer-formatted assessments that are taken out of class. Looking up correct answers is a proven method of exposing students to a thorough review of important concepts. Resources such as the FitSmart package (Zhu, Safrit, & Cohen, 1999) complete with software and manual based on the National Youth Physical Fitness Knowledge Test as well as Ask-Pe: Physical Education Concepts Test (Ayers, 2004) may help high school teachers determine their students' understanding of health-related fitness concepts.

Embed written assessments within physical activity.   Written cognitive and affective assessments can also be combined or embedded within activity. This is an efficient way to check formally for understanding while maintaining overall activity levels. Using a station format for this type of assessment allows students to answer cognitive or affective questions related to each fitness or activity station. Figure 14.14 is from the activity FITT Concentration found in *Physical Best Activity Guide: Middle and High School Level, Third Edition*. It engages students in exercise stations while assessing valuable fitness information. When using this kind of assessment, place pencils at each station rather than have students move between activities carrying sharp objects.

Exit slips.   Exit slips are a form of written assessment that could be used to check for understanding or as a way for students to indicate thoughts, feelings, or attitudes (see figure 14.15). They are short in length, usually containing only one to three questions or items, and therefore do not

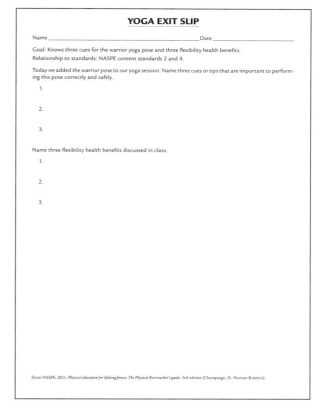

FITT CONCENTRATION

Name _____ Date _____

You will be performing a fitness activity and running to various stations to fill in your activity card. When instructed to go to a station, quickly run and write down the definition. Return to your roll call line for the next exercise. When you have completed each station, you will get into small groups and answer the questions for each category. At the end of the activity, turn in your paper for daily participation points!

Station 1: Principle of Progression
Definition:

Question: How can you apply the principle of progression to muscular strength?

Station 2: Principle of Specificity
Definition:

Question: What component of health-related fitness does core training focus on?

Station 3: Intensity
Definition:

Question: Compute your target heart rate zone using this formula:
208 − (.7 x your age) = _____ (max heart rate)
Threshold heart rate   Target ceiling heart rate
Max HR: _____   Max HR: _____
(x) .65   (x) .90

Station 4: Principle of Overload
Definition:

Question: How can you apply the principle of overload to biceps curls?

Station 5: Frequency
Definition:

Question: What is the recommended number of times to exercise during the week?

Station 6: Time
Definition:

Question: What is the recommended time to exercise for a cardiovascular benefit to occur?

From NASPE, 2011, *Physical education for lifelong fitness: The Physical Best teacher's guide*, 3rd edition (Champaign, IL: Human Kinetics).

YOGA EXIT SLIP

Name _____ Date _____

Goal: Knows three cues for the warrior yoga pose and three flexibility health benefits.
Relationship to standards: NASPE content standards 2 and 4.

Today we added the warrior pose to our yoga session. Name three cues or tips that are important to performing this pose correctly and safely.

1.

2.

3.

Name three flexibility health benefits discussed in class.

1.

2.

3.

From NASPE, 2011, *Physical education for lifelong fitness: The Physical Best teacher's guide*, 3rd edition (Champaign, IL: Human Kinetics).

Figure 14.14 A reproducible version of this rubric is available in appendix A.

Figure 14.15 Exit slip that measures knowledge of yoga and benefits of flexibility. A reproducible version of this rubric is available in appendix A.

take away significantly from activity time, but they serve as means for providing necessary feedback to teachers and students on progress toward cognitive and affective goals. Exit slips are not always answers to written questions; they may also consist of student drawings or prompts that ask students to circle pictures to indicate understanding or feelings about something. See also figures 14.3, 14.4, 14.6, and 14.9.

Logs and journals for assessing the affective domain. Although described previously as a means for recording participation, logs and journals can also be used for affective purposes. Students can record their personal responses to discussion questions in their journals; this provides an opportunity to assess students' levels of understanding. Student reflections provide information on the breadth and depth of knowledge related to the importance of or reasons for participation in activities, and provide opportunities for students to demonstrate what they have learned using their own words. As discussed in

chapter 12, being able to review physical activity information over time can be motivating, resulting in improved approach tendencies or desire to participate regularly in physical activity. Activity charts and graphs help students see how far they have progressed. This process can help students stay motivated as adults as well. Continuous self-monitoring helps create greater awareness of the real-life applications of health-related training principles.

An example related to aerobic training and the use of the PACER is a good illustration. The student records the number of laps completed in three trials over six weeks. The log is the record of the number of laps. Teachers remark on the progress of each student and ask students to write about how they feel at the end of the PACER and to compare feelings based on the first attempt. Teachers can also ask students to reflect on or consider why it would feel easier than before to complete laps, or what they might do to increase the number of laps in the next three weeks.

Logs and journals can also provide a method for individual students to respond privately to the physical educator. Affective entries can simply be individual responses to discussion questions, or they can be more involved, such as logging feelings toward physical activity over several exercise sessions. Hichwa (1998) found it helpful to have his middle school students list the top 10 reasons why students enjoy physical education. He then found it personally and professionally helpful to list the 10 most important aspects of physical education (see the sidebar "Top 10 Lists").

Reports and research assignments. Reports and research assignments can enhance a student's learning while also serving to assess how well students understand, apply, and synthesize fitness knowledge. Most upper elementary through high school students are capable of researching a topic. The ability to use researching tools to create reports on health-related fitness topics is a skill that aligns with most schools' overall educational mission to prepare students to learn how to learn. Through research, students take what they already know about health-related fitness and teach themselves more. Physical educators can encourage use of the Internet, library books, and CD-ROMs as research tools. Have students work with partners or in small groups to collect data. Try assigning topics such as the following:

▶ Select a friend or relative and research what that person does (or does not do) to stay physically active and fit. Pretend to be this person's personal trainer and write an analysis of his or her fitness plan, based on what you have learned about health-related fitness. What does this person do well, and what does this person do less well regarding fitness? Suggest what this person could do to improve his or her plan. Develop an assessment rubric to communicate the strengths of each fitness plan.

▶ Select a specific health condition (e.g., diabetes, asthma, heart disease) and research what benefits physical activity can have in helping a person with this condition improve his or her health.

▶ Find diet ideas and products advertised and analyze them for safety, effectiveness, and value to personal health.

TOP 10 LISTS

John Hichwa had his students create a list of the top 10 reasons that they enjoy physical education, and he then created his own list of what he believed were the 10 most important aspects of effectively teaching physical education.

Students' Top 10 List

10. We get to grade ourselves.
9. We are taught to make goals for ourselves and to try our hardest to achieve them.
8. We have plenty of supplies.
7. The activities are challenging.
6. Physical education relieves stress from our day.
5. We are always doing different things, so it's interesting, and you never get bored.
4. Teachers are supportive, understanding, and are easy to get along with.
3. We get a good workout.
2. We are always active.
1. Teachers make physical education fun!

Teachers' Top 10 List

10. Have enough equipment for each student.
9. Chart each child's progress and motivate him or her to do his or her personal best.
8. Play the game.
7. Make lessons interesting, progressive, and challenging.
6. Keep the development of self-responsibility as a top priority.
5. Develop individual and cooperative skills.
4. Provide equipment that is developmentally appropriate.
3. Present a variety of offerings so that each child can experience success.
2. Keep students physically active as much as possible.
1. Treat each child fairly and with respect.

Reprinted, by permission, from J. Hichwa, 1998, *Right fielders are people too* (Champaign, IL: Human Kinetics) 54-55.

Another option when working with elementary or less experienced students is to provide raw research information in lecture settings and have students briefly summarize it orally or in writing. Examples of developmental approaches to research include the following:

▶ Provide one or two Web sites. Have the students read and explore linked sites and print out the pages explored.

▶ Identify a Web site to open and investigate and provide a list of items that students are to locate, similar to a scavenger hunt.

▶ Progress to having students reflect on Web readings in journals or through responses to specific questions aligned with critical concepts.

Reports and research assignments also create interdisciplinary opportunities. This activity could involve integrating research with other subject areas, such as language arts, math, and science, as a means to help students develop research skills and coordinate the writing of health-related fitness reports. For more information refer to S.F. Ayers and C. Wilmoth, 2003, "Integrating Scientific Subdisciplinary Concepts Into Physical Education," *Teaching Elementary Physical Education,* *14*(4), 10–14.

Projects.　For an explanation of student projects see chapter 12. Projects can be an effective way for students to increase the depth of their knowledge because they have an opportunity to clarify their understanding of health-related fitness through problem solving. For example, students could participate in a project designed to be an enjoyable, challenging way to assess their ability to teach yoga poses to others using at least three cues for five yoga poses as well as explain the health benefits of yoga.

Goals.　Students who can write personal goals and plan a personalized fitness program based on log and journal data are demonstrating the ability to apply fitness knowledge. Teachers can check student goals and their progress toward goals. Students who set goals that are quickly accomplished or lack achievable challenges should be guided to establish more appropriate goals (see chapter 2).

Portfolios.　A well-designed portfolio may provide valuable insight into a student's overall progress toward cognitive and affective outcomes. They can provide valuable insights into a student's overall attitude and motivation level. A portfolio that reflects the minimum activity levels may indicate that the student is not interested in physical activity. In contrast, a portfolio that reflects an enthusiasm for physical activity through up-to-date, detailed logs and thoughtful journal answers may indicate that the student values physical activity. Not all students are capable of expressing their feelings in writing, and those eager to please may mislead. Portfolios should be viewed as personal student reflections. The teacher must guide students as they develop their work.

GRADING IN THE COGNITIVE AND AFFECTIVE DOMAINS

Today's health-related physical fitness education program values knowledge as an important aspect of reaching the ultimate goal of producing adults who value and can independently pursue physical activity. Thus, assessment of knowledge needs to be part of a student's physical education grade. Fitness knowledge is a vital component in a well-designed physical education program, making it well worth the time it takes to assess.

The affective domain can also be an important part of a physical education grade. If teachers choose to include the affective domain as part of a grading system, they are encouraged to focus upon clearly defined student affective behaviors, as opposed to teacher conceptions of effort, and identify the behaviors that are part of the grade. As a result, students will be less threatened by the grade, and more motivated to change. When using journal entries or other forms of assessment that ask students to share thoughts and feelings, avoid grading student work based on the achievement of affective behaviors and focus instead on the accuracy of their self-assessment. If students feel punished for sharing honest thoughts and feelings through assessment, they will no longer share honestly when completing assessments.

Making Cognitive and Affective Assessment Practical

Time constraints and large class sizes can make assessment in the cognitive and affective domains a challenge. A few tips to help overcome such barriers follow:

▶ Make assessment part of instruction. This could be done by using stations during a lesson. At one or more stations leave pencils and short exit slips that allow opportunities for cognitive and affective assessment. This approach also helps to ensure that assessment enhances instruction.

▶ Assess in waves. Avoid trying to assess all students in all classes at the same time. When using teacher observation assessments watch only small groups of students at any one time. While observing, rate only those students who did not reach proficiency and then fill in the other ratings after class. Keep in mind that not assessing all students on the same day is OK. Additionally, when using exit slips, logs, and journals avoid having all classes use them at the same time. For example, use logs and journals with two or three classes while using more informal checks for understanding with other classes. Then rotate so that you are reading logs and journals for only two or three classes at any one time.

▶ Establish routines. Establish efficient routines for ensuring that students get pencils, papers, and so on. Keep sharpened pencils or crayons in several tennis ball cans or other containers that can be placed around the gym where students can pick up pencils quickly without your taking time to pass them all out individually. Using several cans scattered in the gym also prevents students from mobbing one can of pencils, which not only wastes time but may lead to further management problems. Papers and pencils could also be placed in hoops along a wall. There is no one way to manage successful assessment. The idea is to be purposeful, establish a plan, and keeping trying new time-saving ideas to keep assessment practical.

MIDDLE SCHOOL ASSESSMENT EXAMPLE

Effective assessment requires a plan. Here's one example of how to plan assessments for middle school students.

Establish Desired Course Outcome

A physically educated person assesses, achieves, and maintains physical fitness.

Define Domain Analysis (What Will Be Assessed)

- Creation of and participation in a personal plan of activities and exercises to achieve and maintain a level of physical fitness determined by the needs and goals of the student
- Application of principles of training and FITT guidelines
- Management of personal lifestyle and responsibilities for inclusion of participation in regular physical activity

Select Dimension Components (Choosing the Most Important Dimensions)

This assessment is intended to determine mastery of both the processes (principles of training and management of adult life roles) and the product (participation and goals). Assess and score each student individually and use the results to prescribe further sequential instruction, including remediation and enrichment. Focus on achieving cumulative skills and knowledge, resulting from multiple units of study on fitness education, goal setting, and motivation. Achievement will occur through participation in and out of the gymnasium. All students in the system will be assessed as a requirement for promotion to high school level work.

Adapted, by permission, from PSAHPERD, 1994, *Designing assessments: Applications for physical education*, 39-40.

Identify Implementation Characteristics (Other Issues That Need to Be Considered)

The student will design a personal fitness profile to be used to plan a realistic personal program of regular physical activity. The profile will use the results of previous health-related fitness assessments, recognized standards for fitness levels for good health, and personally set goals. Allow instructional time for students to master the skills of fitness assessment, review the requirements of the assessment, and assist students in researching information needed for both the profile and the plan. Conference time outside of class may be needed to provide feedback about accuracy and completeness in designing, implementing, and reporting progress toward achievement of the assessment. The focus of this assessment on life skills for adult roles requires that students solve the same problems related to engaging in regular physical activity that adults do. Therefore, the teacher becomes an advisor who guides the search for information.

Establish Specifications (What the Student Will Do)

Each student will complete a personal fitness profile (assessment results, current status of health fitness levels, and personally established realistic goals), create a personal fitness plan, implement the personal fitness plan (including appropriate warm-up, workout, and cool-down activities and principles of training and conditioning), and report on the results of participation in the plan. (Sample forms are provided in appendix A.) Achievement will be determined based on the following criteria:

- Accurately assess and interpret personal fitness status
- Set appropriate and realistic goals to improve or maintain fitness status
- Apply principles of training and conditioning in designing the personal plan
- Document (accurately and neatly) implementation of the designed plan
- Achieve personal fitness goal
- Reflect on enjoyment, benefits, and risks of participation in physical activity

Administration

This assessment, including scoring, should be presented to the students at the beginning of the school year. You may spend several class periods reviewing the skills required for assessing fitness status, interpreting personal data, and determining research needs and procedures. Time lines for the completion of each component should be established to ensure completion by deadline dates. Students may work in pairs when fitness status, goals, interests, and accessibility for implementing personal plans are similar.

Adapted, by permission, from PSAHPERD, 1994, *Designing assessments: Applications for physical education,* 39-40.

SUMMARY

In quality physical education programs teachers systematically teach and assess in the cognitive, affective, and physical domains using a variety of assessments (NASPE, 2008). To help physical educators provide quality physical education, chapter 13 examined best practices for assessing health-related fitness in the physical domain by presenting information on fitness assessment. Assessment of student learning is one of the greatest challenges that physical educators face today (Gallo, Sheehy, Patton, & Griffin, 2006). Traditionally, physical education teachers assessed using skill and perhaps fitness assessments (the physical domain) but did not always consider the cognitive and affective domains. These two domains are often less familiar to physical educators; therefore, assessment can appear to be a daunting or scary task. The benefits of assessing what students know and can do in relation to the cognitive and affective domains should not be overlooked as an opportunity to increase the likelihood that students will increase and maintain physical activity levels. When teaching and learning about health-related fitness, the cognitive domain includes understanding components of health-related fitness, basic training principles, and nutrition as a means to develop a healthier lifestyle, which is a crucial component of quality physical education. When teaching and learning about health-related fitness, the affective domain includes helping students develop positive feelings, attitudes, values, and social behaviors in physical activity settings as a means to develop a healthier lifestyle, which is another crucial component of quality physical education programs. Therefore, teachers must address affective goals in their programs because students may be skilled and even knowledgeable and still choose not to participate (Rink, 2006).

APPENDIX A
Worksheets and Reproducibles

Appendix A Contents

FITNESS GOALS CONTRACT

To improve my personal fitness level, I, with the help of my teacher, have set the following fitness goals. I will participate in the activities outlined in this plan to achieve improved physical fitness. Based on my current level of fitness, I believe that these goals are reasonable.

Fitness component test item	Score_____ Date_____	My goal	Activities to improve physical fitness	Follow-up score_____ Date_____
Aerobic fitness				
One-mile walk or run				
PACER				
Body composition				
Percent body fat				
Body mass index				
Muscular strength and endurance				
Curl-up				
Trunk lift				
Push-up				
Modified pull-up				
Pull-up				
Flexed-arm hang				
Flexibility				
Back-saver sit and reach				
Shoulder stretch				

Student _____ Date _____ Teacher _____

From NASPE, 2011, *Physical education for lifelong fitness: The Physical Best teacher's guide,* 3rd edition. (Champaign, IL: Human Kinetics).

ACTIVITY GOALS CONTRACT

Week of _____ My plans are to do the following:

	Activity that I plan to do	Time of day	Friends who will be active with me
Monday			
Tuesday			
Wednesday			
Thursday			
Friday			
Saturday			
Sunday			

Student _____ Date _____ Teacher _____

From NASPE, 2011, *Physical education for lifelong fitness: The Physical Best teacher's guide*, 3rd edition (Champaign, IL: Human Kinetics).

FITNESS WORKOUT PLAN

Name _____ Date _____

Week beginning _____

Component	Activity	Mon	Tue	Wed	Thu	Fri	Weekend
	Warm-up						
Aerobic fitness							
Muscular strength and endurance							

(continued)

From NASPE, 2011, *Physical education for lifelong fitness: The Physical Best teacher's guide*, 3rd edition (Champaign, IL: Human Kinetics).

(continued)

Component	Activity	Mon	Tue	Wed	Thu	Fri	Weekend
Flexibility							
Body composition							
	Cool-down						

From NASPE, 2011, *Physical education for lifelong fitness: The Physical Best teacher's guide*, 3rd edition (Champaign, IL: Human Kinetics).

GOAL-SETTING WORKSHEET

Name_____Date_____

M = Measure and monitor

In class, my Fitnessgram scores were as follows: _____ .

My scores falling below the healthy fitness zone were (list) _____ .

O = Outcomes defined that are optimally challenging

Based on my Fitnessgram scores, I wish to improve fitness in the following areas:

(Example: abdominal strength and endurance)

T = Time

I will accomplish my goal in_____weeks.

I = Individualized

I will not compare my scores to my classmates' scores.

To reach the HFZ, I need to increase my score by_____(the exercise).

(Example: 10 curl-ups)

V = Valuable

I have chosen an important goal of _____ .

(Example: increasing abdominal strength)

This is important to me because . . .

A = Active

By completing this sheet, I am taking active responsibility for increasing my health and fitness._____(initial)

T = Type

The following types of activities will help me to reach my goal: (list several activities)

(Example: curl-ups, pelvic thrusts, oblique curls)

I = Incremental

I will add_____(a number of exercises) to my score or add _____ minutes of _____ (activity) each week to achieve my goals.

(Example: two curl-ups each week or five minutes of jogging each week)

(continued)

From NASPE, 2011, *Physical education for lifelong fitness: The Physical Best teacher's guide*, 3rd edition (Champaign, IL: Human Kinetics). Debra Ballinger, PhD, Associate Professor, East Stroudsburg University.

(continued)

O = Overload

I will increase the weight or quantity of my activity each day by _____.

(Example: 10 curl-ups each day)

N = Necessary

The purpose (necessity) of this activity is to help me _____.

A = Authentic assessment

Although I can perform the _____ assessment again to see my improvement, I can also know I am achieving my goal by _____.

(Examples: measuring waist circumference, seeing my clothes fit better)

L = Lifestyle

Unhealthy lifestyle behaviors that I would like to change in the future include the following:

(Examples: Inactive television viewing, snacking on unhealthy foods)

P = Posted but private

I will post this sheet or keep it _____ , where I can see it each day.

My goal partner is _____.

E = Enjoyable

I know that work on this activity may not always be easy or fun, but I will be happier when I am healthy. Enjoyment comes from achieving new goals. My reward to myself when I achieve this goal is _____

_____.

(Example: I will go see a movie with my best friend)

My signature _____

Teacher signature* _____

(*Teacher has reviewed goal and believes it to be achievable for student.)

From NASPE, 2011, *Physical education for lifelong fitness: The Physical Best teacher's guide*, 3rd edition (Champaign, IL: Human Kinetics). Debra Ballinger, PhD, Associate Professor, East Stroudsburg University.

CHILDREN'S OMNI SCALE

Rate Your Perceived Exertion

Name_____Date_____

For each activity, circle the picture, word phrase, or number that best describes how you are feeling during the activity. For an overall RPE, focus on how the body feels as a whole. For chest or limbs RPE, focus on that part of the body.

For use with ages 8 to 15

(continued)

From NASPE, 2011, *Physical education for lifelong fitness: The Physical Best teacher's guide*, 3rd edition (Champaign, IL: Human Kinetics). Reprinted from R. Robertson, 2004, *Perceived exertion for practitioners: Rating effort with the OMNI picture system* (Champaign, IL: Human Kinetics), 145, 146. By permission of R. Robertson.

(continued)

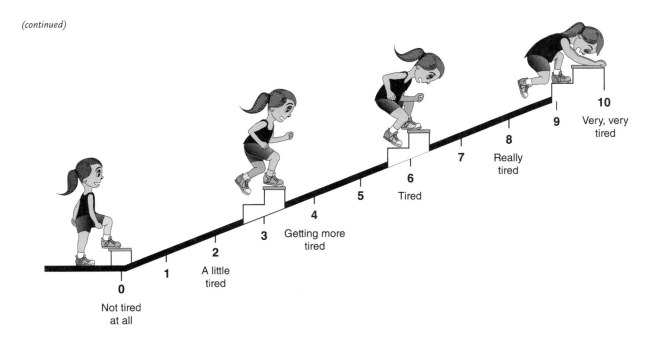

0 — Not tired at all
1
2 — A little tired
3
4 — Getting more tired
5
6 — Tired
7
8 — Really tired
9
10 — Very, very tired

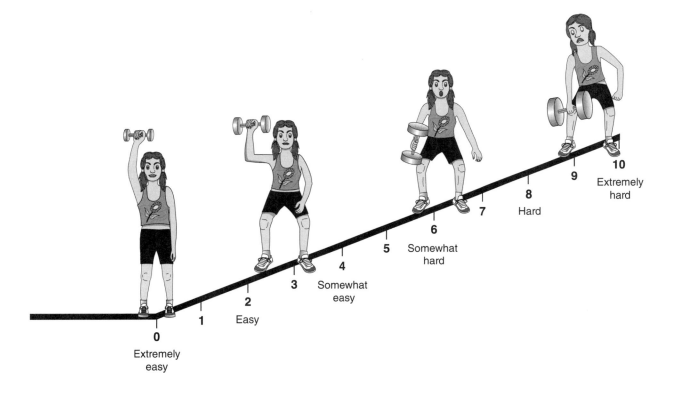

0 — Extremely easy
1
2 — Easy
3
4 — Somewhat easy
5
6 — Somewhat hard
7
8 — Hard
9
10 — Extremely hard

For use with ages 8 to 15

From NASPE, 2011, *Physical education for lifelong fitness: The Physical Best teacher's guide*, 3rd edition (Champaign, IL: Human Kinetics). Reprinted from R. Robertson, 2004, *Perceived exertion for practitioners: Rating effort with the OMNI picture system* (Champaign, IL: Human Kinetics), 148, 150. By permission of R. Robertson.

ADULT'S OMNI SCALE

Rate Your Perceived Exertion

Name_____Date_____

Identify the picture, word phrase, or number that best describes how you are feeling during the activity. For an overall RPE, focus on how the body feels as a whole. For chest or limbs RPE, focus on that part of the body.

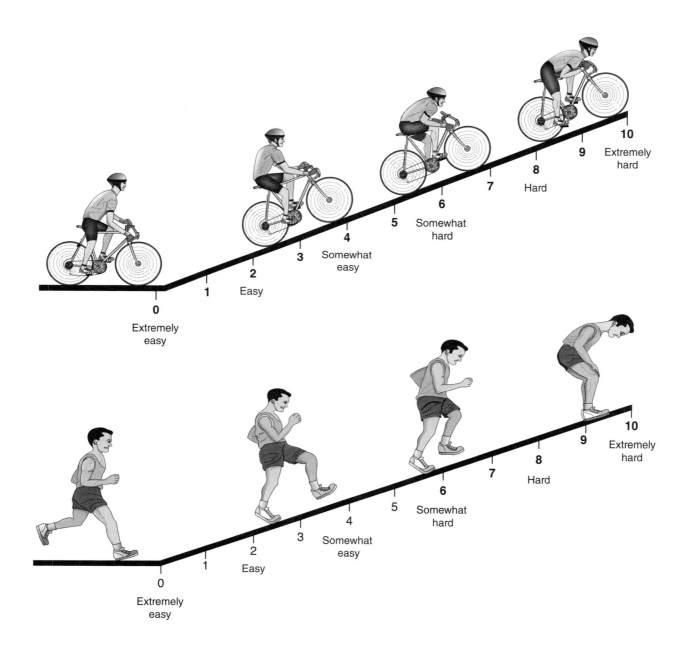

For use with ages 16 and older

(continued)

From NASPE, 2011, *Physical education for lifelong fitness: The Physical Best teacher's guide*, 3rd edition (Champaign, IL: Human Kinetics). Reprinted from R. Robertson, 2004, *Perceived exertion for practitioners: Rating effort with the OMNI picture system* (Champaign, IL: Human Kinetics), 141, 142. By permission of R. Robertson.

(continued)

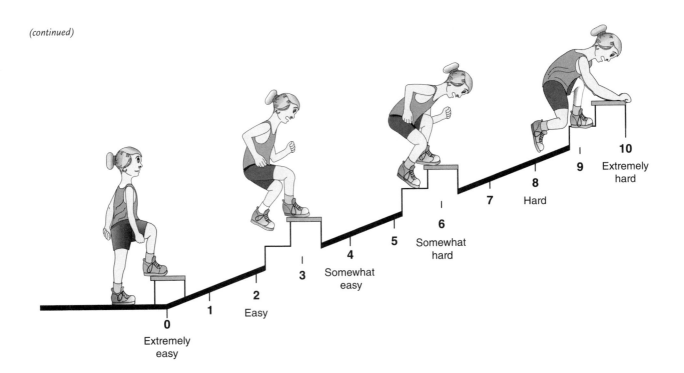

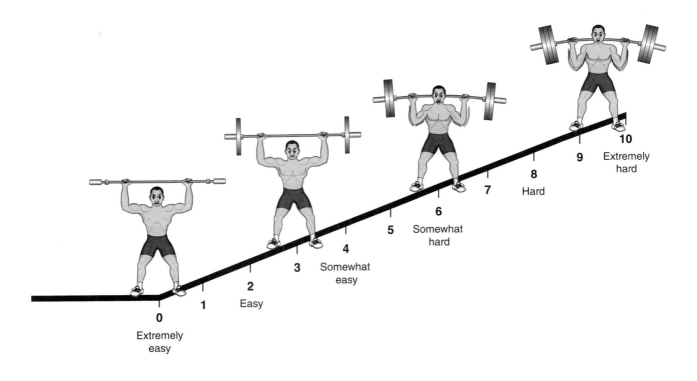

For use with ages 16 and older

From NASPE, 2011, *Physical education for lifelong fitness: The Physical Best teacher's guide*, 3rd edition (Champaign, IL: Human Kinetics). Reprinted from R. Robertson, 2004, *Perceived exertion for practitioners: Rating effort with the OMNI picture system* (Champaign, IL: Human Kinetics), 143, 144. By permission of R. Robertson.

MUSCULAR STRENGTH AND ENDURANCE TRAINING LOG

Name_____Date_____

Exercise	Set 1		Set 2		Set 3	
	Weight	Reps	Weight	Reps	Weight	Reps

From NASPE, 2011, *Physical education for lifelong fitness: The Physical Best teacher's guide*, 3rd edition (Champaign, IL: Human Kinetics). Adapted, by permission, from W. Kraemer and S. Fleck, 2005, *Strength training for young athletes,* 2nd ed. (Champaign, IL: Human Kinetics), 58.

DUMBBELL PRESS TECHNIQUE

Resistance Used

Correct form is essential to avoid injury and get the most from the dumbbell press exercise. Start with a low weight and increase the resistance only if you can maintain proper technique.

Starting Position

Elbows are straight (dumbbells positioned straight above the shoulders); feet are flat on the floor or flat on the end of the bench; buttocks and shoulders touch bench; dumbbells face horizontal to the body (palms up).

Points available: 0–6

Points earned: _____

Lowering (Eccentric) Phase

Descent of dumbbells is controlled; elbows are out to the side; forearms are perpendicular to the floor. Dumbbells are lowered down and a little to the side until the elbows are slightly below the shoulders; roll the shoulder blades back and down like they are being pinched together and raise the chest; feet stay flat on the floor; head stays still.

Points available: 0–7

Points earned: _____

Up (Concentric) Phase

Elbows are out to the sides; both arms straighten at the same controlled speed; motion is smooth and continuous; elbows do not lock; shoulder blades do not rise off the bench; head stays still; feet stay flat on floor.

Points available: 0–9

Points earned: _____

Finishing Position

Same position as starting position.

Points available: 0–3

Points earned: _____

Total points available: 0–25

Total points earned: _____

Technique Tips

- Inhale as you lower the weights and exhale as you lift them.
- A spotter should be behind the lifter's head and should assist the lifter with getting the dumbbells into place and remove them when finished. Impress on young weight trainers the importance of having a spotter during the exercise because the lifter presses the dumbbells over the face, neck, and chest.
- Practice the timing and technique of this exercise using minimal (2- to 5-pound [1 to 2.5 kg]) dumbbells.
- Use only an amount of weight that allows you to maintain proper form and technique throughout the full range of motion.
- Avoid dropping dumbbells when finished. Muscles are under considerable tension and dropping them will release the tension rapidly, potentially causing injury.
- Let your back keep a natural arch so that you have minor gap between the bench and your lower back.

From NASPE, 2011, *Physical education for lifelong fitness: The Physical Best teacher's guide*, 3rd edition (Champaign, IL: Human Kinetics).

INCLUSION PROFILE

Student's name _____

Student's date of birth _____ Classroom teacher _____

Disability code _____ Medications _____

Physical education goals and objectives: _____

_____

_____

_____

_____

Medical information or medical contraindications: _____

_____

_____

_____

_____

Behavior management plan: _____

_____

_____

_____

_____

Activity adaptations: _____

_____

_____

_____

_____

Related service providers; (OT, PT, S/L, hearing, vision, and so on): _____

_____

_____

_____

_____

Locker room accomodations: _____

_____

_____

_____

_____

From NASPE, 2011, *Physical education for lifelong fitness: The Physical Best teacher's guide*, 3rd edition (Champaign, IL: Human Kinetics).

STUDENT PROFILE SHEET

Student _____ Date of birth _____

Classroom teacher _____ Physical education teacher _____

Occupational therapist _____ Physical therapist _____

Speech and language therapist _____

1. Medical information and precautions:

2. Speech and language programs used (devices):

3. Behavior program or protocol:

4. Positioning or adaptive equipment or braces:

5. Nursing plan:

6. Dressing:

From NASPE, 2011, *Physical education for lifelong fitness: The Physical Best teacher's guide*, 3rd edition (Champaign, IL: Human Kinetics). Adapted, by permission, from J. Winnick and F. Short, 1999, *The Brockport physical fitness test manual* (Champaign, IL: Human Kinetics), 131.

CURL-UP ASSESSMENT

Name_____ Date_____

Directions

Circle the level of assistance that the person requires to perform the task. Total each level of assistance column and place the subtotals in the sum of scores row. Total the sum of scores row and place the score in the person's total score achieved row. Determine the percentage independence score based on the chart. Place number of repetitions in the product score row.

Key to Levels of Assistance

IND = Independent—the person is able to perform the task without assistance.

PPA = Partial physical assistance—the person needs some assistance to perform the task.

TPA = Total physical assistance—the person needs assistance to perform the entire task.

Curl-up	IND	PPA	TPA
1. Lie on back with knees bent	3	2	1
2. Place feet flat on the floor with legs slightly apart	3	2	1
3. Place arms straight, parallel to the trunk	3	2	1
4. Rest palms of hands on the mat with fingers stretched out	3	2	1
5. Rest head on partner's hands	3	2	1
6. Curl body in a forward position	3	2	1
7. Curl back down until head touches partner's hand	3	2	1
Sum of scores			
Total score achieved			
Total possible points	21		
Percentage independence score			
Product score			

Percentage of independence

7/21 = 33%	12/21 = 57%	17/21 = 80%
8/21 = 38%	13/21 = 61%	18/21 = 85%
9/21 = 42%	14/21 = 66%	19/21 = 90%
10/21 = 47%	15/21 = 71%	20/21 = 95%
11/21 = 52%	16/21 = 76%	21/21 = 100%

From NASPE, 2011, *Physical education for lifelong fitness: The Physical Best teacher's guide,* 3rd edition (Champaign, IL: Human Kinetics). Reprinted, by permission, from AAHPERD, 1995, *Physical best and individuals with disabilities: A handbook for inclusion in fitness programs* (Champaign, IL: Human Kinetics), 100.

ASSESSING KNOWLEDGE OF CALCULATING AND USING HEART RATE RUBRIC

Student's name _____ Date _____

Score _____ Class _____

Target component	Score 1 point	Score 2 points
Can demonstrate sites at which to count the pulse	Knows one site	Knows two sites
Understands how heart rate information indicates intensity	Some understanding	Clearly understands
Can accurately count the pulse for a fraction of a minute and then accurately calculate heartbeats per minute with a calculator	Sometimes	Most of the time
Can describe ways and reasons to increase or decrease heart rate	Some understanding	Clearly understands

From NASPE, 2011, *Physical education for lifelong fitness: The Physical Best teacher's guide,* 3rd edition (Champaign, IL: Human Kinetics).

FAMILY CHORES STEP LOG

Chore	Guardian	Guardian	Child	Child	Average chore step count
Sweeping					
Dusting					
Raking					
Washing windows					
Doing laundry					
Mowing the grass					
Individual total					

From NASPE, 2011, *Physical education for lifelong fitness: The Physical Best teacher's guide*, 3rd edition (Champaign, IL: Human Kinetics). Adapted, by permission, from R. Pangrazi, A. Beighle, and C. Sidman, 2007, *Pedometer power: 67 lessons for K-12*, 2nd ed. (Champaign, IL: Human Kinetics), 152.

K–2 WARM-UP AND COOL-DOWN ASSESSMENT

Name _____ Date _____

Goal: Knows activities for proper warm-up and cool-down.

Relationship to standards: NASPE content standard 2.

    1. Circle the row of kids who are warming up.

    2. Draw a triangle around the row of kids who are cooling down.

1. Walk   Skip   Jog

2. Jog   Skip   Walk

From NASPE, 2011, *Physical education for lifelong fitness: The Physical Best teacher's guide*, 3rd edition (Champaign, IL: Human Kinetics).

GRADES 3–5 INTENSITY SELF-ASSESSMENT

Goal: Able to determine intensity level using heart rate.

Relationship to standards: NASPE content standard 2.

Try each task 7-10 times and then take your heart rate by placing your hand over your heart. Circle the word that describes your heart beat (level of exertion, or intensity).

1. Jump and spin in the air so that you face the opposite direction.

    Light   Medium   Hard

2. Jump with feet close together.

    Light   Medium   Hard

3. Jump (hop), alternating feet.

    Light   Medium   Hard

4. Jump, alternating landing with feet apart and feet together.

    Light   Medium   Hard

5. Make a V shape with the jump rope on the floor—jump across the rope, starting at the narrow end.

    Light   Medium   Hard

6. Make a circle with a jump rope and jump in and out of the shape.

    Light   Medium   Hard

7. Make a square with a jump rope. Hop in and out of the square.

    Light   Medium   Hard

8. Do criss-cross jumps.

    Light   Medium   Hard

9. Make a triangle and a circle with jump ropes. Lay them next to each other. Jump from one shape to the other.

    Light   Medium   Hard

10. Jump forward and backward across a line.

    Light   Medium   Hard

11. Jump side to side across a line.

    Light   Medium   Hard

From NASPE, 2011, *Physical education for lifelong fitness: The Physical Best teacher's guide*, 3rd edition (Champaign, IL: Human Kinetics).

MIDDLE AND HIGH SCHOOL EXIT SLIP

Name _____ Date _____

_____ is how hard you do your physical activity. Intensity for aerobic activity

can be correlated with heart rate and can affect the _____ that you are able to

participate in the activity.

Hint: If you jog at the upper limits of your target heart rate range, you will not be able to jog as long as you would if you worked at the lower range of your target heart rate.

Word bank (choose from these to fill in the blanks):

   frequency

   intensity

   time

   type

From NASPE, 2011, *Physical education for lifelong fitness: The Physical Best teacher's guide*, 3rd edition (Champaign, IL: Human Kinetics).

EXIT SLIP

Name _____ Date _____

Goal: Correctly identifies aerobic activities.

Relationship to standards: NASPE content standard 4.

Circle the pictures of kids doing aerobic activities that will make their hearts stronger.

From NASPE, 2011, *Physical education for lifelong fitness: The Physical Best teacher's guide*, 3rd edition (Champaign, IL: Human Kinetics).

TEACHER OBSERVATION

Student's name _____ Date _____

Goal: Is self-directed while cooperating and showing compassion for others in small group work.

Relationship to standards: NASPE content standard 5.

Cooperation—willingly worked with the group to accomplish the task.

Self-direction—was focused and worked to complete the task without direct supervision.

Compassion—showed respect and concern for the feelings of others in the group even if their ideas were different from his or hers.

1—needs more work   2—sometimes   3—mastered

Group 1	Cooperation	Self-direction	Compassion

From NASPE, 2011, *Physical education for lifelong fitness: The Physical Best teacher's guide*, 3rd edition (Champaign, IL: Human Kinetics).

AFFECTIVE SELF-ASSESSMENT

Name _____ Date _____

Goal: Remains on task without close teacher monitoring and helps a partner.

Relationship to standards: NASPE content standard 5.

   1. Today I tried hard even if the teacher was not looking.   Yes   I need to work on this

   2. I helped my partner today   Yes   I need to work on this

   3. One thing I said or did to help my partner was _____.

From NASPE, 2011, *Physical education for lifelong fitness: The Physical Best teacher's guide*, 3rd edition (Champaign, IL: Human Kinetics).

PEER OBSERVATION

Name _____ Date _____

Goal: Follows all safety guidelines.

Relationship to standards: NASPE content standard 5.

Today at the yoga stations, my fitness partner

    a. followed all safety rules

    b. followed safety rules sometimes

    c. forgot to follow the safety rules

To help my partner be safe, I told him or her _____

_____ .

From NASPE, 2011, *Physical education for lifelong fitness: The Physical Best teacher's guide*, 3rd edition (Champaign, IL: Human Kinetics).

JOURNAL ENTRY

Name _____ Date _____

Goal: Reflects on personal physical activity choices during choice time.

Relationship to standards: NASPE content standard 5.

During free choice time I _____

_____ .

My top three reasons for choosing to _____ are

1.

2.

3.

Next free choice period I want to _____

because _____ .

From NASPE, 2011, *Physical education for lifelong fitness: The Physical Best teacher's guide*, 3rd edition (Champaign, IL: Human Kinetics)

AFFECTIVE EXIT SLIP

Name _____ Date _____

Goal: Identifies feelings associated with participation in physical activities.

Relationship to standards: NASPE content standard 6.

Today's activities in physical education made me feel

I felt this way because

_____

_____

_____

From NASPE, 2011, *Physical education for lifelong fitness: The Physical Best teacher's guide*, 3rd edition (Champaign, IL: Human Kinetics).

AFFECTIVE ANALYTIC RUBRIC

Name _____ Date _____

Goal: Seeks challenging experiences in physical education.

Relationship to standards: NASPE content standard 6.

How much did you challenge yourself today in class?

    3—I challenged myself the whole time by trying new things even if they seemed hard.

    2—I challenged myself part of the time by trying some of the new things we learned.

    1—I need to work on challenging myself and would like help.

Next time I want to see whether I can _____

_____ .

From NASPE, 2011, *Physical education for lifelong fitness: The Physical Best teacher's guide*, 3rd edition (Champaign, IL: Human Kinetics).

FITNESS JOURNAL

Name _____ Date _____

	I wish I could . . .	I predict that . . .	I feel good about . . .	My fears are . . .
Before my fitness preassessments Date _____				
After my fitness preassessments Date _____				
One month after my fitness program Date _____				
Two months after my fitness program Date _____				
Three months after my fitness program Date _____				

From NASPE, 2011, *Physical education for lifelong fitness: The Physical Best teacher's guide*, 3rd edition (Champaign, IL: Human Kinetics). Reprinted, by permission, from V. Melograno, 1998, *Professional and student portfolios for physical education* (Champaign, IL: Human Kinetics), 128.

THINKING ABOUT PHYSICAL FITNESS AND ACTIVITIES

Name _____ Date _____

1. I would rather exercise or play sports than watch TV.	Yes	No
2. People who exercise regularly seem to have a lot of fun doing it.	Yes	No
3. In school, I look forward to attending physical education class.	Yes	No
4. During physical education class at school, I usually work up a sweat.	Yes	No
5. When I grow up, I will probably be too busy to stay physically fit.	Yes	No
6. How do you feel about your ability to strike a ball with a racket?	☺ ☺ ☹	
7. How do you feel about your ability to kick a ball hard and hit a target?	☺ ☺ ☹	
8. How do you feel about your ability to run a long distance without stopping?	☺ ☺ ☹	
9. How do you feel about your ability to play many different games and sports?	☺ ☺ ☹	
10. How do you feel about your ability to participate in gymnastics?	☺ ☺ ☹	
11. How do you feel about your ability to participate in dance?	☺ ☺ ☹	

From NASPE, 2011, *Physical education for lifelong fitness: The Physical Best teacher's guide*, 3rd edition (Champaign, IL: Human Kinetics). Reprinted, by permission, from G. Graham, 2008, *Teaching children physical education,* 3rd ed. (Champaign, IL: Human Kinetics), 159, 208.

FITT CONCENTRATION

Name _____ Date _____

You will be performing a fitness activity and running to various stations to fill in your activity card. When instructed to go to a station, quickly run and write down the definition. Return to your roll call line for the next exercise. When you have completed each station, you will get into small groups and answer the questions for each category. At the end of the activity, turn in your paper for daily participation points!

Station 1: Principle of Progression
Definition:

Question: How can you apply the principle of progression to muscular strength?

Station 2: Principle of Specificity
Definition:

Question: What component of health-related fitness does core training focus on?

Station 3: Intensity
Definition:

Question: Compute your target heart rate zone using this formula:

$$208 - (.7 \times \text{your age}) = \underline{\hspace{3cm}} \text{ (max heart rate)}$$

Threshold heart rate   Target ceiling heart rate
Max HR: _____   Max HR: _____
(x) .65   (x) .90

Station 4: Principle of Overload
Definition:

Question: How can you apply the principle of overload to biceps curls?

Station 5: Frequency
Definition:

Question: What is the recommended number of times to exercise during the week?

Station 6: Time
Definition:

Question: What is the recommended time to exercise for a cardiovascular benefit to occur?

(continued)

(continued)

Station 7: Type

Definition:

Question: Is core training a skill-related or health-related activity?

Question: What type of activities could I perform if I wanted to improve in the following areas?

• Muscular strength:

• Cardiovascular fitness:

• Flexibility:

Culminating activity question: List one new idea that you learned today and how you can apply it to your personal fitness program.

From NASPE, 2011, *Physical education for lifelong fitness: The Physical Best teacher's guide*, 3rd edition (Champaign, IL: Human Kinetics).

YOGA EXIT SLIP

Name _____ Date _____

Goal: Knows three cues for the warrior yoga pose and three flexibility health benefits.

Relationship to standards: NASPE content standards 2 and 4.

Today we added the warrior pose to our yoga session. Name three cues or tips that are important to performing this pose correctly and safely.

1.

2.

3.

Name three flexibility health benefits discussed in class.

1.

2.

3.

From NASPE, 2011, *Physical education for lifelong fitness: The Physical Best teacher's guide*, 3rd edition (Champaign, IL: Human Kinetics).

YOGA PROJECT

Name _____ Date _____

Goal: Knows at least three cues for five yoga poses as well as health benefits of yoga.

Relationship to standards: NASPE content standards 2 and 4.

The teachers at this school want to increase their strength and flexibility levels while decreasing their stress levels. How fortunate it is that we just finished our study of yoga. A group of the teachers will be coming to the gym next week so that we can help them learn about yoga. Create five yoga pose cards that will help them learn to perform the poses correctly. You may choose to work alone, with a partner, or in a group of three.

Be sure to include the following in the yoga pose card project:

1. Use one page for each of the five yoga poses taught in class.
2. For each yoga pose provide a picture that demonstrates proper form using the cues learned in class. For this portion you will use a digital camera to take photos of properly performed poses.
3. Include at least three cues for each pose.
4. Use one page to list health benefits of yoga.

From NASPE, 2011, *Physical education for lifelong fitness: The Physical Best teacher's guide*, 3rd edition (Champaign, IL: Human Kinetics).

RUNNING STRIDE RUBRIC

Jogging Criteria

Doer 1 _____ Date _____

Doer 2 _____ Date _____

Level III

Observer: Give the doer some pointers about his or her jogging form. Use the tips that follow to help you. Try to be friendly.

Doer: Jog at a moderate pace. When the teacher signals, slow down and then change roles.

	Doer 1			Doer 2		
	Yes	No	Don't know	Yes	No	Don't know
1. Runs tall, leans slightly forward						
2. Swings legs from hip, keeps knees bent						
3. Lands on heels and rolls weight along the outside portion of foot to toes						
4. Points toes straight ahead, lands heel directly under knees						
5. Swings arms straight forward and backward, keeps hands relaxed						
6. Breathes from belly in an even rhythm						

From NASPE, 2011, *Physical education for lifelong fitness: The Physical Best teacher's guide*, 3rd edition (Champaign, IL: Human Kinetics). Adapted, by permission, from S.J. Virgilio, 1997, *Fitness education for children: Team approach* (Champaign, IL: Human Kinetics), 20.

APPENDIX B
Nutrient Content Claims

Easy-to-read food labels can help you find foods low in saturated fat, cholesterol, and sodium. The regulations spell out what terms can be used to describe the level of a nutrient in a food and how those terms can be used. Like the Nutrition Facts label, nutrient content claims are defined for one serving. Alternative spelling of these descriptive terms and their synonyms is allowed—for example, "hi" and "lo"—as long as the alternatives are not misleading. See table B.1 on page 292 for the core terms.

HEALTH CLAIMS

Health claims authorized by the Food and Drug Administration are one of several ways that food labels can win the attention of health-conscious consumers. A health claim alerts shoppers to the health potential of a product, and labeling or advertising may state, suggest, or imply that a relationship exists between what the consumer eats and the risk of a disease. Health claims differ from "structure/function" claims, which also may appear on food or dietary supplement labels. Unlike health claims (that the product may reduce the risk of certain diseases), structure/function claims (i.e., "calcium builds strong bones") do not deal with disease risk reduction. See table B.2 on page 293.

HEALTH CLAIMS ABOUT HEART DISEASE AND FAT, SATURATED FAT, AND CHOLESTEROL

A claim about heart disease means that the food is low in fat, saturated fat, and cholesterol. A diet low in these nutrients will reduce the risk of heart disease in most people, but not everyone. Family health history, smoking, obesity, and diabetes also affect a person's risk of heart disease.

HEALTH CLAIMS ABOUT HIGH BLOOD PRESSURE AND SODIUM

A claim about high blood pressure and sodium means that the food is low in sodium. A low-sodium diet is related to lower blood pressure in some people, but not everyone. Family health history, age, excess weight, and drinking too much alcohol may also be related to high blood pressure.

OTHER DEFINITIONS

The regulations also address other claims. Among them are the following:

► **Healthy**. A food labeled "healthy" must be low in fat and saturated fat and contain limited amounts of cholesterol and sodium. In addition, if it's a single-item food, it must provide at least 10% of the recommended daily amount of one or more of the following: vitamins A or C, iron, calcium, protein, or fiber. Exempt from this 10% rule are certain raw, canned, and frozen fruits and vegetables and certain cereal-grain products. These foods can be labeled "healthy" if they do not contain ingredients that change the nutritional profile, and, in the case of enriched grain products, conform to standards of identity, which call for certain required ingredients. If the food is a meal-type product, such as frozen entrees and multicourse frozen dinners, it must provide 10% of two or three of these vitamins or minerals or of protein or fiber, in addition to meeting the other criteria. The sodium content of meal-type products cannot exceed 360 milligrams per serving for individual foods and 480 milligrams per serving.

Table B.1 Nutrient Content Claim

If the label says	Then one serving of the product has
Calories	
Calorie free	Less than 5 calories
Low calorie	40 calories or less
Reduced or fewer calories	At least 25% fewer calories than regular product
Light or lite	One-third fewer calories or 50% less fat than regular product
Sugar	
Sugar free	Less than 0.5 grams sugar
Reduced sugar or less sugar	At least 25% less sugar than regular product that contain sugars, such as juice or dry fruit
No added sugar	
Fat	
Fat free	Less than 0.5 grams of fat
Low fat	3 grams of fat or less
Reduced fat or less fat	At least 25% less fat than the regular product
Low in saturated fat	1 gram of saturated fat or less, with no more than 15% of the calories coming from saturated fat
Lean	Less than 10 grams of fat, 4 grams of saturated fat, and 95 milligrams of cholesterol
Extra lean	Less than 5 grams of fat, 2 grams of saturated fat, and 95 milligrams of cholesterol
Light or lite	At least one-third less calories or no more than half the fat of the regular product, or no more than half the sodium of the regular product
Cholesterol	
Cholesterol free	Less than 2 milligrams of cholesterol and 2 grams or less of saturated fat
Low cholesterol	20 or less milligrams of cholesterol and 2 grams or less of saturated fat
Reduced cholesterol	At least 25% less cholesterol than the regular product and 2 grams or less of saturated fat
Sodium	
Sodium free or no sodium	Less than 5 milligrams of sodium and no sodium chloride in ingredients
Very low sodium	35 milligrams or less of sodium
Low sodium	140 milligrams or less of sodium
Reduced or less sodium	At least 25% less sodium than the regular product
Fiber	
High fiber	5 grams or more of fiber
Good source of fiber	2.5 to 5.9 grams of fiber
Other claims	
High, rich in, excellent source of	20% or more of daily value
Good source, contains, provides	10% to 19% of daily value
More, enriched, fortifies, added	10% or more of daily value
Lean (meat, poultry, seafood, and game meat)	Less than 10 grams of fat, 4.5 grams of saturated fat, and 95 milligrams of cholesterol
Extra lean	Less than 5 grams of fat, 2 grams of saturated fat, and 95 milligrams of cholesterol
High potency	Individual vitamins or minerals that are present at 100% or more of the RDI

Food and Drug Administration, Center for Food Safety and Applied Nutrition. Available: www.cfsan.fda.gov/~dms/hclaims.html.

Table B.2 Health Claims

To make health claims about . . .	The food must be . . .
Heart disease and fats	Low in fat, saturated fat, and cholesterol
Heart disease and fruits, vegetables, and grain products	A fruit, vegetable, or grain product low in fat, saturated fat, and cholesterol that contains at least 0.6 grams of soluble fiber per serving
Blood pressure and sodium	Low in sodium
Cancer and fat	Low in fat or fat-free
Osteoporosis and calcium	High in calcium and not contain more phosphorus than calcium
Cancer and fruits and vegetables	Good source of fiber, vitamin A, or vitamin C
Neural tube birth defects and folate	At least 40 mcg of folic acid per serving (10% daily value)
Cavities and dietary sugar alcohol	Sugar free or meet the criteria for sugar free
Coronary heart disease and soluble fiber	Whole oats and psyllium seed husk (rolled oats, oat bran, or whole-oat flour)

Food and Drug Administration, Center for Food Safety and Applied Nutrition. Available: www.cfsan.fda.gov/~dms/hclaims/html.

▶ **Percent fat free**. A product bearing this claim must be a low-fat or a fat-free product. In addition, the claim must accurately reflect the amount of fat present in 100 grams of the food. Thus, if a food contains 2.5 grams of fat per 50 grams, the claim must be "95% fat free."

▶ **Implied**. These types of claims are prohibited when they wrongfully imply that a food contains or does not contain a meaningful level of a nutrient. For example, a product claiming to be made with an ingredient known to be a source of fiber (such as "made with oat bran") is not allowed unless the product contains enough of that ingredient (for example, oat bran) to meet the definition for a good source of fiber. As another example, a claim that a product contains no tropical oils is allowed—but only on foods that are low in saturated fat because consumers have come to equate tropical oils with high saturated fat.

▶ **Meals and main dishes**. Claims that a meal or main dish is free of a nutrient, such as sodium or cholesterol, must meet the same requirements as those for individual foods. Other claims can be used under special circumstances. For example, "low calorie" means that the meal or main dish contains 120 calories or less per 100 grams. "Low sodium" means that the food has 140 milligrams or less per 100 grams. "Low cholesterol" means that the food contains 20 milligrams of cholesterol or less per 100 grams and no more than 2 grams of saturated fat. "Light" means that the meal or main dish is low fat or low calorie.

▶ **Standardized foods**. Any nutrient content claim, such as "reduced fat," "low calorie," or "light," may be used in conjunction with a standardized term if the new product has been specifically formulated to meet the FDA's criteria for that claim, if the product is not nutritionally inferior to the traditional standardized food and if the new product complies with certain compositional requirements set by the FDA. A new product bearing a claim also must have performance characteristics similar to the referenced traditional standardized food. If the product doesn't and the differences materially limit the use of the product, its label must state the differences (for example, "not recommended for baking") to inform consumers.

FRESH

The FDA has issued a regulation for the claim "fresh," although it is not mandated by NLEA. The agency took this step because of concern over the possible misuse of the term on some food labels.

The regulation defines the claim "fresh" when it is used to suggest that a food is raw or unprocessed. In this context, "fresh" can be used only on a food that is raw, has never been frozen or heated, and contains no preservatives. (Irradiation at low levels is allowed.) "Fresh frozen," "frozen fresh," and "freshly frozen" can be used for foods that are quickly frozen while still fresh. Blanching (brief scalding before freezing to prevent nutrient breakdown) is allowed. Other uses of the term "fresh," such as in "fresh milk" or "freshly baked bread," are not affected.

Food and Drug Administration, Center for Food Safety and Applied Nutrition. Available: www.cfsan.fda.gov/~dms/hclaims.html.

APPENDIX C
Exercises for Prepuberty

From the multitude of exercises for strength training, the following exercises are offered as guidelines only. You can use other exercises, depending on the environment and facilities.

Adapted, by permission, from T.O. Bompa, 2000, *Total training for young champions* (Champaign, IL: Human Kinetics), 115-123.

DUMBBELL OR RESISTANCE BAND SIDE RAISE

Area worked: deltoids (shoulders)

1. The student stands with the feet apart and the arms at the side.
2. He or she lifts the dumbbells or resistance band parallel to the floor and then returns to the starting position.

DUMBBELL OR RESISTANCE BAND CURL

Area worked: biceps (front of upper arm)

1. The student stands with the arms extended down in front of the hips and the palms facing upward.
2. He or she flexes the right elbow, lifting the dumbbell or resistance band toward the right shoulder.
3. The student returns to the starting position and then repeats with the left arm.

   *Note: Can be done with both arms at the same time.

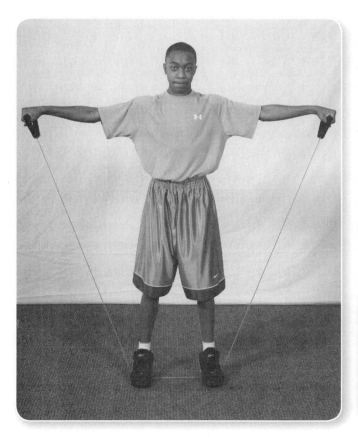

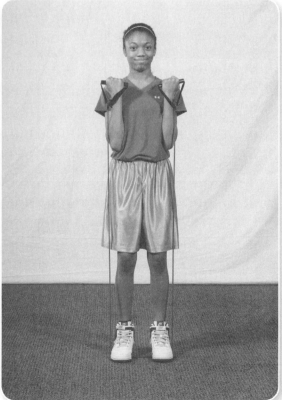

DUMBBELL SHOULDER PRESS

Area worked: deltoids (shoulders)

1. The student sits with back supported and holds the dumbbells at shoulder level.
2. He or she presses the dumbbells straight above the shoulders and then returns them to the starting position.

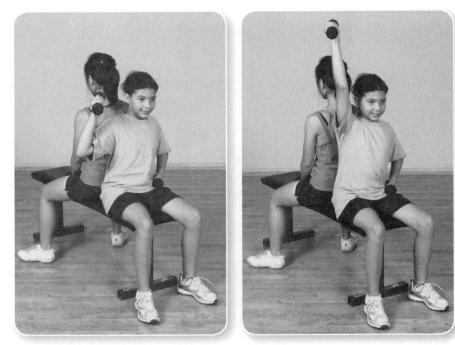

DUMBBELL FLY

Area worked: pectoralis (chest) and deltoids (shoulders)

1. The student lies on back with the arms extended to the sides.
2. He or she raises both arms to vertical (above the chest) and then returns to the starting position.

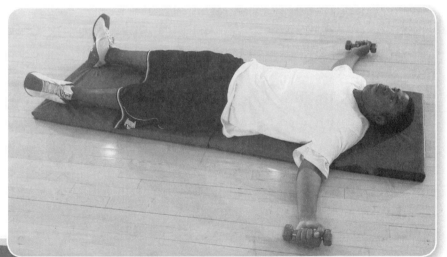

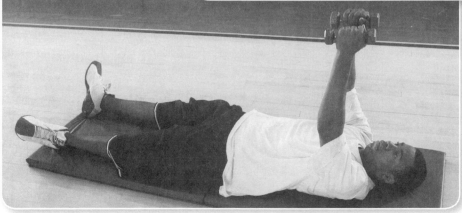

MEDICINE BALL CHEST THROW

Area worked: deltoids (shoulders) and triceps (back of upper arm)

1. Two partners face each other, standing 8 to 10 feet (2.5 to 3 m) apart. Partner A holds a medicine ball in front of the chest.
2. Partner A extends the arms up and forward to throw the ball toward the chest of partner B.
3. After catching the ball, partner B throws the ball back to partner A.

MEDICINE BALL ZIGZAG THROW

Area worked: biceps (front of upper arm), triceps (back of upper arm), and deltoid (shoulders)

1. Two equal lines face each other 10 feet apart (3 m). The first person in each line holds a medicine ball.
2. Students throw the ball with two hands from line to line in a zigzag pattern.

Variation

Students throw the ball with one hand, overhead with two hands, or from the side.

MEDICINE BALL TWIST THROW

Area worked: biceps (front of upper arm), triceps (back of upper arm), and oblique and abdominal muscles

1. Partner A holds the ball at hip level and stands with his or her left side facing partner B.

2. Partner B faces partner A and anticipates the ball with arms extended forward.

3. Partner A turns the body to the left, extends the arms, and releases the ball to the side toward partner B.

4. After catching the ball, partner B takes the same starting position (side facing partner A), performs a rotation, and returns the ball to partner A in the same manner.

MEDICINE BALL FORWARD OVERHEAD THROW

Area worked: pectoralis (chest), deltoids (shoulders), biceps (front of upper arm), triceps (back of upper arm), and abdominal muscles

1. Partners face each other, standing 8 to 10 feet (2.5 to 3 m) apart. Partner A holds the ball above the head.

2. Partner A extends the arms backward and then immediately forward to release the ball toward the chest of partner B.

3. After catching the ball, partner B returns it to partner A with the same motion.

MEDICINE BALL SCOOP THROW

Area worked: Hip extensors; and arm, shoulder, and back muscles

1. The student stands with the feet apart and holds the ball between the legs.
2. He or she bends the knees and then immediately extends them to throw the ball vertically with the arms (self-toss).
3. The student extends the arms upward to catch the ball and then returns to the starting position.

Variation

The student can perform the same exercise with a partner.

ABDOMINAL CRUNCH

Area worked: upper and lower abdominal muscles

1. The student lies on the floor with the arms along the body. The knees are slightly bent.
2. He or she raises the upper body up and forward and then relaxes and brings the trunk slowly back to the starting position. The student slides the hands along the floor throughout the range of motion.

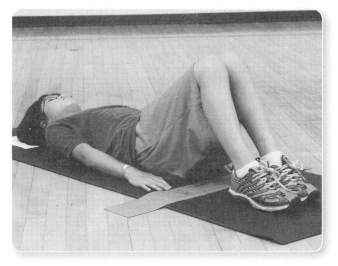

MEDICINE BALL BACK ROLL

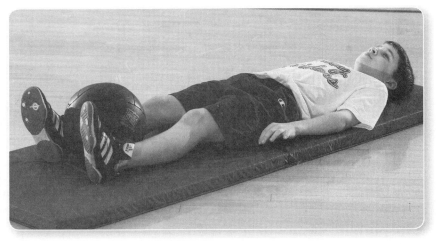

Area worked: abdominal muscles and hip flexors

1. The student lies on back, with the arms along the body, holding a medicine ball between the feet. The knees are slightly bent.

2. He or she raises the legs until the medicine ball is above the head, takes the ball with his or her hands, and then lowers the legs back to the starting position and touches the ball to the floor above the head.

Variation

The student can perform the same exercise with a partner, throwing the ball backward overhead.

Safety Note

When the ball is above the face, the student should place the palms over the face to catch the ball if it falls toward the face or head.

MEDICINE BALL SIDE PASS RELAY

Area worked: oblique abdominal muscles and shoulders (deltoids)

1. Two equal teams sit with their feet apart. The players on each team line up in a straight line. (Set the distance between players so that they can perform the pass comfortably.) The first player on each team holds a medicine ball.

2. The first player rotates to the right and passes the ball to the next player.

3. The players continue this sequence as fast as possible to the end of the line.

4. After receiving the ball, the last player stands up, runs to the front as quickly as possible, sits down, and starts the series again.

5. The relay is over when the first player is at the end of the row.

Variations

▶ Players pass the ball alternately to each side.

▶ Players pass the ball back over the head.

▶ Players hold the ball between the feet, roll over, and pass the ball to the feet of the next player.

TRUNK TWIST

Area worked: internal and external oblique abdominal muscles

1. The student sits with the feet resting under a heavy object or stall bars or with a partner holding the feet. The hands are over the ears, and the knees are slightly bent.

2. The student leans slightly back, with the trunk in an oblique position, and turns the trunk to the left as far as possible.

3. He or she returns to the starting position and then turns the trunk to the right as far back as possible.

4. Repeat on alternating sides.

SINGLE-LEG BACK RAISE

Area worked: hip extensors and spine muscles

1. The student lies face down with the arms extended forward.

2. He or she lifts the right leg upward as high as possible, keeping belly button on the floor.

3. The student lowers the right leg to the floor and lifts the left leg.

4. Repeat with alternating legs.

CHEST RAISE AND CLAP

Area worked: lumbar extensor (lower back)

1. The student lies face down with the arms extended forward on the floor.

2. He or she raises the chest with the arms extended and performs claps two or three times.

3. The student relaxes the trunk and lowers the arms to the floor.

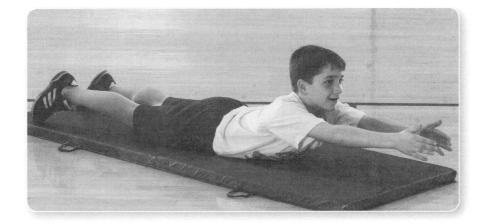

APPENDIX D
Alternatives for Questionable Exercises

Stretching can be harmful when the routine is too vigorous or too lengthy or when bouncing at the extreme ROM. The wrong choice of exercises also imposes serious risk of injury to joints. In fact, many popular stretching exercises used in the past are potentially harmful. Unfortunately, most people acquire their stretching knowledge by watching others. This informal, copycat approach has spawned a series of popular but dangerous exercises capable of damaging the knees, neck, spinal column, ankles, and lower back. The following material identifies nine popular stretching exercises that should be avoided and offers safe substitutes that will effectively stretch the same muscle groups.

Adapted, by permission, from J.S. Greenberg, G.V. Dintiman, and B. Myers Oakes, 2004, *Physical fitness and wellness: Changing the way you look, feel, and perform*, 3rd edition (Champaign, IL: Human Kinetics), 151-153.

Questionable exercises	Safer alternative exercises
Neck roll (circling) Danger: Drawing the head backward could damage the disks in the neck area and may even precipitate arthritis.	Head look Description: Look in all four directions and hold in position (only looks right and left are shown).

Questionable exercises	Safer alternative exercises
Quadriceps stretch holding toes Danger: If the ankle or toe box of shoe is pulled too hard, muscle, ligament, and cartilage damage may occur.	Quadriceps stretch holding ankle Description: Grasp one ankle with the corresponding hand. Instead of pulling, attempt to straighten the leg that you are stretching.
Hurdler's stretch Danger: Subjects hip, knee, and ankle to abnormal stress.	Everted hurdler's stretch Description: Bend the left leg at the knee and slide the foot next to the right knee. Pull yourself forward slowly by using a towel or by grasping the toe.

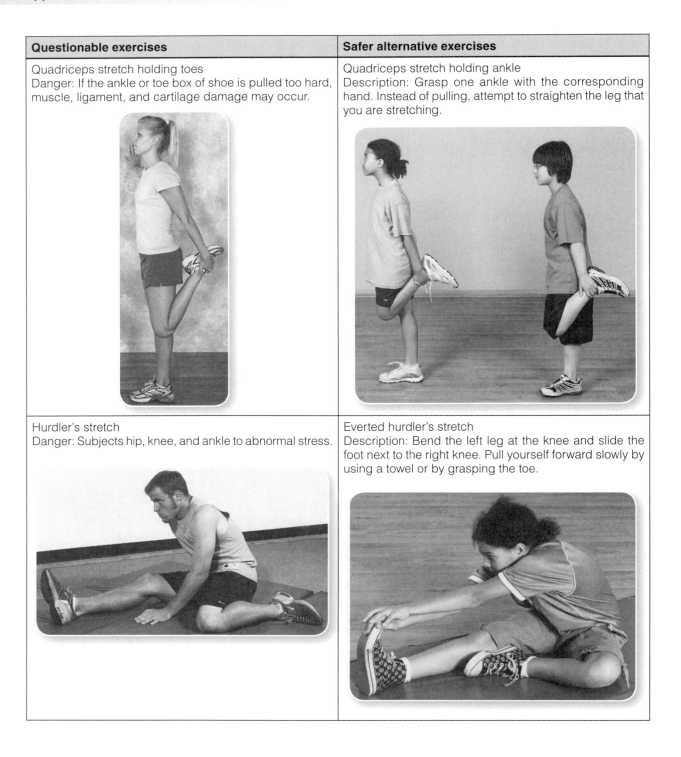

Questionable exercises	Safer alternative exercises
Deep knee bend (or any exercise that bends the knee beyond a right angle) Danger: Places excessive stress on ligament, tendon, and cartilage tissue.	Single-knee lunge Description: Place one leg in front of your body and extend the other behind it. Bend forward at the trunk as you bend the lead leg to a right angle.
Yoga plow Danger: This exercise could overstretch muscles and ligaments, injure spinal disks, or cause fainting.	Extended one-leg stretch or back-saver sit and reach Description: Extend one leg and bend at the knee. With your foot on the floor, draw the knee of the other leg toward your chest. Bend forward at the trunk as far as possible.

Questionable exercises	Safer alternative exercises
Straight-leg curl-up Danger: Produces back strain and sciatic nerve elongation. It also moves the hip flexor muscles and does not flatten the abdomen. 	Bent-knee curl-up Description: Cross both hands on your chest and bend the knees slightly. Raise the upper body slightly to about 25 degrees on each repetition. Note: Fitnessgram suggests that the arms remain straight along the body.
Double-leg raise Danger: Stretches the sciatic nerve beyond its normal limits and places too much stress on ligaments, muscles, and disks. 	Knee-to-chest stretch Description: Clasp both hands beside the head or on the ears. Draw the knee toward the chest and hold that position of maximum stretch for 15 to 30 seconds.
Prone arch Danger: Hyperextension of the lower back places extreme pressure on spinal disks. 	Belly push-up Description: Lie flat on your belly, resting on your elbows. Push with your arms slowly to raise the upper body as the lower torso remains pressured against the floor. Use caution to avoid hyperextending your back.

Questionable exercises	Safer alternative exercises
Back bends Danger: Spinal disks can easily be damaged. 	No alternative exercise has been approved.

APPENDIX E

Body Mass and Body Composition Measures

2 to 20 years: Boys
Body mass index-for-age percentiles

NAME _____

RECORD # _____

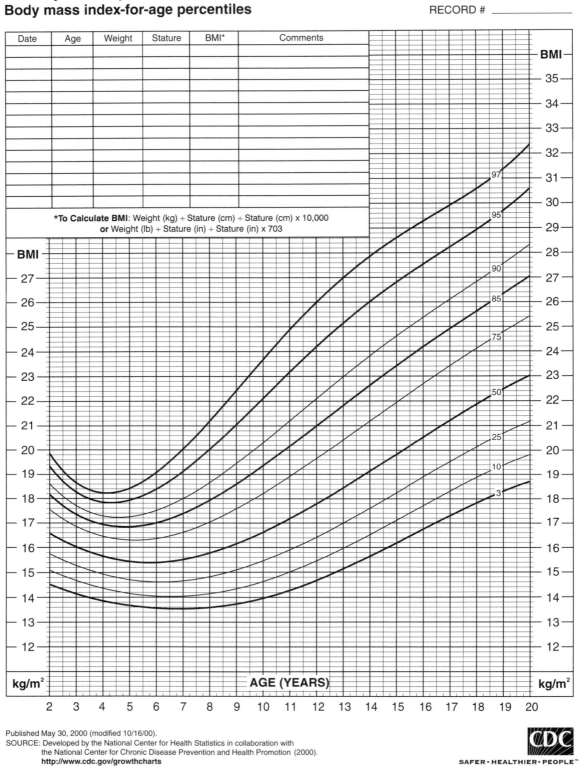

Date	Age	Weight	Stature	BMI*	Comments

*To Calculate BMI: Weight (kg) ÷ Stature (cm) ÷ Stature (cm) x 10,000
or Weight (lb) ÷ Stature (in) ÷ Stature (in) x 703

AGE (YEARS)

Published May 30, 2000 (modified 10/16/00).
SOURCE: Developed by the National Center for Health Statistics in collaboration with
the National Center for Chronic Disease Prevention and Health Promotion (2000).
http://www.cdc.gov/growthcharts

SAFER · HEALTHIER · PEOPLE™

Figure E.1 BMI chart for males ages 2 to 20

From http://www.cdc.gov/nchs/data/nhanes/growthcharts/set2clinical/cj411073.pdf

2 to 20 years: Girls
Body mass index-for-age percentiles

NAME _____

RECORD # _____

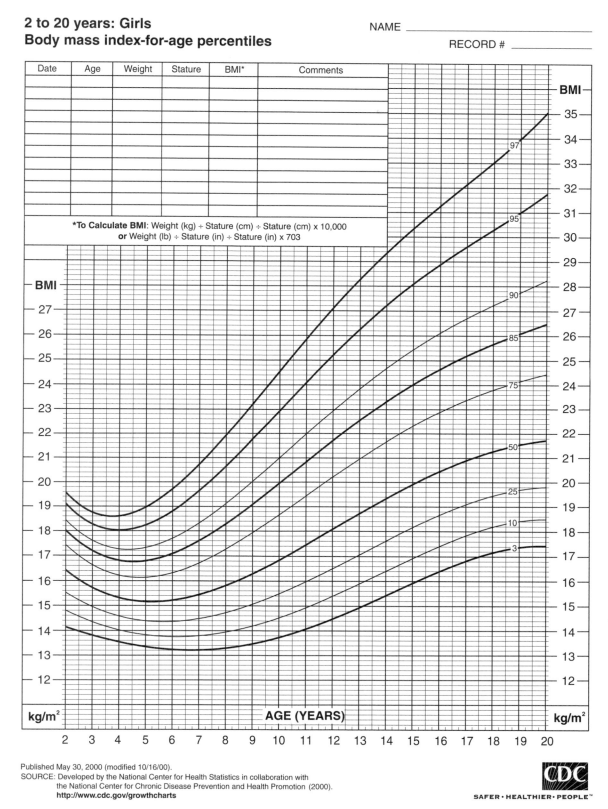

Date	Age	Weight	Stature	BMI*	Comments

*To Calculate BMI: Weight (kg) ÷ Stature (cm) ÷ Stature (cm) x 10,000
or Weight (lb) ÷ Stature (in) ÷ Stature (in) x 703

BMI

27
26
25
24
23
22
21
20
19
18
17
16
15
14
13
12

kg/m²

AGE (YEARS)

2 3 4 5 6 7 8 9 10 11 12 13 14 15 16 17 18 19 20

BMI

35
34
33
32
31
30
29
28
27
26
25
24
23
22
21
20
19
18
17
16
15
14
13
12

kg/m²

97
95
90
85
75
50
25
10
3

Published May 30, 2000 (modified 10/16/00).
SOURCE: Developed by the National Center for Health Statistics in collaboration with
the National Center for Chronic Disease Prevention and Health Promotion (2000).
http://www.cdc.gov/growthcharts

SAFER · HEALTHIER · PEOPLE™

Figure E.2 BMI chart for females ages 2 to 20

From http://www.cdc.gov/nchs/data/nhanes/growthcharts/set2clinical/cj411073.pdf

SKINFOLD MEASUREMENTS

This section provides information on measuring skinfolds, including suggestions on how best to learn to do skinfold measurements.

Test Objective

To measure the triceps and calf (and abdominal for college students) skinfold thicknesses for calculating percent body fat.

Equipment and Facilities

A skinfold caliper is necessary to perform this measurement. The cost of calipers ranges from US$5 to $200. Both the expensive and inexpensive calipers have been shown to be effective for use by teachers who have had sufficient training and practice.

Testing Procedures

The triceps and calf skinfolds have been chosen for Fitnessgram because they are easily measured and highly correlated with total body fatness. The caliper measures a double layer of subcutaneous fat and skin.

Measurement Location

The triceps skinfold is measured on the back of the right arm over the triceps muscle, midway between the elbow and the acromion process of the scapula. Using a piece of string to find the midpoint is a good method. The skinfold site should be vertical. Pinching the fold slightly above the midpoint will ensure that the fold is measured right on the midpoint.

The calf skinfold is measured on the inside of the right leg at the level of maximal calf girth. The right foot is placed flat on an elevated surface, and the knee is flexed at a 90-degree angle. The vertical skinfold should be grasped just above the level of maximal girth, and the measurement is made below the grasp.

Measurement Technique

- Measure skinfolds on the person's right side.
- Instruct the student to relax the arm or leg being measured.

- Firmly grasp the skinfold between the thumb and forefinger and lift it away from the other body tissue. The grasp should not be so firm as to be painful.
- Place the caliper .5 inches (1.25 cm) below the pinch site.
- Be sure that the caliper is in the middle of the fold.
- The recommended procedure is to do one measurement at each site before taking a second measurement at any site. Likewise, complete the second set of measurements before doing the third set.

Scoring

The skinfold measure is registered on the caliper. Each measurement should be taken three times. The recorded score is the median (middle) value of the three scores. To illustrate, if the readings were 7.0, 9.0, and 8.0, the score would be recorded as 8.0 millimeters. Each reading should be recorded to the nearest 0.5 millimeters. For teachers who do not use the computer software, a percent fatness look-up chart is provided in tables E.1 and E.2. Fitnessgram uses the formula developed by Slaughter and Lohman to calculate percent body fat (Slaughter et al., 1988).

Suggestions for Test Administration

- Skinfolds should be measured in a setting that provides the child with privacy.
- Interpretation of the measurements may be given in a group setting as long as individual results are not identified.
- Whenever possible, the same tester should administer the skinfold measurement to the same students at subsequent testing periods.
- Practice measuring the sites with another tester and compare results on the same students. As you become familiar with the methods you can generally find agreement within 10% between testers.

Learning to Do Skinfold Measurements

Using video training tapes or participating in a workshop are excellent ways to begin to learn how to do skinfold measurements. The videotape *Prac-* *tical Body Composition Video* (available from Human Kinetics) illustrates the procedures described in this manual.

Adapted, by permission, from The Cooper Institute, 2010, *Fitnessgram/ Activitygram test administration manual,* 5th ed. (Champaign, IL: Human Kinetics), 42.

Table E.1 Fitnessgram Body Composition Conversion Chart

Total MM	% fat	Total MM	% fat	Total MM	% fat	Total MM	% fat	Total MM	% fat
Boys										
1.0	1.7	16.0	12.8	31.0	23.8	46.0	34.8	61.0	45.8
1.5	2.1	16.5	13.1	31.5	24.2	46.5	35.2	61.5	46.2
2.0	2.5	17.0	13.5	32.0	24.5	47.0	35.5	62.0	46.6
2.5	2.8	17.5	13.9	32.5	24.9	47.5	35.9	62.5	46.9
3.0	3.2	18.0	14.2	33.0	25.3	48.0	36.3	63.0	47.3
3.5	3.6	18.5	14.6	33.5	25.6	48.5	36.6	63.5	47.7
4.0	3.9	19.0	15.0	34.0	26.0	49.0	37.0	64.0	48.0
4.5	4.3	19.5	15.3	34.5	26.4	49.5	37.4	64.5	48.4
5.0	4.7	20.0	15.7	35.0	26.7	50.0	37.8	65.0	48.8
5.5	5.0	20.5	16.1	35.5	27.1	50.5	38.1	65.5	49.1
6.0	5.4	21.0	16.4	36.0	27.5	51.0	38.5	66.0	49.5
6.5	5.8	21.5	16.8	36.5	27.8	51.5	38.9	66.5	49.9
7.0	6.1	22.0	17.2	37.0	28.2	52.0	39.2	67.0	50.2
7.5	6.5	22.5	17.5	37.5	28.6	52.5	39.6	67.5	50.6
8.0	6.9	23.0	17.9	38.0	28.9	53.0	40.0	68.0	51.0
8.5	7.2	23.5	18.3	38.5	29.3	53.5	40.3	68.5	51.3
9.0	7.6	24.0	18.6	39.0	29.7	54.0	40.7	69.0	51.7
9.5	8.0	24.5	19.0	39.5	30.0	54.5	41.1	69.5	52.1
10.0	8.4	25.0	19.4	40.0	30.4	55.0	41.4	70.0	52.5
10.5	8.7	25.5	19.7	40.5	30.8	55.5	41.8	70.5	52.8
11.0	9.1	26.0	20.1	41.0	31.1	56.0	42.2	71.0	53.2
11.5	9.5	26.5	20.5	41.5	31.5	56.5	42.5	71.5	53.6
12.0	9.8	27.0	20.8	42.0	31.9	57.0	42.9	72.0	53.9
12.5	10.2	27.5	21.2	42.5	32.2	57.5	43.3	72.5	54.3
13.0	10.6	28.0	21.6	43.0	32.6	58.0	43.6	73.0	54.7
13.5	10.9	28.5	21.9	43.5	33.0	58.5	44.0	73.5	55.0
14.0	11.3	29.0	22.3	44.0	33.3	59.0	44.4	74.0	55.4
14.5	11.7	29.5	22.7	44.5	33.7	59.5	44.7	74.5	55.8
15.0	12.0	30.0	23.1	45.0	34.1	60.0	45.1	75.0	56.1
15.5	12.4	30.5	23.4	45.5	34.4	60.5	45.5	75.5	56.5

Reprinted, by permission, from The Cooper Institute, 2010, *Fitnessgram/Activitygram test administration manual,* 5th ed. (Champaign, IL: Human Kinetics), 101.

Table E.2 Fitnessgram Body Composition Conversion Chart

					Girls				
Total MM	% fat	Total MM	% fat	Total MM	% fat	Total MM	% fat	Total MM	% fat
1.0	5.7	16.0	14.9	31.0	24.0	46.0	33.2	61.0	42.3
1.5	6.0	16.5	15.2	31.5	24.3	46.5	33.5	61.5	42.6
2.0	6.3	17.0	15.5	32.0	24.6	47.0	33.8	62.0	42.9
2.5	6.6	17.5	15.8	32.5	24.9	47.5	34.1	62.5	43.2
3.0	6.9	18.0	16.1	33.0	25.2	48.0	34.4	63.0	43.5
3.5	7.2	18.5	16.4	33.5	25.5	48.5	34.7	63.5	43.8
4.0	7.5	19.0	16.7	34.0	25.8	49.0	35.0	64.0	44.1
4.5	7.8	19.5	17.0	34.5	26.1	49.5	35.3	64.5	44.4
5.0	8.2	20.0	17.3	35.0	26.5	50.0	35.6	65.0	44.8
5.5	8.5	20.5	17.6	35.5	26.8	50.5	35.9	65.5	45.1
6.0	8.8	21.0	17.9	36.0	27.1	51.0	36.2	66.0	45.4
6.5	9.1	21.5	18.2	36.5	27.4	51.5	36.5	66.5	45.7
7.0	9.4	22.0	18.5	37.0	27.7	52.0	36.8	67.0	46.0
7.5	9.7	22.5	18.8	37.5	28.0	52.5	37.1	67.5	46.3
8.0	10.0	23.0	19.1	38.0	28.3	53.0	37.4	68.0	46.6
8.5	10.3	23.5	19.4	38.5	28.6	53.5	37.7	68.5	46.9
9.0	10.6	24.0	19.7	39.0	28.9	54.0	38.0	69.0	47.2
9.5	10.9	24.5	20.0	39.5	29.2	54.5	38.3	69.5	47.5
10.0	11.2	25.0	20.4	40.0	29.5	55.0	38.7	70.0	47.8
10.5	11.5	25.5	20.7	40.5	29.8	55.5	39.0	70.5	48.1
11.0	11.8	26.0	21.0	41.0	30.1	56.0	39.3	71.0	48.4
11.5	12.1	26.5	21.3	41.5	30.4	56.5	39.6	71.5	48.7
12.0	12.4	27.0	21.6	42.0	30.7	57.0	39.9	72.0	49.0
12.5	12.7	27.5	21.9	42.5	31.0	57.5	40.2	72.5	49.3
13.0	13.0	28.0	22.2	43.0	31.3	58.0	40.5	73.0	49.6
13.5	13.3	28.5	22.5	43.5	31.6	58.5	40.8	73.5	49.9
14.0	13.6	29.0	22.8	44.0	31.9	59.0	41.1	74.0	50.2
14.5	13.9	29.5	23.1	44.5	32.2	59.5	41.4	74.5	50.5
15.0	14.3	30.0	23.4	45.0	32.6	60.0	41.7	75.0	50.9
15.5	14.6	30.5	23.7	45.5	32.9	60.5	42.0	75.5	51.2

Reprinted by permission, from The Cooper Institute, 2010, *Fitnessgram/Activitygram test administration manual,* 5th ed. (Champaign, IL: Human Kinetics), 102.

APPENDIX F
Asthma Action Card

Asthma and Allergy Foundation of America

STUDENT ASTHMA ACTION CARD

National Asthma Education and Prevention Program ⚕EPA

Name: _____ Grade: _____ Age: _____

Homeroom Teacher: _____ Room: _____

Parent/Guardian Name: _____ Ph: (h): _____

                   Address: _____ Ph: (w): _____

Parent/Guardian Name: _____ Ph: (h): _____

                   Address: _____ Ph: (w): _____

ID Photo

Emergency Phone Contact #1 _____

                        Name   Relationship   Phone

Emergency Phone Contact #2 _____

                        Name   Relationship   Phone

Physician Treating Student for Asthma: _____ Ph: _____

Other Physician: _____ Ph: _____

EMERGENCY PLAN

Emergency action is necessary when the student has symptoms such as, _____ , _____ ,

_____ , _____ or has a peak flow reading of _____ .

• **Steps to take during an asthma episode**:
1. Check peak flow.
2. Give medications as listed below. Student should respond to treatment in 15-20 minutes.
3. Contact parent/guardian if _____

4. Re-check peak flow.
5. Seek emergency medical care if the student has any of the following:
   - ✔ Coughs constantly
   - ✔ No improvement 15-20 minutes after initial treatment with medication and a relative cannot be reached.
   - ✔ Peak flow of _____
   - ✔ Hard time breathing with:
     - • Chest and neck pulled in with breathing
     - • Stooped body posture
     - • Struggling or gasping
   - ✔ Trouble walking or talking
   - ✔ Stops playing and can't start activity again
   - ✔ Lips or fingernails are grey or blue

IF THIS HAPPENS, GET EMERGENCY HELP NOW!

• **Emergency Asthma Medications**

	Name	Amount	When to Use
1.			
2.			
3.			
4.			

See reverse for more instructions

Daily Asthma Management Plan

- **Identify the things which start an asthma episode (Check each that applies to the student.)**

☐ Exercise   ☐ Strong odors or fumes   ☐ Other _____

☐ Respiratory infections   ☐ Chalk dust / dust   _____

☐ Change in temperature   ☐ Carpets in the room

☐ Animals   ☐ Pollens

☐ Food _____   ☐ Molds

Comments _____

- **Control of School Environment**

(List any environmental control measures, pre-medications, and/or dietary restrictions that the student needs to prevent an asthma episode.) _____

_____

_____

_____

- **Peak Flow Monitoring**

Personal Best Peak Flow number: _____

Monitoring Times: _____   _____   _____   _____

- **Daily Medication Plan**

Name	Amount	When to Use
1.		
2.		
3.		
4.		

Comments / Special Instructions

_____

_____

_____

For Inhaled Medications

☐ I have instructed _____ in the proper way to use his/her medications. It is my professional opinion that _____ should be allowed to carry and use that medication by him/herself.

☐ It is my professional opinion that _____ should not carry his/her inhaled medication by him/herself.

_____   _____
Physician Signature   Date

_____   _____
Parent/Guardian Signature   Date

AAFA • 1233 20th Street, N.W., Suite 402 , Washington, DC 20036 • www.aafa.org • 1-800-7-ASTHMA

02/00

GLOSSARY

active stretch—A stretch in which the person stretching provides the force of the stretch by contracting the opposing (antagonist) muscle.

Activitygram—A feature of Fitnessgram that provides physical activity assessments. It includes detailed information about the student's activity habits and prescriptive feedback about how active he or she should be.

affective domain—Personal responsibility, attitudes, and values that a student has toward and during physical activity.

alternative assessment—Using tools other than traditional standardized testing—including tools such as portfolios, journals, and role playing—to collect evidence about student learning and achievement of program objectives.

anorexia nervosa—A serious and potentially fatal disease characterized by self-induced starvation and extreme weight loss.

assessment—Continuous collection and interpretation of information on student behaviors to provide information about students' improvement in specific components.

ballistic stretching—A type of stretching that involves moving quickly, bouncing, or using momentum to produce the stretch.

binge eating—A type of eating disorder not otherwise specified and characterized by recurrent binge eating without the regular use of compensatory measures to counter the binge eating.

bodybuilding—A sport in which competitors are judged on size, symmetry, and definition of muscle.

body composition—The amount of lean body mass compared with the amount of body fat. This quantity is typically expressed in terms of percent body weight (i.e., percent fat as a percent of weight).

body mass index (BMI)—A ratio of height to weight that correlates with body fat in the general population.

bulimia—An eating disorder characterized by a destructive cycle of bingeing and purging of food.

carbohydrate—A category of nutrient that provides four kilocalories per gram and is the preferred source of energy for the body, particularly the brain.

circuit training—Training that involves several different exercises or activities. This type of training allows variation in the intensity or type of activity from station to station.

cognitive domain—Refers to knowledge, comprehension, application, analysis, synthesis, and evaluation.

complex carbohydrate—Foods such as pasta, cereals, breads, and grains that supply longer, sustained energy.

concentric contraction—A muscle-shortening contraction.

continuous activity—Movement that lasts at least several minutes without rest periods.

cool-down—A period of light activity that allows the body to slow down and gradually return to near resting levels. The body needs this gradual recovery following activity bouts to ensure proper blood flow back to the heart, reduce muscle stiffness, remove lactic acid, and prevent light-headedness, dizziness, or even fainting.

cooperative learning—A teaching style that involves students working together to complete a specified task or assignment.

criterion-referenced health standards—Standards associated with good health. Scientific information is used to determine the amount of fitness needed to meet minimum health levels.

cue words—Key terms or phrases that a student repeats while executing a skill so that he or she will learn the vocabulary that goes with the actions.

developmentally appropriate activities—Activities that are appropriate based on a student's developmental level, age, ability level, interests, and previous experience and knowledge.

discretionary calorie allowance—The balance of calories remaining in a person's energy allowance after accounting for the calories needed to meet the recommended nutrient intakes.

diet—The total intake of food and beverages consumed.

duration—How long an activity should be performed (time).

dynamic flexibility—The range of joint movement in the performance of a physical activity at a normal or rapid speed.

dynamic stretch—Involves moving parts of the body and gradually increasing ROM, speed of movement, or both.

eccentric contraction—A muscle-lengthening contraction; also known as negative exercise.

effort—Infers how hard a student tries.

energy balance—State in which calories consumed equal calories expended.

exercise—Physical activity that is planned, structured, and repetitive bodily movement done to improve or maintain one or more of the components of health-related fitness.

exercise-induced asthma—A narrowing of the airways brought on by exercise, making breathing difficult. Symptoms include wheezing, coughing, tightness of the chest, and breathlessness.

exercise prescription—The process of designing a routine of physical activity in a systematic and individualized manner (ACSM, 2010).

external factors—Environmental, demographic, and social influences on behavior that the person cannot change.

extrinsic motivation—A person's desire to perform a particular task based on environmental or other personal influences. Occurs when a desired object or socially enhancing consequence is presented to increase the likelihood that a behavior will be repeated.

fartlek training—A modification of continuous training in which periods of increased intensity are interspersed with continuous activity over varying and natural terrain. Also referred to as speed play.

fat—A category of nutrient that provides nine kilocalories per gram.

fat-soluble vitamins—Vitamins that dissolve in fat and can be stored in the body; includes vitamins A, D, E, and K.

Fitnessgram—A health-related fitness assessment and computerized reporting system that has been endorsed as the assessment tool to be used in conjunction with the Physical Best program.

FITT guidelines—Describe how to safely apply the five principles of training (overload, progression, specificity, regularity, and individuality) by manipulating the frequency, intensity, time, and type of activity.

flexibility—The ability to move a joint through its complete range of motion.

frequency—How often a person performs an activity.

Gardner's theory of multiple intelligences—A theory of learning that asserts that different individuals are strong in different "intelligences." The types of intelligence include bodily-kinesthetic intelligence, spatial intelligence, interpersonal intelligence, musical intelligence, logical-mathematical intelligence, intrapersonal intelligence, naturalistic intelligence, and linguistic intelligence.

grades—A product based on previous performance.

growth plates—Section of cartilage at the end of long bones in children.

health-related fitness—A measure of a person's ability to perform physical activities that require endurance, strength, or flexibility and are achieved through a combination of regular exercise and inherent ability. The components of health-related physical fitness are aerobic fitness, muscular strength, muscular endurance, flexibility, and body composition as they relate specifically to health enhancement.

healthy fitness zone (HFZ)—Designates the range of fitness scores associated with good health; used by Fitnessgram. The healthy fitness zone is based on criterion-referenced standards because they represent the age- and gender-appropriate fitness levels that a child needs for good health.

heart rate monitor—A device that provides heart rate data.

heart rate reserve—The difference between a person's maximal heart rate and resting heart rate.

hydrogenation—The process of adding hydrogen under pressure to unsaturated oils to produce a solid product such as shortening or margarine.

hyperextension—Moving a joint well beyond its normal range of motion (extension), which can cause an increased risk for the development of joint laxity and possible injury.

hyperflexion—Moving a joint well beyond its normal range of motion (flexion), which can increase the risk of developing joint laxity and can possibly cause injury.

hypermobility—Excess range of motion at a joint. This condition may predispose a person to injury.

inclusion—The process of creating a learning environment that is open to and effective for all students whose needs and abilities fall outside of the general range of those for children of similar age or whose cultural or religious beliefs differ from that of the majority group.

individuality principle—The principle of training that takes into account that each person begins at a different level of fitness, each person has personal goals and objectives for physical activity and fitness, and each person has different genetic potential for change.

intensity—How hard a person exercises during a physical activity period. Appropriate intensity should be determined based on the age, fitness level, and fitness goals of the participant.

internal factors—Personal (i.e., biological and psychological) influences on behavior that can be influential in changing levels of motivation.

interval training—Training that involves alternating short bursts of activity with rest periods.

intrinsic motivation—A person's internal desire to perform a particular task.

journal—A written account from the perspective of the individual. Often a reflection on daily events or logged activities.

kettle bells—These ball-shaped weights vary in size. Lifting and controlling a kettle bell forces the muscles in the entire body (especially the core) to contract together, building strength and stability at the same time.

kilocalorie—A measure of heat energy required to raise the temperature of one kilogram of water one degree Celsius. Popular sources often shorten the term *kilocalories* to simply *calories*.

lanugo—A downy layer of hair growth that occurs as a side effect of anorexia nervosa.

laxity—The degree of abnormal motion of a given joint. Abnormal joint laxity means that the ligaments connecting bone to bone can no longer provide stability to the joint.

log—A systematic record or accounting of behavior (usually without reflection) that is used mainly for recording performance and participation data. Logs provide a baseline record of behaviors that can be used to help set personal goals related to exercise frequency, intensity, duration, or type.

macronutrients—Nutrients that provide the greatest amount of energy and include carbohydrate, protein, and fat.

maximal heart rate (MHR)—The fastest rate at which the heart can beat. Used when determining the appropriate exercise heart rate for monitoring training intensity. Maximal heart rate is calculated using this formula: $207 - (.7 \times age)$.

maximal oxygen consumption ($\dot{V}O_2max$)—Considered the best measure of aerobic fitness. It is a laboratory test measuring the maximum amount of oxygen that a person can consume despite an increase in the workload during a graded exercise test. May also be referred to as maximal oxygen uptake (MOU).

medicine ball—A heavy ball that weighs between 1 and 20 pounds (.5 and 9 kg) and is made of leather or rubber. Medicine balls can be employed in muscular fitness activities.

micronutrients—Vitamins and minerals that are required in the human diet in very small amounts.

mineral—A nonorganic substance necessary for the normal functioning of the body, especially for growth and health maintenance. Minerals contain zero calories.

moderate physical activity—Activity of an intensity equal to brisk walking that can be performed for relatively long periods without fatigue.

motivational factors—Factors that push or pull to create behavior change. The behaviors of people are influenced by both internally and externally controlled factors.

muscular–tendon unit—The area of the muscle where the muscle and tendon connect to the bone. Stretching increases the length of the muscular–tendon unit.

muscular endurance—The ability of a muscle or muscle group to exert a submaximal force repeatedly over a period of time.

muscular fitness—In the Physical Best program, muscular fitness refers to the development of a combination of muscular strength and muscular endurance.

muscular power—The ability to exert a force rapidly. It can be calculated as force times distance divided by time.

muscular strength—The ability of a muscle or muscle group to exert a maximal force against a resistance one time through the full range of motion.

normative standards—Provide comparisons relative to others in a group but do not provide information concerning how the values relate to individual health.

nutrient density—The amount of a given nutrient per calorie in a food. For example, a vegetable has a higher nutrient density than a candy bar.

obesity—A condition of excess body fat, typically defined as 120% of ideal body weight or greater.

one-repetition maximum (1RM)—The amount of weight that can be lifted one time through the full range of motion. This assessment technique is not recommended for children, but it can be determined by performing either a 10RM or 12RM and then using a table to estimate the 1RM.

overload principle—States that a body system (cardiorespiratory, muscular, or skeletal) must perform at a level beyond normal to adapt and improve physiological function and fitness.

overtraining—A condition caused by training too much or too intensely and not allowing sufficient recovery time. Symptoms include lack of energy, decreased performance, fatigue, depression, aching muscles, loss of appetite, and proneness to injury.

passive stretch—A stretch with the assistance of a force other than the opposing (antagonist) muscle. The force can be from the person, a partner, gravity, or an implement.

pedometer—A device used to count steps taken.

peer assessment—An assessment method whereby students analyze the performance of other students.

physical activity—Any bodily movement produced by skeletal muscles that results in expenditure of energy.

phytonutrients—Organic components of plants thought to promote health and protect humans against certain cancers, heart disease, and age-related macular degeneration.

plyometrics—A muscular fitness training technique used to develop explosive power. It emphasizes prestretching (eccentric contraction) the muscle before engaging in concentric contractions, and it often involves hops, jumps, and throws.

PNF (proprioceptive neuromuscular facilitation)—A static stretch that uses combinations of active and passive stretching techniques. Generally involves a precontraction of the muscle to be stretched and a contraction of the antagonist muscle during the stretch.

portfolio—A collection of a student's work—usually a combination of student-chosen and required material—that demonstrates achievement of program goals.

powerlifting—A competitive sport involving the dead lift, the squat, and the bench press.

progression principle—Refers to how a person should increase the overload. Proper progression involves a gradual increase in the level of activity, which is manipulated by increasing frequency, intensity, time, or a combination of all three components.

protein—A category of nutrient that provides four kilocalories per gram and is primarily for cell growth and replacement.

psychomotor domain—Refers to skills and motor or movement patterns. It is commonly assessed during drills, skill tests, and gamelike activities.

purging—The use of laxatives, vomiting, or diuretics to prevent absorption of calories in the body and weight gain.

regularity principle—States that physical activity must be performed on a regular basis to be effective and that long periods of inactivity can lead to a loss of the benefits achieved during the training session.

repetition—The number of times that an exercise is performed during one set.

resistance training or strength training—A systematic, preplanned program using a variety of methods (e.g., a person's own body weight or tension bands) or equipment (e.g., machines or free weights) that progressively stresses the musculoskeletal system to improve muscular strength, endurance, or power.

resting energy expenditure (REE)—The energy that the body uses at rest.

rubric—A scoring tool that identifies the criteria used for judging student performance. Rubrics range in complexity from checklists to tools that are holistic in nature. Rubrics can be used to assess skills, attitudes, and knowledge.

saturated fat—The main contributor of high cholesterol, it tends to be hard at room temperature and comes predominantly from animal sources.

self-assessment—An assessment method whereby students use rubrics of critical elements, journals, or logs to monitor their own progress.

set—A group of repetitions followed by a rest period.

simple carbohydrate—Food that is high in sugar (e.g., candy, soda pop).

skill-related fitness—Skill-related fitness (sometimes referred to as sport-related fitness) components often go hand in hand with certain physical activities and are necessary for a person to accomplish or enhance a skill or task. The skill-related components include agility, balance, coordination, power, reaction time, and speed.

skinfold—A double layer of skin and subcutaneous fat measured to assess body composition.

skinfold caliper—Equipment used to measure a skinfold in body composition assessment.

specificity principle—States that explicit activities that target a particular body system must be performed to bring about fitness changes in that area.

spotting—A technique whereby someone helps ensure the safety of the person performing an exercise or activity.

stability balls—Large, inflatable balls used as exercise equipment. Comfortable and highly supportive, they are generally heavy duty and capable of holding large amounts of weight.

stages of change (also transtheoretical model)—A model for behavioral change that focuses on motivation to change as it relates to stages of readiness and awareness. The model identifies typical behaviors of people at each stage and provides recommendations for moving through the stages of change, including precontemplation, contemplation, preparation, action, and maintenance.

static flexibility—The range of motion at a joint or group of joints. The limits of static flexibility are determined by a person's tolerance of the stretched position.

static stretch—A slow sustained stretch of the muscle that is held for 10 to 30 seconds. The person stretches the muscular–tendon unit to the point where mild discomfort is felt and then backs off slightly, holding the stretch at a point just before discomfort is felt.

stride length—The distance between two heel strikes.

task analysis—A process that involves breaking down a task into its component parts to help determine the level and type of support that must be provided for a person to learn the task.

tidal volume—The volume of air either inhaled or exhaled in a normal resting breath.

time—How long an activity is performed (duration).

traditional assessment—A process in which results of tests are the main data used to measure or quantify student learning outcomes. In physical education, this kind of assessment has often taken the form of rules tests (e.g., for specific games and sports), skill tests, fitness tests, and teacher observation.

training adaptations—The basic physiological changes that occur over the course of a training period.

trans fatty acid—A type of unhealthy fat that is the result of the hydrogenation of vegetable oils.

type—Refers to mode or what kind of activity a person chooses to perform in each area of health-related fitness.

underweight—Typically defined as less than 90% of ideal body weight or a body mass index lower than the 5th percentile.

unsaturated fat—Fat that is liquid at room temperature and comes from plant sources. Unsaturated fat can help lower cholesterol level and is beneficial when consumed in moderation.

ventilation—The movement of air into and out of the lungs. The volume of air moved is generally expressed in liters per minute and is calculated by multiplying respiratory rate by tidal volume.

vigorous physical activity—Movement that expends more energy or is performed at a higher intensity than brisk walking.

volume—In muscular fitness, the number of sets and repetitions in a workout.

warm-up—A low-intensity activity done before a full-effort or main activity to prepare the body for upcoming more intense activity. A proper warm-up improves muscle function, maximizes blood flow to the muscles, and improves flexibility.

water-soluble vitamins—Vitamins that need to dissolve in water before the body can absorb them; includes the numerous B-complex (such as B_6, B_{12}, niacin, riboflavin, and folate) vitamins and vitamin C.

weightlifting—A competitive sport involving maximal lifts.

yogic stretching—Involves unique stretching maneuvers that are mainly static and focus primarily on the trunk musculature (ACSM, 2009).

REFERENCES AND RESOURCES

AAHPERD. (2004). *Physical Best activity guide: Elementary level* (2nd ed.). Champaign, IL: Human Kinetics.

AAHPERD. (2004). *Physical Best activity guide: Middle and high school level* (2nd ed.). Champaign, IL: Human Kinetics.

AAHPERD. (2010). *Physical Best activity guide: Elementary level* (3rd ed.). Champaign, IL: Human Kinetics.

AAHPERD. (2010). *Physical Best activity guide: Middle and high school* (3rd ed.). Champaign, IL: Human Kinetics.

Alter, M.J. (2004). *Science of flexibility* (3rd ed.). Champaign, IL: Human Kinetics.

American Academy of Pediatrics (AAP). (2000a). Intensive training and sports specialization in young athletes (RE9906). *Pediatrics, 106*(1), 154-157.

American Academy of Pediatrics (AAP). (2000b). Physical fitness and activity in schools (RE9907). *Pediatrics, 105*(5), 1156-1157.

American Academy of Pediatrics (AAP). (2000). *Promoting physical activity.* www.aap.org/family/physicalactivity/physicalactivity.htm [Web excerpt from American Academy of Orthopaedic Surgeons, American Academy of Pediatrics. *Care of the young athlete.* Elk Grove Village, IL: American Academy of Pediatrics; 2000; 36-41], retrieved April 2, 2010.

American Academy of Pediatrics (AAP), Committee on Sports Medicine and Fitness. (2001). Policy statement: Strength training by children and adolescents. *Pediatrics, 107*(6): 1470-1472.

American Academy of Pediatrics. (2010). *A teenagers nutritional needs.* www.healthychildren.org

American Association for Active Lifestyles and Fitness–American Alliance for Health, Physical Education, Recreation and Dance (AAALF–AAHPERD). (1995). *Physical Best and individuals with disabilities: A handbook for inclusion in fitness programs,* ed. J.A. Seaman, Champaign, IL: Human Kinetics.

American College of Sports Medicine (ACSM). (2003). *ACSM fitness book* (3rd ed.). Champaign, IL: Human Kinetics.

American College of Sports Medicine (ACSM). (2006). www.acsm.org/AM/Template.cfm?Section=Home.

American College of Sports Medicine (ACSM). (2009). *ACSM's guidelines for exercise testing and prescription* (8th ed.). Philadelphia: Lippincott, Williams, and Wilkins.

American Heart Association (AHA). (2006). Promoting physical activity in children and youth: A leadership role for schools. *Circulation, 114,* 1214-1224.

Anderson, P.M., & Butcher, K.E. (2006). Childhood obesity: trends and potential causes. *Future Child, 16*(1), 19-45.

Armstrong, N., Williams, J., Balding, J., Gentle, P., & Kirby, B. (1991). The peak oxygen uptake of British children with reference to age, sex, and sexual maturity. *European Journal of Applied Physiology, 62,* 369-375.

Asthma and Allergy Foundation of America. (2000). *Student asthma action card.* www.aafa.org/public/pdfs/student.pdf.

Ayers, S.F. (2004). Ask-pe physical education concepts test. AAHPERD.

Baechle, T.R., & Earle, R. (2008). *Essentials of strength training and conditioning* (3rd ed.). Champaign, IL: Human Kinetics.

Baechle, T.R., & Groves, B. (1998). *Weight training: Steps to success* (2nd ed.). Champaign, IL: Human Kinetics.

Bailey, D.A., Ross, W.D., Mirwald, R.L., & Weese, C. (1978). Size dissociation of maximal aerobic power during growth in boys. *Medicine and Science in Sport and Exercise, 11,* 140-151.

Bailey, R. (2006). Physical education and sport in schools: A review of benefits and outcomes. *Journal of School Health, 76,* 397-401.

Bailey, R.C., Olson, J., Pepper, S.L., Porszaz, J., Barstow, T.J., & Cooper, D.M. (1995). The level and tempo of children's physical activities: An observational study. *Medicine and Science in Sport and Exercise, 27,* 1033-1041.

Banks, J.A. (1988). *Multiethnic education: Theory and practice.* Needham Heights, MA: Allyn & Bacon.

Barfield, J.P., Rowe, D.A., & Michael, T.J. (2004). Interinstrument consistency of the Yamax Digi-walker pedometer in elementary school-aged children. *Measurement in Physical Education and Exercise Science, 8*(2), 109-116.

Bar-Or, O. (1984). Children and physical performance in warm and cold environments. In R.F. Boileau (Ed.), *Advances in pediatric sport sciences,* Vol. 1 (pp. 117-130). Champaign, IL: Human Kinetics.

Bar-Or, O. (1993). Importance of differences between children and adults for exercise testing and exercise prescription. In J.S. Skinner (Ed.), *Exercise testing and exercise prescription for special cases* (2nd ed., pp. 57-74). Philadelphia: Lea and Febiger.

Bar-Or, O. (1994). Childhood and adolescent physical activity and fitness and adult risk profile. In C. Bouchard, R.J. Shephard, & T. Stephens (Eds.), *International proceedings and consensus statement* (pp. 931-942). Champaign, IL: Human Kinetics.

Bar-Or, O., & Rowland, T.W. (2004). *Pediatric exercise medicine.* Champaign, IL: Human Kinetics.

Baumgartner, T., & Jackson, A. (1999). *Measurement for evaluation in physical education and exercise science* (6th ed.) Boston: WCB-McGraw-Hill.

Beets, Michael W., Foley, John T., Tindall, Daniel W.S., & Lieberman, Lauren J. (2007). *Adapted Physical Activity Quarterly, 24*(3), 218-227.

Beets, M.W., Patton, M.M., & Edwards, S. (2005). The accuracy of pedometer steps and time during walking in children. *Medicine and Science in Sports and Exercise, 37*(3), 513-520.

Beighle, A., Pangrazi, R.P., & Vincent, S.D. (2001). Pedometers, physical activity, and accountability. *Journal of Physical Education, Recreation & Dance, 72*(9), 16-19.

Beunen, G.P., Lefever, J., Philippaerts, R.M., Delvaux, K., Thomis, M., Claessens, A.L., et al. (2004). Adolescent correlates of adult physical activity: A 26-year follow-up. *Medicine and Science in Sports and Exercise, 36*, 1930-1936.

Biddle, S.J.H., Whitehead, S.H., O'Donovan, R.M., & Nevill, M.E. (2005). Correlates of participation in physical activity for adolescent girls; A systematic review of recent literature. *Journal of Physical Activity and Health, 2*, 423-434.

Blair, S.N. (1995). Youth fitness: Directions for future research. In L.W.Y. Chueng & J.B. Richmond (eds.), *Child health, nutrition, and physical activity* (pp. 147-152). Champaign, IL: Human Kinetics.

Blair, S.N., Kohl, H.W., 3rd, Barlow, C.E., Paffenbarger, R.S., Jr., Gibbons, L.W., & Macera, C.A. (1995). Changes in physical fitness and all-cause mortality: A prospective study of healthy and unhealthy men. *JAMA, 273*, 1093-1098.

Blankenship, B.T. (2008). *The psychology of teaching physical education: From theory to practice.* Scottsdale, AZ: Holcomb Hathaway.

Bompa, T.O. (2000). *Total training for young champions.* Champaign, IL: Human Kinetics.

Bompa, T. & Carerra, M. (2005). *Periodization training for sports* (2nd ed.). Champaign, IL: Human Kinetics.

Boreham, C.A., Twisk, J., Murray, L., Savage, M., Strain, J.J., & Cran, G.W. (2001). Fitness, fatness, and coronary heart disease risk in adolescents: The Northern Ireland Young Hearts Project. *Medicine and Science in Sport and Exercise, 33*, 270-274.

Boreham, C.A., Twisk, J., Savage, M., Cran, G.W., & Strain, J.J. (1997). Physical activity, sports participation, and risk factors in adolescents. *Medicine and Science in Sport and Exercise, 29*, 788-793.

Borg, G. (1970). Perceived exertion as an indicator of somatic stress. *Scandinavian Journal of Rehabilitation Medicine, 2*(2), 92-98.

Brooks, G.A., Fahey, T.D., & White, T.P. (1996). *Exercise physiology: Human bioenergetics and its application* (2nd ed.). Mountainview, CA: Mayfield.

Brown, J. (2002). *Nutrition now* (3rd ed.). Belmont, CA: Wadsworth Thomson Learning.

Bukowski, B.J., & Stinson, D. (2000). Physical educators' perceptions of block scheduling in secondary physical education. *JOPERD, 71*(1): 53-57.

California Department of Education. (2002). *State study proves physically fit kids perform better academically.* www.cde.ca.gov/news/ releases2002/rel37.asp (accessed February 5, 2004).

Campbell, W., Crim, M., Young, V., & Evans, W. (1994). Increased energy requirements and changes in body composition with resistance training in older adults. *American Journal of Clinical Nutrition, 60*, 167-175.

Cardinal, B.J. (2000). Are sedentary behaviors terminable? *Journal of Human Movement Studies, 38*, 137-150.

Carrico, M. (1997). *Yoga Journal's yoga basics: The essential beginner's guide to yoga for a lifetime of health and fitness* (p. xiv, 191). New York: Henry Holt.

Carron, A.V., Hausenblas, H.A., & Estabrooks, P.A. (2003). *The psychology of physical activity.* New York: McGraw-Hill.

Carson, R.L., Blankenship, B., & Landers, R.L. (in press). Concluding comments and recommendations [Special feature: Promises and pitfalls of sport specialization in youth sport]. *Journal of Physical Education, Recreation and Dance.*

Centers for Disease Control and Prevention (CDC). (1996). *National Health and Nutrition Examination Survey III (1988-1994).* Hyattsville, MD: National Center for Health Statistics.

Centers for Disease Control and Prevention (CDC). (1997). Guidelines for school and community programs to promote lifelong physical activity among young people. *MMWR Morbidity and Mortality Weekly Report, 46*(RR-6), 1-36.

Centers for Disease Control and Prevention (CDC). (2000b). *CDC growth charts.* www.cdc.gov/nchs/data/nhanes/growthcharts/set2clinical/cj411073.pdf (accessed February 5, 2004).

Centers for Disease Control and Prevention (CDC). (2001a). *Profiles of the nation's health.*

Centers for Disease Control and Prevention (CDC), Department of Health and Human Services. (2001b). *CDC fact book 2000-2001.*

Centers for Disease Control and Prevention (CDC). (2002). *Improving nutrition and increasing physical activity.* www.cdc.gov.

Centers for Disease Control and Prevention (CDC). (2004). Trends in intake of energy and macronutrients, United States 1971-2000. *Morbidity & Mortality Weekly Report, 53* (4).

Centers for Disease Control and Prevention (CDC). (2008). Youth risk behavior surveillance—United States, 2007. *Morbidity & Mortality Weekly Report, 57* (No. SS-4).

Centers for Disease Control and Prevention (CDC). (2010). *National Health and Nutrition Examination Survey 2003-2006.* Available: www.cdc.gov/nchs/nhanes.htm.

Center for Disease Control and Prevention (CDC). (2010). *U.S. obesity trends. Trends by state 1985-2008.* Available: www.cdc.gov/obesity/data/trends.html.

Center for Disease Control and Prevention (CDC). (2010). *National physical activity plan.* Available: www.physicalactivityplan.org.

Cohen, G. (1993). *Women in sport*. Newbury Park, CA: Sage.

Cone, T.P., & Cone, S.L. (2005). *Assessing dance in elementary physical education*. Reston, VA: American Alliance for Health, Physical Education, Recreation and Dance.

Cooper Institute. (2004). *FITNESSGRAM/ACTIVITYGRAM test administration manual* (3rd ed.), Gregory J. Welk & Marilu D. Meredith (Eds.). Champaign, IL: Human Kinetics.

Cooper Institute. (2007). *FITNESSGRAM/ACTIVITYGRAM test administration manual* (4th ed.), Gregory J. Welk & Marilu D. Meredith (Eds.). Champaign, IL: Human Kinetics.

Corbin, C.B. (1994). The fitness curriculum: Climbing the stairway to lifetime fitness. In R.R. Pate & R.C. Hohn (Eds.), *Health and fitness through physical education* (pp. 59–66). Champaign, IL: Human Kinetics.

Corbin, C., Le Masurier, G., & Lambdin, D. (2007). *Fitness for life middle school*. Champaign, IL: Human Kinetics.

Corbin, C., & Lindsey, L. (2007). *Fitness for life* (6th ed.) Champaign, IL: Human Kinetics.

Corbin, C.B., & Pangrazi, R.P. (2002). Physical activity for children: How much is enough? In G.J. Welk, R.J. Morrow, & H.B. Falls (Eds.), *FITNESSGRAM reference guide* (p. 7). Dallas, TX: Cooper Institute.

Corbin, C., & Pangrazi, R. (2008). FITNESSGRAM and ACTIVITYGRAM: An introduction. In G.J. Welk & M.D. Meredith (Eds.), *Fitnessgram/Activitygram reference guide* (pp. 1–3). Dallas, TX: Cooper Institute.

Corbin, C.B., Pangrazi, R.P., & Le Masurier, G.C. (2004). Physical activity for children: Current patterns and guidelines. *President's Council on Physical Fitness and Sports Research Digest, 5*(2), 1–8.

Corbin, C.B., Welk, G.J., Corbin, W.R., & Welk, K.A. (2009). *Concepts of fitness and wellness: A comprehensive lifestyle approach* (8th ed.). New York: McGraw Hill.

Corbin, C.B., Welk, G.J., Lindsey, R., & Corbin, W.R. (2004). *Concepts of fitness and wellness*. (5th ed.). New York: McGraw-Hill.

Cowen, V., & Adams, T. (2005). Physical and perceptual benefits of yoga asana practice: Result of a pilot study. *Journal of Bodywork and Movement Therapies, 9*, 211–219.

Coyle, E.F. (1990). Detraining and retention of training-induced adaptations. *Sports Science Exchange, 2*(23). Chicago: Gatorade Sports Science Institute.

Coyle, E.F., Martin, W.H., Sinacore, D.R., Joyner, M.J., Hagberg, J.M., & Hollozy, J.O. (1984). Time course of loss of adaptations after stopping prolonged intense endurance training. *Journal of Applied Physiology, 57*, 1857–1864.

Craft, D. (1994). Strategies for teaching inclusively. *Teaching Elementary Physical Education, 5*(5), 8–9.

Crouter, S.E., Schneider, P.L., & Bassett, D.R. Jr. (2005). Spring-levered versus peizo-electric pedometer accuracy in overweight and obese adults. *Medicine and Science in Sports and Exercise, 37*(10), 1673–1679.

Crouter, S.E., Schneider, P.L., Karabulut, M., & Bassett, D.R. Jr. (2003). Validity of 10 electronic pedometers for measuring steps, distance, and energy cost. *Medicine and Science in Sports and Exercise, 35*(8), 1455–1460.

Cuddihy, T.F., Pangrazi, R.P., & Tomson, L.M. (2005). Pedometers: Answers to FAQs from teachers. *JOPERD, 76*(2), 36–40, 55.

Cumming, G.R., Everatt, D., & Hastman, L. (1978). Bruce treadmill test in children: Normal values in a clinic population. *American Journal of Cardiology, 59*, 60–75.

Cumming, G.R., & Langford, S. (1985). Comparison of nine exercise tests used in pediatric cardiology. In R.A. Binkhorst, H.C.G. Kemper, & W.H.M. Saris (Eds.), *Children and exercise XI, 58*–68. Champaign, IL: Human Kinetics.

Dale, D., & Corbin, C. (2000). Physical activity participation of high school graduates following exposure to conceptual or traditional physical education. *Research Quarterly for Exercise and Sport, 71*, 61–68.

Dale, D., Corbin, C.B., & Dale, K.S. (2000). Restricting opportunities to be active during school time: Do children compensate by increasing physical activity levels after school? *Research Quarterly for Exercise and Sport, 71*, 240–248.

Daley, A.J. (2002). School based physical activity in the United Kingdom: Can it create physically active adults? *Quest, 54*, 21–33.

Daniels, S.R., Arnett, D., Eckel, R.H., Gidding, S.S., Hayman, L., Kumanyika, S., Robinson, T.N., Scott, B.J., St. Jeor, S., & Williams, C.L. (2005). Overweight in children and adolescents: Pathophysiology, consequences, prevention, and treatment. *Circulation, 111*, 1999–2012.

Darst, P., & Pangrazi, R. (2007). *Dynamic physical education for secondary school students* (6th ed.). San Francisco: Benjamin Cummings.

Davison, B. (1998). *Creative physical activities and equipment: Building a quality program on a shoestring budget*. Champaign, IL: Human Kinetics.

Deci, E.L., & Ryan, R.M. (1985). *Intrinsic motivation and self-determination in human behavior*. New York: Plenum.

DePauw, K. (1996). Students with disabilities in physical education. In S. Silverman & C. Ennis (Eds.), *Student learning in physical education: Applying research to enhance instruction* (pp. 101–124). Champaign, IL: Human Kinetics.

Deurenberg, P., Van der kooy, K., Leenan, R., Westrate, J.A., & Seidell, J.C. (1991). Sex and age specific population prediction formulas for estimating body composition from bioelectrical impedance: A cross validation study. *International Journal of Obesity, 15*, 17–25.

Dietary guidelines for Americans 2005. (2005). U.S. Department of Health and Human Services (DHHS) and U.S. Department of Agriculture (USDA). Available: www.healthierus.gov/dietaryguidelines.

Dietary reference intakes: Guiding principles for nutrition. Report. Dietary reference intakes: Guiding principles for nutrition labeling and fortification. (2003). Institute of Medicine of the National Academies.

Dishman, R.K., & Sallis, J.F. (1994). Determinants and interventions for physical activity and exercise. In C.

Bouchard, R.J. Shepard, & T. Stephens (Eds.), *Physical activity, fitness, and health: International proceedings and consensus statement* (pp. 214-238). Champaign, IL: Human Kinetics.

Duncan, J.S., Schofield, G., Duncan, E.K., & Hinckson, E.A. (2007). Effects of age, walking speed, and body composition on pedometer accuracy in children. *Research Quarterly for Exercise and Sport, 78*(5), 420-428.

Ennis, C.D. (1996). Designing curriculum for quality physical education programs. In B.F. Hennessy (Ed.), *Physical education sourcebook* (pp. 13-37). Champaign, IL: Human Kinetics.

Epstein, L.H., Paluch, R.A., Gordy, C.C., & Dorn, J. (2000). Decreasing sedentary behaviors in treating pediatric obesity. *Archives of Pediatric and Adolescent Medicine, 154,* 220-226.

Epstein, L.H., Valoski, A., Wing, R.R., Perkins, K.A., Fernstrom, M., Marks, B., & McCurley, J. (1989). Perception of eating and exercise in children as a function of child and parent weight status. *Appetite, 12,* 105-118.

Faigenbaum, A.D. (2001). Physical activity for youth: Tips for keeping kids healthy and fit. *ACSM Fit Society Page,* April-June, 3-4.

Faigenbaum, A.D. (2003). Youth resistance training. *PCPFS Research Digest, 4*(3), 1-8.

Faigenbaum, A.D. (2007). Resistance training for children and adolescents: Are there health outcomes? *American Journal of Lifestyle Medicine, 1,* 190-200.

Faigenbaum, A., Bellucci, M., Bernieri, A., Bakker, B., & Hoorens, K. (2005). Effects of different warm-up protocols on fitness performance in children. *Journal of Strength and Conditioning Research, 19,* 376-381.

Faigenbaum, A., & Chu, D. (2001). Plyometric training for children and adolescents. *American College of Sports Medicine Current Comment,* December.

Faigenbaum, A., Kang, K., McFarland, J., Bloom, J., Magnatta, J., Ratamess, N., & Hoffman, J. (2006). Acute effects of different warm-up protocols on anaerobic performance in teenage athletes. *Pediatric Exercise Science, 17,* 64-75.

Faigenbaum, A.D., Kraemer, W.J., Cahill, B., Chandler, J., Dziados, J., Elfink, L.D., Forman, E., et al. (1996). Youth resistance training: Position statement paper and literature review. *Strength and Conditioning, 18*(6): 62-75.

Faigenbaum, A., & McFarland, J. (2007). Guidelines for implementing a dynamic warm-up for physical education. *Journal of Physical Education, Recreation, and Dance, 78,* 25-28.

Faigenbaum, A.D., & Westcott, W.L. (2000). *Strength and power for young athletes.* Champaign, IL: Human Kinetics.

Faigenbaum, A.D., & Westcott, W.L. (2009). *Youth strength training: Programs for health, fitness, and sport.* Champaign, IL: Human Kinetics.

Faigenbaum, A.D., Westcott, W.L., Loud, R., & Long, C. (1999). The effects of different resistance training protocols on muscular strength and endurance development in children. *Pediatrics, 104*(1), e5.

Faigenbaum, A.D., Zaichkowsky, L.D., Westcott, W.L., Micheli, L.J., & Fehlandt, A.F. (1993). The effects of a twice-a-week strength training program on children. *Pediatric Exercise Science, 5,* 339-346.

Falk, B., & Tenenbaum, G. (1996). The effectiveness of resistance training in children: A meta-analysis. *Sports Medicine, 3,* 176-186.

FDA Center for Food Safety and Applied Nutrition. (2010). Medline Plus: Nutrition. wwwnlm.nih.gov/medlineplus/nutrition.html.

Fernandez, J.R., Redden, D.T., Pietrobelli, A., & Allison, D.B. (2004). Waist circumference percentiles in nationally representative samples of African-American, European-American, and Mexican-American children and adolescents. *Journal of Pediatrics, 145,* 439-44.

Ferraro, K.F., Thorpe, R.J. Jr., & Wilkinson, J.A. (2003). The life course of severe obesity: Does childhood overweight matter? *Journal of Gerontology, 58B*(2), S110-S119.

Finding your way to a healthier you: Based on the "Dietary Guidelines for Americans." DHHS and USDA. (2005). Available: www.health.gov/dietaryguidelines/dga2005/document/pdf/brochure.pdf.

Fleck, S.J. (1988). Cardiovascular adaptations to resistance training. *Medicine and Science in Sport and Exercise, 22,* 265-274.

Flegal, K.M., Carroll, M.D., Ogden, C.L., & Curtin, L.R. Prevalence and trends in obesity among US adults, 1999-2008. (2010). *Journal of the American Medical Association, 303*(3): 235-241.

Food and Drug Administration (FDA). (2008). *Guidance for industry: A food labeling guide.* Available: www.fda.gov/Food/GuidanceComplianceRegulatoryInformation/GuidanceDocuments/FoodLabelingNutrition/FoodLabelingGuide/default.htm.

Foster, E.R., Hartinger, K., & Smith, K.A. (1992). *Fitness fun.* Champaign, IL: Human Kinetics.

Franks, B.D., & Howley, E.T. (1998). *Fitness leader's handbook* (2nd ed.). Champaign, IL: Human Kinetics.

Fredette, D.M. (2001). Exercise recommendations for flexibility and range of motion. In *ACSM's resource manual for guidelines for exercise testing and prescription,* 4th ed. (pp. 468-477). Philadelphia: Lippincott, Williams, and Wilkins.

Freedman, D.S., Khan, L.K., Dietz, W.H., Srinivasan, S.R., & Berenson, G.S. (2001). Relationship of childhood obesity to coronary heart disease risk factors in adulthood: The Bogalusa heart study. *Pediatrics, 108,* 712-718.

Gallo, A.M., Sheehy, D., Patton, K., & Griffin, L. (2006). Benefits and barriers: What are you committed to? *Journal of physical education, recreation, and dance, 77*(8), 46-50.

Gardner, H. (1983). *Frames of mind: The theory of multiple intelligences.* New York: Basic Books.

Gardner, H. (1993). *Multiple intelligences: The theory in practice.* New York: Basic Books.

Gellish, R.L., Goslin, B.R., Olson, R.E., Mcdonald, A., Russi, G.D., & Moudgil, V.K. (2007). Longitudinal modeling of the relationship between age and maximal heart rate. *Medicine and Science in Sports and Exercise, 39*(5), 822–829.

Goldberg, L., & Twist, P. (2007). *Strength ball training* (2nd ed.). Champaign, IL: Human Kinetics.

Graham, G. (1992). *Teaching children physical education: Becoming a master teacher.* Champaign, IL: Human Kinetics.

Graham, G. (2008). *Teaching children physical education* (3rd ed.). Champaign, IL: Human Kinetics.

Graham, G., Holt/Hale, S.A., & Parker, M. (2010). *Children moving: A reflective approach to teaching physical education* (8th ed.). St. Louis, MO: McGraw-Hill.

Graser, S.V., Pangrazi, R.P., & Vincent, W.J. (2009). Step it up: Activity intensity using pedometers: If you think pedometers can't measure MVPA, think again. *JOPHERD, 22*(3), 22–24.

Greenberg, J.S., Dintiman, G.V., & Myers Oakes, B. (2004). *Physical fitness and wellness: Changing the way you look, feel, and perform* (3rd ed.). Champaign, IL: Human Kinetics.

Greene, L., & Pate, R. (1997). *Training for young distance runners.* Champaign, IL: Human Kinetics.

Griffin, J.C. (2006). *Client-centered exercise prescription* (2nd ed.). Champaign, IL: Human Kinetics.

Grunbaum, J., Kann, L., Kinchen, S., Williams, B., Ross, J., Lowry, R., & Kolbe, L. (2002). *Youth risk behavior surveillance—United States, 2001.* June 28, 2002/51 (SS04); 1–64 www.cdc.gov/mmwr/preview/mmwrhtml/ss5104a1.htm (accessed February 5, 2004).

Guidance on how to understand and use the nutrition facts panel on food labels. (2004). U.S. Food and Drug Administration Center for Food Safety and Applied Nutrition. Available: www.cfsan.fda.gov/˜dms/foodlab.html.

Guo, S.S., Roche, A.F., Chumlea, W.C., Gardner, J.D., & Siervogel, R.M. (1994). The predictive value of childhood BMI values for overweight at age 34 y. *American Journal of Clinical Nutrition, 59,* 1810–1819.

Harris, J., & Elbourn, J. (1997). *Teaching health-related exercise at key stages 1 and 2.* Champaign, IL: Human Kinetics.

Harrison, J.M., Blakemore, C.L., & Buck, M. (2001). *Instructional strategies for secondary school physical education* (5th ed.). New York: McGraw-Hill.

Harter, S. (1999). *The construction of the self: A developmental perspective.* New York: Guilford Press.

Harter, S., Waters, P.L., & Whitesell, N.R. (1998). Relational self-worth: Differences in perceived worth as a person across interpersonal contexts among adolescents. *Child Development, 69,* 756–766.

Haskell, W.L., Lee, I.M., Pate, R.R., Powell, K.E., Blair, S.N., Franklin, B.A., et al. (2007). Physical activity and public health: Updated recommendation for adults from the American College of Sports Medicine and the American Heart Association. *Medicine and Science in Sports and Exercise, 39*(8), 1423–1434.

Hass, C.J., Faigenbaum, M.S., & Franklin, B.A. (2001). Prescription of resistance training for healthy populations. *Sports Medicine, 31*(14), 953–964.

Hastie, P. (2003). *Teaching for lifetime physical activity through quality high school physical education.* San Francisco: Benjamin Cummings.

Hatano, Y. (1993). Use of the pedometer for promoting daily walking exercise. *International Council for Health, Physical Education and Recreation, 29,* 4–8.

Hayes, E., & Silberman, L. (2007). Incorporating video games into physical education. *Journal of Physical Education, Recreation and Dance, 78*(3): 18–24.

Haynes-Dusel. (2001). Block scheduling: A catalyst for change in middle and high school physical education. *Research Quarterly for Exercise and Sport, 72,* A-67.

Hellison, D. (2003). *Teaching responsibility through physical activity* (2nd ed.). Champaign, IL: Human Kinetics.

Heyward, V.H. (2002). *Advanced fitness assessment and exercise prescription* (4th ed.). Champaign, IL: Human Kinetics.

Heyward, V.H. (2010). *Advanced fitness assessment and exercise prescription* (6th ed.). Champaign, IL: Human Kinetics.

Heyward, V.H., & Wagner, D.R. (2004). *Applied body composition* (2nd ed.). Champaign, IL: Human Kinetics (pp. 1–280).

Heyward, V.H., & Stolarczyk, L.M. (2004). *Applied body composition assessment* (2nd ed.). Champaign, IL: Human Kinetics.

Hichwa, J. (1998). *Right fielders are people too: An inclusive approach to teaching middle school physical education.* Champaign, IL: Human Kinetics.

Himberg, C., Hutchinson, G., & Roussell, J. (2002). *Teaching secondary physical education: Preparing adolescents to be active for life.* Champaign, IL: Human Kinetics.

Hopple, C. (2005). *Performance-based assessment in elementary education* (2nd ed.). Champaign, IL: Human Kinetics.

Hopple, C.J. (2005). *Elementary physical education teaching and assessment: A practical guide.* Champaign, IL: Human Kinetics.

Horn, T.S., & Hasbrook, C.A. (1986). Informational components influencing children's perceptions of their physical competence. In M.R. Weiss & D. Gould (Eds.), *Sport for children and youth* (pp. 81–88). Champaign, IL: Human Kinetics.

Horn, T.S., & Hasbrook, C.A. (1987). Psychological characteristics and the criteria children use for self-evaluation. *Journal of Sport Psychology, 9,* 208–221.

Houston-Wilson, K. (1995). Alternate assessment procedures. In J.A. Seaman (Ed.), *Physical Best and individuals with disabilities: A handbook for inclusion in fitness programs* (pp. 91–109). Reston, VA: AAHPERD.

Houtkeeper, L.B., Going, S.B., Westfall, C.H., Roche, A.F., & Van Loan, M. (1992). Bioelectrical impedance estimation of fat-free body mass in children and youth: A cross-validation study. *Journal of Applied Physiology, 72,* 366–373.

Houtkeeper, L.B., Lohman, T.G., Going, S.B., & Hall, M.C. (1989). Validity of bioelectrical impedance for body composition assessment in children. *Journal of Applied Physiology, 66,* 814–821.

Huitt, W. (2004). Bloom et al.'s taxonomy of the cognitive domain. Educational Psychology Interactive. Valdosta, GA: Valdosta State University. Retrieved [4/22/09], from http://chiron.valdosta.edu/whuitt/col/cogsys/bloom.html.

Hutchinson, G.E. (1995). Gender-fair teaching in physical education. *Journal of Physical Education, Recreation and Dance, 60*(2), 23-24.

Institute of Medicine of the National Academies. (2001). *Dietary reference intakes: Applications in dietary assessment.* Washington, DC: National Academies Press.

Institute of Medicine of the National Academies. (2005). *Dietary reference intakes: Water, potassium, sodium, chloride, and sulfate.* Available: www.iom.edu/Reports/2004/Dietary-Reference-Intake-Water-Potassium-Sodium-Chloride-and-Sulfate.

International Life Sciences Institute (ILSI). (1997). *Physical activity message for parents from new survey: No more excuses.* Press release, July 1.

Jackson, A., Morrow, J., Hill, D., & Dishman, R. (2004). *Physical activity for health and fitness.* Champaign, IL: Human Kinetics.

Jacobs, J.E., & Eccles, J.S. (2000). Parents, task values, and real-life achievement related choices. In C. Sansone & J.M. Harackiewicz (Eds.), *Intrinsic motivation* (pp. 405-439). San Diego: Academic Press.

Jacobs, J.E., Lanza, S., Osgood, D.W., Eccles, J.S., & Wigfield, A. (2002). Changes in children's self-competence and values: Gender and domain differences across grades one through twelve. *Child Development, 73*(2), 509-527.

James, A.R., Griffin, L.L. and Dodds, P. (2008). The relationship between instructional alignment and the ecology of physical education. *Journal of teaching physical education, 27*(3) 308-326.

Janz, K.F., Golden, J.C., Hansen, J.R., & Mahoney, L.T. (1992). Heart rate monitoring of physical activity in children and adolescents: The Muscatine study. *Pediatrics, 89*, 256-261.

Janz, K.F., Levy, S.M., Burns, T.L., Torner, J.C., Willing, M.C., & Warren, J.J. (2002). Fatness, physical activity and television viewing in children during the adiposity rebound period: The Iowa Bone Development Study. *Preventative Medicine, 35*, 563-571.

Jobe, M. (1998). Disabilities awareness field days. *Teaching Elementary Physical Education, 9*(1), 10-11.

Joint Committee on National Health Education Standards. (1995). *National health education standards: Achieving health literacy.* American Cancer Society. Atlanta, GA.

Jones, A.M. (2002). Running economy is negatively related to sit-and-reach test performance in international-standard distance runners. *International Journal of Sports Medicine, 23*, 40-43.

Jones, B.H., & Knapik, J.J. (1999). Physical training and exercise-related injuries. *Sports Medicine, 27*, 111-125.

Karlsson, M.K., Ahlborg, H., Obrant, K.J., Nyquist, F., Lindberg, H., & Karlsson, C. (2002). Exercise during growth and young adulthood is associated with reduced fracture risk in old ages. *Journal of Bone Mineral Research, 17*(suppl. 1), S297.

Katzmarzyk, P.T., Srinivasan, S.R., Chen, W., Malina, R.M., Bouchard, C., & Berenson, G.S. (2004). Body mass index, waist circumference, and clustering of cardiovascular disease risk factors in a biracial sample of children and adolescents. *Pediatrics, 114*(2), e198-205.

KidsHealth>Teens>Food and Fitness>Nutrition Basics>Food Labels. (2010). http://kidshealth.org/teen/food_fitness/nutrition/food_label.htl#.

Kim, H.K., Tanaka, K., Nakadomo, F., Watanabe, K., & Marsuura, Y. (1993). Fat-free mass in Japanese boys predicted from bioelectrical impedance and anthropometric variables. *Medicine and Science in Sport and Exercise, 25*, S59. (Abstract).

Kirkpatrick, B., & Birnbaum, B. (1997). *Lessons from the heart: Individualizing physical education with heart rate monitors.* Champaign, IL: Human Kinetics.

Kleiner, S. (1999). Water: An essential but overlooked nutrient. *JADA (Journal of the American Dietetic Association), 99*, 200-206.

Knudson, D.V., Magnusson, P., & McHugh, M. (2000). Current issues in flexibility fitness. In C. Corbin and B. Pangrazi (Eds.), *The president's council on physical fitness and sports digest*, 3rd ser., no. 10, Washington, DC: Department of Health and Human Services.

Kraemer, W.J., & Fleck, S.J. (2005). *Strength training for young adults* (2nd ed.). Champaign, IL: Human Kinetics.

Krishnamoorthy, J.S., Hart, C., & Jajalian, E. (2006). The epidemic of childhood obesity: Review of research and implications for public policy. *Soc Policy Rep., 20*(2), 3-17.

Kurtzweil, P. (2003). "Daily Values" encourage healthy diet. www.fda.gov/fdac/special/foodlabel/dvs.html.

Kushner, R.F., Schoeller, D.A., Field, C.R., & Danford, L. (1992). Is the impedance index (ht2/R) significant in predicting total body water? *American Journal of Clinical Nutrition, 56*, 835-839.

Lacy, A., & Hastad, D. (2007). *Measurement and evaluation in physical education and exercise science* (5th ed.). San Francisco: Benjamin Cummings.

Lambert, L. (2007). *Standards based assessment of student learning: A comprehensive approach* (2nd ed.). Reston, VA: American Alliance for Health, Physical Education, Recreation and Dance.

Lavay, B., French, R., & Henderson, H. (2006). *Positive behavior management in physical activity settings* (2nd ed.). Champaign, IL: Human Kinetics.

LeFevre, D. (2002). *Best new games.* Champaign, IL: Human Kinetics.

Le Masurier, G.C., Beighle, A., Corbin, C.B., Darst, P.W., Morgan, C., Pangrazi, R.P., Wilde, B., & Vincent, S. (2010). Pedometer-determined physical activity levels of youth. *Journal of Physical Activity and Health 2*(2): 153-162.

Le Masurier, G.C., Lee, S.M., & Tudor-Locke, C. (2004). Motion sensor accuracy under controlled and free-living conditions. *Medicine & Science in Sports & Exercise, 36*(5), 905-910.

Let's Move. America's Move to Create a Healthier Generation of Kids. (2010). Retrieved February 22, 2010 from www.letsmove.gov.

Levi, J., Vinter, S., St. Laurent, R., & Segal, L. (2008). *F as in fat: How obesity policies are failing in America, 2008.* Washington, DC: Trust for America's Health & Robert Wood Johnson Foundation.

Lieberman, L., & Houston-Wilson, C. (2002). *Strategies for inclusion: A handbook for physical educators.* Champaign, IL: Human Kinetics.

Lindsey, E. (2003). *Strengthening your physical education program with innovative fitness strategies and activities (grades 6–12): Resource handbook.* Bellevue, WA: Bureau of Education and Research.

Lindsey, R., & Corbin, C. (1989). Questionable exercises—some safer alternatives. *Journal of Physical Education, Recreation and Dance,* (October), 60: 26–32.

Lohman, T.G. (1992). *Advances in body composition assessment: Current issues in exercise science series.* Monograph no. 3. Champaign, IL: Human Kinetics.

Lowry, S. (1995). A multicultural perspective on planning. *Teaching Elementary Physical Education, 6*(3), 14–15.

Lubans, D.R., Morgan, P.J., & Tudor-Locke, C. (2009). A systematic review of studies using pedometers to promote physical activity among youth. *Preventive Medicine, 48*(4), 307–315.

Lukaski, H.C., Johnson, P.E., Bolonchuk, W.W., & Lykken, G.I. (1985). Assessment of fat-free mass using bioelectric impedance measurements of the human body. *American Journal of Clinical Nutrition, 41,* 810–817.

Lund, J. (2010). *Creating rubrics for physical education* (2nd ed.). Reston, VA: American Alliance for Health, Physical Education, Recreation and Dance.

Lund, J.L., & Kirk, M.F. (2002). *Performance-based assessment for middle and high school physical education.* Champaign, IL: Human Kinetics.

Malina, R.M. (1996). Tracking of physical activity and physical fitness across the life span. *Research Quarterly for Sport and Exercise, 67,* 48–57.

Malina, R.M. (2001). Tracking of physical activity and physical fitness across the life span. *PCPFS Research Digest, 3*(14), 1–8.

Marcus, B.H., & Forsyth. (2003). *Motivating people to be physically active.* Champaign, IL: Human Kinetics.

Marshall, S.J., Levy, S.S., Tudor-Locke, C.E., Kolkhorst, F.W., Wooten, K.M., MingMing, J., Macera, C.A., & Ainsworth, B.E. (2009). Translating physical activity recommendations into a pedometer-based step goal: 3000 steps in 30 minutes. *American Journal of Preventive Medicine, 36*(5), 410–415.

Martens, R. (2004). *Successful coaching.* Champaign, IL: Human Kinetics.

Mayo Clinic. (2009). *Nutrition and healthy eating: Is vitamin water a healthier choice than plain water?* Available: www.mayoclinic.com/health/vitamin-water/ANO1734.

McAtee, R.E., & Charland, J. (1999). Facilitated stretching. Champaign, IL: Human Kinetics.

McCraken, B. (2001). *It's not just gym anymore: Teaching secondary students how to be active for life.* Champaign, IL: Human Kinetics.

McDowell, M., Briefel, R., Alaimo, K., et al. (1994). Energy and macronutrient intakes of persons ages 2 months and over in the United States: Third national health and nutrition examination survey, phase 1, 1988–1991. *Advance Data from Vital and Health Statistics,* no. 255. Hyattsville, MD: National Center for Health Statistics.

McKenzie, T., & Kahan, D. (2008). Physical activity, public health, and elementary schools. *Elementary School Journal, 108*(3), 171–180.

Mears, B. (2006). Making wise technology purchases. *Journal of Physical Education, Recreation and Dance, 77*(8).

MedlinePlus: Teen health. DHHS. NIH National Library of Medicine. *Health headlines: Vitamin D.* NIH publication #09-4328.

Melograno, V.J. (2006). *Professional and student portfolios for physical education* (2nd ed.). Champaign, IL: Human Kinetics.

Middle and Secondary School Physical Education Council (MASSPEC). (1995). *Appropriate practices for middle school education.* Reston, VA: NASPE.

Mitchell, M., Barton, G., & Stanne, K. (2000). The role of homework in helping students meet physical education goals. *Journal of Physical Education Recreation and Dance, 71*(5).

Mohnsen, B.J. (1997). *Teaching middle school physical education: A blueprint for developing an exemplary program.* Champaign, IL: Human Kinetics.

Mohnsen, B.J. (2003). *Teaching middle school physical education: A standards-based approach for grades 5–8.* Champaign, IL: Human Kinetics.

Morris, G.S.D., & Stiehl, J. (1998). *Changing kids' games* (2nd ed.). Champaign, IL: Human Kinetics.

Mosston, M., & Ashworth, S. (2002). *Teaching physical education* (5th ed.). San Francisco: Benjamin Cummings.

Mujika, I., & Padilla, S. (2001). Cardiorespiratory and metabolic characteristics of detraining in humans. *Medicine and Science in Sports and Exercise, 33*(3), 413–421.

My Pyramid Food Guidance System. USDA Center for Nutrition Policy and Promotion. www.mypyramid.gov.

Nader, Philip R., Bradley, Robert H., Houts, Renate M., McRitchie, Susan L., & O'Brien, Marion. (2008). Moderate-to-vigorous physical activity from ages 9 to 15 years. *JAMA, 300*(3), 295–305.

National Association for Sport and Physical Education (NASPE). (1995). *Moving into the future: National standards for physical education.* Reston, VA: NASPE.

National Association for Sport and Physical Education (NASPE). (1998). *Physical activity for children: A statement of guidelines.* Reston, VA: NASPE.

National Association for Sport and Physical Education (NASPE). (1999). Healthy people 2010. *NASPE News,* no. 52 (winter), 1.

National Association for Sport and Physical Education (NASPE). (2004a). *Moving into the future: National standards for physical education* (2nd ed.). Reston, VA: NASPE.

National Association for Sport and Physical Education (NASPE). (2004b). *Physical activity for children: A statement of guidelines for children ages 5–12* (2nd ed.). Reston, VA: NASPE.

National Association for Sport and Physical Education (NASPE). (2005a). *Physical Best activity guide: Elementary level* (2nd ed.). Champaign, IL: Human Kinetics.

National Association for Sport and Physical Education (NASPE). (2005b). *Physical Best activity guide: Middle and high school levels* (2nd ed.). Champaign, IL: Human Kinetics.

National Association for Sport and Physical Education (NASPE). (2008). *Comprehensive school physical activity programs* [Position statement]. Reston, VA: NASPE.

National Association for Sport and Physical Education (NASPE). (2009). *Appropriate instructional practice for elementary school physical education* (3rd ed.). Reston, VA: NASPE.

National Association for Sport and Physical Education (NASPE). (2010a). Guidelines for participation in youth sport programs: Specialization versus multiple-sport participation [Position statement]. Reston, VA: Author. Retrieved from www.aahperd.org/naspe/standards/upload/Participation-in-Youth-Sport-Programs-2010.pdf.

National Association for Sport and Physical Education (NASPE). (2010b). *Shape of the nation: Status of physical education in the USA*. Reston, VA: NASPE.

National Center for Chronic Disease Prevention and Health Promotion (NCCDPHP), U.S. Centers for Disease Control and Prevention. (2003). *Physical activity and good nutrition: Essential elements to prevent chronic diseases and obesity.* www.cdc.gov/nccdphp/aag/.

National Cholesterol Education Program. (1991). Report of the expert panel on population strategies for blood cholesterol reduction program. *Circulation, 83,* 2154–2232.

National Consortium for Physical Education and Recreation for Individuals With Disabilities. (1995). *Adapted physical education national standards.* Champaign, IL: Human Kinetics.

National Dance Association. (1996). *National standards for dance education: What every young American should know and be able to do in dance.* Reston, VA: National Dance Association.

National Eating Disorders Association. (2003). *Anorexia nervosa and bulimia nervosa.* www.nationaleatingdisorders.org.

National Strength and Conditioning Association (NSCA). (2008). *Essentials of strength training and conditioning* (3rd ed.). Champaign, IL: Human Kinetics.

National Strength and Conditioning Association (NSCA). (2007). *Strength training.* L.E. Brown, Ed. Champaign, IL: Human Kinetics.

Nestle, M., & Ludwig, D.S. (2010). Front-of-package food labels: Public health or propaganda? *JAMA, 303*(8), 771–2.

Nieman, D. (2008). You asked for it: Question authority. *ACSM'S Health & Fitness Journal, 12,* 5–6.

Nilges, L. (1996). Ingredients for a gender equitable physical education program. *Teaching Elementary Physical Education, 7*(5), 28–29.

Norman, G.J., Nutter, S.K., Ryan, S., Sallis, J.F., Calfas, K.J., & Patrick, K. (2006). Community design and access to recreational facilities as correlates of adolescent physical activity and body-mass index. *Journal of Physical Activity and Health, 3*(Suppl 1), S118–S128.

Nutrition for Weight Loss: What You Need to Know About Fad Diets, Information about fad diets from the American Academy of Family Physicians. familydoctor.org/online/famdocen/home/healthy/food/improve/784.html–33.

Ogden, C.L., Carroll, M.D., & Flegal, K.M. (2008). High body mass index for age among US children and adolescents, 2003–2006. *JAMA, 299*(20), 2401–2405.

Ogden, C., Carrol, M., Curtin, L., Lamb, M., & Flegel, K. (2010). Prevalence of high body mass index in US children and adolescents, 2007–2008. *Journal of the American Medical Association, 303*(3), 242–249.

Ogden, C.L., Flegal, K.M., Carrol, M.D., & Johnson, C.L. (2002). Prevalence and trends in overweight among U.S. children and adolescents, 1999–2000. *Journal of the American Medical Association, 288,* 1728–32.

Ormrod, J.E. (1995). *Educational psychology principles and applications.* Columbus, OH: Merrill.

Pangrazi, R., Beighle, A., & Sidman, C.A. (2007). *Pedometer power: Using pedometers in school and community* (2nd ed.). Champaign, IL: Human Kinetics.

Pangrazi, R.P., & Corbin, C. (1994). *Teaching strategies for improving youth fitness* (2nd ed.). Reston, VA: AAHPERD.

Pangrazi, R.P., & Corbin, C.B. (2008). Factors that influence physical fitness in children and adolescents. In G.J. Welk & M.D. Meredith (Eds.), *Fitnessgram/Activitygram Reference Guide.* Dallas, TX: Cooper Institute.

Pate, R.R. (1995). Promoting activity and fitness. In L.W.Y. Cheung & J.B. Richmond (Eds.), *Child health, nutrition, and physical activity* (pp. 139–145). Champaign, IL: Human Kinetics.

Payne, V.G., & Morrow, J.R. Jr. (1993). Exercise and $\dot{V}O_2max$ in children: A meta-analysis. *Research Quarterly for Exercise and Sport, 64,* 305–313.

Pettifor, B. (1999). *Physical education methods for classroom teachers* (Champaign, IL: Human Kinetics.

Powers, S.K., & Dodd, S.L. (1997). *The essentials of total fitness: Exercise, nutrition, and wellness.* Boston: Allyn & Bacon.

President's Council on Fitness and Sports. (2008a). *The president's challenge: Physical activity and fitness awards program.* www.presidentschallenge.org.

President's Council on Physical Fitness and Sports. (2008b). *Get fit and be active: A handbook for youths ages 6–17.* www.presidentschallenge.org/pdf/getfit.pdf

President's Council on Physical Fitness and Sports. (2009). Promoting positive youth development through physical activity. *Research Digest* 10(3): 1-8.

Prochaska, J.O., Norcross, J.C., & DiClemete, C.C. (1994). *Changing for good: The revolutionary program that explains the six stages of change and teaches you how to free yourself from bad habits.* New York: William Morrow.

PSA/HPERD. (1994). *P.E.–L.I.F.E. project, designing assessments: Applications for physical education.*

Raffini, J.P. (1993). *Winners without losers: Structures and strategies for increasing student motivation to learn.* Needham Heights, MA: Allyn & Bacon.

Rink, J. (2009). *Teaching physical education for learning* (4th ed.). New York: McGraw-Hill.

Rink, J. (2010). *Teaching physical education for learning* (6th ed.). St. Louis, MO: McGraw-Hill.

Ross, R., Freeman, J., & Janssen, P. (2000). Exercise alone is an effective strategy for reducing obesity and related comorbidities. *Exercise and Sport Science Review, 28,* 165-170.

Rowland, T.W. (1990). *Exercise and children's health.* Champaign, IL: Human Kinetics.

Rowland, T.W. (1996). *Developmental exercise physiology.* Champaign, IL: Human Kinetics.

Rowland, T.W. (2002). Telephone conversation and email with Jennie Gilbert, 3 December.

Rowland, T.W. (2005). *Children's exercise physiology.* Champaign, IL: Human Kinetics.

Rowland, T.W. (2007). Physical activity, fitness, and children. In C. Bouchard, S.N. Blair, & W.L. Haskell (Eds.), *Physical activity and health* (pp. 247-257). Champaign, IL: Human Kinetics.

Rowlands, A.V., & Eston, R.G. (2005). Comparison of accelerometer and pedometer measures of physical activity in boys and girls, ages 8-10, *Research Quarterly for Exercise and Sport, 76(3),* 251-257.

Ryan, R.M., & Deci, E.L. (2000). Self-determination theory and the facilitation of intrinsic motivation, social development, and well-being. *American Psychologist, 55,* 68-78.

Sadker, M., & Sadker, D. (1995). *Failing at fairness: How our schools cheat girls.* New York: Simon & Schuster.

Sallis, J.F. (1994). Determinants of physical activity behavior in children. In R.R. Pate & R.C. Hohn (Eds.), *Health and fitness through physical education* (pp. 31-43). Champaign, IL: Human Kinetics.

Sallis, J.F. (2000). Age-related decline in physical activity: A synthesis of human and animal studies. *Medicine and Science in Sports and Exercise, 32*(9), 1598-1600.

Sallis, J.F., & Patrick, K. (1994). Physical activity guidelines for adolescents: Consensus statement. *Pediatric Exercise Science, 6,* 302-314.

Sallis, J.F., Prochaska, J.J., Taylor, W.C., Hill, J.O., & Geraci, J.C. (1999). Correlates of physical activity in a national sample of girls and boys in grades 4 through 12. *Health Psychology, 18,* 410-415.

Saltman, P., Gurin, J., & Mothner, I. (1993). *The University of California at San Diego nutrition book.* Boston: Little, Brown.

Schincariol, L. (1994). Including the physically awkward child. *Teaching Elementary Physical Education, 5*(5), 10-11.

Schmidt, R.A., & Wrisberg, C. (2000). *Motor learning and performance* (2nd ed.). Champaign, IL: Human Kinetics.

Schneider, P.L., Crouter, S.E., Lukajic, O., & Bassett, D.R. (2003). Accuracy and reliability of 10 pedometers for measuring steps over a 400-m walk. *Medicine and Science in Sports and Exercise, 35*(10), 1779-1784.

Schneider, P.L., Crouter, S.E., & Bassett, D.R. Jr. (2004). Pedometer measures of free-living physical activity: Comparison of 13 models. *Medicine and Science in Sports and Exercise, 36*(2): 331-335.

Secretary of Health and Human Services and Secretary of Education. (2000). *Promoting better health for young people through physical activity and sports: A report to the president.* www.hhs.gov/news/factsheet/physactive.html.

Segal, K.R., Gutin, B., Presta, E., Wang, J., & Van Itallie, T.B. (1985). Estimation of human body composition by electrical impedance. *Federation Proceedings, 46,* 1334. (Abstract).

Segal, K.R., Van Loan, M., Fitzgerald, P.I., Hodgdon, J.A., & Van Itallie, T.B. (1988). Lean body mass estimation by bioelectrical impedance analysis: A four-site cross-validation study. *American Journal of Clinical Nutrition, 47,* 7-14.

Sharman, M., Cresswell, A., & Riek, S. (2006). Proprioceptive neuromuscular facilitation stretching: mechanisms and clinical implications. *Sports Medicine, 36,* 929-939.

Sheldon, K.M. (2002). The self-concordance model of healthy goal striving: When personal goals correctly represent the person. In E.L. Deci & R.M. Ryan (Eds.), *Handbook of self-determination research* (pp. 65-86) Rochester, NY: University of Rochester Press.

Sheldon, K.M., & Elliot, A.J. (1998). Not all personal goals are personal: Comparing autonomous and controlled reasons for goals as predictors of effort and attainment. *Personality and Social Psychology Bulletin, 24,* 546-557.

Sheldon, K.M., & Elliot, A.J. (1999). Goal striving, need satisfaction, and longitudinal well-being: The Self-Concordance Model. *Journal of Personality and Social Psychology, 76,* 482-497.

Sheldon, K.M., & Kasser, T. (1998). Pursuing personal goals: Skills enable progress, but not all progress is beneficial. *Personality and Social Psychology Bulletin, 24,* 1319-1331.

Sheldon, K.M, Ryan, R.M., Deci, E.L., & Kasser, T. (2004). The independent effects of goal contents and motives upon well-being: It's both what you pursue and why you pursue it. *Personality and Social Psychology Bulletin, 30,* 475-486.

Sherman, K., Cherkin, D., Erro, J., Miglioretti, D., & Deyo, R. (2005). Comparing yoga, exercise, and a self-care book for chronic low back pain a randomized, controlled trial. *Annals of Internal Medicine, 143,* 849-856.

Shrier, I. (2004). Does stretching improve performance?: A systematic and critical review of the literature. *Clinical Journal of Sport Medicine, 14*, 267-273.

Slaughter, M.H., Lohman, T.G., Boileau, R.A., Horswill, C.A., Stillman, R.J., Van Loan, M.D., & Benben, D.A. (1988). Skinfold equations for estimation of body fatness in children and youth. *Human Biology, 60*, 709-723.

Smith, A., Ntoumanis, N., & Duda, J. (2007). Goal striving, goal attainment, and well-being: Adapting and testing the self-concordance model in sport. *Journal of Sport and Exercise Psychology, 29*, 763-782.

Sonstroem, R.J. (1984). Exercise and self-esteem. *Exercise and Sports Science Reviews, 12*, 123-155.

Sportline, Inc. *Sportline's guide to walking* (brochure), Walk4Life. Campbell, CA: Sportline.

Sullivan, J.A., & Anderson S.J., eds. (2000). *Care of the young athlete.* Elk Grove Village, IL: American Academy of Pediatrics.

Tanaka, H., Monahan, K.D., & Seals, D.R. (2001). Age-predicted maximal heart rate revisited. *Journal of the American College of Cardiology, 37*(1), 153-156.

Task Force on Community Preventive Services. (2002). Recommendations to increase physical activity in communities. *American Journal of Preventive Medicine, (4S)*, 67-72.

Telama, R., Yang, X., Hirvensalo, M., & Raitakari, O. (2006). Participation in organized youth sport as a predictor of adult physical activity: A 21-year longitudinal study. *Pediatric Exercise Science, 17*, 76-88.

Thacker, S., Gilchrist, J., & Stroup, D. (2004). The impact of stretching on sports injury: A systematic review of the literature. *Medicine and Science in Sports and Exercise, 36*, 371-378.

Thomas, K., Lee, A., & Thomas, J. (2003). *Physical education methods for elementary teachers* (2nd ed.). Champaign, IL: Human Kinetics.

Tipton, J., & Tucker, S. (1998). Fund-raising can be fun! *Teaching Elementary Physical Education, 9*(3), 14.

Trout, J., & Christie, B. (2007). Interactive video games in physical education. *Journal of Physical Education Recreation and Dance, 78*(5).

Tudor-Locke, C., Hatano, Y., Pangrazi, R.P., & Kang, M. (2008). Revisiting "How Many Steps are Enough?" *Medicine and Science in Sports and Exercise, 40*(7), July, Suppl. 537-543.

Tudor-Locke, C., Pangrazi, R.P., Corbin, C.B., Rutherford, W.J., Vincent, S.D., Raustorp, A., Tomson, L.M., & Cuddihy, T.F. (2004). BMI-referenced standards for recommended pedometer determined steps/day in children. *Preventive Medicine, 38*(6), 857-864.

Turner, C.H., & Robling, A.G. (2003). Designing exercise regimens to increase bone strength. *Exercise and Sports Science Reviews, 31*(1), 45-50.

Ulrich, D. (2000). *Test of gross motor development.* Austin, TX: Pro-Ed.

U.S. Department of Agriculture. (2002). *Food guide pyramid.* www.nal.usda.gov/fnic/Fpr/pyramid.html.

USDA Agricultural Research Services. (2005). *Childhood obesity: Regulation of energy balance and body composition.* Available: www.ars.usda.gov/research/projects/projects.htm?accn_no=408082.

USDA Agricultural Research Services. (2005). *Phytonutrient FAQs.* Available: www.ars.usda.gov/Aboutus/docs.htm?docid=4142.

USDA Center for Nutrition Policy and Promotion. (2000). *Dietary guidelines for Americans* (5th ed.). Atlanta, GA: U.S. Department of Health and Human Services, Government Printing Office.

U.S. Department of Education. (1994). *Prisoners of time: Report of the National Education Commission on Time and Learning.* Washington, DC: U.S. Department of Education.

U.S. Department of Health and Human Services and U.S. Department of Agriculture. (2005). *Dietary guidelines for Americans, 2005* (6th ed.). Washington, DC: U.S. Government Printing Office.

U.S. Department of Health and Human Services (USDHHS). (1999). *Promoting physical activity.* Champaign, IL: Human Kinetics.

U.S. Department of Health and Human Services (USDHHS). (2000a). *Healthy people 2010: Understanding and improving health.* Washington, DC: U.S. Department of Health and Human Services, Government Printing Office.

U.S. Department of Health and Human Services (USDHHS). (2000b). *Promoting better health for young people through physical activity and sports.* Washington, DC: U.S. Department of Health and Human Services, Government Printing Office.

U.S. Department of Health and Human Services. (2008). *Physical activity guidelines advisory committee report.* Washington, DC: U.S. Department of Health and Human Services.

U.S. Department of Health and Human Services. (2008). *2008 physical activity guidelines for Americans.* Washington, DC: U.S. Department of Health and Human Services.

U.S. Department of Health and Human Services. (2010). *The surgeon general's vision for a healthy and fit nation 2010.* Rockville, MD: U.S. Department of Health and Human Services.

U.S. Department of Health and Human Services (USDHHS), Centers for Disease Control and Prevention, National Center for Chronic Disease Prevention and Health Promotion. (1996). *Physical activity and health: A report of the surgeon general.* Atlanta, GA: U.S. Department of Health and Human Services, Government Printing Office.

U.S. Department of Health and Human Services (USDHHS), Centers for Disease Control and Prevention. (2000a). *Physical activity and the health of young people: Fact sheet.* [Online]. Available: www.cdc.gov.

U.S. Department of Health and Human Services (USDHHS), Centers for Disease Control and Prevention. (2000b). *Fact sheet: Physical education and activity, school health policies and programs study.* [Online]. Available: www.cdc.gov.

U.S. Department of Health and Human Services (USDHHS), Centers for Disease Control and Prevention. (2000c). *Promoting lifelong physical activity, CDC guidelines for school and community programs.* [Online]. Available: www.cdc.gov.

U.S. Department of Health and Human Services (USDHHS). (2001). *Surgeon General's Call to Action to Prevent and Decrease Overweight and Obesity.* Washington, D.C.: U.S. Government Printing Office. Available: www.surgeongeneral.gov/calltoaction/fact_adolscents.html.

U.S. Food and Drug Administration. (1999). *The food label.* www.fda.gov/opacom/backgrounders/foodlabel/newlabel/html [May 1999].

U.S. Food and Drug Administration, Center for Food Safety and Applied Nutrition. (2003). Claims that can be made for conventional foods and dietary supplements. www.cfsan.fda.gov/~dms/hclaims.html (accessed February 6, 2004).

U.S. Food and Drug Administration, Office of Food Labeling. (2003). *FDA's food label information on the Web.* www.cfscan.fda.gov.label.html.

U.S. Food and Nutrition Board, Institute of Medicine. (2002). *Dietary reference intakes for energy, carbohydrates, fiber, fat, protein, and amino acid (micronutrients).* Washington, DC: National Academics Press.

Vallerand, R.J. (2001). A hierarchical model of intrinsic and extrinsic motivation in sport and exercise. In G.C. Roberts (Ed.), *Advances in motivation in sport and exercise.* Champaign, IL: Human Kinetics.

Vanden Auweele, Y., Bakker, F., Biddle, S., Durand, M., & Seiler, R. (1999). *Psychology for physical educators.* Champaign, IL: Human Kinetics.

Van Loan, M., & Mayclin, P.L. (1987). Bioelectrical impedance analysis: Is it a reliable estimator of lean body mass and total body water? *Human Biology, 59,* 299–309.

Vincent, S.D., Pangrazi, R.P., Raustorp, A., Tomson, L.M., & Cuddihy, T.F. (2003). Activity levels and body mass index of children in the United States, Sweden, and Australia. *Medicine and Science in Sports and Exercise. 35*(8), 1367–1373.

Virgilio, S.J. (1997). *Fitness education for children: A team approach.* Champaign, IL: Human Kinetics.

Wall, A.E. (1982). Physically awkward children: A motor development perspective. In J.P. Das, R.F. Mulcahy, & A.E. Wall (Eds.), *Theory and research in learning disabilities* (pp. 253–268). New York: Plenum Press.

Ward, D.S.; Saunders, R.P.; & Pate, R.R. (2007). *Physical activity interventions in children and adolescents.* Champaign, IL: Human Kinetics.

Wardlaw, G. (1999). *Perspectives in nutrition* (4th ed.). Boston: WCB/McGraw-Hill.

Wardlaw, G. (2002). *Contemporary nutrition* (5th ed.). Boston: WCB/McGraw-Hill.

Watanabe, K., Nakadomo, F., Tanaka, K., Kim, K., & Maeda, K. (1993). Estimation of fat-free mass from bioelectrical impedance and anthropometric variables in Japanese girls. *Medicine and Science in Sports and Exercise, 25,* S163. (Abstract).

Weiss, M.R., & Horn, T.S. (1990). The relation between children's accuracy of estimates of their physical competence and achievement-related characteristics. *Research Quarterly for Exercise and Sport, 61*(3), 250–258.

Welk, G.J., & Blair, S.N. (2008). Health benefits of physical activity and fitness in children. In G.J. Welk & M.D. Meredith (Eds.), *Fitnessgram/Activitygram reference guide.* Dallas, TX: Cooper Institute.

Welk, G.J., Differding, J.A., Thompson, R.W., Blair, S.N., Dziura, J., & Hart, P. (2000). The utility of the Digiwalker step counter to assess daily physical activity patterns. *Medicine and Science in Sports and Exercise, 32*(9 suppl), S481–488.

Westcott, W.L. (2003). *Building strength and stamina* (2nd ed.). Champaign, IL: Human Kinetics.

Weston, A.T., Petosa, R., & Pate, R.R. (1997). Validation of an instrument for measurement of physical activity in youth. *Medicine and Science in Sports and Exercise, 29*(1), 138–143.

Wickelgren, I. (1998). Obesity: How big a problem? *Science, 280* (May), 1364–1367.

Williams, D.P., Going, S.B., Lohman, T.G., Harsha, D.W., Srinivasan, S.R., Webber, L.S., & Berenson, G.S. (1992). Body fatness and the risk of elevated blood pressure, total cholesterol and serum lipoprotein ratios in children and adolescents. *American Journal of Public Health, 82,* 358–363.

Winnick, J.P. (1995). Personalizing measurement and evaluation for individuals with disabilities. In J.A. Seaman (Ed.), *Physical best and individuals with disabilities: A handbook for inclusion in fitness programs* (pp. 21–31). Reston, VA: AAHPERD.

Winnick, J.P. (1999). Individualized education programs and the development of health-related physical fitness. In J.P. Winnick & F.X. Short (Eds.), *The Brockport physical fitness training guide* (p. 6). Champaign, IL: Human Kinetics.

Winnick, J.P. (2005). *Adapted physical education and sport* (4th ed.). Champaign, IL: Human Kinetics.

Winnick, J.P., & Short, F.X. (1999). *The Brockport Physical Fitness Test manual.* Champaign, IL: Human Kinetics.

Woods, A.M. (1997). Assessment of the cognitive domain. *Teaching elementary physical education, 8*(3), 28–29.

Youth Risk Behavior Surveillance (YRBS). (2001). June 28, 2002, Vol. 51, No. SS04, 1–64 (retrieved Nov. 30, 2003, www.cdc.gov/mmwr/preview/mmwrhtml/ss5104a1.htm).

Youth Risk Behavior Survey (YRBS). (2007). Youth Risk Behavior Survey as reported in *Morbidity and Mortality Weekly Report,* June 6, 2008, Vol. 57, No. SS-4, www.cdc.gov/mmwr.

Youth Risk Behavior Surveillance (YRBS). (2009). *Youth Risk Behavior Survey, 2009.* Available: www.cdc.gov/mmwrhtml/ss5905al.htm#tab80.

Zavatto, L., Schilling, E., Docheff, D.M., Crawford, S., et al. (2005). Should physical educators make greater use of homework? *Journal of Physical Education Recreation and Dance, 76*(2), 15–17.

Zeigler, E., & Filer, L. (2000). *Present knowledge in nutrition* (7th ed.). Washington, DC: International Life Sciences Press.

Zhu, W., Safrit, M., & Cohen, A. (1999). *Fitsmart test user manual: High school edition*. Champaign, IL: Human Kinetics.

Zwiren, L.D. (1988). Exercise prescription for children. In American College of Sports Medicine (Ed.), *Resource manual for guidelines for exercise testing and prescription* (pp. 309-314). Philadelphia: Lea and Febiger.